January, 2015

To Deepak,

All the best,

Ron

OPTIMIZING
Organization
Design

RONALD G. CAPELLE

OPTIMIZING
Organization
Design

A PROVEN APPROACH TO ENHANCE
Financial Performance,
Customer Satisfaction,
AND Employee Engagement

JB JOSSEY-BASS™
A Wiley Brand

Published by Jossey-Bass, a Wiley brand
One Montgomery Street, Suite 1200,
San Francisco, CA 94104-4594—www.josseybass.com

For general information about our other products and services, please contact our Customer Care Department within Canada at 1-800-567-4797, outside Canada at (416) 236-4433 or fax (416) 236-8743.

Wiley publishes in a variety of print and electronic formats and by print-on-demand. Some material included with standard print versions of this book may not be included in e-books or in print-on-demand. If this book refers to media such as a CD or DVD that is not included in the version you purchased, you may download this material at http://booksupport.wiley.com. For more information about Wiley products, visit www.wiley.com.

Library and Archives Canada Cataloguing in Publication
Capelle, Ronald G., 1948-, author

Optimizing organization design : a proven approach to enhance financial performance, customer satisfaction and employee engagement / Ronald G. Capelle.
Includes index.
Issued in print and electronic formats.
ISBN 978-1-118-76373-5 (bound).—ISBN 978-1-118-76382-7 (pdf).—
ISBN 978-1-118-76379-7 (epub)
1. Organizational change. I. Title.
HD58.8.C36 2013   658.4'06   C2013-904508-2
                                                   C2013-904509-0

Printed in the United States of America
FIRST EDITION
HB Printing 10 9 8 7 6 5 4 3 2 1

To Karen, Geoff, and Graeme

CONTENTS

List of Research Studies

Capelle Associates Research Paper #1
Optimizing Organization Design: Improvements in Manager–Direct Report Alignment, Financial Performance and Employee Satisfaction (January 1, 1999)

Capelle Associates Research Paper #2
Optimizing Organization Design: Improvement in Employee Satisfaction (March 1, 2000a)

Capelle Associates Research Paper #3
Optimizing Organization Design: Improvements in Manager–Direct Report Alignment, Employee Satisfaction and Customer Satisfaction (June 23, 2000b)

Capelle Associates Research Paper #4
Optimizing Organization Design: Improvements in Manager–Direct Report Alignment and Employee Satisfaction (March 1, 2000c)

Capelle Associates Research Paper #5
Optimizing Organization Design: Improvements in Manager–Direct Report Alignment, Leadership and Direction, and Employee Commitment (March 1, 2000d)

Capelle Associates Research Paper #6
The Information Processing Capability of an Employee and the Job Grade of a Position: Is There a Relationship? (Oct 16, 2000e)

Capelle Associates Research Paper #7
Information Processing Capability, Time Span, and Job Grade (Sept 14, 2000f)

Capelle Associates Research Paper #8
Appropriateness of Compensation, Overall Employee Satisfaction, and Employee Satisfaction with Compensation: Review of 20 Organizations (March 28, 2003a)

Capelle Associates Research Paper #9
Organization Design, Manager–Direct Report Alignment and Organization Performance in Canadian Private Sector Companies: Results from Surveys of CEOs and Heads of Human Resources (March 28, 2003a)

Capelle Associates Research Paper #10
Task Alignment: A More Micro Organization Alignment Approach (Dec 16, 2004a)

Capelle Associates Research Paper #11
Equitable Differential Pay Scale for the Canadian Market (Mar 9, 2004b)

Capelle Associates Research Paper #12
Relationship between Time Span, Compensation Span, and Actual Compensation: Review from 57 Organizations (June 23, 2005a)

Capelle Associates Research Paper #13
Organization Design: From Improvement to Decline (Sept 27, 2005b)

Capelle Associates Research Paper #14
Manager–Direct Report Alignment Is Directly Related to Employee Satisfaction: A Review of 30 Organizations (March 15, 2005c)

Capelle Associates Research Paper #15
Organization Design, Manager–Direct Report Alignment, and Employee Satisfaction (Oct 26, 2011)

Capelle Associates Research Paper #16
Manager–Direct Report Alignment, Delegation and Compensation from Capelle Associates Benchmarking Database (July 10, 2012a)

Capelle Associates Research Paper #17
Capelle Associates Employee Satisfaction Questionnaire (July 5, 2012b)

Capelle Associates Research Paper #18
Relationship among Time Span, Self Span, and Compensation Span from Capelle Associates Benchmarking Database (July 30, 2012c)

Capelle Associates Research Paper #19
Relationship among Manager–Direct Report Alignment, Delegation, and Compensation from Capelle Associates Benchmarking Database (Aug 1, 2012d)

Capelle Associates Research Paper #20
Span of Control and Employee Satisfaction from Capelle Associates Benchmarking Database (Aug 9, 2012e)

Capelle Associates Research Paper #21
Manager–Direct Report Alignment and Employee Satisfaction for an Analyst Role (Aug 7, 2012f)

Capelle Associates Research Paper #22
Manager–Direct Report Alignment and Employee Satisfaction in Three Organizations (Aug 9, 2012g)

Capelle Associates Research Paper #23
Potential Annual Cost Savings from Organization Design Assessments (August 22, 2012h)

ACKNOWLEDGMENTS

A book such as this is not the output of just one person. I have been influenced by the writings of those who came before me; by teachers, mentors, colleagues, clients, and family along the way; and by current friends, colleagues, clients, and family who have directly contributed to this book. It is not possible to acknowledge everyone, but I will attempt to provide some highlights.

The foundation of who one is goes back to parents, family, and community. Within this framework one develops values and skills that serve as the basis for later development. I studied psychology and obtained a BA (Honors), MA, and PhD (with a primary focus on clinical counseling psychology and a secondary focus on organizational psychology) degrees. Along the way, I worked for a year with the Manitoba Department of Education in Winnipeg under the direction of David Hemphill and John Banmen, received training in California with Carl Rogers, and led and completed published research on encounter groups. During my PhD program, I had numerous internships in clinical counseling settings, and learned much about groups and organizations at NTL Institute.

During an internship in family therapy at the Hospital for Sick Children in Toronto, I was supervised by three psychiatrists, each with a different orientation (one more psychoanalytic, one more systems oriented, and one more eclectic). The therapy sessions were videotaped and I had a supervisory meeting with Paul Steinhauer, an outstanding therapist and an even better person. He asked me for my diagnosis of the family to which I had been assigned. I responded that the identified patient was one of the two sons (issues at school, etc.), but the real issue was that the mother and father had conflict that was not resolved. The mother was angry and confrontational and the father was passive and withdrawn. Paul Steinhauer said, "I agree with your assessment—and how are you contributing to their problem?" I was naturally taken aback. However, he was right. I was taking an individual focus with the mother, with the idea that I was helping her to develop insight. However, when one looked at the system (the family), it was not changing. The father was sitting back, pleased that he didn't have to do anything, and the family system stayed stuck. This insight was a profound one: it taught me the difference between the individual and the system.

As I was finishing my PhD dissertation and becoming certified as a psychologist (CPsych), I worked with a small industrial-organizational psychology firm in Toronto under the supervision of David Jackson. I learned a lot, and developed a strong friendship with Dave.

I set up my own practice in 1977, which developed an organizational focus. I realized that I didn't know enough about business so I completed the process necessary to become a Certified Management Consultant (CMC), a Certified Organization Development Consultant, and a Certified Human Resources Professional (CHRP).

In 1979, I wrote *Changing Human Systems*, in which I developed a framework for human systems: individual, interpersonal, group and family, intergroup, organization, interorganization, and community. The book focused on how human systems function, how they change, and the role of a third party in the change process. My view was that the disciplines in each of these areas functioned as silos with a different language, that this was dysfunctional, and that the similarities were greater than the differences. Therefore, I believed that integrated models would add value.

My practice in the first 10 years included management training and performance management. However, my primary interest was on large scale organization change—how does one help to improve the performance of a whole organization or a major part thereof? I became more involved in working with organizations that wanted to improve performance, and started to develop methods for both the assessment of organizations and the implementation of agreed improvements.

In the late 80s, I met Elliott Jaques. He and his colleagues developed an approach to understanding organizations and the people within them that was not confined to some ivory tower but was grounded in real field research. While there are many facets to this approach, I believe that its foundation is a measure of the complexity of work (time span) and a measure of individual information processing capability. This approach has had various names over the years, including "Stratified Systems Theory," and most recently "Requisite Organization." Elliott was a teacher and mentor, and also a colleague and friend. While my firm has changed some aspects of this approach for our practice, and developed numerous additional aspects, Elliott's core concepts remain part of its foundation.

Our firm expanded in the early 90s when I hired Chris Becker. He joined as a business student and then left a few years later with an MBA and Certified Management Consultant designation. He helped to develop our approaches to assessment and implementation, and also laid the foundation for our research. Research has been an important part of our practice throughout. This stems at least partially from my PhD training and valuing the relationship between professional practice and research.

Dwight Mihalicz joined the firm in the late 90s and continues to work with us. Dwight provided consulting services, was accountable for our marketing, oversaw our research, and was the General Manager of the firm until 2010. Dwight was instrumental in further developing our implementation approach and materials. Raymond Daigneault joined the firm in the early 2000s. He is providing consulting services, and has recently taken over the general manager duties. He has contributed to the further enhancement of our implementation approach and materials. Other consultants have included Karen King and John Young, who continue with the firm; Charlotte Bygrave, who has left; and Chris Harcourt Vernon, who unfortunately passed away far too soon. Other key staff who have provided important support over the years include Donna Lalonde, Sandra Rayner, and Christine Rothman.

Part of the substance of this book comes from material that we have developed as part of our client work. Dwight Mihalicz and Raymond Daigneault have made significant contributions to this. They have also taken the lead in preparing our case studies. For these studies, I thank our clients. Bob Lavery, who joined the firm in the early 2000s and leads our assessment and research function, has played a significant role in most of the research that we have done, including the research papers in this book.

I would like to thank those who reviewed drafts of this book. Their insights have added great value. They include Ken Craddock, Raymond Daigneault, Jerry Gray, Ruth Hubbard, Owen Jacobs, Karen King, Herb Koplowitz, Dwight Mihalicz, and Paul Tremlett. I would also like to thank Ken Shepard and the Global Organization Design Society for support of this book.

The worth of an approach to organization performance has two proofs. The first is the research that supports it. This book provides considerable support of this nature. The second is in the executives who have implemented it and obtained the desired benefits. While some of these benefits may be quantitative, many are qualitative.

While I am sometimes disappointed that so few executives seem to get that organization design is important, and fewer still take the initiative to do it well or do it at all, I believe that we have been blessed with clients who have worked with us. By and large, they tend not to be in organizations in serious trouble. On the contrary, they tend to have (a) higher capability (which we will define in the book), (b) an internal sense of excellence that drives them to be the best and not settle for the (easier) status quo, and (c) a moderate risk-taking orientation.

It is only through working with clients, and doing related research, that one can really develop theory, research, and practice. We are grateful to our clients for the opportunities they have provided. While it is not possible to mention them all, I have listed some with whom we have worked most intensively. These are in reverse chronological order:

- Gerry Savaria and Vadim Motlik (LS Travel Retail)
- Fred Green, Peter Edwards, and Bob MacIntyre (Canadian Pacific Railway)
- Brian Vaasjo and Peter Arnold (Capital Power Corporation)
- Don Lowry and Robert Petryk (EPCOR)
- Naseem Somani and Pierre Belanger (Gamma-Dynacare)
- Jim Baumgartner and Joan Mitchell (Moneris Solutions)
- Claude Lamoureux and Bob Bertram (Ontario Teachers' Pension Plan)
- Mike Donoghue and Eric Pickering (Allstate Insurance)
- Paul Lucas and Ruth Kemp (GlaxoSmithKline)
- Isadore Sharp and John W. Young (Four Seasons Hotels and Resorts)
- Keith Ambachtsheer (K.P.A. Advisory Services)
- Dale Reeson (Canadian Tire)
- Ruth Hubbard (Revenue Canada and Public Service Commission of Canada)
- Robert W. Pearce and April Taggart (BMO Financial Group)
- George Weber (International Federation of Red Cross and Red Crescent Societies, Canadian Dental Association, Royal Ottawa Health Care Group)
- Derek Fry (Visa)

- Keith Willard (Zeneca)
- Michael J. Brophy (Baxter and *The Globe and Mail*)
- Peter C. Reid (Fulcrum Technologies)
- Bob MacPhee (Canadian Passport Office)

Naturally, while many have contributed to this book, I remain accountable for all errors of omission and commission.

INTRODUCTION

Everything that we measure has improved markedly.
Our financial performance is up. Our customer
service scores are up. Our employee morale and the
general attitude around all of this is up ... I can say
with just absolute conviction that getting the
organization design right ... has been fundamental
to the improvements around this place.

—Robert W. Pearce, President and Chief
Executive Officer, Personal and Commercial
Client Group, BMO Financial Group,
September 2002

You want to improve your organization performance, and it is getting more difficult to do so. Customers are becoming more knowledgeable and demanding. Competition is increasing. It is more difficult to recruit, fully engage, and retain employees. Strategies and business plans are developed, but they don't always deliver the expected outcomes. There are difficulties in growing revenues and reducing costs that make it more difficult to hit financial performance targets.

What if there was an approach that could help you to deal with all of these issues? What if this approach was supported by extensive research and had been successfully used by executives for the past 25 years? The good news is that there is such an approach. The better news is that this book will show you how to use it to improve your organization performance. By using our insights and methods, you can

- improve financial performance (both short term cost savings and longer term financial improvement)
- improve customer satisfaction (better organization design supports better customer focus)
- improve employee satisfaction (this can include engagement and retention)
- develop competitive advantage (some competitive advantages can easily be copied; this one requires capability and commitment and can be better sustained)
- achieve a significant return on investment (while all improvements require investment, this one provides a significant return)
- improve implementation of strategy and business plans (organization design provides the foundation for strategy implementation)
- improve human resources performance (this approach provides the foundation for human resources management)

Our comprehensive approach provides methods for both assessing organization design and implementing improvements. You will learn about the key factors in assessing organization design:

- Align positions vertically and functionally: Learn about a proven method to determine how many layers your organization should have and place every position in the appropriate layer. Learn why the manager–direct report alignment is the single most important organization design factor . . . and why it is wrong about half the time.
- Align accountabilities and authorities (both managerial and cross functional): Learn how to break down organization silos and develop a better alternative to matrix organization.

- Align people to positions: Learn why the information processing capability of an individual is critical to matching people to positions and for promotion, and how you can use it to improve employee satisfaction and performance.
- Align deliverables to positions: Learn why employees are often doing work below their pay grade—and what you can do about it.
- Align tasks to positions: Learn why professionals spend about 50 percent of their time doing work you could pay someone less money to do at least as well—and free up professionals' time to do the more complex work they should be doing.

You will learn about the key factors for implementing organization design improvements:

- project scope, structure, and process
- project management
- people change management
- best practices for aligning positions, accountabilities and authorities, people, deliverables, and tasks
- a cascading iterative process, with natural work teams, including education and training, real managerial work, and feedback
- sustainable improvement through systems improvement and skill development

For the past 25 years, we at Capelle Associates® have focused exclusively on helping executives improve organization performance with our Optimizing Organization Design® approach. During that time, we have completed more than 100 comprehensive organization design assessments and been involved in the implementation of many of the resulting agreed recommendations. We consider research to be a fundamental part of our practice and have completed 24 research projects (one of which was previously published). This book is a synthesis of this experience.

Anyone with an interest in improving organization performance should find value in this book. Individuals who would find value in this include all executives and managers, particularly heads of organizations and business units; heads of Human Resources and related specialists (this model provides a framework for all human resources systems and practices); strategic and business planners (this book provides the foundation for strategic implementation); organization design professionals; project management professionals; process management (e.g., Lean and Six Sigma) professionals; members of boards of directors; management consultants; individuals involved in mergers and acquisitions; and organizational development professionals.

In Chapter 1 you will learn why organization design matters: how it is related to financial performance, customer satisfaction, and employee satisfaction. You will learn about how it can provide competitive advantage, a significant return on investment, and a foundation for strategy implementation and for human resources management. If someone claims that a method or program improves organization performance (as we are claiming), we believe that two types of evidence are important. The first is that executives have judged it to have been successful. I have included comments by many of them in this book. The second is that there is research demonstrating its effectiveness. We have the results of 24 research studies, 23 of which are published here for the first time.

In Chapter 2 you will learn about organization design assessment, or how organizations function. Our view is that organizations can be thought of as stratified human systems. Understanding an organization as a human system has tremendous power for understanding how it functions and changes, as well as providing linkages to strategy. I introduce systems models for this purpose. Understanding them as stratified (with the levels differentiated by compensation and title) means that there is a hierarchy, i.e., there are manager positions accountable for direct report positions. Therefore one should have a good method for determining how many levels there should be in an organization, and what the optimal vertical alignment should be. I believe that the best work in this area comes from Jaques (1996) and his colleagues. In particular, there are two aspects that have strong research support and are fundamental to our practice. The first is a measurement of the complexity of work called "time span." The second is a measure of individual capability called "information processing capability." These are complementary work–person factors that provide a foundation for understanding the nature of work and of working relationships in an organization.

I discuss models and practices for the optimal alignment of several parts of the system. This includes the optimal alignment of positions (vertically and functionally), accountabilities and authorities (managerial and cross functional), people, deliverables, and tasks. Our Optimizing Organization Design® approach is about far more than moving boxes on an organization chart. Rather, it is about the "content," i.e., the parts of an organization and their alignment. We use models to help understand organization functioning. It should be noted that a model is a representation of reality, but not the full reality. Organizations are far too complex: no model can represent all aspects of their functioning. However, models can be extremely valuable if they are descriptive (accurately rendering various components), prescriptive (doing it in a particular way, under particular circumstances, is better than offering alternatives), and predictive (anticipating likely outcomes). For example, the complexity of work can be measured by a method called "time span analysis" and organized into levels or strata (descriptive); a manager should be exactly one level or stratum above a direct report (prescriptive); and if a manager and direct report are actually operating at the same level or stratum, the manager will likely micromanage and the direct report will likely not be able to use full capability, resulting in reduced satisfaction and financial performance (predictive).

In Chapter 3, you will learn about organization design implementation or how organizations change. This is more the "process" of the organization design. Change management is required for any organization improvement (e.g., quality, re-engineering, etc.). It is not sufficient to know what you want to change: you have to know how you are going to go about doing it. This chapter includes implementation objectives, an organization design implementation components model, an organization design implementation process model, principles, a specific approach for strengthening the implementation, and discussion of the value of an internal–external team.

In Chapter 4, I provide an overview of the Optimizing Organization Design® approach. This approach consists of four main steps: initial discussion, proposal, and contract; assessment, report, and meetings; implementation; and sustainment. These are important steps for executives and managers to understand, whether they directly lead a project or set up a project that others lead. The degree of detail will vary with the complexity and scope of the organization design initiative. However, a minimal condition should be that each of the steps be considered, and none missed.

In Chapter 5, I describe four topics related to our approach that deserve attention. The first focuses on the role of a board of directors with respect to governance. While our focus is mainly on the organization itself, boards play a critical role that impacts the organization. I believe that boards, in their role related to risk management, should ensure optimal organization design. This tends not to happen.

The second topic is project management. I believe that project management methodology adds significant value in areas such as project definition and scope, work breakdown structures, scheduling, budgeting, and monitoring. However, project management often is extremely weak in areas related to organization design, such as position alignment, accountabilities and authorities (managerial and cross functional), and matching people to positions. I believe that this is a major cause of suboptimal outcomes and numerous failures, particularly in the information systems/information technology field, including large-scale enterprise resource planning (ERP) implementations.

The third topic is process management. While our focus is primarily on positions, accountabilities, etc., I show that our approach is integrally related to process management in three ways. First, our approach provides a framework for the ongoing accountability for processes. Second, our systems model provides a framework for determining macro processes that go across the organization. Third, our task alignment method provides valuable information that can be used in improving micro processes.

The fourth topic is compensation. Time span, as a measure of the complexity or work, is also a job evaluation method, and can be used to determine appropriate compensation. There is research showing that it is strongly related to felt fair pay (Richardson, 1971). I discuss opportunities for organizations to use time span to enhance their approaches to compensation.

In Chapter 6, I provide a call to action. I respond to several reasons we have heard for not optimizing organization design. Hopefully more executives will become aware of, and achieve, the benefits of taking action.

There are also three appendices. Appendix A includes comments by executives of companies with whom we have worked describing their experience with the Capelle Associates approach. In Appendix B we publish for the first time 23 Capelle Associates Research Papers and in Appendix C we offer four case studies. These case studies come from quite different sectors: financial services, power generation, railways, and health care. They are also quite different in the challenges that they overcame. One was a comprehensive organization design improvement that was completed nearly 10 years ago and is still thriving. A second was a large-scale (16,000 employee) improvement that was completed in a high speed, high quality manner. A third involved the splitting of an organization through an IPO (initial public offering) and the creation of a new organization. The fourth was the successful organization design improvement of a health care organization (hospital and other related entities). Health care organizations are among the most difficult to successfully change.

There is also a glossary. Too often, in organizations people use the same word to mean different things. As a result, what seems to be clear communication is not. While our definitions would not necessarily be used by everyone (there are often no universally agreed definitions), they make clear what I mean. Our clients tell us that these operationally defined words help to change the language and culture of their organizations.

In summary, I have set out to demonstrate why organization design matters. Its benefits include improving employee satisfaction, customer satisfaction and financial performance. Organizations that adopt our methods often gain and sustain a competitive advantage. And they build the foundations for both strategy implementation and human resources management. In these pages, I explain organization design *assessment* or how organizations function. Here, the emphasis is on a systems approach, the alignment of positions, accountabilities and authorities, people, deliverables and tasks. I explain our approach to organization design *implementation* or how organizations change. Many books focus solely on organization design assessment and leave out this critical area. I elaborate on the full process for *optimizing* the organization design approach, from the initial meetings to the subsequent sustainment of the organization design improvements. Finally, I show that this approach can help you with several related areas, including the board of directors, project management, process management, and compensation.

OPTIMIZING
Organization
Design

CHAPTER 1

WHY ORGANIZATION DESIGN MATTERS

Organization design, as we define it, is one of the most powerful tools available for improving organization performance. Our Optimizing Organization Design® approach

- is related to better employee satisfaction
- is related to better customer satisfaction
- is related to better financial performance
- can give you a competitive advantage that is more sustainable than most
- provides a significant return on investment
- provides a foundation for strategy implementation
- provides a foundation for human resources management

We define organization design as the relationship of an organization to its environment and the interrelationships of its parts. This includes the alignment of positions, accountabilities and authorities, people, deliverables, and tasks.

Within organization design, there is one factor that is powerful enough to be directly related to improved outcomes. That factor is the manager–direct report alignment. Following on the work of Jaques and his colleagues (Jaques, 1996), the basic idea is that every employee should have a manager exactly one level or "stratum" (our technical term which will be discussed shortly) above. We believe that this precise stratification is a necessary but not sufficient condition for an optimal manager–direct report relationship. Buckingham and Coffman (1999) have conducted significant research showing the importance of relationship with manager and how it is related to productivity, profitability, retention, and customer satisfaction.

The important relationships among these factors have also been demonstrated by Heskett and his colleagues in their development of the service profit chain (Heskett et al., 1994; Heskett, Sasser & Schlesinger, 1997; Heskett, Sasser & Schlesinger, 2003; Heskett, Sasser & Wheeler, 2008). They have shown that there is a relationship between the employee (satisfaction and loyalty); the customer (value equation, satisfaction, and loyalty); and financial performance (revenue growth and profitability). This research is further discussed in Appendix B.

EMPLOYEE SATISFACTION

Productivity in the department has improved, and user satisfaction has increased remarkably while employee morale and team work have shown exceptional gains.

—John W. Young, Executive Vice President,
Human Resources, Four Seasons Hotels and
Resorts, April 2002

We would expect that better organization design would lead to better employee satisfaction. Organization design provides better manager–direct report alignment (as well as overall better position alignment), better clarity of accountabilities and authorities, better matching of people to positions, and better alignment of deliverables. Any one of these alone might have a positive impact on employee satisfaction. The combination of all or most of them would seem to significantly improve that probability.

The relationship between organization design and employee satisfaction is strongly supported by our research (see Appendix B).

While these outcomes would have been expected, we have also shown the power of the manager–direct report alignment. Manager–direct report alignment also is based on the work of Jaques (1996) and his colleagues. They developed a measure of the complexity of work called "time span." With it, one can determine how many layers or strata an organization should have and place every position in the correct layer or stratum. More specifically, one can develop optimal manager–direct report alignment. This is a situation in which a manager is exactly one layer or stratum above a direct report, in terms of both the complexity of work done and capability to work at that level.

While there is one optimal situation, there are two suboptimal situations. The first is when a manager and direct report are operating at the same level or stratum (called "compression"). We would expect that the manager in this situation would be micromanaging and not adding sufficient value and that the direct report could not use her full capability. The second situation arises when a manager and direct report are operating more than one level or stratum apart (called "gap"). We would expect that the manager in this situation could feel "pulled down into the weeds" and see the direct report as having no "initiative" while the direct report would see the manager as providing inappropriate direction.

This manager–direct report alignment would therefore appear to be fundamental to manager and employee satisfaction. One can see how it could be related also to customer satisfaction and financial performance. There are relationships among all of these factors. Quite frankly, we have been surprised at the robustness of manager–direct report alignment. While we would have expected that organization design would be related to these outcome measures, we would not have expected that any of the sub factors would be robust enough to have a similar effect. Our experience with manager–direct report alignment has proved us wrong.

The relationship between manager–direct report alignment and employee satisfaction is shown in our survey of top 2000 Canadian companies (Capelle Associates Research Paper #9, 2003b). Nine other studies reinforce these findings. The first six are organization design assessment and implementation projects (Capelle Associates Research Paper #1, 1999; Capelle Associates Research Paper #3, 2000b; Capelle Associates Research Paper #4, 2000c; Capelle Associates Research Paper #5, 2000d; Capelle Associates Research Paper #13, 2005b; Capelle Associates Research Paper #15, 2011). In each of the studies both the manager–direct report relationship and employee satisfaction improved following the organization design intervention. Three more studies focus on situations where there was no organization design intervention. Capelle Associates Research Paper #14 (2005c) shows a significant relationship between manager–direct report alignment and employee satisfaction. Capelle Associates Research Paper #21 (2012f) looks at one role (analyst). It shows that individuals in analyst positions, who have requisite or optimal alignment with their managers (exactly one stratum below), have higher satisfaction than those who are in gap or compression situations. Finally, Capelle Associates Research Paper #22 (2012g) shows a significant relationship between manager–direct report alignment and employee satisfaction in three interrelated organizations.

It is clear that organization design in general, and the manager–direct report alignment in particular, are both directly related to employee satisfaction. We believe that better organization design and better manager–direct report alignment both lead to better employee satisfaction.

CUSTOMER SATISFACTION

We found that better aligning positions, clarifying accountabilities and authorities, matching people to positions, and developing business plans has resulted in improved employee performance and customer satisfaction.

—Naseem Somani, President and CEO,
Gamma-Dynacare Medical Laboratories,
October 2011

We would expect that better organization design would lead to better customer satisfaction. Improvements in alignment of positions, accountabilities and authorities, people, and deliverables should provide better clarity and a foundation to focus on customers. Our research supports the relationship between organization design and customer satisfaction. This is shown in our survey of top 2000 Canadian companies (Capelle Associates Research Paper #9, 2003b), as well as one additional study (Capelle Associates Research Paper #3, 2000b). We also find that there is a relationship between manager–direct report alignment and customer satisfaction (Capelle Associates Research Paper #9, 2003b; Capelle Associates Research Paper #3, June 23, 2000b; Capelle Associates Research Paper #14, 2005c).

In addition to our research studies, Heskett and his colleagues have developed the service profit chain (Heskett et al., 1994; Heskett, Sasser & Schlesinger, 1997; Heskett, Sasser & Schlesinger, 2003; Heskett, Sasser & Wheeler, 2008). They have shown that there is a relationship between the employee (satisfaction and loyalty), the customer (value equation, satisfaction, and loyalty), and financial performance (revenue growth and profitability). We believe that this adds further credence to the impact of better organization design and better manager–direct report alignment on both employee satisfaction and customer satisfaction.

FINANCIAL PERFORMANCE

We were indeed able to establish a statistically positive relationship between organization design and performance using our performance data and your organization design framework. We found that Capelle Associates' approach to better organization design is related to better financial performance in the global pension fund industry. This includes governance, layering, and delegation.

—Keith P. Ambachtsheer, President, K.P.A.
Advisory Services, and co-author, Pension Fund
Excellence: Creating Value for Stakeholders,
October 1999

We would expect better organization design in general, and better manager–direct report alignment in particular, would lead to better financial performance. There are three factors related to this.

First, it seems logical and reasonable that improvements in the alignment of positions, accountabilities and authorities, people, and deliverables should lead to better financial performance. As well, the absence of optimal or requisite manager–direct report alignment leads to problems such as gaps or compression. These elements are fundamental to the operation of an organization. Our research supports this expectation. It is shown in our survey of top 2000 Canadian companies (Capelle Associates Research Paper #9, May 12, 2003b). It is also shown in a longitudinal study (Capelle Associates Research Paper #1, 1999) and a previously published study of financial performance in the global pension fund industry (Ambachtsheer, Capelle & Scheibelhut, 1998).

Second, organization design assessments can produce cost savings. These are all directly related to the manager–direct report alignment. The Capelle Associates Benchmarking Database shows average potential annual cost savings of $2,505 per position (Capelle Associates Research Paper #23, 2012h). The total in each case would be found by multiplying this number by the number of positions in the review (e.g., in a 1,000-employee organization, the average potential annual cost savings would be $2,505,000).

The third factor comes from related research. Buckingham and Coffman 1999 show a relationship between the manager–direct report relationship and profitability. Heskett and his colleagues (Heskett et al., 1997) have developed the service profit chain showing the relationship between employee satisfaction, customer satisfaction, and financial performance (revenue growth and profitability). So, not only do we show a direct relationship between organization design and financial performance, we would also expect that improvements in relationship with manager, employee satisfaction, and customer satisfaction would further drive financial performance. This hypothesis is further supported by the statistically significant relationships found in our survey of top 2000 Canadian companies (Capelle Associates Research Paper #9, 2003b).

In conclusion, we have three streams of support for the relationships between both organization design and manager–direct report alignment with financial performance: three studies showing direct relationships; one study showing cost savings; and a number of related studies showing that the relationships between manager, employee, and customer satisfaction align with financial performance.

COMPETITIVE ADVANTAGE

The advice came at significant turning points in our history and helped to keep the fund competitive and focused on identifying unexpected risks while remaining at the top of our game.

—Bob Bertram, *Executive Vice President, Investments, Ontario Teachers' Pension Plan, November 2007*

Better organization design, as we define it, can provide a competitive advantage. It is clearly related to better organization performance, as shown by employee satisfaction, customer satisfaction, and financial performance. However, there is more to the story. This Optimizing Organization Design® approach can and should be done in such a way as to be sustainable. Much of my focus in this book is on how to accomplish this. Further, because this approach requires both skill and commitment, I contend that it can be a more sustainable competitive advantage than many that can be more easily copied.

SIGNIFICANT RETURN ON INVESTMENT

The icing on the cake is that, although organization design did not start for us as a cost cutting exercise, it ended up paying for itself within the first year of implementation and that's a recurring benefit.

—Gerry Savaria, President and CEO, LS
Travel Retail North America, July 2011

Improvements in organizations generally require some forms of investment. The critical question then becomes, "What is the return on investment?"

We track this information in our consulting work. We have information on 19 organizations. There were significant potential annual cost savings, mainly resulting from the elimination of redundant managerial positions (i.e., positions that are in the same stratum as their immediate manager). The average potential annual cost savings was $2,994,298 per organization. The average investment in the assessment was significantly lower at $454,779. The average potential annual return on investment (ROI) was 589 percent. It should be noted that while the investment is one time, the savings recur on an annual basis (e.g., if there are savings because a position is eliminated, those savings recur each year). The average potential annual cost savings per employee was $2,505.

This number is calculated by dividing the annual cost savings by the number of employees in the organization.

Two of the 19 organizations we tracked had no potential annual cost savings. It is important that these numbers have integrity, and be based on the best interest of the organization. In these two cases, the organizations were in a significant growth mode. Not only were there no redundant positions, but there were requirements to add positions. We have included these numbers in our averages because these are actual situations that one might also encounter.

We believe that the number of redundant positions that we identify is quite conservative (i.e., quite low). The average percentage of compressed situations in this study was 37.1 percent while the average number of redundant positions was only 2.2 percent per organization. If more aggressive criteria were employed, it would be possible to further elevate this number.

FOUNDATION OF STRATEGY IMPLEMENTATION

We have accomplished much over the years. Accountabilities are clearer. Administration is appropriately centralized. We created a new Product Development function to deal with the increasing complexity of this area. This separate focus helped us to accomplish much more than would otherwise have been the case. Similarly, we created a new function to deal with our fastest growing business line, which further enhanced its growth. In summary, we designed our organization to better achieve our strategy. In fact, I believe that organization is part of strategy, and is divorced from it to the peril of both.

—Derek Fry, President, Visa Canada
Association, March 2006

Often we find that there is often a focus on strategy (e.g., front-end analysis and planning), but less on strategy implementation.

One without the other is meaningless. I was a founding member of the Strategic Management Society in 1980. The society is dedicated to the principle that overall strategic management is important, and that strategic planning is a necessary but not sufficient condition for good performance: strong implementation is critical.

An organization has to be capable of delivering its strategy. This entails the optimal alignment of positions, accountabilities and authorities, people, deliverables, and tasks. If these are not well aligned, performance will be suboptimal. Our research shows that only about 50 percent of manager–direct report relationships are optimally aligned, so it seems unlikely that most organizations are best positioned to deliver their strategies. Further, I would hypothesize that most organizations do not even have the information necessary to know whether or not this is the case.

Our approach provides the foundation for an integrated organization planning and review system. This ensures that deliverables at each level are integrated and at the requisite level of complexity. Without this foundation, more complex, higher-level work is often not done well, or at all. Our approach also makes it possible to integrate strategic planning, business planning, and performance management systems into one more effective and better aligned system. This adds more power by aligning and integrating all work to the necessary outcomes.

FOUNDATION OF HUMAN RESOURCES MANAGEMENT

We have been able to utilize these principles to strategically realign several critical Human Resources systems and practices. Of greatest significance is the impact they have had in the areas of Talent Management, Talent Pool Assessment, Compensation and Job Evaluation.

—Eric Pickering, Vice President, Human
Resources, Allstate Canada Group,
February 2006

Key questions to consider in human resources management include "How effective are our human resources policies and practices?" "How well are our human resources policies aligned to strategic requirements?" and "Are they changing for better or for worse?" While managers throughout an organization are accountable for their human resources (i.e., managers are accountable for their direct reports), the human resources function should ensure that the human resources systems and practices are optimal.

The foundation for answering these questions, and for improving systems and practices, can be found in this Optimizing Organization Design® approach. This would include the alignment of positions, accountabilities and authorities, people, deliverables, and tasks. This organization framework provides unique added value to human resources management. It can be used to

- Provide more strategic value to the organization, and have a broader impact on its outcomes.
- Determine how many strata an organization should have and place each position in the correct stratum. Each stratum is different in the nature of work, the complexity of work, and the information processing capability that is required for an individual to be successful.
- Organize each stratum into three parts (low, medium, and high), that provides a framework for job evaluation, career progression, and compensation.
- Better clarify accountabilities and authorities. Most organizations complain about having silos. This approach provides a solution by addressing cross functional accountabilities and authorities.
- Develop more powerful managerial leadership training.
- Better develop the talent pool. Matching people to positions requires that they have the appropriate knowledge, application, and (unique to this approach) information processing capability. With this information the organization can make better

recruiting, selection, promotion, and talent development decisions.

- Increase employee retention. We have found that the manager–direct report relationship is fundamental to maintaining employee loyalty. Our approach can measure and improve this relationship.
- Ensure that employees are delivering the outcomes that are required for their strata. Too often, the deliverables produced by employees are at a stratum lower than their level of compensation.
- Ensure that employees are doing appropriate tasks for their stratum. Our research shows that professionals spend about 50 percent of their time doing lower-level tasks than someone at a lower level could be paid less money to do as well. This situation is not only a waste of money, but also results in lower employee satisfaction because it means that some individuals are working below their capability. This design approach ensures that the right work is done by the right positions at the appropriate level of compensation.

CLIENT EXPERIENCE

Numerous executives have experienced success in using our approach to organization design to improve organization performance. This is probably the best test of an approach—does it work in real life?

In Appendix A, we have comments from more than 30 executives about their experience in utilizing our organization design approach to improving organization performance. These comments are all dated and go back almost 20 years. While we are grateful for the expressions of thanks we received in these commentaries for the support that our firm provided, that is not why we added them to the book. The most important point is that executives are accountable for improving the performance of their organizations. They are the ones who have to ensure that improvement takes place and is sustained. A consultant doesn't improve an organization—an executive does. These executives have been able to utilize our support and make something happen.

As I reread the commentaries I was struck both by the differences among the executives and by the variety of their insights. With respect to the first point, while we have a comprehensive approach, not all parts are implemented all the time. Even when they are, there are differences in the organization priorities and emphasis. Our approach is not, and cannot be, "one size fits all." While the underlying principles and systems and practices are the same, the actual application has to be tailored to the unique differences in each organization. As for the second point, I find that, as a consultant, I have certain views of the world. What I find is that the executives with whom I work often have different insights and perspectives. I think that there is much to be learned from them.

These executive comments account for about half of the approximately 100 comprehensive organization assessment and implementation projects that we have done over the past 20 years. I think that it would be fair to conclude that in these cases, executives have been able to improve organization design and achieve benefits that one would expect. It should be noted that in many of these situations we also have client research (that is covered later) demonstrating the changes and improvements.

RESEARCH SUPPORT

As is evident from the positive comments made by executives reprinted in this book, the experience of a great many organizations has proven the benefits of our program. A second important validation for our approach is the research support showing its effectiveness. We have been conducting research on organization design for almost 20 years. Some of this work has been alluded to already. It includes one published paper (Ambachtsheer,

Capelle & Scheibelhut, 1998) and the 23 papers that can be found in Appendix B.

This body of work includes the following:

- nonequivalent control group design (there is a control group, but it is not assigned on a random basis)
- one group pretest posttest design (measurement before and after organization design)
- a survey of the top 2,000 companies in Canada
- a measurement and survey within the global pension fund industry
- analysis from the Capelle Associates Benchmarking Database of more than 59,000 manager–direct report relationships from 76 organizations, and more than 13,000 employee satisfaction responses from 38 organizations (this benchmarking database includes managers and their direct reports from the United States, Canada, and many other countries)
- numerous other studies showing relationships among variables

There is consistency in the outcomes from different approaches in different situations over many years. Our research supports the importance of organization design. The following points are important:

- Organization design is (statistically significantly) related to employee satisfaction, customer satisfaction, and financial performance.
- Manager–direct report alignment is (statistically significantly) related to employee satisfaction, employee satisfaction, and financial performance.
- Despite the importance of the manager–direct report alignment, we find that it is misaligned about 50 percent of the time. This is a horrendous waste of human capability—and a tremendous opportunity for improvement.
- Organization design assessments produce average potential annual cost savings of $2,505 per position (total savings are

found by multiplying this number by the number of positions in the review). For example, in an organization of 1,000 employees, this would be average potential annual cost savings of $2,505,000.

- Task alignment assessments can produce average potential annual cost savings of approximately $10,951 for each higher level position included in the review. This is because professionals spend about half of their time doing tasks that someone at a lower level could be paid less to do at least as well.

All of the research papers can be found in Appendix B. You may not be interested in reviewing all of them, but we recommend that you read the introduction and those studies that are of particular interest. It should be comforting for you to know that this approach is supported by both executives who have had success with it and a substantial body of research.

SPECIAL TOPICS

Three special topics need to be addressed as you begin to think about organization design. The first is to understand the strategy, which is an important early step in this Optimizing Organization Design® approach. The second is to understand the work, which is an oft-repeated refrain in organization design. The third is the mistaken belief found in some (often high tech) organizations that a clear organization design will make them bureaucratic.

Understand the Strategy

While we do not provide strategy consulting services, strategy and organization design are integrally linked. We believe that understanding the strategy of an organization is an important early step in enhancing organization design. However, we would have a few caveats.

The first is that strategy is often thought of as being relatively one dimensional and precise (e.g., we will get the strategy and then do the design). Our experience is that it is both complex and evolving. What's more, written documents often do not best describe strategy: it is better to derive it from discussions with senior executives.

The second is that strategy often refers to a plan. The strategy implementation system, which we would call "organization planning and review," is at least equally important, but often overlooked. Complicating matters further is that the term "strategy" can be vague: we prefer "strategic positioning." This is discussed in detail in a later section of the book on aligning deliverables.

The third caveat is that strategy and organization design are generally thought to be sequential: One first does strategy and then design. We find that these phases are more iterative (i.e., each informs the other). An organization design should be both robust and flexible so it can be modified as strategy evolves.

Despite these caveats, it remains true that strategy does inform organization design. This starts with position alignment. Strategy informs both vertical alignment (e.g., how many strata do we need and how do we place each position in the appropriate stratum) and functional alignment (e.g., do we need business units, and how do we make choices about organizing by functions, customers, products/services, geography, etc.).

Much has been written on strategy (far more than on organization design). We have found the following books to be particularly useful in understanding strategy: Ansoff (1979, 1988), Buzzell & Gale (1987), Kim & Mauborgne (2005), Mintzberg (1994), Mintzberg et al. (1998), Pearce & Robinson (1991), and Porter (1980, 1985).

Understand the Work

This could be our mantra. The starting point always is to understand the work. It forms the foundation on which other information gathering and analysis can take place.

In understanding the work of a larger organization, it is important to determine at an early stage the fundamental delivery unit or driver. This is the focal point around which one can design the rest of the organization. For example, in a banking network the delivery unit could be the branch manager. In a hospital, it might be a ward delivering patient care. In a railway, it could be the operational units that move the goods. In a government fisheries department the migratory patterns of fish species might be the unit that makes sense of the system. In each case there is a "key" that provides a fundamental design factor.

In assessing only a part of an organization, it is more difficult to start with a support function (e.g., Human Resources) than a core function (e.g., Production). There are two reasons for this. First, the support functions are designed to provide support to core functions. One has to have some understanding of these in order to properly align the support function. This is doable but complex. The second reason is that a support function is more interconnected with the rest of the organization than some core functions are, which also adds complexity to the analysis.

"A Clear Organization Design Will Make Us Bureaucratic"

Some organizations take the position that clarity of organization design is a problem. Specifically, they argue that it will increase bureaucracy and reduce innovation. These organizations are a small minority and generally found in the high tech sector, where innovation and speed to market are particularly important. We believe this view is extremely dysfunctional. It makes the mistake of confusing clarity with rigidity (i.e., "we can't move quickly enough"). We see it differently.

Some of these (often high tech) organizations often need to deal with developing and managing a complex set of relationships with suppliers, outsourcers, partners, customers (of many varieties), and competitors (who are sometimes partners). This complex set of relationships can include a substantive supply chain. Due to this complexity, there is often a requirement for a sophisticated set of systems, skills, and practices.

Einstein said that everything should be made as simple as possible—but no simpler. We would argue that an organization design must have the "requisite complexity" necessary to deliver its business requirements. If an organization does not have clarity internally, how can it provide clarity to its supply chain and related relationships? A clear organization design does not equate to rigidity and bureaucracy. The reality is quite the contrary. The approach we are describing is principle and research based. If one understands these factors, it is possible to make the necessary changes to the organization more quickly and accurately, and in a way that makes it possible for others to better appreciate where things are going and how they will get there.

A number of our clients are growing quickly, making acquisitions and operating in a turbulent environment. They require a design that is robust and flexible. Our approach supports their specific requirements.

CONCLUSION

You can use our approach to significantly improve your organization performance. In fact, it could be one of the most important methods in your toolkit. You can employ it to improve employee satisfaction, customer satisfaction, and financial performance. You can achieve a competitive advantage that is more sustainable than most. While organization improvements generally require a financial outlay, this one has a significant return on investment (ROI). Organization design also provides a foundation for both strategy implementation and human resources management.

Finally, you can know that this approach is solidly grounded in 25 years of experience. Our approach has demonstrated success in implementation and achieving expected benefits. Organization design tends to not be a central preoccupation for most executives. This constitutes a significant missed opportunity. We encourage you to take advantage of some of the unique opportunities that this book provides.

CHAPTER 2

ORGANIZATION DESIGN ASSESSMENT

*Capelle Associates has provided organization design
support to us for over ten years. They have
conducted four major organization assessments.
Each assessment has been rich in insight, thorough,
comprehensive, very well documented, and focused
in terms of recommendations.*

—April Taggart, Senior Vice President, Talent
Management and Diversity, BMO Financial
Group, April 2006

Organization design assessment is the "content" of organization design. You have to understand how organizations function in order to design them in optimal ways.

The starting point for this discussion is the definition of an organization. We attempt to provide definitions for the terms that we use. Not everyone uses particular terms in the same way, so it is essential to establish our meaning and intention. For our purposes, an organization is a stratified human system. A system is a set of interrelated parts with a boundary separating it from its environment. Systems have inputs, throughputs, outputs, and feedback systems. A human system is a system composed of people and their roles. There are many groupings of human systems, including individual, interpersonal, group and family, intergroup, organization, interorganization, and community (Capelle, 1979). Roles are defined parts of a human system that carry a name and related expectations (e.g., parent or manager).

A stratified system is one in which there is a hierarchy of positions and position relationships based on the differential complexity of the positions. We define a position as a role within an organization. A position should have a description that includes a number of details such as accountabilities, authorities, and requirements.

Organizations clearly have hierarchies. For example, there is differential pay based upon some measure of the complexity of work (e.g., job evaluation system). There are reporting relationships that further define the hierarchy. Of course, we are referring here to employment hierarchies. This does not include partnerships, which are a different type of organization form. Nor are we referring to nonemployees (e.g., contractors). Their treatment is related but different. In such cases one does not manage an employee, but has accountability for a contract.

We define organization design as the relationship of an organization to its environment and the interrelationship of its parts. By optimizing organization design we aim to make the organization design as perfect as possible and appropriate in order to meet its purpose. This requires approaches for assessment and implementation based upon sound theory, research, and practice. Models are invaluable for this purpose.

We use models to understand how organizations function and change. This includes a model for how human systems function, and a model for how human systems change. These models include a view of a system relative to its environment. We also use a model for the parts of a human system and their interrelationships. We call this the organization alignment model. A model can be a useful tool to assist in decision making. For a model to be useful, it should meet the following criteria:

- It should be descriptive, providing a reasonable representation of reality (by definition a model does not replicate reality). It should be understandable.

- It should be prescriptive, meaning that it is useful for decision making. Ideally a model prescribes different actions for different circumstances.

While these are baseline requirements, we would add several other higher-level features for organization design models. They should

- be based on theory that seems reasonable and cohesive
- be supported by research demonstrating their validity and reliability
- have been used in organizations and demonstrated expected results

In our Optimizing Organization Design® approach, we use three main models to understand how organizations function and change: an organization systems functioning model, an organization systems change model, and an organization alignment model. I will outline them here and later discuss them more comprehensively.

- Organization systems functioning model: This model provides a framework for understanding how an organization functions. For example, an organization is a system, and it operates in an environment made up of other organizations, clients, and customers, etc. The organization has inputs (receives resources from the environment), throughputs (transforms the inputs), and outputs (provides products and services). There is a boundary between the organization and the environment and feedback to the organization. This model also provides a basis for developing an organization systems change model.
- Organization systems change model: We can take the organization systems functioning model and think about how it functions over time. We can create a current state model, and then create a future/desired state model. This gives us a framework for thinking about what must change to improve performance over time.

- Organization alignment model: While the organization systems functioning model provides an important framework for understanding an organization as a system in an environment, we also need a model to better understand what does and should happen inside the organization. For this we have an organization alignment model. This model describes the alignment of positions (vertical and functional), accountabilities and authorities (employee, supervisor, manager, manager once removed, and cross functional), people, deliverables, and tasks.

ORGANIZATION SYSTEMS FUNCTIONING MODEL

We believe that the best framework (and therefore model) for understanding organizations is systems theory. Systems theory was initially developed by Ludwig von Bertalanffy (1968) in his book *General Systems Theory*. Miller (1965a, 1965b, 1965c, 1971, 1972 & 1975) extensively developed this approach for what he called "living systems." The framework was further developed for human systems by my book *Changing Human Systems* (1979). In this book, I looked at seven groupings of human systems (intrapersonal, interpersonal, group, intergroup, organization, interorganization, and community) in terms of how they function and change, and the role of a third party in the change process.

An organization can be thought of as a system operating in an environment (see Figure 2.1). The system consists of two parts. There is a governance function (e.g., a Board of Directors) and there is the organization itself. The governance function is accountable to the "owners" whose identity varies (they may be shareholders, members, taxpayers, etc., depending on the nature of the organization). The governance function has overall accountability and authority for the organization. If the Board of Directors can't do the work of the organization, it appoints a head (e.g., a CEO) and delegates accountability and authority to this individual.

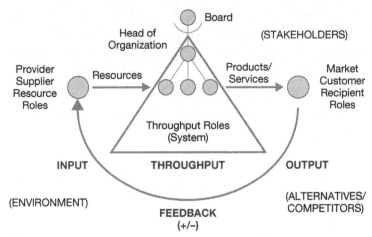

FIGURE 2.1.   Organization Systems Functioning Model

The ongoing governance accountability and authority includes providing context and prescribed limits; approving resources and results; and the selection, oversight, and potential termination of the CEO. The CEO is accountable for the development and operation of the organization within context and prescribed limits.

The organization receives resources from the environment (e.g., providers and suppliers, including external partners); transforms them (throughput); and produces products and services for the market/customers/recipients. There should be a feedback loop with positive and negative feedback to make ongoing changes. The environment also includes stakeholders (e.g., government), alternatives/competitors, and general factors (e.g., economics, politics).

Understanding these factors is critical to organization performance. In fact, the essence of strategic positioning (which I shall describe later) is providing better value to market/customer/recipient than alternatives/competitors. Applying this model for a more comprehensive understanding of the organization supports both organization planning and review, and organization design.

This model becomes important when we start to work with an organization. One of the early steps we take is to determine what is

in scope for the assessment. It might be a full stand-alone organization (as shown in Figure 2.1) or it might be a part of a larger entity
(e.g., a business unit or function). In the latter case, whatever is
in scope for the review is the system and whatever is not in scope
is the environment. Clearly, understanding the environment (at
least to some extent) is critical. At the very least, an appreciation
of the environment provides an understanding of the potential
limits of the review. (It's much more difficult to change basic
systems such as job grading, compensation, etc., if they are not
in scope.)

This raises an important point. We believe that a professional
should make diagnostic decisions about what work to do and what
work not to do. In what situations would one decide that the
intervention was unlikely to lead to benefits? Our rule of thumb
is that the area in scope should be at least a whole subsystem
(e.g., business unit or function) headed by a single individual. This
provides clear accountability for the organization design initiative.
Everything else being equal, the more stand-alone the subsystem
is, the better the chance for success.

We have some reluctance to engage in a "piecemeal" analysis
(e.g., working with a few individuals or a very small unit). The
reason is related to the power of a system. If you change a few
individuals within a larger system where there are significant
differences (practices, values, etc.) in play, the odds are always that
the larger system's way of working will prevail. Some professionals
learned this lesson years ago with training that involved taking
individuals out of a system, "changing" them, and putting them
back in. This was often both demoralizing and a waste of money.
We see similar things happening with piecemeal approaches to
organization design.

With regard to making decisions about whether or not to inter-
vene, Capelle (1979) developed a change readiness model. The basic
idea was that one needed to have at least a medium degree of readiness on all of three factors: power, motivation, and skill.

In translating this into organization design work, the power condition would be satisfied if the head of the unit in scope (and ideally the head of Human Resources) were committed to the improvement and both had sufficient flexibility to actually make the changes. We have found that sometimes this lack of readiness is difficult to discern. Understanding the broader organization can be helpful. Some organizations rotate managers too frequently to develop sustainable change, and sometimes (especially in government) central agencies are so powerful and change resistant that apparent power turns out to be illusory.

The motivation condition would be satisfied either if the organization had an issue that was substantive and needed to be addressed, or the head of the organization was driven by a keen desire to achieve excellence. One might expect that executive motivation would be driven chiefly by a desire to resolve serious issues. That is not our experience. When organizations have serious problems, they often become more cost averse and eliminate discretionary spending. In one way, this seems ironic, because they need the kind of intervention that requires some investment. But we have found that our clients tend to be executives who habitually strive for excellence and are moderate risk takers rather than those whose organizations are in trouble. While we are often disappointed that so many executives don't seem to get that organization design is fundamental to performance, we also feel fortunate that our clients often are more capable and committed than one might reasonably expect.

We have found that the third factor, skill, is less important. Skill can be brought into and/or developed within the organization. For example, as the consultant, we have spent many years developing assessment and implementation skills, methods, and materials. These can be brought into the organization, adapted to it, internal resources trained, and changes sustained.

So, this organization systems functioning model is important in general, and very helpful when we begin working with an organization. We find that background information on the following topics is helpful:

- the context in which the accountable manager (for the area in scope) works
- the market and customers (e.g., a customer satisfaction survey)
- products/services
- positions and employees (e.g., position descriptions, employee satisfaction surveys, etc.)
- providers/suppliers of resources, including contracted and outsourced work
- competitors and alternatives to products/service
- other relevant stakeholders
- the feedback system and the nature of the boundary between the organization and the environment (e.g., how open or closed is the system?)
- strategy/business planning

Two final comments: First, when we review an organization, we undertake a comprehensive assessment of the complete system in scope. This includes both the systems models we have already discussed, as well as the alignment models that are covered later. A more common approach is to analyze one part at a time—the top two or three strata for example. Our view is that it's worth looking at the entire system. This makes the initial review more complicated (it is easier to do one piece at a time), but it gives us a valuable foundation on which to make changes. We're able to look at the whole system and its interdependencies at one time, rather than trying to overlay separate parts on one another.

Second, this model is especially helpful for your thinking about both strategy and organization design. In fact, you will find that this organization systems functioning model operates at the boundary between strategy and organization design.

ORGANIZATION SYSTEMS CHANGE MODEL

Organizations are not static. They change over time. Systems operate in both time and physical space. Space can be measured in many different ways. It can be important in understanding organizations. For example, the physical layout of a railway is critical to understanding both its operation in general and its optimal organization design in particular.

Time is particularly important. It is relatively easy to conceive of time in three periods: past, present, and future. The past is important in terms of understanding history and the developments that have led up to the present. The present is important since the current state is the basis for the future state. The future is important with respect to the natural evolution and enhancement of the system.

The organization systems change model, Figure 2.2, shows the organization in its current and future/desired state. The grid shows both time and performance. The ideal, indicated by the change arrow, is to improve performance over time.

I have discussed the current state of the organization through the organization systems functioning model. What about the future

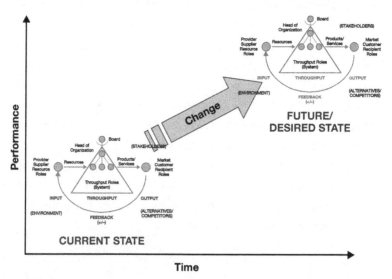

FIGURE 2.2.   Organization Systems Change Model

state? This is also critical as part of the initial understanding of an organization. An organization should be designed to achieve as nearly as possible its desired future state. To the extent that this is understood, the design can be more focused.

Most organizations have documents that deal with their future or desired state. These go by different names. They might be called strategic or business plans. At this point we would be interested in the plan for the total organization in scope. If this happens to be part of a larger organization, then the broader plan is also of value.

These plans may or may not include discussion of vision, mission, and values, which we consider to be important factors. There often tends to be little strategic positioning (e.g., starting with the point of providing better value to alternatives). There is usually a fairly detailed one-year or annual plan, while longer-term plans often are sketchier or absent. The connection between the operating and resource plans and between strategic plans, business plans, and performance management systems may be vague or overlooked. I discuss later in the book, in the section on aligning deliverables, how these systems should be set up and operate.

Two final points: First, we usually find that time is better spent talking to the head of the organization (and perhaps some other key people) about the plans, rather than poring over documents. Written plans are often not up to date with evolving thinking, and tend to be more one dimensional than nuanced. Written documents, while important, may be dated and oversimplified. Second, you should have some clarity on your future or desired state. This model simply introduces the point. You will develop a greater understanding of this in the later section on aligning deliverables.

ORGANIZATION ALIGNMENT MODEL

The organization systems functioning model and organization systems change model provide a broad perspective. They do this in terms of both the relationship of the organization to its environment

FACTOR	DESCRIPTION
ALIGNMENT OF POSITIONS	• Vertical and functional alignment • Provides the spine of the organization • Includes manger–direct report alignment
ALIGNMENT OF ACCOUNTABILITIES AND AUTHORITIES	• Employee, supervisor, manager, manager once removed, and cross functional
ALIGNMENT OF PEOPLE	• Current matching and future requirements
ALIGNMENT OF DELIVERABLES	• Vision, mission, values, strategic, positioning, operational plan, resource plan
ALIGNMENT OF TASKS	• Getting the right tasks done at the right levels

FIGURE 2.3.   Organization Alignment Model

and to its future direction. This information provides the context for a more in-depth look at the alignment within an organization. Our organization alignment model, which evolved from the work of Jaques (1996) and his colleagues, is about the alignment of five factors, as shown in Figure 2.3.

The five critical alignments relate to positions, accountabilities and authorities, people, deliverables, and tasks:

• Alignment of positions: The combination of vertical and functional alignment, constitutes, in effect, the organization structure—its spine. To the extent that it is misaligned, all other factors will be suboptimal. This is also the basis for the manager–direct report alignment, which we believe is one of the most important factors in optimal organization design.

Time span is a critical variable in the alignment of positions.

- Alignment of accountabilities and authorities: These include basic employee, supervisor, manager, and manager once removed accountabilities and authorities, along with cross functional accountabilities and authorities, which are among the most important and most difficult to understand and implement. Alignment of accountabilities also involves the development of position descriptions that include position specifications (i.e., requirements for individuals to fill positions).
- Alignment of people to positions: People are matched to positions based on their skilled knowledge, information processing capability, and application. While the primary purpose in getting this alignment right is the current state of the organization, it also provides the framework for planning future requirements, including succession planning. Understanding potential is an important byproduct of the process.
- Alignment of deliverables: This includes vision, mission, values, strategic positioning, operational plan, and resource plan. It can include the integration of strategic planning, business planning, and performance management systems in an organization.
- Alignment of tasks: Often, some parts of the organization have issues with clarity respecting the tasks required of them and their effectiveness and cost efficiency (e.g., professionals are often paid more to do tasks that employees in lower level positions could do as well for less money).

You can now see the five alignment factors that we consider to be most critical. Each of them has significant potential to help you improve your organization design and your organization performance. I will now begin to look at these five alignment factors in greater detail.

VERTICAL ALIGNMENT OF POSITIONS

The implementation of better role alignment and
related leadership processes, enterprise wide, lead to
new found organizational capabilities and
opportunities. One of the major benefits we gained is
higher level of contribution from managers. We
reframed the expected contribution and are now
having managers think, talk, and act with broader
and longer-term perspectives than we had before.
This is to me a key foundation in ensuring that we
deliver, by the appropriate roles and in a coordinated
way, the right mix of short and long-term results we
require to materialize our strategic plan.

—Christianne Dostie, Vice President, Allstate
Brand, November 2006

We have defined an organization as a stratified human system. It is stratified because there is a hierarchy in terms both of
position titles (e.g., manager, director, and vice president) and
of compensation (job evaluation systems determine different levels of compensation for different positions). It is also stratified
because there is a hierarchy of reporting relationships (one position
"reports to" another).

Hierarchy is a fact: It is universal and incontestable. Our
approach does not create hierarchy—we find it in every organization we go into. We find different levels of position titles,
compensation, and reporting relationships. Some may prefer to not
have a hierarchy—some even pretend that it does not exist. We do
not consider this to be helpful. However, it is important to remem-
ber that this is a hierarchy of work, not of human worth. All human
beings should be valued and treated with respect. Further, all levels
of work in an organization are critical to its success. To think that
people who occupy lower positions in the work hierarchy have less
value as human beings is misguided and harmful. The question is

not how you can get rid of a hierarchy. Rather, it is how to set it up in the most effective, efficient, and fair way.

Jaques (1996) and his colleagues discovered a method to measure a position's complexity. The method is "time span," which is the deliverable with the longest target completion time in a position. They determined that there is a universal system of organization strata. Each stratum is different in terms of the nature of the work, its complexity, and the information processing capability that an individual requires to function in that stratum (this is described that later in the section on aligning people). In the next few sections, I will discuss a number of factors affecting vertical alignment.

Time Span

Time span is a method to determine the complexity of a position. It has considerable research support to which we have added (see Appendix B). It is a fundamental part of our practice and our research.

The time span of a position is determined by the deliverable within the position that has the longest target completion time. This is a measure of the complexity of work in the position. Three points about time span are critical. First, a position with a longer time span is more complex than a position with a shorter time span. The reason is not the complexity of the specific deliverable, but rather the complexity of managing this deliverable and all other deliverables and variables within the specified period. For example, a position with a time span of six months (e.g., in which the task is to manage a six month development project) would be more complex than a position with a time span of two weeks (e.g., in which the task is to contribute a two-week piece of development work to the development project).

The second point is that the higher up the organization one goes, the longer the time span of the position should be. You would not expect the time span of a clerical employee to be 18 months (e.g., managing the development of six new offices). Neither would you expect the time span of a CEO to be limited to three months (e.g., tied to quarterly results). You would anticipate problems in both situations.

The third point is that the full term is time span of discretion. Time span refers to a deliverable that has been delegated, and for which an individual has appropriate accountability and authority. For example, if there is an 18 month deliverable to be completed, it might be delegated either as one 18 month deliverable, or as three six-month chunks. These would be very different deliverables.

More than 50 years of research and practice support time span's efficacy. It can be used to determine how many strata an organization should have and the placement of every position in the correct stratum (vertical alignment). Our own research has shown that better organization design (based upon time span analysis) is related to better organization performance.

Universal Pattern of Organization Strata

There is a universal pattern of organization strata that transcends organization types, countries and cultures (Jaques, 1996). Each stratum is discrete and discontinuous from the adjoining one, and the nature of work in each stratum is different. The research suggests that a reason for this is that people have different information processing capabilities that are discontinuous. In other words, there are transitions in moving from one state to another: a good analogy would be the change from ice to water to steam. Therefore, work at each stratum of the organization requires a different level of individual information processing capability.

The following stratum descriptions are based upon the work of Jaques, (1996). Since both our practice and research are closely linked to these, we have tried to keep the definitions as close as possible to the original.

Positions from Stratum 1 to Stratum 4 operate at a symbolic verbal level (information processing and language used by most adults), while positions from Stratum 5 to Stratum 8 operate at a conceptual abstract level (information processing and language required for more complex, higher-level positions). Stratum 1 positions have a time span of up to three months. Work at this level is focused on one issue at a time, requires a clear set of procedures, and involves overcoming obstacles to reach a goal. Both methods and outcomes can be concretely specified. Individuals require declarative information processing (reasoning by one or more unconnected arguments). The logic is disjunctive (or–or), as in, "Do this or this or this or come and see me." This work includes first-level production, service and administrative employees, as well as supervisory positions.

Stratum 2 positions have a time span of 3 to 12 months. Work at this level involves accumulating data, reflecting, diagnosing, initiating actions, and being accountable for subsequent deliverables that may require as long as three to twelve months. Individuals require cumulative information processing (reasoning by two or more linked arguments). The logic is conjunctive (and-and), as in, "Look at this and this and this, give me your diagnosis, and manage an improvement process that may require 3 to 12 months to complete." This work includes first-level managers and most professionals.

Stratum 3 positions have a time span of one to two years. Work at this level involves selecting a pathway to a solution; implementing it over an extended period of time; and having alternative pathways available to meet the objective if required. Individuals require serial processing (reasoning by chains of two or more cause and effect sequences). The logic is conditional (if-then-then). "If I do this, then I can do this, and then I can do this." This work includes being accountable for (i.e., managing) Stratum 2 managers and professionals, as well as any more senior individual contributors accountable for somewhat longer-term development work.

Stratum 4 positions have a time span of two to five years. Work at this level involves creating and implementing parallel and inter-connected pathways, and managing them to completion. Individuals require parallel processing capability (reasoning by two or more series of cause and effect sequences that are linked and interwoven). The logic is bi-conditional (if-and-only-if): two or more if-then-then processes, one dependent upon the other. This work includes general managers and individuals accountable for longer-term development work (e.g., a three year project to develop and implement a new integrated computer system for a larger enterprise, with related training and process improvement). It is important to note that this stratum is general management and not the direct management found in the previous two strata.

Stratum 5 positions have a time span of 5 to 10 years. Work at this level involves developing whole systems (e.g., developing new products for new markets over a 5-to-10-year period). Individuals require third order declarative information processing (reasoning by one or more unconnected arguments). The logic is disjunctive (or-or). However, the third order of information complexity is at the abstract conceptual level. Abstract concepts are used as tools to do the work. These positions include heads of most standalone Stratum 5 organizations, as well as heads of substantial business units and major functions in larger organizations. This seems to be the natural level to organize full business units. A Stratum 5 head should work in two directions by providing direction below while influencing the strategic context above.

Stratum 6 positions have a time span of 10 to 20 years. Stratum 6 generally marks the transition from business unit (Stratum 5) work to corporate work (Strata 6 to 8) in large organizations. It requires broad networking to accumulate diagnostic information. It involves judging corporate priorities, enhancing the value of corporate assets, and contributing to longer-term corporate performance. Work at the Stratum 6 level moves from one bounded whole system to two or more whole systems. An executive accountable for a group of business units or functions would be accountable (within the context of the work) for their creation (green field, acquisition, merger, joint venture), development (including investment), modification, amalgamation, and divestment. Individuals in this stratum require third order cumulative information processing (reasoning by two or more linked arguments). The logic is conjunctive (and-and). However, the third order of information complexity is at the abstract conceptual level. Abstract concepts are used as tools to do the work. Titles of positions doing this work include CEO, COO, president, and executive vice president.

Stratum 7 positions have a time span of 20 to 50 years. Work at this level moves to executive leadership of more complex organizations. The work involves judging longer-term international societal requirements, and translating this into the required business directions. An individual accountable for Stratum 6 groupings of Stratum 5 business units or functions can create, develop, modify, amalgamate, and/or divest them. Conceptual pathways, with alternatives, are constructed to provide paths into the future. The logic is conditional (if-then-then). However, the third order of information complexity is at the abstract conceptual level. Abstract concepts such as culture, values, and economies become key working tools. Titles of positions doing this work include CEO, COO, and president of large organizations.

Stratum 8 positions have a time span of more than 50 years. Work at this level is limited to executive leadership of a limited number of the most complex worldwide, multi-business organizations. The work focuses on Stratum 7 groups of Stratum 6 groups of Stratum 5 business units. Such higher-level groupings can be created, developed, modified, amalgamated, and divested. Parallel and inter-connected conceptual pathways into the future are created. The logic is bi-conditional (if-and-only-if): two or more if-then-then processes, one dependent upon the other. However, the third order of information complexity is at the abstract conceptual level. Abstract concepts such as economies are key working tools. Titles of positions doing this work include a limited number of CEOs of the most complex organizations. It is interesting to note that the language is one of generations (e.g., future generations).

As incumbents evolve through these positions they sometimes develop a keener interest in longer-term societal issues rather than corporate issues.

It is interesting to consider the delegation of work within this framework. For example, a Stratum 4 head of Information Technology might have three years to develop and implement a new integrated computer system for a larger enterprise. This work requires parallel processing (i.e., developing and managing parallel and interconnected pathways, which could include hardware, software and people plans). This individual might delegate one of these pathways to a Stratum 3 direct report. This would become a serial path for this individual (e.g., develop and implement an 18-month deliverable to develop the required skills sets in the organization through hiring and training). This Stratum 3 individual might delegate a six-month diagnostic deliverable to a Stratum 2 individual (do an assessment, develop a training program, and complete a pilot project). The Stratum 2 individual might delegate a one-month deliverable to a Stratum 1 direct report (e.g., gather information and complete an inventory of the offerings of all service providers in this field).

You can see that each level is doing work at a different level of complexity, and the work is delegated so that all strata are contributing to the desired outcome. As well, each manager in this example is doing higher-level work than the direct report, and each provides the context that is necessary for getting the work done. It all fits together.

You can also see what might happen if the manager of an individual was not one stratum higher. For example, a Stratum 1 individual doing proceduralized work requires a Stratum 2 manager who has the diagnostic capability necessary to provide direction and develop new proceduralized approaches. If a Stratum 1 individual had a Stratum 1 manager, they would both be operating at the same level, and the diagnostic capability necessary of oversight would be missing. As well, if a Stratum 1 individual has a Stratum 3 manager, there is too much distance between the two. Both of these other situations would be sub optimal. We will address this further in the next section.

Manager–Direct Report Alignment

One of the significant implications of appropriate stratification is that every employee should have a manager exactly one stratum above, in terms of both the complexity of work and information processing capability. This is called requisite manager–direct report alignment (Jaques, 1996). There are two suboptimal alignments.

The first is when a manager and direct report are in the same stratum. This is called compression. This situation is not reflected in an organization chart, which is just boxes drawn on a piece of paper. It is only when you understand the complexity of the work that you can identify the problem. Some symptoms of compression are lack of clarity, redundancy, confusion, and conflict. The manager is being paid extra money to be a manager but is not providing the necessary level of work and the organization is not getting full value for its money. The direct report will often be micromanaged and consequently not use all of his capability. This is a good example of how poor organization design results in both employee dissatisfaction and reduced financial performance.

The second suboptimal alignment is when a manager and direct report are more than one stratum apart. This is called a gap. The manager is at too high a level relative to the direct report: there is a missing position between the two. Symptoms of a gap may include a manager complaining that the direct report has no initiative and/or the manager being "pulled down into the weeds." Another symptom of a gap can be a direct report complaining that the manager gives no direction. These complaints generally are treated as a performance issue when there is actually a structural defect caused by a missing position. Although rarely discussed, a gap is an effectiveness issue that can kill an organization. For example, the collapse of Barings Bank was caused by the financial losses incurred

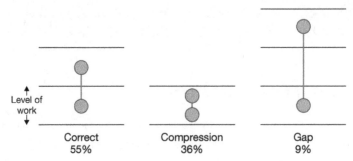

FIGURE 2.4.   Layering Compression and Gaps

by a rogue trader (Nick Leeson), who was in a gap situation with inadequate management (Leeson & Whitley, 1996).

Manager–direct alignment is one of the most powerful factors related to improving organization performance. Figure 2.4 shows, compression, gaps, and optimal vertical alignment based on the Capelle Associates benchmarking database of over 59,000 manager–direct report relationships in 76 organizations. This shows that vertical alignment is only optimal only about half the time.

Poor alignment is a significant barrier to optimal performance. The alignment of manager–direct report relationships provides the spine on which other factors are overlaid. If it is not properly aligned, other factors will be sub-optimal. This is a horrendous waste of human resources. Many organizations unintentionally create barriers preventing employees from doing optimal work.

Our client research shows that the removal of redundant positions provides average potential annual savings of about $2,505 per position. The savings can be considerable. For example, for a 1,000 person organization, it would be $2,505 × 1,000 = $2,505,000). This provides an average potential annual ROI of 589%. This result would be based on a comprehensive assessment that pinpoints compression situations.

There are a few situations in which it may be appropriate to have a gap between a manager and direct report. This might occur when the primary purpose of the direct report is to provide direct output support (DOS) to the manager. The most common example is a support position such as executive assistant. It can also apply to a professional position in which, due to the complexity, the output should be at a higher level. For example, an executive may be accountable for a more complex deliverable (e.g., business plan, design or development) and may receive direct output support (DOS) from a professional position more than one stratum below.

Determining Vertical Alignment

The first step in assessing vertical alignment is to understand the organization (in scope for the review) from a broader perspective. You need to understand the organization in its environment. This analysis comes from the organization systems functioning model and related information drawn from documents and interviews. You also need to know the direction in which the organization is headed. This would come from the organization systems change model and related information from documents and interviews.

The next step is to interview managers to determine the time spans of their direct reports. This provides information on the current organization. It is also useful to find out what managers think that their time span is (self span) and the actual level of compensation for the position (compensation span). This provides additional information for understanding the nature and complexity of work. However, these are not required. It is also possible to verify the information with the manager of the manager, but we do not consider this to be essential.

This information should then be analyzed. What are the issues? Analysis of manager–direct report alignment is particularly useful. Gaps and compressions are serious impediments to optimal performance.

The next step is the most difficult and integrates the science and art of organization design. It involves understanding the future direction of the organization and its current position alignment, and then creating the future position alignment that can best serve the organization. While only vertical alignment has been discussed to this point, this future position alignment also includes functional alignment, which will be covered in the next section. There are different ways that one can develop this future position alignment. For example, you could do one or two strata of the organization at a time. We prefer to provide recommendations on the full organization in scope to our client. While this is a more complex undertaking, we find that it adds more value than doing it one piece at a time. This full organization position alignment becomes the blueprint for the full organization. Further fine tuning and improvement can be undertaken in the cascading management team meetings that are part of the implementation.

Several related points should be made. First, in designing positions, it is important to ensure that there is consistency between the time span and the information processing requirement of the position. A discrepancy between these two is an indication of a suboptimally designed position. An example might be a position that has a Stratum 1 time span (e.g., one month deliverable) and a Stratum 2 information processing requirement (e.g., one that calls for diagnostic capability). However, there can be situations in which younger employees with a high information processing capability are required to develop skilled knowledge before moving to higher-level positions. For example, a newly recruited university graduate with Stratum 3 information processing capability may not yet have the skilled knowledge to function in a Stratum 3 director position. There may be an array of skilled knowledge that must be acquired first. This is a difficult balancing act, and these situations need to be managed carefully.

Second, while I have emphasized the primary managerial accountability within each stratum, it is also possible to have individual contributor positions at different strata. For example, individuals in research, development, and policy positions could be found at a Stratum 2 level or up to several strata above.

Third, work at each stratum includes some work from all lower levels. For example, individuals at a Stratum 3 level also will do Stratum 2 and Stratum 1 work. Further, they retain the information processing capability to do so. Position descriptions specify the maximum rather than the minimum level of work and complexity of information processing at each stratum.

Special Topics

While it is important to understand the general framework (e.g., time span, universal pattern of organization strata, manager–direct report alignment and how to determine vertical alignment), a few special topics provide more in depth examples of how vertical alignment works and some of the related issues and opportunities. We have encountered the following three issues in organizations that have not been properly stratified. Many readers may recognize them from their own experience:

- job grades substituted for reporting levels
- an extra layer inserted for career planning
- arbitrary removal of management layer

Next, I will discuss several additional special topics pertaining to properly stratified organizations, as follows:

- span of control
- Stratum 1 employees, Stratum 1 supervisors, and Stratum 2 managers
- organization complexity and the need for more strata
- executive assistant return on investment
- Stratum 1 or Stratum 2?
- three-level teams
- one manager, two positions in two different strata
- organizations and democracy
- work levels shifting

Job Grades Substituted for Reporting Levels

When we go into organizations and see too many layers, often the cause is confusion between job grade and reporting level. For example a position with a job grade of 4 reports to a position with a job grade of 5 which reports to a position with a job grade of 6. In these cases, we often find that such job grades are actually in the same stratum. The failure to understand this can result in too many levels and compressed positions.

A difficulty with most job grade systems is that it is not clear what the requirements should be for each reporting level. This is another example of the value of determining the strata of positions. We know that every employee should have a manager exactly one stratum above, as reflected both by the complexity of work done and by the information processing capability at that level. Both are measurable, making a robust system.

Further, each stratum can be divided into three sub strata: Low, Medium, and High. For example, at Stratum 2 (e.g., professional positions), we could establish:

- Stratum 2 Low: entry level professional positions
- Stratum 2 Medium: full professional positions
- Stratum 2 High: senior professional positions

This framework can be used for compensation and development purposes.

An Extra Layer Inserted for Career Planning

Sometimes an organization adds an extra layer in order to have "better career planning." The following is a cautionary tale that bears repeating. An organization had director positions, which should have been at a Stratum 3 level, and professional positions, which should be at a Stratum 2 level. They wanted to have an in-between position so that the professionals could develop more managerial skill and to reduce the distance between professional and director. So, they added assistant director positions. All of this was well intentioned. However, the effect was to create compressed positions between Stratum 2 and Stratum 3. We know the outcomes of compression. The manager positions micromanaged and the direct report positions couldn't use their full capabilities. It got worse. Our experience is that people generally want to do real work. So these new assistant directors took some work from the directors and took some work from the professionals. The organization then had three levels without sufficient real work!

Beware of assistant titles! They are often a sign of compression. The worst title that we have come across was in government department where we encountered the Assistant Associate Assistant Deputy Minister. (I did not make this up!) How compressed do you think that position was?

Arbitrary Removal of Management Layers

We have seen instances where management has decided in the interest of, say, increased efficiency, to arbitrarily remove one or more layers. This is done without first analyzing the nature of the work or determining the optimal number of strata required for the particular situation. When we have gone into organizations that have done this, we have generally found that gaps were created, there were disconnects between managers and direct reports, and that employee satisfaction was reduced (particularly in terms of the relationship with the manager).

The starting point should always be an understanding of the work. We find that time span analysis is essential in determining the complexity of work, the number of strata that are necessary, and in placing each position in the correct stratum. The complexity of work in an organization will determine how many strata it requires. For example, a mom and pop store might require two levels or strata, whereas a worldwide multibusiness organization might require eight. It is not a matter of reducing strata: it is a matter of getting them right. However, it remains the case that optimizing the vertical alignment often does result in identifying and removing redundant positions, and thereby reducing costs and increasing satisfaction. But these steps should be taken on the basis of an analysis and understanding of the work, and not with some arbitrary target in mind.

Span of Control

Some executives tend to focus on span of control (the number of direct reports of a manager) to the exclusion of other factors. Often they do this because it is easily measured. The exclusive attention paid to span of control often leads to simple (and simplistic) prescriptions for "improving" organization design. For example, you might hear someone say, "Determine the current average span of control and reduce it by X." We have often heard that the span of control should be between 6 and 8. Some have been bold enough to say that the span of control should be 7!

Our view is that these simplistic recommendations are fundamentally wrong. There is no consistent research supporting an ideal span of control that can be implemented across any organization. The starting point should always be to understand the nature of work, and to then design the positions, the alignment of positions, and the accountabilities and authorities based on that understanding. The span of control is an output of understanding the nature of work, not a rigid input to designing an organization. It depends on a number of factors such as level of complexity, nature and measurability of work, experience and capability of manager and direct reports, amount of change, and so on.

Admittedly, we sometimes find legitimate patterns. For example, a manager of first-level employees with relatively proceduralized, measurable work can have considerably more direct reports than a manager of professionals doing quite diverse work. But, fundamentally, the design of the organization should enable managers to be effective and cost efficient. This means not having too many or too few direct reports. It also means having a manager accountable for work that is functionally aligned and that the manager can understand. For example a manager of first-level employees should know the work very well and ideally be able to do it. A more senior manager does not have to understand the work in as much detail, but does need to have sufficient understanding to direct it. Work gets more diverse and complex at higher strata and consequently requires differences in management. So a CEO, for example, cannot (and should not) understand the details of the work of all direct reports. One of the problems that comes from relying on a simplistic span of control prescription is that quite diverse areas are often put together with the result that the manager cannot understand them well enough to provide proper direction.

In summary, start with an understanding of the work. Set up optimal spans of control based upon this understanding. And don't fall victim to a simplistic prescription for a "one size fits all" span of control.

Stratum 1 Employees, Stratum 1 Supervisors, and Stratum 2 Managers

The relationship among Stratum 1 employees, Stratum 1 supervisors, and Stratum 2 managers is critical to effective performance. This was originally suggested by Jaques (1996) and his colleagues, and has become an important part of our practice. We often find that these relationships are not properly aligned.

Much of the output of most organizations comes from Stratum 1. This includes many front line employees (e.g., production and service employees) and support staff. Stratum 1 positions have time spans of less than three months. Employees in Stratum 1 positions require managers in Stratum 2 positions. These Stratum 2 manager positions have time spans of 3 to 12 months, and the incumbents should have the capability to work at that level.

Before looking at the accountability relationships, it is important to understand the difference between Stratum 1 and Stratum 2 work. Work at a Stratum 1 level is more procedural, and involves overcoming obstacles to reach a goal. The logic set is or-or: "Try this or this or this, or, if that does not work, go and discuss it with your manager or supervisor." Judgment is required in Stratum 1 work, but only within a fairly clear set of parameters or procedures. For example, a Stratum 1 customer service representative may have a set of procedures to follow in dealing with customers. Issues that fall outside of these parameters would be elevated to another position (e.g., a manager or supervisor).

Stratum 2 work, on the other hand, involves accumulating data, reflecting, diagnosing, and initiating action. The logic set is and-and: "Look at this and this and this, and give me your diagnosis and action plan." Stratum 2 work generally involves getting beneath the surface, looking at connections, making judgments and action plans, and completing implementations that will range from 3 to 12 months. For example, a Stratum 2 manager of a call center finds that a new product line in a new geographic area requires significant changes in the way the center works. The manager would be accountable, with appropriate support, to develop new systems, procedures, and training and development. The initial work may be completed in one month, but the full implementation may require four months.

With this understanding of the basic difference between Stratum 1 and Stratum 2, we can now look at the relationships between Stratum 2 managers and Stratum 1 employees. Stratum 2 managers should be accountable for (i.e., manage) Stratum 1 employees. The manager should know the employees (their capabilities and issues), know the work (and ideally be able to do it), and continually improve both.

However, there may come a point when a Stratum 2 manager has more Stratum 1 direct reports than she can comfortably manage. The manager does not know either the direct reports or the work well enough, and does not improve them enough. When there are too many direct reports to do the work, one solution is to create another manager position. This may be the best solution, particularly where more than one manager position already exists. Another solution is to appoint a supervisor (other titles, such as foreman, group leader or team leader, can also be used). A supervisor is a Stratum 1 employee who should have very good technical and interpersonal skills. The role of the supervisor, within the context and prescribed limits set by the manager, is to assist the manager by assigning and monitoring work; providing oral feedback to employees; and making recommendations to the manager on hiring, performance appraisal, and performance issues. However, the manager remains the individual who is accountable for both the employees and the supervisor, including hiring, appraisal, etc. The manager must continue to know the employees and the work, and improve both. This relationship is illustrated in Figure 2.5.

A Stratum 1 supervisor position does not perform at a Stratum 2 manager level. Stratum 1 supervisors are operating within the same stratum as the employee, and do not add Stratum 2 value (context, prescribed limits, and diagnostic work). If they are used as a management layer, they block the Stratum 2 manager from doing his diagnostic work (i.e., knowing the employees and the work and improving both). This is extremely dysfunctional. Over time, the lack of diagnostic work can lead to a decline in performance. We often find this on night and weekend shifts. A Stratum 1 supervisor

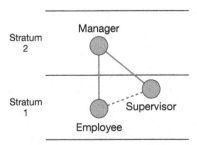

FIGURE 2.5.   Manager, Supervisor and Employee Relationship

is left in charge and virtually alone, the Stratum 2 manager having abdicated his or her accountability. The Stratum 2 manager does not have to be there all the time, but must have sufficient contact to do the Stratum 2 managerial work. The situation in which the Stratum 2 manager does not maintain the requisite relationship with the Stratum 1 supervisor and employees tends to result in both reduced performance and reduced employee satisfaction.

I have already shown that Stratum 1 and Stratum 2 work is different. The language of the two strata also is different. Those with experience around a production area (manufacturing or service) usually get this. In response to "How are things going?" a Stratum 1 supervisor tends to make a number of unconnected declarative statements. She might say, for example, that we had this problem and fixed it, we had another problem and fixed it, etc. A Stratum 2 manager tends to respond in a diagnostic way, along the lines of "we had several problems, I think that they are interrelated, and I need to do some analysis to find out what is really going on."

I have also shown that each stratum of work requires individuals with different capabilities. Promotion from a Stratum 1 employee to a Stratum 1 supervisor, with the required technical and interpersonal skills, is a reasonably manageable progression. The requirement for information processing capability is the same. However, moving from a Stratum 1 supervisor to a Stratum 2 manager is a much bigger jump because it requires a fundamentally different information processing capability. The research indicates that the development of this capability is a growth process. Some individuals, throughout their careers, stay at the level of disjunctive information processing (or-or) suitable for Stratum 1 work. Some mature to the level of conjunctive information processing (and-and) suitable for Stratum 2 work. Some individuals move to higher levels. Clearly, selection processes (internal talent pool and external recruiting) should be developed to ensure that work requirements and individual capabilities are properly aligned. The objective should be to match individuals to work so that they will use their capabilities and be successful. Problems are created when individuals are in positions that do not use their full capabilities. However, problems may also emerge when individuals are promoted to positions for which they do not have the required capabilities (e.g., information processing capability).

Organization Complexity and the Need for More Strata

A lot of management literature focuses on delayering—how can we have the fewest layers? We focus instead on understanding the complexity of work, creating the optimal number of strata, and placing each position in the right stratum. If an organization has too few strata for the complexity of work it needs to do, it may be lacking the higher-level positions that will be necessary to be successful. Lower-level positions with lower levels of individual capability will not be able to do this. The organization will likely not reach its potential.

A couple of situations demonstrate this point. We once assessed an international nonprofit organization that dealt with world bodies such as the United Nations. This organization had five strata and it was clear it needed six. Higher-level work, especially in relation to these other global organizations, was not being adequately performed. An extra stratum was added and higher stratum positions were created and filled by capable individuals, and it made a significant positive difference. No organization wants its representatives matched up with higher capability individuals from other organizations. The less capable individuals would likely "underrepresent" their organization and be less successful in moving its agenda ahead in a broader forum.

Another issue we have seen several times is the case of an organization that grows in complexity and responds by adding more high-level positions. These positions are generally compressed within the existing strata alignment. However, what the organization needs is to add an extra stratum. We call this "stress cracks," when an organization is moving towards adding an additional stratum but has not yet done so. It is necessary is to make the decision and then realign positions accordingly. For example, we had one client that started as a fairly focused Stratum 5 business unit. Over time, it added more business lines, increased its geographic scope, and found itself competing in an industry that was consolidating with fewer, larger firms. In other words, its business was becoming increasingly complex. The firm shifted to a Stratum 6 organization, and made the necessary changes, particularly at the higher levels. It had been performing well, but moved the performance to a still higher level.

Executive Assistant Return on Investment

Over the years, we have noticed considerable variability in executive assistant positions (and, indeed, in most positions). These EA positions are often set up in Stratum 1 and filled by individuals with Stratum 1 information processing capability. Our view is that the capability of the executive assistant makes a significant difference in the performance of an executive.

We sometimes suggest that executive assistant positions should be at a Stratum 2 level. This creates much stronger support for the executive. Provided the executive assistant had the skilled knowledge and application required for the position, he also would have the diagnostic capability to handle more complex situations without the more detailed involvement of the executive. Naturally, the executive would have to create the position and delegate to it optimally. Once this is done, however, the executive would be freed up to focus on the unique added-value work that the position requires. This move can be one of the best investments an executive can make.

There are situations in which executive assistant positions, and the information processing capabilities of the incumbents, can beneficially be at levels higher even than Stratum 2. A rule of thumb would be that executive assistants ideally are no more than two strata below an executive. So, for example, it would be beneficial to look at having a Stratum 3 executive assistant for a Stratum 5 executive. It is interesting to note that some government (particularly on the political side) and military organizations have such positions.

Stratum 1 or Stratum 2?

Deciding whether a position should be at a Stratum 1 or Stratum 2 level, staffing it with individuals with the right level of information processing capability, and delegating the right level of tasks are critical for effective and efficient work. The first step is to accurately determine the level of the position.

We have found that certain positions are particularly problematic. The worst seems to be an analyst position. This could be at Stratum 1 or Stratum 2 depending on the requirements. For example, a Stratum 1 analyst may do statistical analysis using predetermined spreadsheets and methods. This would be proceduralized work at a Stratum 1 level. However, there are situations in which an analyst may be required to assess more complex situations and determine the best methods to apply. For example, she may have to measure the performance of a company, and be required to pull together both the required information and methods of analysis, in order to arrive at a conclusion. This would put the position into Stratum 2. However, we find that few organizations understand the difference between Stratum 1 and Stratum 2 positions and capabilities and consequently these distinctions are rarely made. This failure could result in Stratum 2–capable individuals who are underutilized in a Stratum 1 position, or Stratum 1–capable individuals who fail in a Stratum 2 position. As well, tasks often are inappropriately delegated, leading to additional issues.

It is relatively easy to come up with other examples of this lack of clarity between Stratum 1 and Stratum 2 positions. In hospitals, it is often unclear whether nursing positions are at a Stratum 1 or Stratum 2 level. This is somewhat unfortunate, because health care costs are such an important issue, but something as fundamental as the level of the position often does not get addressed. Another example is found in banking. In the search for higher value added, teller positions (also called customer service representative positions) are eliminated and loans or investment positions are created. Teller positions are Stratum 1. Loans or investments positions can be at either Stratum 1 or Stratum 2 (or higher, although not usually in a branch location). The failure to understand the difference has resulted in some Stratum 1–capable individuals from teller positions being put into Stratum 2 loans or investments positions. Not surprisingly, many of them fail to thrive in their new situation. This has resulted in unnecessary damage to customer and employee satisfaction and in financial performance.

Determining a position's stratum is a critical early step in building organizations. It creates the foundation for other vital moves, such as staffing and delegation. Getting it right makes a big difference in organization performance.

Three-Level Teams

We have often encountered situations in which a manager is accountable for direct report positions that are in two different strata. The managers are generally not aware of what strata are. They are aware of the problems the issue gives rise to, even though they do not understand source of the problem and are incapable of resolving it.

The situation generally occurs when the direct reports are in both Stratum 1 and Stratum 2 positions. The manager generally is in a position that should be Stratum 3. This would provide appropriate alignment for the Stratum 2 positions, but leave a gap with the Stratum 1 positions. This disconnect will result in the Stratum 1 employees getting insufficient direction while the manager may feel "pulled down into the weeds" and believe that the Stratum 1 employees lack initiative.

We have found numerous examples of this situation. For example, in sales organizations, a Stratum 3 manager may be accountable for sales positions at a Stratum 2 level (relationship management) and a Stratum 1 level (transactional sales). The manager usually does not understand strata, but is aware of issues. If the manager delegates more broadly (appropriate for the Stratum 2 level), the Stratum 1 employees can't operate properly. If the manager delegates in a more detailed way (appropriate for the Stratum 1 employees), the Stratum 2 employees feel constrained and unable to use their full capability. This is a catch-22. This problem is also obvious in meetings. There is a tug of war between a more conceptual (Stratum 2) and a more concrete (Stratum 1) focus. The manager has to keep "translating" between the two levels. This takes time and energy and can be frustrating for both the manager and the direct reports. People intuitively know there is a problem, but they don't have the conceptual framework necessary to understand and rectify it.

Another example of this kind of dysfunction is found in health care where the head of a nursing unit (which often should be Stratum 3) is accountable for both registered nurses (usually Stratum 2) and nursing assistants (Stratum 1). There is a gap between the head of the nursing unit and the nursing assistants with the result that the nursing assistants receive suboptimal direction and do suboptimal work.

The problem also sometimes occurs with Stratum 4 manager positions. These Stratum 4 managers would be accountable for managers who run geographically separate units. Examples of such units would include manufacturing plants, retail stores, transportation terminals, health care units, power generation plants, bank branches, or sales offices. As one can gather from the list, the problem ranges across diverse fields. In each case the assumption is that since these units do a similar kind of work, they are the same and should report to the same manager. This assumption is often not warranted. The different units can be at either Stratum 2 or Stratum 3 level (or even higher in some cases). Having them report to the same individual often creates gaps and all of the problems that go with them.

In all of these situations, two remedial steps are necessary. First determine the strata of the direct report positions. Second, ensure that each of these direct reports has a manager exactly one stratum higher. The result will be a much stronger manager–direct report alignment. Further, as the research shows, this relates to better employee satisfaction, customer satisfaction, and financial performance.

One Manager, Two Positions in Two Different Strata

We have seen situations in which organizations have removed a manager. Rather than realigning the work and positions, they've taken a shortcut. Either the manager of the unfilled position, or a direct report manager of the unfilled position, retains her current position and takes over the unfilled position. She is therefore expected to occupy positions in two adjacent strata and manage direct reports in two different strata. This looks like a slick solution. It might get the work done and save money.

Generally, however, it does not work. There are two issues. The first is that when there is an unfilled position (or a position has been removed), it is necessary to understand the work done by the position in order to make appropriate decisions on its elimination or reallocation. Different aspects of the work might properly be assigned to different positions. This is often not done.

The second issue is that an individual may have information processing capability suitable for managing in one stratum but not for managing in two. If the individual has information processing capability in line with the higher of the two positions, there will be a gap with lower-level positions. If she has information processing capability in line with the lower of the two positions, there will be a gap with the immediate manager position. So, a suboptimal position alignment is created with all of the attendant problems.

Organizations and Democracy

An association is generally a democracy. It elects a governing body. This could be shareholders electing a Board of Directors, members of a nonprofit organization electing a Board of Directors, or citizens electing a government.

The governing body generally cannot directly do the work, so it appoints a head of the organization. It could be the CEO of a company, the executive director of a nonprofit organization, or the deputy minister of a government organization. The head of the organization is accountable to the governing body for the performance of the organization. This individual cannot do all the work, so he delegates accountability and authority to direct reports. This sequence of delegation cascades down through the organization. Because there are hierarchies of positions, accountabilities and authorities, and delegation of work, organizations are not democracies.

So there is a profound, demonstrable difference between an association, which is a democracy, and an organization, which is not.

Although organizations are not democracies, this in no way entitles anyone to treat employees badly. While there is a moral rationale for this, there is also a business rationale: Research shows that there is a strong linkage between employee satisfaction and both customer satisfaction and financial performance.

It also is a mistake for an organization to pretend that it is a democracy. Employees usually see through this guise. Further, if organization and business conditions deteriorate, and executives take cost-cutting measures, it soon becomes clear that any claim to democratic process is patently untrue. Consider, for example, what happened at the time of the high tech crash in the early 2000s. Many high tech companies perpetuated the egalitarian myth, only to demonstrate its illusory nature when they cut back on staff. When pretense is exposed, it results in serious distrust issues.

Work Levels Shifting

Fairfield (2002, 2007) developed a concept he calls "work levels shifting." The basic idea is to identify a critical factor in an industry, and then raise the level of complexity for the client company. For example, if quality is a critical factor in manufacturing, and competitors are using end-of-the-line inspection, a company could shift to a higher level of quality assurance, or an even higher level of statistical quality control. These enhancements would require higher levels of work and capability. However, they also should provide better results, and, if the factor was a critical success factor, they should also provide competitive advantage.

We have not done this in the same strategic way, with a competitive analysis, as suggested by Fairfield. However, we have often been in situations where a function was at too low a level to do the required work. In these cases—most frequently with product development—the level of work of the function was increased. We have also found situations where a whole organization did not have enough strata to do the required level of work. In these cases we have worked with the organization to add a stratum with all that entails.

Conclusion

Better organization design, as we define it, is related to better employee satisfaction, customer satisfaction, and financial performance. One subfactor, manager–direct report alignment, is also directly related to these outcomes.

FUNCTIONAL ALIGNMENT OF POSITIONS

In particular, the recommendations ... on the vertical and functional alignment in the Secretariat including our country and regional delegations have stood the test of time. The way we operate has improved significantly because of a clearer understanding of the relationships amongst these critical operating areas.

—George Weber, Secretary General, International Federation of Red Cross and Red Crescent Societies, October 1999

Vertical alignment is a critical piece of position alignment; functional alignment is another. Functional alignment begins with the definition of the corporate function, including its added value, and the potential creation of business units. It looks at the interrelationships between the corporate and business unit level, and at the interrelationships among business units. A useful perspective on strategy and added value at these levels is provided by Goold et al (1994).

At the business unit level, functional alignment includes both core and support functions. The core functions that an organization has are externally focused on the market and clients, and on the products and/or services of an organization. There are three main core functions related to the organization's products and services:

- development
- delivery
- communication, marketing and sales

The support parts of an organization are more internally oriented. These would typically include

- finance
- human resources
- information technology

When you create the functional alignment, the starting point is an understanding of the strategy. There are a number of options with respect to how functions are organized, including the following:

- geography (e.g., six country heads are direct reports of the organization head)
- client type (e.g., the heads of small business clients, medium business clients, and large business clients are direct reports of the organization head)

- product/service type (e.g., the heads of small products, medium products, and large products are direct reports of the organization head)
- function (e.g., heads of development, marketing and sales, and manufacturing are direct reports of the organization head)

An initial decision, related to strategy, determines which would be the primary way of organizing. This becomes the framework for setting up managerial accountabilities and authorities. A decision then is made with respect to the secondary (or even tertiary) way of organizing. For example, if you organize primarily on the basis of client type, then geography and function are still important. One of these may become the secondary way of organizing. The secondary way of organizing requires cross functional accountabilities and authorities to be effective. Accountabilities and authorities are discussed in the next section. We have found that Galbraith (1977, 2002) and his colleagues provide some helpful perspectives on making these grouping choices and their subsequent linkages. As well, Galbraith (2000) has provided some useful insights on the design of the global corporation.

Note that the distinction between core and support functions is not always complete. For example, I have listed information technology as a support function. This is accurate for some aspects of IT, such as developing and maintaining the information technology system so that people within the organization can communicate. However, in financial services organizations, information technology is an important core function, essential to delivering electronic financial services. So, care must be taken in setting up this function and ensuring that there is also proper alignment with the core functions.

Functional alignment of positions does not have the research based foundation that exists with respect to vertical alignment (e.g., time span, universal pattern of organization strata, etc.). It requires judgment based on current design and future direction. Vertical alignment of course plays a part in functional alignment.

One question that frequently arises has to do with the complexity of work associated with a particular function, and therefore the stratum in which it belongs. For example, we had a situation in a fast growing organization where one of the most important issues was attracting and developing the necessary talent pool. This was a one to two year deliverable requiring a Stratum 3 position. However, the most senior position was at a Stratum 2 level. The function had to be enhanced accordingly and a Stratum 3 managerial position created that would be accountable for it.

Special Topics

In this section, a number of special topics are discussed to provide a better sense of the issues and opportunities in functional alignment. Some of these topics are linked to vertical alignment as well as functional alignment. The special topics include the following:

- co-CEOs
- position titles
- core functions for today and tomorrow
- missing core functions
- sales challenges
- asset management
- policy: a critical government function
- information technology challenges
- outsourcing

Co-CEOs

Although it tends to be an exception, some organizations have co-CEOs. The rationale is sometimes that they are "equal" and they have complementary expertise that is critical to the organization (e.g., operations and sales). We believe this is a dysfunctional design. It violates a fundamental principle, which is that an organization should have a single point of accountability or integration. This single point of accountability would be the cross over point manager. This is defined as the lowest level manager who controls most or all of the resources necessary to deal with a particular issue or opportunity. For example, there is a requirement for a clearly defined cross over point manager for product development, which requires resources from across the organization including marketing, sales, technology, procurement, manufacturing, distribution, etc.

With co-CEOs, the lowest level point of integration would be the Board of Directors. This is too high. Also, because the Board of Directors is the lowest point accountable for the whole organization, it can end up playing the CEO role. This would be inappropriate. The Board cannot properly take on the CEO's role. It also takes the Board away from its unique added value role of governance.

When issues go beyond the two co-CEO silos, their resolution can become difficult. Each of the co-CEOs has a preferred orientation (e.g., sales vs. operations) and may explicitly or implicitly give direction that is in conflict with the other view or a better integrated view. The integrative mechanism that is important for a well-functioning organization is broken.

As is the case with human nature, when times are good, differences may be papered over. Differences may not seem significant. However, when there is conflict (which is, not surprisingly, prevalent in organizations), the issues are often exacerbated. Conflicts get resolved by power of personality rather than appropriate accountability mechanisms. Issues that should be dealt with are not, and come back to haunt the organization at a later stage. The issues at the top reverberate and create dysfunction down through the whole organization. In short, co-CEOs is a bad idea. It may seem okay for a while, but the day of reckoning will come.

Position Titles

Position titles are often not helpful in understanding the work done in the position. This may seem surprising. It is often assumed that a position title provides a good shorthand indication of what a position does. However, in our experience, they provide less useful information than one might expect. There are a couple of reasons for this.

The first, and probably most fundamental reason, is that most organizations are not properly stratified. As a result, there is no framework for understanding what a position at a particular level should do. For example, one may have manager positions at one level and director positions at the next higher level. Although we may know that one is higher than the other, we don't know what the expectations are for each of them. This changes if we understand that directors are Stratum 3 positions accountable for Stratum 2 positions, and managers are Stratum 2 positions accountable for Stratum 1 positions. We now know the complexity of work (time span), the information processing capability required, and the nature of managerial work required at each level. When an organization is stratified, titles should consistently be used in a stratum-specific way.

A second reason for title failure has to do with the lack of precision related to functional accountability. If someone is a manager, then what is she accountable for? The term "finance" may be suitable for the top position in this function. However, we would expect more precision at lower levels (e.g., Manager, Accounts Payable). A title should have two parts, the second part should describe the functional accountability as precisely as possible.

Even with this degree of specificity encapsulated in the title, there will be differences among individuals with the same position title. This is quite appropriate if the work is both stratum and function appropriate. Much can be done to ensure that position titles are accurate and convey useful information. Even in situations where titles have been conscientiously thought out, however, it would be a mistake to assume that the work across positions with the same title is necessarily identical.

Core Functions for Today and Tomorrow

One of the most critical questions in organization design is how to determine what the core functions should be, and then how to organize them. Getting this right can confer advantages on a business in both the short and long term.

We worked with the credit card function of a large financial services organization. The title of the function was relatively amorphous. It was organized by credit card type, and there was one unit that really didn't fit. As we began to understand the work of this area, and the industry more broadly, it became clear that the most fundamental distinction was related to customer type: there was a consumer area (Card Holder) and a business area (Merchant). As a result of this analysis and subsequent consultation, the decision was made to make these two areas key business units. Support Services was consolidated into a third area—having two Support Services units would have created too much redundancy. The third unit that did not fit was moved to another part of the institution. These changes resulted in much greater clarity and focus. Other changes were made to improve alignment of positions, accountabilities and authorities, employees, and deliverables. The net result was considerably higher performance on numerous fronts.

Interestingly as the industry evolved, there was consolidation in both the consumer and business card areas. The changes made within the organization not only provided better short to midterm performance, but also positioned the firm to take advantage of this later consolidation.

Missing Core Functions

In a generic sense, there are three core functions. These are product/service development, marketing and sales, and product/service delivery.

In our experience, the marketing/sales and delivery functions are usually present, albeit sometimes in somewhat disguised form. However, the product/service development function is often either underdeveloped or missing. Manufacturing firms generally are more likely to have a product development function. It is sometimes called "research and development." This can be problematic because undue emphasis on research, rather than product development, can lead to activities that lack focus central to the organization's mission. In service organizations (e.g., consulting) there often is no a formal service development function. Service development may be undertaken as part of the delivery to clients. This means that there is a need for a coordinative role, which may be missing or weak.

The other function that can be important in organizations that are larger and more complex, and is often missing, is a corporate development function. This function would have a focus outside of the firm's main business lines. It could include supporting the development of new business lines and incubating small business units that have the potential to evolve into more substantive units. We find that in larger, more complex organizations this function often does not have clear accountabilities and authorities. This can sometimes be traced back to the lack of clarity in the strategic plan, and sometimes results from lack of clarity between the development accountabilities within business units and the broader development accountabilities in a corporate development function.

Sales Challenges

Organizations have a tendency to want to make sales more "pure." Sales people are exhorted to let someone else do the service work and get out there and sell! Distinctions are made between "hunters" and "farmers." Hunters are the ones who go out and get new business from new customers. Farmers are the ones who maintain current customers. Hunters are the "real sales people" and are "more important" than the farmers.

We believe that there are some fundamental misunderstandings about sales that lead to conflict and bad organization design. We saw one organization that had separated sales and service at lower levels. Sales people sold and service people provided service. This resulted in a split in which sales people enjoyed higher status than service people. However, when one examined the actual work, it was apparent that this dichotomy was false. Customers interacted with both and were not bothered by the distinction. The so-called sales people needed to provide some service, and the so-called service people had significant opportunities both to sell directly and to refer sales prospects to others.

We saw a different situation in another organization in which hunters were valued and farmers were not. However, when we looked at the work, the hunters actually did lower-level transactional selling to small accounts. The farmers were accountable for the largest accounts with the largest customers. Not only that, but they had significant opportunities to sell even more. This organization was so enamored with the hunter role that they had the relative value of hunter and farmer exactly reversed.

One final example sometimes used to demonstrate a pure sales role is the so-called "rainmaker." He can be found in businesses such as law firms. The primary objective is to sell rather than deliver services (which other partners in the law firm might do). However, even in this case, the role often is only superficially understood. It is really about developing and maintaining a network, and the managing the relationships that nurture the network. There are definitely relationship management and service components—and both are critical to success.

In sum, by defining sales too narrowly, some firms show a misunderstanding of the nature of sales, which leads to unnecessary conflict and poor organization design.

Asset Management

In production organizations (e.g., manufacturing, oil and gas, mining, railway, etc.), one of the most critical and complex functions is asset management. This function often tends to be fragmented and at too low a level. There are generally operating, maintenance, and procurement functions. All three are related to asset management. A piece of equipment is bought, operated, maintained, and disposed. All three tend to be at too low a level.

The procurement function tends to be transactional. It often does not evolve to supplier relationship management or, as it should, to the establishment of a strong supplier network. Maintenance, similarly, is often neglected. Routine maintenance is carried out as needed. Preventative maintenance is inadequate and relevant information is not maintained. It often does not further evolve to higher-level, longer-term maintenance plans.

The same pattern applies to operations. Equipment is operated but the focus is often short term. There is limited appreciation of the interdependent relationship with procurement and maintenance. There can be conflict in that the maintenance function wants to do maintenance work on equipment and the operations function wants to keep operating it.

There is a concept that can link these functions together: asset life cycle management. It involves understanding the life cycle from procurement to disposal of assets. The starting point is to determine the cross over point manager (the lowest level manager who is accountable for most or all of the resources necessary to accomplish the task). The cross over point manager sets up an optimal position alignment with accountabilities and authorities to optimize overall performance. This should clearly involve at least procurement, maintenance, and operations.

It's worth noting an interesting implication of this process. Life cycle management will often be the deliverable with the longest target completion time (time span) of a senior position. Time spans can sometimes be measured in decades. For example, one could make the case that the deliverable with the longest target completion time and most complexity in a nuclear power plant is the life cycle management of the plant in general and the reactor in particular. Unfortunately, the most complex work that should be done by the most senior executives is often neither understood nor undertaken. The negative consequences, while disturbing, should not be surprising.

Policy: A Critical Government Function

A government is elected by the population to represent it. The essence of government is ensuring that there are desirable outcomes for this population, as understood and interpreted by the government. There are several fundamental mechanisms of governance. They include establishing policy, monitoring to assess compliance and performance, and applying rewards and sanctions to enforce compliance. These three functions (policy, monitoring, and rewards and sanctions) are interdependent. They reinforce and strengthen one another. Policy is a core function of government, not a support function. It is externally focused and a direct mechanism for doing the work of government.

It would be useful to pause and examine what we mean by policy. First, policy is not writing a piece of paper by oneself and tossing it over the wall to an operations person to implement (the latter having had no involvement in its formulation). Policy should rather be thought of as a process to shift behavior over time, as government policy is focused on changing society. The process of policy should include the following characteristics:

- An individual should have ultimate accountability for the policy process.
- A policy process generally requires several phases. The first is initiation, the start of the policy process. The second is negotiation, which often includes outside parties and requires more senior approval. The third is implementation. The fourth is monitoring and feedback. The accountability for each phase should be clear (it will often be in different parts of an organization). This is actually a feedback loop that allows for continuous improvement.

- A policy process often requires a team. The members may bring diverse skills to the process, including policy writing, implementation, and monitoring. The team will often involve clients and other stakeholders.
- The policy process requires a related client relations (marketing, selling, and communicating) function. This is often a key ingredient in the success or failure of policy.
- The policy process requires networking to develop the necessary information and relationships to be successful.

Information Technology Challenges

We have had an opportunity to review many Information Technology (IT) functions. (They are sometimes called Information Systems.) There are probably few areas in an organization that provide as much promise and as much heartbreak. We would consider the following to be among the major issues (and therefore opportunities) that we have seen.

IT is a significant function. It should be designed with the appropriate strata and position alignment to allow it to deliver the complex outcomes that are required. The head of IT should generally be a direct report of the head of the organization (although there may be exceptions).

IT is generally thought of as a support function (it was originally data processing within finance).This is now an outdated concept. While it does have a support aspect (providing infrastructure for people within the organization), it is generally directly involved with the core functions of developing and delivering products and services. Linkages to these areas are critical.

The head of IT is often called the Chief Information Officer (CIO). We understand this: after all, these "Chief" titles are becoming quite popular, and the head of Finance is often called the Chief Financial Officer (CFO). However, we believe that the real CIO is the head of the organization because using information technology to develop and deliver products and services requires both the IT side and the business side. The cross over point manager (lowest level manager controlling most or all of the resources necessary to be successful) is the top person. He has real work to do in this area. Unfortunately, heads of organizations generally don't understand this role and don't do it. It doesn't have to take a lot of time, but is critical. Abdication of this function by the top person is a major reason why IT projects often fail.

IT projects use typical project management methods in designing their projects. They may engage sponsors, champions, steering committees, and operating committees. But project management literature is extremely weak on organization design and these terms obscure accountability and authority. It is essential that the cross over point manager ensure that the position alignment is set up with appropriate managerial and cross functional accountabilities and authorities. Eliminate sponsors, champions, steering committees, and operating committees!

A project should have one project manager, not two. But many IT projects have two managers, one from the business side and one from IT. Not surprisingly, when the project fails to deliver the expected results (and it often does), the fickle fingers of blame point in all directions. A project manager should have the capability to operate at the interface between the business and IT. That is to say, she should know enough about each to be effective. Such individuals are relatively rare—more effort should go into their development.

The final point is also important: The complexity of projects should be recognized, and the project managers should have the necessary information processing capability to work at the required level. Project managers are often one stratum too low for the level of work required. For example, a Stratum 2 IT professional is appointed as project manager for a one- to two- year project requiring Stratum 3 capability. (Unfortunately, IT tends not to understand these terms). This individual would likely not have sufficient information processing capability for this level of work.

Projects with even more complexity (e.g., time spans of two to five years) require project managers with Stratum 4 capability (often Vice President or equivalent). Our suggestions to executives about this point are often met with the question "Why would we waste such a position on a project?" They would rather have the project fail, which often is exactly what happens!

In sum, IT is a critical and often underperforming function. Many of its problems have to do with suboptimal organization design. Rectifying these issues can go a long way to significantly improving organization performance.

Outsourcing

One organization outsourcing certain functions to another organization has become very common. The reasons are generally financial: the other organization can complete the work at a lower cost. However, the reasons may also have to do with doing better work: the other organization may specialize in a particular area, do more of it, and be further along the experience curve. While there is little doubt that outsourcing can provide advantages, we have seen numerous situations in which the outcome was suboptimal. The following are suggestions that make success more likely.

First, there may be an assumption, explicit or implicit, that because we have outsourced something, we are no longer accountable for it. Wrong! The host organization is still accountable. Rather than a managerial accountability (i.e., managing direct report employees), it becomes an accountability through managing a contract. This is still complex work and should be undertaken at an appropriate stratum. Some organizations make the mistake of assuming that the relationship is transactional and can be handled by a lower level position such as an accounts payable clerk. It's not.

When an organization outsources, it may actually require more capabilities than it previously required, but in different areas. The most obvious area is in the legal implications of contracting. In addition, there may be additional requirements to establish specifications (more difficult when someone else is doing the work) and to establish appropriate monitoring (again, different from managing the work inside).

Some of the same practices that are important inside an organization should be specified in the outsourcing process. What is the organization design that you expect the outsourced organization to have? We know that better organization design leads to better performance. Shouldn't the organization that you are outsourcing to also have this? Too picky, you suggest? Not really. For example, there is a difference between Stratum 1 positions (proceduralized) and Stratum 2 positions (diagnostic). Further, there is a difference between individuals with Stratum 1 information processing capability and Stratum 2 information processing capability. Do you know the difference? Does the organization you are outsourcing to know the difference? We have seen situations in which the organization doing the outsourcing assumed that the other organization would provide Stratum 2 positions filled by Stratum 2 capable individuals, in order to do the more complex, diagnostic, professional work that was required. At the time they didn't understand this framework so they couldn't be specific about requirements. The outcome was that Stratum 1 positions were created and filled by Stratum 1 capable individuals. This was not sufficient to do the required work. The output was not satisfactory—not a pretty picture!

Conclusion

The functional and vertical alignments of positions are complementary. Together they create the organization structure or spine. Whereas the vertical alignment has a strong research-based framework (e.g., time span and universal pattern of organization strata), functional alignment does not. It requires judgment, which starts with understanding the organization and its environment, as well as its future direction. Functional alignment, in larger organizations, starts with the alignment of the corporate office and the related business units and other parts of the organization. Within business units, there is a distinction between core and support functions.

You have numerous choices with your functional alignment. Keys to success include starting with the strategy, determining the primary alignment for managerial accountabilities and authorities, and determining the secondary alignment for cross functional accountabilities.

ALIGNING ACCOUNTABILITIES AND AUTHORITIES

We have accomplished a lot. Interestingly, one of the important outcomes was better understanding why we weren't able to accomplish some things. This understanding was critical in our change process. For example, we understood that being caught up in silos was related to misaligned roles and unclear cross functional accountabilities and authorities. Roles are now clearer, and jobs are deeper and more robust ... Breaking down silos results in better customer focus and leads to better retention and satisfaction of customers.

—Joan Mitchell, Vice President, Human
Resources, Moneris Solutions, February 2006

The first step in the organization design is to align positions from both vertical and functional perspectives. The next step would be to ensure that positions have appropriate accountabilities and authorities. There should be generic accountabilities and authorities that apply to all employees, including managers. As well, there should be additional generic accountabilities and authorities for those in managerial positions. These include managers and managers once removed, as well as supervisors (which is not a full managerial position, as previously discussed). The advantage of generic accountabilities and authorities is that they establish shared expectations and a framework for consistency across an organization.

In addition to these generic accountabilities and authorities, there should be position-specific accountabilities and authorities. For example, while all managers have generic accountabilities and authorities, each manager would have accountabilities and authorities specific to the requirements of her particular position.

In the next sections, these accountabilities and authorities are discussed, as well as cross functional accountabilities and authorities, types of work and delegation, and a few special topics.

It should be noted that we use types of human systems to assist in describing accountabilities and authorities. We start at the level of individual. We would expect all employees to behave in ways that were consistent with organization values and accepted practices. The next level is interpersonal. We would expect all employees to have effective interpersonal working relationships. In addition, we would expect managers to have effective manager–direct report relationships. The next level is group or team. We would expect all employees to participate effectively in teams, and for managers to develop and lead their own teams. The next level is intergroup. We would expect those in manager once removed positions to develop effective intergroup relations through cross functional accountabilities and authorities. The next level is organization. We would expect the head of the organization (generally at least a Stratum 4 position and usually higher) to develop an effective organization.

Employee Accountabilities and Authorities

The first step is to determine the basic expectations for any employee, at whatever level. The first and primary accountability would be giving one's best effort. This is the essence of an employee contract. Other accountabilities include the following:

- operating within the context and prescribed limits provided by your manager (this provides the framework for all other accountabilities)

- behaving in ways consistent with the values of the organization
- planning, executing, reviewing, and improving your work
- using delegated authority and resources to accomplish deliverables
- providing leadership when appropriate
- developing your skilled knowledge
- having effective working relationships with others
- keeping your manager informed and providing appropriate feedback and suggestions
- participating effectively as a member of a team

I would suggest the following authorities:

- have access to your manager to inform and provide feedback and suggestions
- have access to your manager once removed to appeal decisions or report complaints in predefined circumstances (e.g., abuse of various sorts, etc.)

Manager Accountabilities and Authorities

Managers are employees who are accountable for direct reports. They should provide context and prescribed limits and ensure clarity and appropriateness of direct reports' accountabilities and authorities. Within a clear accountability framework, employees will better understand their positions, and be better able to take initiative and apply their full capability in a way that is consistent with the organization's requirements.

Earlier I stated that the manager–direct report alignment is the single most important factor in organization design. That factor, alone, relates directly to an organization's employee satisfaction, customer satisfaction, and financial performance. Even so, I consider appropriate vertical position alignment to be a necessary but not sufficient condition for good managerial work. Compression (the manager and direct report are operating in the same stratum) often leads to micromanagement. Gaps (the manager is more than one stratum above the direct report) often lead to a lack of direction. Having a manager exactly one stratum above the direct report, in both the manager's level of work and capability to work at that level, provides the necessary framework.

Since managers are first of all employees, they have the same basic accountabilities and authorities of all employees plus some additional ones. The first of these is to develop and maintain effective manager–direct report relationships. The fundamentals of the related accountabilities are shown in Figure 2.6.

The manager should provide the appropriate context and prescribed limits. The context includes factors such as the organization framework (e.g., vision, mission, values, etc.); the manager's business plans and work plans; organization limits (e.g., legal and fiscal responsibility); and the manager's personal limits (e.g., "Give me important bad news early; I don't want to hear it from others").

The manager should be clear about the outputs or deliverables expected and to adjust them as appropriate. The range of adjustments would include quantity, quality and timeliness. He is responsible for undertaking the current work while also finding ways to improve work processes and methods. The manager should be clear and fair about the inputs or resources provided, and link these to the deliverables expected. Resources could include people (time and expertise), money (budget), and technology (equipment and information technology). Within this framework, the manager

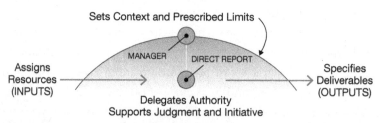

FIGURE 2.6. Fundamental Managerial Framework

should ensure that the direct report has appropriate authority to do the required work, and should support the employee in using her judgment and initiative.

In addition to this fundamental managerial framework, there are other important accountabilities. Managers should provide the following kinds of support to their direct reports:

- coaching for development in current position
- performance appraisals and recommended consequences
- appropriate processes within area of accountability
- leadership and development (ensures effective team working and collateral relationships)

Managers should have at least minimal managerial authority in relation to direct reports. They would be able to

- veto any new appointment (They may not unilaterally hire anyone they want, although the choice may be from a predetermined talent pool, and they should have the right to refuse an unacceptable employee being forced upon them.)
- decide the nature of the work
- decide performance appraisal and recommend related consequences/rewards (e.g., compensation)
- decide removal from position (The manager may not unilaterally fire someone, but, within due process, has the authority to determine that a direct report will no longer work for him.)

It should be noted that union contracts may impose limitations on these authorities. A fundamental part of this approach is to be respectful of people. Naturally, this respect extends to union contracts and other working agreements.

Manager and Direct Report Accountabilities and Authorities

What should managers and direct reports be held accountable for? In most approaches, direct reports are fully accountable for achieving their deliverables and the related accountabilities and means of achieving the outputs. There are problems with this approach. First, managers are accountable for many of the factors that shape success and failure: selecting the individual, providing resources, establishing deliverables, delegating accountabilities and authorities, performance appraisal, coaching, etc. Second, there is a tendency for managers to place undue reliance on numbers regardless of circumstances. For example, if 7/10 is the target and it is achieved, some would say that is very good performance. However, depending on the circumstances, this outcome could be excellent, average, or poor.

Another approach, which comes from the historical framework we use, is that direct reports are accountable for their best effort and managers are accountable for the output of direct reports. The rationale is the significant impact that the manager has on the outcomes beyond what the direct report controls (e.g., manager is accountable for the direct report's selection, management, development, etc.).

I recommend a different approach. Accountability and authority start at the top of the organization and are delegated down. For example, the Board of Directors delegates to the CEO, and holds her accountable for the performance of the organization. The CEO delegates to her direct reports, and so on down the organization. The important point is that delegation does not absolve one from the prior established accountability. For example, it should not be acceptable for the CEO to tell the Board that she is not really accountable for performance because one of the CEO's direct reports performed badly (although this is sometimes how the blame game works).

I would argue that all employees (including managers, etc.) be held accountable for providing their best effort and for their stated accountabilities (generic and position specific) and their deliverables. The manager of the employee (i.e., direct report of the manager) is accountable for making a judgment on the performance of a direct report. Clearly measured performance (from both qualitative and quantitative perspectives) is an important input in making that judgment, but not a substitute for it. A key factor is whether or not a direct report applied best effort.

The manager once removed continues to hold the direct report manager accountable for the performance of her unit (including the direct reports) and for appropriate managerial behavior. This ensures an important balance is maintained between the manager and direct report. The manager once removed should ensure that appropriate managerial practices are in place to ensure fairness to the direct report. The judgment of the performance of the direct report by the manager would take place within this framework.

I believe that this approach provides a better balance of accountability between a manager and a direct report. It maintains the principle that a manager needs to make a judgment, and best effort on the part of the direct report is a fundamental factor. However, it places direct report performance more strongly in the foreground.

Leadership and Managerial Leadership   There is a considerable body of published work on leadership in general and the relationship between leaders and managers. Some observers say that leaders provide vision and direction, while managers have a more administrative, bureaucratic role. We define a manager as someone accountable for the work of others regardless of level. I have listed what we consider to be the related accountabilities and authorities. I have not yet covered deliverables, but it is clear that managers have to mobilize others to determine and accomplish relatively complex deliverables over extended periods of time.

We define leadership as the process of influencing others to move in a particular direction. Leadership can be found in most if not all social situations. It does not require an individual to assume a specific role. Different people provide leadership in different circumstances. Some roles—teaching and parenting, for example—require leadership. It also is required of managers as a fundamental part of what they do.

For our purposes, there is no significant dichotomy between leaders and managers. I believe insisting on the distinction between them is denigrating to managers. I expect managers to provide leadership as part of their managerial role. Bearing this in mind, we use the term "managerial leadership," by which we mean leadership that is related to the accountabilities and authorities of a manager. Managerial leadership includes the following:

- selection and induction of direct reports
- definition of context and prescribed limits
- provision of resources
- determination and delegation of accountabilities, authorities, and deliverables
- provision of feedback, development, and coaching
- performance management, including appraisal and recommended consequences/rewards (e.g., compensation)
- development of an effective team of direct reports, including meetings
- recommendation for removal from position

Manager Once Removed Accountabilities and Authorities

A manager once removed is a manager of managers. He has direct reports once removed, who are also the direct reports of the manager. He has the same accountabilities as both an employee and a manager, since the manager once removed is also in these two roles. In addition, the manager once removed has additional accountabilities and authorities. He is required to do the following:

- Ensure that direct report managers fulfill their managerial accountabilities (these were specified in the last section), including fair treatment of employees.
- Oversee performance appraisals by managers of their direct reports.

- Maintain effective relationships with direct reports once removed. The focus is potential, career development, and mentoring. These people are potential direct reports (with promotion), so they are an important part of the talent pool.
- Oversee talent pool meeting and approve decisions about direct reports once removed.
- Decide new positions at direct report once removed level.
- Veto appointments of direct reports once removed.
- Decide appeals from direct reports once removed.
- Oversee deselection of direct reports once removed.
- Establish appropriate three-level team working, including meetings.
- Ensure effective intergroup relationships at direct report once removed level through appropriate cross functional accountabilities and authorities.

Supervisor Accountabilities and Authorities

A supervisor is a Stratum 1 employee who supports a Stratum 2 manager in doing her work. A supervisor should not be a level or stratum of management. A supervisor has Stratum 1 information processing capability and should have very good technical and social process skills. A Stratum 2 manager would be accountable for both a Stratum 1 supervisor and other Stratum 1 employees.

A Stratum 1 supervisor would have the employee accountabilities and authorities that were previously described. In addition, a Stratum 1 supervisor would have various accountabilities depending on the circumstances and within the context and prescribed limits of the manager. These could include assigning and checking work, providing feedback, training, coaching, and handling disciplinary problems. The supervisor would have the authority to make recommendations to the manager on a wide range of actions.

Cross Functional Accountabilities and Authorities

While the managerial accountabilities and authorities are important, much of the work in organizations is done through cross functional accountabilities and authorities. These are sometimes referred to as lateral relations. They include the relationships that support functions (e.g., human resources, finance, and information technology) have with other parts of an organization. They also include other relationships across core functions (e.g., product/service development, product/service delivery, marketing and sales, etc.). While these cross functional accountabilities and authorities are important, they are seldom properly articulated and virtually never part of position descriptions.

The delegation of cross functional accountabilities and authorities starts, as always, at the top of the organization (see Figure 2.7). The head of the organization (I will use the term "CEO") determines the core and support functions of the organization. Core functions are the basic work of the organization. They have an external client focus and include:

- developing the products and services
- obtaining necessary materials, producing and delivering the products and services
- marketing, selling, and communicating the products and services

Support functions facilitate the core work and consequently have a mainly internal focus. This would include functions such as human resources, finance, and information technology.

The CEO has direct reports accountable for each support function (although one direct report may be accountable for more than one area). The most fundamental accountability of the head of a support function is to ensure that the support function is operating optimally. This requires two activities: first, to recommend policies, standards, and procedures for the support function, and second,

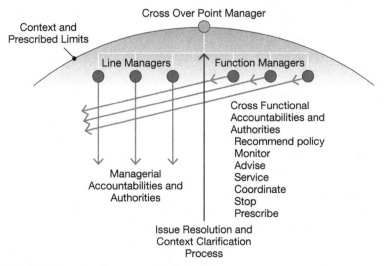

FIGURE 2.7. Cross Functional Relationships

to monitor the organization to ensure the required compliance and performance. The recommending and monitoring functions together allow the CEO to determine how well a function is doing. For example, the CEO would likely want to know if the organization's human resources are doing better or worse than in previous years, what standards have been set up, what mechanisms are used to measure performance, etc. These support activities are fundamental to optimal performance.

Both activities should be assessed from the perspective of added value. What policies, standards, procedures and monitoring mechanisms are necessary to provide added value? Two types of error are possible. The first is to do too much of low value and bureaucratize the system. This tends to occur when organizations are fat. The second is to do too little in this area, and run the risk of significant exposure. This tends to occur when organizations are downsizing and/or are very lean. The first error is a lack of efficiency and a waste of money. The second error is a lack of effectiveness and suboptimal risk management. While the latter is more easily overlooked, it also is more likely to have significant negative consequences.

There are five additional types of cross functional account-abilities and authorities. The next two are providing advice and providing services. Their provision should be assessed on a value-added basis. Depending on the findings, these could be provided within the organization or outsourced.

The final three types of cross functional accountabilities and authorities are coordinating, stopping, and prescribing. The seven types of cross functional accountabilities and authorities are shown in Table 2.1. These have been adapted from the work of Jaques (1996) and his colleagues.

One additional point should be noted. The cross over point manager is the lowest level manager who controls all or at least most of the resources needed to be successful with a particular issue or opportunity. The identity of the cross over point manager will vary, but it is an important role. When properly established, it can set the framework for successful cross functional relationships and projects. When not identified or properly used, which unfortunately is common, the chances of success are significantly reduced.

Cross Functional Grid   We sometimes find it useful to show the cross functional relationships in a cross functional grid (see Figure 2.8).

This grid uses the managerial and cross functional accountabilities and authorities that we have previously discussed. However, in this case the cross over point manager has direct reports in execution positions (e.g., production) and some direct reports ensuring the "goodness of function" (e.g., technology, quality assurance, industrial engineering, etc.). The execution managers are accountable for the delivery. The "goodness of function" managers are accountable for ensuring high-level consistent performance across the execution positions. Cross functional accountabilities and authorities are used to do this.

This situation is quite common. An organization wants both excellent delivery and excellent, continuously improving, consistent output across all delivery units. Achieving these objectives

Table 2.1.   Cross Functional Accountabilities and Authorities

Recommend Policies, Standards, Procedures and Objectives:	While this is actually direct output support work (it is a recommendation to one's immediate manager) rather than a true cross functional relationship, it is the foundation for cross functional work. It provides a framework within which all cross functional work can be performed.
Monitoring:	Monitoring relates to ensuring adherence to approved policies, standards, and procedures. Monitoring interactions occur when an individual is authorized to be informed about what others are doing; try to persuade others to change; or, if a mutually satisfactory resolution cannot be reached on a substantive issue, ask others to delay their actions until the matter is reviewed at a higher level.
Advising:	Advisory interactions occur when specified experts/specialists are authorized to take the initiative to offer unsolicited advice to specified others. The specified others must listen to the advice, but are not obliged to follow it. This is an issue for the specified others to decide within the context established by their own immediate managers.
Service Providing:	Service providing occurs when an authorized service is provided to another. A broad range of services would be included. Clear definitions/policies about which services are to be provided and the specified levels are a key to success.
Coordinating:	Coordinative interactions occur when an individual is authorized to be informed about the tasks or work of others directed toward the achievement of an integrated program or goal (e.g., product launch). The coordinator can call people together, make suggestions on how work is to be done, resolve bottlenecks or problems; and must take substantive matters higher if issues cannot be resolved. This authority can be useful for project managers.
Stopping:	Stopping interactions occur when an individual has the authority to inspect work and to stop work that is outside of standards. This interaction can be useful in high-risk situations. For example, a health and safety inspector can require a plant manager to stop a process while it is being made safe.
Prescribing:	Prescribing interactions occur rarely. This is when an individual has the authority to prescribe an activity to an individual that is not her direct report. For example, a doctor could require certain actions to take place by those who are not her direct reports (e.g., requesting a nurse to administer a prescription).

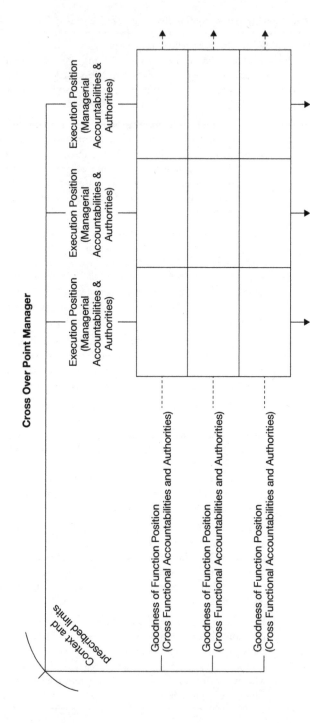

FIGURE 2.8. Cross Functional Grid

requires a delicate balance. The role of the cross over point manager, in setting context and prescribed limits and delegating managerial and cross functional accountabilities and authorities, is fundamental to success.

When we consult with organizations we generally find that cross functional relationships are inadequately defined and working suboptimally. The problems include the following:

- The cross over point manager does not realize that he has this role.
- There is no context and prescribed limits.
- There is lack of clarity of managerial accountabilities and authorities.
- There is a virtual absence of cross functional accountabilities and authorities.

In this veritable vacuum, decisions are likely to be made on the basis of personal power rather than on what is required by the organization.

Type of Work

While seldom discussed, there actually are three types of work: delegated direct output; direct output support; and direct output within context. These are shown in Figure 2.9.

Delegated direct output is the most familiar type. A manager has one or more direct reports. He delegates work to the direct

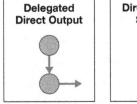 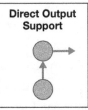 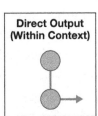

FIGURE 2.9.   Types of Work

report and the direct report does the work. This occurs in situations where the output is appropriate for the position of the direct report. For example on a production line, the first-level production work would be delegated to first-level employees.

Direct output support is less well understood and this leads to problems. The fundamental questions are, first, what is the complexity of the work, and second, at what stratum should it be done? The common assumption seems to be that a good manager delegates everything and doesn't have any direct output. This is suboptimal. A manager needs to determine what work is complex enough to do at his or her level, and what work has the right degree of complexity to delegate.

For example, it is our view that every manager should complete her own business plan. Managers are in a position in the right stratum to do this complexity of work and should have the necessary skilled knowledge and application to do so. At one time, there was a proliferation of strategic planning units that tended to do this work. They have faded away over time because they often did not deliver what was expected. The fundamental problem was not understanding the type of work required. These units were considered to be delegated direct output units: managers requested these units to do their plans for them. The managers were abdicating their accountability and the plans were suboptimal. The individuals in the units tended to have information processing capability at too low a level, and insufficient skilled knowledge (especially related to the business). This should be direct output support work—here is my overall plan, please do these pieces for me, and I will use them to further develop *my* plan.

For example, if a Stratum 4 manager develops a three-year plan to improve product and geographic scope, it would be at a parallel processing level. This would involve multiple and interconnected serial paths going out into the future. These paths can then be delegated to Stratum 3 managers (e.g., to develop a new product over an 18-month period). However, if a Stratum 3 manager developed the plan for a Stratum 4 manager, it would likely be unfit for purpose because (a) it would lack the optimal serial paths, (b) it would be connected in suboptimal ways, and (c) it would not have the optimal time spans. The level of capability and the corresponding output are different.

The third and final type of work is direct output within context. This occurs at all levels of an organization, although it tends to be more common at higher levels where more of the work can be self-initiated within the established context and prescribed limits. For example, professionals do not have all deliverables specifically delegated. They would understand the context and prescribed limits, and initiate work within them. It should be understood that this is not a free for all: The output must still be within context and prescribed limits—and these should be clear.

Delegation of Work

Delegation comes into play with all three types of work. See Figure 2.10 for an example in Stratum 3, Stratum 2, and Stratum 1.

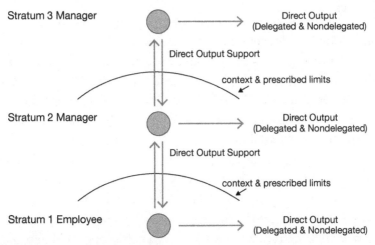

FIGURE 2.10.   Delegation of Work

There are three positions in this chart representing a Stratum 3 manager, a Stratum 2 manager, and a Stratum 1 employee. The Stratum 3 manager has work to be done. Some will be direct output by the Stratum 3 manager. This could be work delegated by the Stratum 4 manager, or it could be nondelegated work that is done within the established context. The Stratum 3 manager may also ask the Stratum 2 manager to provide direct output support for some of the Stratum 3 manager's output.

The Stratum 3 manager delegates some work to the Stratum 2 manager. The Stratum 2 manager output could include some of this delegated work and also some nondelegated work within context. The Stratum 2 manager may delegate some work to the Stratum 1 employee, and may ask the Stratum 1 employee to provide direct output support to some work that will be done by the Stratum 2 manager.

The Stratum 1 employee is not a manager and does not delegate. The Stratum 1 employee provides direct output that may be delegated or may be nondelegated but within context.

Working across Organizations: A Better Alternative to Matrix Organization

As organizations become more complex, aligning on only one dimension is no longer sufficient. It is necessary to plan for working across functions, across geographies, across business lines, etc. One solution to this complexity—matrix organization—has been around for some time. This basically involves setting up different reporting relationships, some of which have "solid lines" and some of which have "dotted lines."

We hear two common complaints: "We have silos, and don't work across them very well" and "We have a matrix organization that doesn't work very well." The latter complaint may refer to a matrix design either for an organization or for a specific project. Our view is that matrix organization is an unclear approach and that ours is superior. These are the steps we think should be followed.

Start with Strategy   Understanding the strategy (or as we prefer to say, "strategic positioning") is the first step. Organization design is a foundation for strategy implementation, so we start with understanding strategy.

Align Positions Vertically   We have discussed the importance of vertical alignment. We have described a method (time span) to ensure that the organization has the optimal number of strata and that each position is placed in the appropriate stratum. This procedure also supports manager–direct report alignment, which is the single most important organization design factor. We would want to eliminate gaps (manager and direct report more than one layer or stratum apart) and compression (manager and direct report operating in the same layer or stratum).

Quite simply, if positions have not been properly aligned vertically, the work across the organization will be sub optimal. For example, if there is an extra position in the vertical alignment (e.g., a Stratum 3 director position and a compressed, redundant assistant director position), which of the two positions do you invite to meetings? Both of them, which is a waste of money? Only one, in which case, you don't know if there will be proper communication with the other? Save yourself these problems and get the vertical alignment set up properly.

Align Positions Functionally   Many executives stumble here. Reexamine your strategy, and determine what your primary, secondary and perhaps tertiary ways of organizing are. For example, you may decide that product line is your primary organizing principle, while geography, and then business function (e.g., production, marketing, etc.) come second and third respectively. Your primary way of organizing determines your managerial accountability hierarchy. This is what you would see on your organization charts. Your secondary (and perhaps tertiary) ways of organizing become the foundation for your cross functional accountabilities and authorities, which we will discuss shortly.

Executives are often not explicit about the secondary (and perhaps tertiary) ways of organizing. This can lead to issues in working across the organization.

Establish the Cross Over Point Manager   This is a critical success factor. The cross over point manager is the lowest- level manager who controls most if not all of the resources necessary to be successful. It we were considering working across a total organization, the cross over point manager would be the head of the organization. For some projects, depending on scope, this role could be at a lower level.

The cross over point manager sets context and prescribed limits, establishes a conflict resolution and context improvement mechanism, and ensures appropriate accountabilities and authorities. Incidentally, the work of the cross over point manager does not have to be overly time consuming. This is particularly the case when these important mechanisms are put in place.

Most executives (including CEOs) don't understand the role of a cross over point manager and don't do the required work. This creates all kinds of problems, the most common of which is giving someone accountability ("Improve the organization performance management system") without authority (e.g., "Just talk to them—I'm sure they will cooperate"). Then, when the initiative fails, the individual gets blamed ("It would have been okay if you had better influencing skills ... better personality ... " etc.).

Establish Appropriate Employee, Supervisor, Manager and Manager Once Removed Accountabilities and Authorities
Accountabilities and authorities should be established for employees, supervisors, managers and managers once removed. Some of these are essentially generic for anyone in a particular position, while some are specific to the unique circumstances of the position. The next point is critical: Every employee can have only one manager. This is set up through the primary way of organizing that we have previously discussed. However, each employee

can (as required) have multiple cross functional relationships, accountabilities, and authorities.

For example, let's assume that the primary way an organization is functional (e.g., Operations, Human Resources, etc.) and secondarily on a geographic basis (Western, Central, and Eastern regions). My manager may be a human resources executive, and I may have a cross functional (service providing) relationship with the executive accountable for Western Region operations.

The Foundation Is In Place   Working across an organization is the most difficult aspect of establishing effective working relationships. Unless you have the foundation in place, you will not be successful. Now you have created that foundation, you can set up cross functional accountabilities and authorities that have a high probability of success.

Establish Appropriate Cross Functional Accountabilities and Authorities   There is a taxonomy of cross functional accountabilities and authorities that we have previously discussed. Each accountability has related authority. So this cross functional system is quite robust, and supports work being done across the organization in a much more powerful and clear way than is usually the case. The accountabilities, with their commensurate authorities, include recommending policies, standards, objectives, and procedures; monitoring; advising; service providing; coordinating; stopping and prescribing. This system is much more powerful than having some "reporting relationships" with "solid lines" or "dotted lines."

Eliminate Champions, Steering Committees, and Operating Committees   You have the system in place. You don't need champions, steering committees, and operating committees (other than any that are legally required). These entities tend to obscure accountability and authority. They often involve people sitting around the table, lacking clear accountabilities and authorities, and producing suboptimal outcomes.

A Closing Note on Trust   In the absence of optimal organization design, we often encounter vague terms and phrases, such as "we need better communication," or "collateral relationships." One word that is often invoked is "trust," as in "We need be more trusting." Rather than invoke these terms, we would suggest that you create an organization design that produces better clarity and communication, and provides the framework that encourages trust inducing because it is transparent and explicit. People are far more likely to do what they say they will do with the clarity and specificity of this system.

Special Topics

In this section, I address a number of topics related to aligning accountabilities and authorities. The topics include the following:

- What a manager should not delegate.
- Self-directed teams.
- Regionalization: striking the right balance.
- Specialization is not free.
- The siren song of synergy.
- If trust is so important, why is it so elusive?
- When an owner is not an owner.
- A recipient is not a client ... and why it matters.

What a Manager Should Not Delegate   Effective work in an organization requires delegation. A manager (from the head of the organization on down), within the context and prescribed limits provided by her manager, chooses to either do work directly or delegate it. However, there are two key accountabilities that a manager should not delegate.

The first is the business plan. While others can support the planning, fully delegating it is not appropriate. When an organization is properly stratified, the full capability of the manager is required to develop (and execute) the plan. If it is delegated to a lower-level individual, the plan comes out at too low a level; it doesn't have the required complexity and nuance. This has been a major problem with so-called strategic planning units. These units, instead of supporting managers in doing their work, have actually done the work due to the abdication of managers. The resulting outcomes have often been unsatisfactory.

The second key item that should not be delegated is the integrative accountability. For example, only a Stratum 5 president should integrate the core and support functions that are organized at a Stratum 4 level. While some aspects of the work clearly can be delegated, much of it is at the interface of these functions. The manager should ensure the appropriate interplay, and make the appropriate trade-offs. Our view is that many executives do not recognize the importance of this integrative accountability and do not perform it adequately.

Self-Directed Teams   Effective teams are critical for optimal organization performance. This would include "natural teams" (manager and direct reports), project teams, and cross functional teams. These teams also require clear and appropriate accountabilities and authorities.

We have run into self-directed teams numerous times: they are almost invariably dysfunctional. They usually operate on a concept of "team accountability" (meaning that the team, rather than a single position, is accountable). The underlying assumption is that a manager is unnecessary. Our view is that accountability is individual: when the team is accountable, then no one is accountable. Reliance on the team in these conditions can lead to very negative outcomes.

Of course, a manager may delegate accountabilities and authorities to a group of direct reports. However, in this case, the team would not be self-directed. It would be working within the context and prescribed limits, and delegation framework established by the manager. The manager still has an important ongoing role. Further, since the manager is one stratum above, it establishes the necessary manager–direct report relationships. Within this framework, a team can use mutual adjustment mechanisms to get the work done. One finds this arrangement in production and military combat situations. However, the key is that there is a managerial role to provide and continuously improve the framework. Most self-directed teams lack this important framework. The result often is significantly lower employee satisfaction—a key success factor is the relationship with the manager.

One way of identifying the problem is to ask the question "Who is accountable?" The answer may be unclear. However, if the answer, delivered with great certainty, is that "the team is accountable," then you know that no one is.

The most frightening situation that we have encountered was in a hospital where the staff, of course, was dealing with issues of life and death. Hospitals are complex organizations, their work made more complex by having to deal with issues 24 hours a day, 7 days a week. We asked who was accountable for the patient. The answer was the team. But it was not clear which accountabilities different team members had. Nor was it clear how problems would be picked up. We then asked about the accountability for contact with the patient's family—in the jargon, an important stakeholder. Again the answer was the team. So, the patient's family would not get the whole picture, but only the part of the picture that a particular team member was familiar with at that point in time. We believe that the concept of self-directed teams, without the framework we have discussed, is ill conceived, and that it leads to suboptimal performance.

Regionalization: Striking the Right Balance   Our experience
has led to an interesting conclusion with regard to regions, a
phenomenon we notice chiefly in government organizations, but
also see in business.

The most critical parts of an organization are the top (which
provides comprehensive vision, mission, values, strategic positioning, plans, standards, monitoring, and services) and the bottom
(which delivers the products and/or services). In larger organizations there is also a need for an intermediate level, which is
often called a regional level. In these cases there is a tendency for
the upper levels to "decentralize." This often results in the upper
level delegating so much to the middle level that they abdicate
their upper-level accountabilities and authorities. The middle level
holds on to these accountabilities and authorities without sufficient
further delegation to the lower levels. This results in the worst of
situations: there is suboptimal work at the top and the bottom and a
bloated middle. Regionalization should be balanced to ensure that
the appropriate accountabilities and authorities are established at
all levels.

Specialization Is Not Free   A yin and yang of organization
design is differentiation and integration. There can be value in
differentiation, which sometimes is a product of functional alignment. So, for example, instead of having one position accountable
for both sales and manufacturing, there are two different positions.
Each position would be filled by someone with the specific skills
required for the position. This is generally called specialization. It
allows us to develop deeper skill sets and methods.

Most people fail to realize is that there is a flip side to special-
ization/differentiation, and that is the requirement for integration.
What has been separated must be brought together again. Organizations generally differentiate quite readily but are slow to recognize
the need for integration. A useful rule of thumb is that for every act
of differentiation, there should be an act of integration with equal

focus and intensity. While this may be an overstatement, having a strong focus on both will add value.

We frequently hear the complaint that an organization operates in silos—units or divisions that do not function together effectively. More complex work that requires connections across the organization does not get done well. This is the classic outcome of differentiation (specialization) without sufficient integration. Integration requires a strong organization design. It starts with the optimal alignment of positions vertically and functionally. It then moves to employee and manager accountabilities and authorities. Only on this framework is it possible to apply the integrating mechanism that is the antidote to silos: cross functional accountabilities and authorities.

Rarely do we find organizations that exhibit a reluctance to differentiate or specialize. However, specialization is not free. The flip side, integration, is virtually never sufficiently in place. The cost of the lack of integration can be seen every day in organizations with silos and failed projects.

The Siren Song of Synergy   Synergy is defined by a combination of elements producing a result that is greater than the individual parts: the proverbial 1+1=3.

While synergy is both desirable and valuable, we have seen numerous organizations reduce performance because they don't really understand the process and their attempts to make it happen are unsuccessful. The plan usually involves putting together two organizations or two parts of one or more organizations that are dissimilar, but seen to have some aspects that can lead to enhanced performance. For example, if we put together a unit focused on selling X with a unit focused on selling Y, we will have synergy because both sell, and both can sell both X and Y. Or, if we put together two different business units in the same territory, we will get synergy, despite the fact that they have nothing in common except location.

The failure in these situations comes from not understanding the underlying work, and from assuming that one common feature is enough to produce the desired result. Failures that we have seen are often driven by one variable (e.g., cost savings) without considering others. Pulling together different functions or units requires considerable coordinative effort, which in turn requires time and effort. The forced union can easily divert each function or unit from focusing on its core deliverables, and this lack of focus can result in reduced performance.

We have seen this happen most frequently (although not only) in government organizations. When the maneuver involves, for example, removing one or more senior-level positions, it may look like an easy way to reduce expenses. However, the coordinative costs and the energy absorbed, which are more difficult to understand and measure, are seldom given sufficient consideration. Done properly, achieving synergy requires enhanced cross functional accountabilities and authorities.

The search for synergy should include really understanding the underlying work and putting in place the necessary cross functional accountabilities and authorities. Otherwise, the outcome can be something like $1+1=1.5$.

If Trust Is So Important, Why Is It So Elusive?   Trust is a foundation for all human relationships, and organizations are not an exception. Trust, or its lack, is a critical part of employee satisfaction and the relationship with one's manager. Trust is often thought of as being related to integrity. If a person has integrity, then that person will be trusted. If one doesn't intentionally lie or deceive, then one will be trusted.

Covey (1991) provides a broader perspective. Trust is related to people fulfilling their commitments or doing what they say they will do. It is possible to be a person of integrity but still not be trusted, because of unfulfilled commitments. This principle can be applied to organizations. Unfortunately, organizations also sometimes lack integrity and are capable of intentional deceit. However, the more substantive issue for both individuals and organizations is whether or not they will do what they have said they will do.

We believe that there are two parts to this issue. First, people are not careful enough about making commitments. And second, accountabilities and authorities in organizations are often unclear. The result can be that an individual thinks he has authority and then it turns out that he doesn't. The individual promises certain resources to a direct report, but someone else takes them. The issue goes beyond this of course. Are positions aligned properly? Are people properly matched to positions that they are capable of performing in? Are deliverables clear and appropriate? A strong organization design is an important foundation on which to develop trust. It is not the only part of the solution, but an important one.

When Is an Owner Not an Owner? We go into a number of organizations that use the term "owner". This generally occurs where there are cross functional relationships. For example, some people (e.g., production managers) are accountable for the delivery, and one person or function is accountable for ensuring that there is consistency (e.g., in processes) across all production areas. There is a tendency to say that this latter person or function "owns the process." We have also seen this occur with regard to assets. Again, some people (e.g., again, the production managers) are accountable for the delivery, and one person or function is accountable for the maintenance of the assets. There is a tendency to say that this latter person or function "owns the assets."

The problem here is that a complex relationship is reduced to a simplistic duality: I own it and you don't. The actual situation is much more nuanced. Both parties have interrelated account-abilities and authorities. One is positioned to utilize the processes and assets within parameters. This generally requires considerable planning and skilled execution. The other is positioned to rec-ommend policies and standards to the cross over point manager, monitoring, providing advice and service, etc. This combination of managerial and cross functional accountabilities and authorities provides much clearer and more accurate language, and is much more likely to develop and enhance the working relationships that are required.

A Recipient Is Not a Client ... and Why It Matters   There is an important distinction between a client (or customer) and a recipient. Most services within an organization are provided to recipients and not to clients. Our operational definitions and the implications are as follows.

A client is someone who, in a relatively open market (i.e., where there is real choice), is both the recipient of and payer for a product or service. If one does not meet both conditions, then one is not a client. Therefore, both the recipient and payer have to be identified in order to have an accurate analysis. For example, the users of internal services generally do not make decisions to buy and pay for the services in a relatively open market. Therefore they are recipients and not clients.

If internal users are recipients, who is the payer? The ultimate payer is the shareholder, and, through the shareholder, the payer accountability and authority is delegated through executive level (for present purposes, let's say the executive is the President) in order to make decisions on the allocation of resources. The President has to establish the context and prescribed limits for the service, and directly make significant trade-off decisions. For example, if there was a decision to reduce a support service staff by X percent (which could have been a reasonable decision from a total organization perspective), the payer (President) has decided that the recipients will have fewer resources from which to draw for their support services. There may be some legitimate reductions in the level of service. This should be communicated. Naturally, the related details are the accountability of the head of the support department and not the President. However, the President needs to be clear about the generally acceptable levels of service and significant trade-offs. The President needs to set the context and prescribed limits and establish a conflict resolution channel to deal with any significant issues.

Several implications flow from this distinction between client and recipient. Providers of services to recipients must balance the requirements of the recipients with the requirements of the payer. For example, if the payer expects services to be relatively evenly divided among recipients, it would not likely be appropriate for a provider to agree to a request from one recipient to receive three times as many services as they were due. If a provider doesn't understand the difference between a client and a recipient, it is easier to fall into this trap of meeting all service demands from recipients—treating them, in effect, as clients. The fact that not all requests from recipients have to be fulfilled in no way absolves a provider from delivering optimal agreed services. Service contracts can be useful for facilitating this.

Internal services are provided on the basis of cross functional accountabilities and authorities. This includes recommending, monitoring, advising, providing services, coordinating, stopping, and sometimes prescribing. There can be an inherent conflict in these roles: a recipient may want as many services as possible, but may not want to be monitored since this can be restricting. For example, a finance department provides services to other departments but also has a watchdog (monitoring) role. This role can be critical to the payer (e.g., keeping her out of jail!) but not popular with the recipient. Having different objectives quite naturally leads to conflict; conflict resolution mechanisms should be in place for this reason.

In sum, there is a critical difference between clients and recipients. Internal providers and recipients require a clear cross functional accountability and authority framework in order to most effectively do their work.

Conclusion

Once positions are aligned vertically and functionally, you move on to determining accountabilities and authorities with respect to employee, supervisor, manager and manager once removed.

Establishing cross functional accountabilities and authorities also is a part of this process. And so is ensuring appropriate position descriptions, with accountabilities and authorities and specifications indicating what an individual requires to fill a position. These descriptions provide a foundation for making decisions about aligning people with positions.

ALIGNING PEOPLE WITH POSITIONS

I believe that we can better match people to positions and have better succession planning. We have eliminated some jobs, and invested in other higher value added jobs. We can better coach employees in this system, and this is related to lower turnover.

—Joan Mitchell, Vice President, Human
Resources, Moneris Solutions, February 2006

Once positions are aligned vertically and functionally, it is possible not only to better align accountabilities and authorities, but also to align employees to positions. Developing position specifications provides a foundation for this alignment of people to positions. There are three key factors in aligning people to positions:

- skilled knowledge
- information processing capability
- application, or fully applying an individual's capabilities to the work

Of these, information processing capability in particular is part of the unique added value of this organization design method. This framework is based on the work of Jaques (1996) and his colleagues. While we have modified some aspects of this framework, we adhere quite closely to the definitions of information processing capability. This is one of two measures (the other is time span) that are at the core of stratification. Time span and information processing capability have become a critical part of our practice and research.

Therefore, consistency in definitions is critical. We have adapted this framework with the work of Macdonald, Burke, and Stewart (2006). They discuss knowledge, technical skill, and social process skill, which we have specified under skilled knowledge. As well, they use "application" instead of "values/commitment," which we have found to be helpful.

Skilled Knowledge

Three specific components of skilled knowledge are knowledge, technical skills and social process skills. Knowledge includes conceptual understanding and any related certification. Technical skills relate to doing the specific work in a position. Social process skills include relations with others (important for all positions in the organization), and managerial skills for all management positions.

Skilled knowledge can generally be acquired and learned. Skilled knowledge requirements should be vertically differentiated to the extent possible (i.e., by strata and levels within strata). Some skilled knowledge requirements are more amenable to vertical differentiation than others, so care must be exercised. While many organizations use competencies for position requirements, we believe that skilled knowledge is more useful. It is more specific to a position, and is therefore more easily adapted to training and learning.

Information Processing Capability

Information processing capability determines the maximum level or stratum at which the individual could work at the present time given the following conditions:

- opportunity
- the necessary skilled knowledge
- full application to the position requirements

Information processing capability is the way in which an individual processes information (i.e., takes information, understands it, reasons with it, and draws conclusions). This is a capability that an individual carries, and can be seen when an individual is fully engaged in problem solving. One could think of it as "processing power." By itself, it is not sufficient to be successful in a position (skilled knowledge and application are also important), but to be successful in a position in a particular stratum, an individual should have information processing capability appropriate to that stratum.

Information processing capability changes through a growth process. Some people stay at Stratum 1 all their lives; some may go up to Stratum 8 or higher. Many are in between.

It is important to understand the level of information processing capability in order to best match people to the appropriate stratum of a position. If an individual has a higher information processing capability, then the individual will not be using full capability. This "underemployment" may lead to employee dissatisfaction. If an individual has a lower information processing capability than the stratum of the position, then the individual will not be successful in the position. This is often referred to as the "Peter Principle." The key is to find the right match so that the individual is successful and the organization derives the benefits.

Complexity of information processing can be evaluated by observing the categories of information processing that an individual uses. The resulting evaluation is a measure of the stratum of work that an individual is currently capable of doing, assuming skilled knowledge and appropriate application in the particular position.

It should be noted that the immediate requirement is to match people to positions. However, individual information processing capability seems to mature along relatively predictable paths (Jaques, 1996). Therefore, this information can also assist with understanding future individual capabilities, "bench strength," career planning, and succession planning.

Application

A necessary condition for optimal success in a position is that an individual applies to it his full capability and commitment. This is a function of motivation and commitment, and valuing and putting energy into the work. The individual should fully apply himself to the type of work (accountabilities and authorities) of the position. This could include the professional/technical work (such as, sales, finance, information technology, etc.) and also managerial work for those in managerial positions.

Application is particularly important when an individual moves from a technical or professional to a managerial position. Does the individual really value doing managerial work, and will there be full application? Sometimes individuals apply for management positions because it is a way to "move up the organization" but do not really value management work. The organization loses one of its best technical or professional individuals, and gets one of their worst managers, all in one move.

Talent Pool Review

When work in an organization is properly stratified, a management process called "talent pool review" can be used to determine an individual's information processing capability, skilled knowledge, and application. The manager once removed and direct report managers would meet to review individuals in the next stratum down. In other situations, information processing capability can be determined through an assessment process conducted by a trained assessor. The purpose of undertaking a talent pool review is to provide information that can be used for the following purposes:

- to assess the current talent pool and develop a better understanding of the individuals comprising the talent pool
- to make decisions to match people to positions (staffing decisions)

- to identify strengths and weaknesses related to current organization bench strength (replacement capability)
- to assist with the longer-term development of the talent pool (individual development and organizational succession planning)
- to formulate employee development plans
- to assist all managers and managers once removed in fulfilling their accountability to develop and sustain an effective team of employees.

The talent pool review process evaluates the managers' direct reports on the three dimensions discussed previously (information processing capability, skilled knowledge, and application).

While a primary outcome is optimizing the current situation, there can be an additional benefit. Information processing capability seems to mature over time in relatively predictable patterns. Future capability can be estimated through progression curves, providing valuable information on bench strength. This is particularly important in situations where demographics show that there will likely be high turnover in senior positions (e.g., as baby boomers retire).

It can also be instructive to consider where an individual is on the progression curve and extrapolate back in time. We often find that around the time when an individual's information processing capability moves up one stratum, there is significant dissatisfaction and often a significant change (e.g., a job change, going back to school, etc.).

Individuals with higher information processing capabilities tend to continue to move to higher levels throughout their lifetime. Therefore, the societal practice of forced retirement can be extremely dysfunctional in removing these individuals from the work force.

The talent pool review process is used to plan current and future human resources requirements. It can be used diagnostically to determine the distribution of talent across functions and strata within the organization.

Special Topics

The following four topics are worth special attention:

- the "best person"
- career planning systems
- training that never works
- the leadership pipeline

The "Best Person"   Don't hire the "best person" for the job!

On the face of it, this seems like poor advice. However, we have seen two organizations that had reason to regret hiring the "best person." In both cases, the organization defined best as more highly educated and recruited people according to that criterion.

In the first case, although the organization was hiring for first-level customer service positions in which the work was proceduralized and routine, a decision was made to only hire university graduates. In the second case, the organization was hiring for first-level positions in a quality assurance function. Although the work did require some specialized technical skills, it too was quite proceduralized. Nevertheless, a decision was made to hire individuals with PhD degrees.

In both cases, there was a mismatch between the position requirements and the incumbent capabilities. The incumbents had higher-level capability than the level of work, and were bored and frustrated. As a result, there were issues with work that was improperly done, poor morale, absenteeism, and turnover. So, don't hire the "best person"; hire the person best suited for the position.

Career Planning Systems   Career planning systems, which are used in many organizations, often are inhumane. Generally, they involve the individual and her manager and are meant to map out the individual's career. There is often paper work reflecting what is expected of the individual over time.

While the purpose is noble, the process and outcome often are not. These systems are based on the premise that an individual should want to move up in the organization. A first-level employee should want to be a supervisor, a supervisor should want to be a manager, a manager should want to be a director, and so on up the organization. In fact, since this is a built-in premise, employees are often explicitly or implicitly made to feel guilty about not wanting to move up the organization ("You don't want to be a manager! Don't you have any ambition?").

We know that different individuals have different information processing capabilities. We also know that different strata require different capabilities to be successful. Therefore, one of the important outcomes is to have individuals properly matched to the stratum of work. We don't want individuals promoted to their level of incompetence (Peter Principle). We also don't want individuals held back from using their full capability. We want the right match.

So, if someone is in a job, and is suited to this job in terms of information processing capability, skilled knowledge and application, and is successful in the job, then this is an achievement to honor and celebrate. A planning process that makes the individual feel guilty or uncomfortable serves neither her best interest nor that of the organization.

Training That Never Worked   To be successful in a position, an individual requires the necessary information processing capability, skilled knowledge, and application. In order to understand this, it is necessary to understand the requirements of the position, including the information processing requirement.

Financial institutions have been seeking ways to create more "added value" positions and remove less "added value" positions (generally ones that are more transactional in nature). This has often meant reducing the number of teller positions and creating new positions related to loans or investments. Tellers have been taken out of their old positions and put in these new positions.

They have been given training that generally involves what we would call skilled knowledge. The outcomes we have seen and heard about have included many failures. Why is that? Was the training not good?

The problem in our view is twofold. First, the financial institutions did not understand the difference between Stratum 1 positions (e.g., tellers) and Stratum 2 positions (some, but not all, of the loan and investment positions). Second, they did not understand the difference between individuals with Stratum 1 information processing capability and those with Stratum 2 information processing capability. We would expect that many (although not all) of the individuals in teller positions have only Stratum 1 capability and are therefore not suited for these Stratum 2 positions. The financial institutions could have saved a lot of time and money, the individuals involved could have been spared an unnecessary failure, and many customers could have been spared having to deal with an individual who was not capable of doing the work (stories about this were legion).

If you have a mismatch in information processing capability, you can train as long as you want, but it won't produce the desired results.

The Leadership Pipeline   Charan et al. (2001) wrote *The Leadership Pipeline*, in which the authors describe the GE system of leadership development. In this system, there are vertical levels (managers of individuals, managers of managers, etc.) and each level has different requirements. Individuals are assessed for their readiness to move to the next level and then, at the time of transition, given training. There also is a strong system of coaching and development (as well as high expectations for performance). The GE system is rightly regarded as the epitome of leadership development.

We share a common ancestry with the GE leadership program. Charan et al. (2001) note that the GE system came initially from a consultant to GE named Walter Mahler. Mahler sold to GE, and helped to further develop, an approach called "Career Crossroads." Mahler also wrote several books (Mahler, 1973, 1975). Wilfred Brown was the CEO with whom Elliott Jaques did most of his early development work. Brown also wrote several books (Brown, 1960, 1971). Craddock (2004) points out that Mahler (1975) refers to Brown (1960). At this time, the only extensive vertical alignment work was being done by Jaques, Brown, and their colleagues.

So, the GE system and the one developed by Jaques, Brown, and their colleagues have similar origins. While the GE system is unparalleled in its execution and impact, the system developed by Jaques, Brown, and their colleagues has also progressed. It provides certain specificity that the GE system lacks. Features that make our system unique include the following:

- There is a clearer delineation of levels of work (called strata). Each stratum is different in the nature or work and the complexity of work.
- There is a clearer delineation of the individual capability required to work at each level or stratum. One of the most critical is information processing capability.
- Direct measures for the complexity of work in each stratum are provided. These are time span and information processing requirement.
- Direct measures for the individual capability required in each stratum are provided. These include information processing capability and time horizon.
- There is better differentiation of managers of individuals according to strata. For example, there are significant differences between being a manager of Stratum 1 first-level employees and of Stratum 2 professionals.
- There is better differentiation of manager requirements at different strata. For example, Stratum 4 is a general manager level, while Stratum 5 is business unit head level. Each has unique requirements.

The GE system has evolved to be the epitome of leadership development. It seems to be particularly good at helping individuals to move from one level to the next higher level. However, the Jaques/Brown system has also evolved and contains many elements that could be beneficial to the GE system and others like it.

Conclusion

Aligning people to positions is a critical part of optimizing your organization design. The most fundamental part is matching people to current positions. However the Talent Pool method also provides a foundation for the development of employees to meet future requirements. You can use this to make a significant difference in talent acquisition and retention, and also in improving your organization performance.

ALIGNING DELIVERABLES

One of our biggest improvements has been in business planning. Because we had taken the time to properly align the organization, we have been able to create and overlay a cascading business planning and review system in which employees have clearer deliverables with more appropriate complexity at each level. This is extremely powerful.

—Mike J. Donoghue, President and CEO,
Allstate Canada Group, February 2006

What are the outputs that individuals in different strata and different functions should be providing? How can the deliverables of the whole organization be synchronized to provide the greatest impact? There are two factors to consider in answering these questions. One is the individual: each individual should be accountable for appropriate deliverables. The other aspect relates to the systems the organization uses. We usually find a number of relatively unrelated systems. These include strategic planning, business planning, budgeting, and performance management. One solution that has great power is an integrated organization planning and review system.

Earlier in this chapter I introduced our organization systems functioning model and our organization systems change model (see Figure 2.1 on page 24 and Figure 2.2 on page 28). These models provide the foundation for aligning deliverables to positions. These two models provide the framework for aligning deliverables and provide the basis for our organization planning and review model.

Organization Planning and Review Model

Our organization planning and review model is important to move an organization from its current state to a higher-performing future/desired state. The basic idea is that each manager (defined as being accountable for the work of another employee, regardless of level or title) should have a plan. The organization planning and review model provides a framework to ensure that managerial positions in each stratum are working at the right level of complexity and in concert to move the organization in the desired direction. Our model has two components: content and process.

Organization Planning and Review Model: Content Our content model is shown in Figure 2.11.

The content (Figure 2.11) is the six aspects of an organization plan (vision, mission, values, strategic positioning, operational plan, and resource plan):

- Vision: what we want to be (i.e., desired future state)
- Mission: why we exist (our basic business, i.e., current state)
- Values: how we relate/behave, our principles or standards
- Strategic positioning: optimal positioning to provide better value to stakeholders than alternatives (or in the case of a monopoly, better value than comparable monopolies provide)

Organization Plan

- Vision
- Mission
- Values
- Strategic Positioning
- Operational Plan
- Resource Plan

FIGURE 2.11.   Organization Planning and Review Model: Content

- Operational plan: what we are going to accomplish in terms of quality, quantity, timeliness, etc.; this would include appropriate time spans (target completion times) for different levels or strata of an organization
- Resource plan: obtaining and optimally utilizing the required resources, particularly human, financial, material, information, and technology

Organization Planning and Review Model: Process   For organization planning and review to be successful, the process as well as the content are important. The process can be thought of as operating at two levels: individual and organization.

At an individual level, the importance of process is shown in Figure 2.12. The process includes plan, do, review, and feedback (+/-). This can be thought of as a continuous improvement loop or a learning loop. It should be noted that the feedback loop can include any reward system that the organization uses.

FIGURE 2.12.   Organization Planning and Review Model: Individual Process

The six content pieces of a strategic plan combined with the individual process are necessary but not sufficient conditions for effective organization planning and review. It is also necessary to develop an effective organization wide system.

We believe that organization planning and review is too important to be limited to senior managers. Each manager (defined as being accountable for others regardless of level or title) should have his own plan. It doesn't matter whether the manager is accountable for the whole organization or a small unit. A manager's plan will always be within the context and prescribed limits of his direct manager's plan. It would include vision, mission, values (these are usually the same throughout an organization), strategic positioning, operational plan, and resource plan. As well, each manager ensures that each nonmanagerial direct report has an operational plan and a resource plan.

It is important to have one comprehensive organization planning and review process instead of two or more disjointed plans. We often find organizations whose systems for strategic planning (often for most senior executives), business planning, budgeting, and performance management are disconnected and fail to drive the organization in a consistent direction. This is dysfunctional.

The model for a cascading and iterative organization planning and review process shown in Figure 2.13 facilitates the entire workforce working in concert to move the organization in the desired direction.

The head of the organization is accountable for a plan that encompasses the entire organization. This plan is constrained by the context and prescribed limits set by the Board. The head of the organization is accountable for implementing the plan. As part of this implementation, she or he will delegate accountabilities and authorities to each direct report.

These direct reports will, in turn, translate these accountabilities into a plan for themselves. At this step there will be iteration between the direct report and the manager for approval of the

Planning Framework

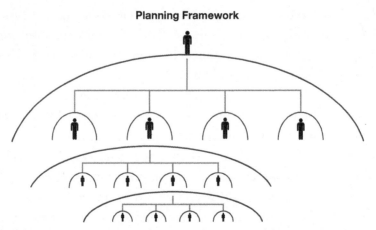

FIGURE 2.13.   Organization Planning and Review Model: Organization Process

plan and possible modifications. In implementing the plan, the manager will carry out some work personally and delegate some to direct reports. These direct reports then develop their plans. This iterative process cascades down throughout the organization to the lowest level of managers. Such a cascading process ensures that the plans at lower levels in the organization are subsets of plans at higher levels. The iterative loop is important at each level to ensure that there are opportunities to revise plans based on feedback from the managers who are developing their own plans.

One of the key added-value functions of a manager is to differentiate the deliverables that the manager receives from her manager into deliverables that the manager should carry out directly and those that can be (or parts of which can be) delegated to direct reports. Part of this process is to "translate" into deliverables that are appropriate for direct reports, and that can be accomplished within the resources available, while at the same time contributing to the success of the department and the organization as a whole.

Organization planning and review is a major task. It may require dedicated planning and review resources to support the process. If so, it is important to recognize that the role is to assist managers in developing their plans (direct output support), and not developing them for them. The latter case would be inappropriate delegation.

Since this approach is different than most, I would like to highlight some of the differences and what I perceive to be some of the advantages of this approach:

- It provides an integrated organization planning and review system, which replaces existing disjointed systems (e.g., strategic planning, business planning, performance management, etc.).
- It pulls together what I consider to be the important content (vision, mission, values, strategic positioning, operational plan, and resource plan).
- It provides a simple yet powerful process (learning loop).
- It operates within the framework of context and prescribed limits at each level, with the appropriate stratification (i.e., proper complexity of work at each stratum).
- It eliminates the undefined term "strategy" and replaces it with "strategic positioning." We find the former term to lack clarity: "strategic positioning" is much more precise and provides a different and more focused approach.
- It requires managers at each level to develop and deliver a more comprehensive plan. We believe that expectations for managers generally are far too low. I would suggest (a bit tongue in cheek) that strategic work is too important to leave to senior executives.

Organization Planning and Review Model: Content and Process   Figure 2.14 shows the content and process of the organization planning and review model.

Delegation is from the top of the organization to the bottom. This is both a cascading and iterative process. Each manager develops a plan for his unit within the context and prescribed limits of his immediate manager. A couple of examples will illustrate what I mean.

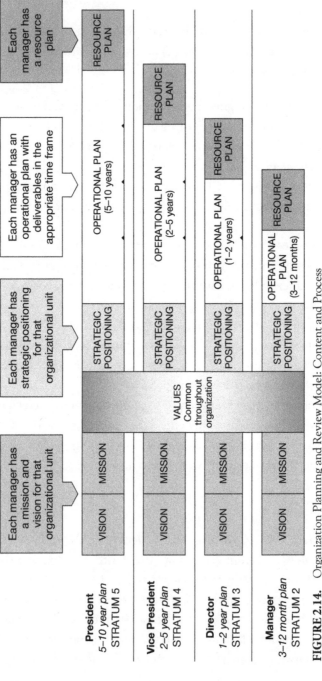

FIGURE 2.14. Organization Planning and Review Model: Content and Process

In the first case, the president develops a business plan, which becomes the business plan for the total organization. It contains a vision (what we want to be, our desired future state, etc.), mission (why we exist, our basic business, current state, etc.), values (how we relate/behave, our principles or standards, etc.), strategic positioning (optimal positioning to provide better value to stakeholders than alternatives), operational plan (what we are going to accomplish in terms of quality, quantity, timeliness, and resource requirements), and resource plan (obtaining and optimally utilizing the required resources, particularly human, financial, material, and information). Each manager should have a similar plan for her particular unit within the context and prescribed limits of the immediate manager. The failure to follow this process underutilizes managers and weakens organizations.

In the second case, a Stratum 3 director in charge of a training and development function within a human resources department should have a business plan that answers the following questions:

- What is the mission of the department? What business are we in? How we define this is important. Is it all modes of training for all functions? Are there restrictions?
- What is the vision of the department? Where do we want to be in two years? Do we want to double our electronic learning offerings and cut our classroom training in half?
- What are our values? While we expect each manager to consider this question, it is generally the case that the values are common throughout an organization. However, there may be some variance in focus (e.g., a production unit may put greater emphasis on safety than an office unit).
- What is our strategic positioning? How can our training unit provide greater value to our organization than other training units provide to their organizations? We might purchase generic training (e.g., meeting skills) in which we can provide little unique added value, but develop our own managerial program in which we can add particular added value due to the uniqueness of our organization approach.

- What is our operational plan? What are we going to accomplish? How will we measure that? What is our two-year plan and what are our shorter-term plans?
- What is our resource plan? What are our current resource requirements and availability? What resource changes will be required through our vision (e.g., developing and adding electronic learning resources and reducing classroom learning resources)?

Special Topics

The following special topics merit discussion:

- when a whole organization is compressed
- business plan issues
- an excessive focus on costs
- managerial judgment
- iterative strategy and organization design
- the myth of customer service

When a Whole Organization Is Compressed   One of the objectives of our organization planning and review system is to ensure that everyone is doing the appropriate complexity of work. This is critical. We often find individuals not working at the right level. However, one sometimes finds that whole organizations are compressed and need to be pulled up to the right complexity of work (e.g., time span). This also better matches complexity of work with compensation. This is demonstrated in Figure 2.15.

Business Plan Issues   Organizations generally have annual plans. The fundamentals make sense: you want to have a time frame to plan, execute, and review, and one year is a convenient time frame. Problems emerge when it is assumed that this is the actual cycle of work, and that this is the appropriate time frame for

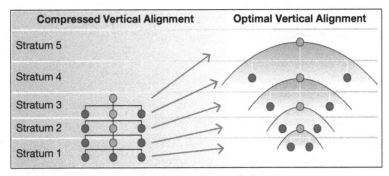

FIGURE 2.15.   Compressed and optimal vertical alignment

all levels in the organization. This is not the case. Bear in mind the time spans associated with various strata: one year is the time span at the boundary between Stratum 2 and Stratum 3. If your role is at this level, then one year coincides with your time span. For all other roles, it is artificial and potentially misleading and dysfunctional.

Let's start with Stratum 1 positions. The time span is between a day and three months, and is usually at the lower end of this range. Those who have worked on a shop floor know that daily and/or weekly measurements can often be the most useful in providing feedback and improving behavior. One year is not very useful, except as a very macro summation (and often not then).

Now consider Stratum 3 positions. The time span should be between one and two years. However, one seldom finds time spans in this range. Much of the work tends to be compressed into the one-year time frame (annual plan). Much of the unique added-value Stratum 3 work does not get done.

At Stratum 4, there may be two-to-five-year plans, but these (if they exist) tend to be vague and aspirational. They are usually not the robust plans that one would expect to see at this level.

So the one-year plan definitely has some value, but don't be lulled into thinking that this is what all work is about. Understand the real time spans of positions at various levels, and supplement this one-year cycle to plan, measure, and provide feedback on the real time spans of different positions in different strata.

An Excessive Focus on Costs   One of the key accountabilities of an executive is to ensure that the organization is profitable (government and nonprofit organizations would have somewhat different financial targets). Profit is a function of revenues and costs. Increasing profitability can result from some combination of increasing revenues and decreasing costs. So, a cost focus is important. However, we have seen numerous situations in which the cost orientation has been excessive—where it has become the primary management focus to the relative exclusion of other variables.

There are several problems with this excessive cost focus. First, it tends to produce a very short-term outlook: how were our costs last month? By the same token, it often eliminates a longer-term perspective that is necessary to building the business. Development projects don't get done. A commitment to the fundamental building blocks of the organization is abandoned. There may be five levels in the organization, but no one is working beyond Stratum 2—or Stratum 1! Everything is compressed.

An excessive focus on costs also leads to dysfunctional game playing. Particularly in organizations in which people are moved from one position to another fairly quickly, some individuals may strive to significantly reduce costs in their immediate area of accountability and then move on before the substantive problems emerge. The next person to occupy the position gets blamed for the previous incumbent's inappropriate short-term behavior. Unfortunately, organizations are often not smart enough to recognize and deal with this kind of tactical maneuvering.

A related issue is that it is difficult to know the point at which profitability is artificially enhanced by depleting assets (e.g., a failure to maintain old equipment and invest in new). Asset depletion like this does not yield true profit; it just weakens the balance sheet. Unfortunately many accounting practices tend not to do a good job of assessing this.

On top of all of the above, costs are not a good primary focus because they are a lagging rather than a leading indicator. Leading indicators would be measures such as productivity, quality, and customer satisfaction—these are the drivers of financial performance. An excessive focus on costs is analogous to driving with one's eyes firmly fixed on the rear view mirror: neither a very safe nor productive way to move ahead.

Managerial Judgment   Measurement systems and managerial work often are misunderstood. Managers are paid to make judgments. The essence of management is to be in a situation with relatively complex and often confusing information, and to make judgments and decisions about the best course of action. One might argue that this is also the essence of life.

Measurement systems are valuable because they can provide more specificity to assist managers in making judgments. Measurement systems can become dangerous when managers start believing they are a substitute for judgment. There is no substitute for management judgment.

The problem often occurs with performance management systems, particularly when applied to sales. A target is set; let's say it is 8 out of 10. Someone gets 8 out of 10. What does this mean? The simplistic answer is that the individual has been successful. After all, this system is "objective." People who favor this kind of measurement argue that they wouldn't want to fall back on something that was "subjective," often meaning management judgment. We would argue that, on the contrary, 8 out of 10 doesn't mean anything. It is useful input to a judgment, but until you understand the broader situation, you cannot reasonably come to a conclusion about performance. What if the sales environment was worse than expected (this can happen) and everyone else got 6 out of 10? Then you could conclude, assuming the measurement had some value, that the individual who made 8 out of 10 performed very well. However, if conditions were significantly better than anticipated, and everyone else got 10 out of 10, then the outcome was relatively poor. The bottom line is relatively simple: measurement is input to managerial judgment, not a substitute for it.

Iterative Strategy and Organization Design   The general view is that strategy precedes organization design. There is some truth in this proposition, but it is more complex than it first appears.

An organization strategy is part of the context for designing the organization. Not all organization designs are equal, and some will be better for achieving particular strategies. When people talk about strategy, they are generally referring to the strategic plan. However, the issues around strategy often have less to do with the plan and more to do with the implementation. We believe that organization design provides the foundation for strategy implementation and is therefore a critical aspect of the strategy.

A questionable but widely held belief is that you first work on developing a perfect strategy and only later begin work on the organization design. Developing a strategy is generally not a "blank piece of paper" exercise. It is limited by numerous factors including the existing organization design. So waiting for the perfect strategy to begin organization design may have more disadvantages than advantages. It may unnecessarily postpone the benefits that are possible from a better organization design. Further, a strong organization design method based on research and principle should be robust enough to deal with current circumstances but flexible enough to deal with future changes.

We have seen a newly appointed executive decide to improve both strategy and organization design at the same time. There was a great deal of interaction between the two teams established to work on the separate streams. It turned out that it was entirely possible to do both simultaneously. What was interesting is that organization design informed strategy as much as strategy informed organization design.

The Myth of Customer Service   Optimal customer service is critical for any organization. Without satisfied customers, an organization will perform suboptimally (there may be some exceptions for monopolies). But how is customer service defined?

We have seen several organizations make a fundamental mistake in this area. They have defined optimal customer service as doing whatever the customer wants. Late order? That's okay; we will still fulfill it. Want something that is not part of our service package? That's okay; we will produce/deliver it.

These one-off decisions often create more problems than they solve. They disrupt manufacturing schedules. They disrupt delivery schedules. They introduce variability into the system that reduces both reliability and financial performance. In fact, these decisions often weaken customer satisfaction because they weaken quality and reliability. They often weaken financial performance too, because the organization is not getting a higher price to compensate for the higher costs.

Organizations that routinely bend their own rules in this way often seem to have weak performance measurement systems. They don't understand the costs, financial and otherwise, and they certainly don't receive the required benefits. The key is to strategically position a business to provide better value to stakeholders than is offered by alternative sources. Customer service is critical, but it needs to be defined properly and delivered consistently.

Conclusion

Organization planning and review is critical to optimizing your organization design. It provides an initial framework (i.e., organization plan of whole organization) that assists in designing the organization to best attain the desired results. However, it also becomes an important part of organization design itself, since it helps to ensure that deliverables throughout the organization are integrated and stratum specific. If deliverables are not delegated appropriately, and if the context within which employees are to make decisions is not clear, then the result is a combination of decisions that can be counterproductive to the overall strategy of the organization. If there is clear delegation within a framework that helps every employee to understand how their deliverables relate to the overall strategy of the organization, then the likelihood of combined actions pulling the organization in the optimal direction is greatly enhanced.

ALIGNING TASKS

We have defined positions as roles that should have a position description. That description should include details such as accountabilities and authorities, requirements for people to fill the position, and deliverables that would be part of an organization planning and review system. Positions have varying degrees of complexity that can be measured in two ways. The first is time span, which is the deliverable with the longest target completion time. The second is the information processing requirement, which is the information processing capability that an individual must have to function in the position (at that particular stratum).

These factors provide the broader framework that we regard as important to successful organization design. However, it is also possible to move to a more micro analysis and alignment focusing on tasks. We would define a task as an activity carried out by an individual. A task would generally have input (receiving something); throughput (doing something); and output (delivering something). In defining tasks, it is necessary to decide how micro or macro to be.

While improving the alignment of tasks is important in its own right, this level of analysis has an additional benefit. There is considerable discussion about the relationship between positions and processes. We believe that the task is the "molecule" that underlies both. One can align tasks either into positions or into processes. The two approaches tend to be quite complementary. We have already discussed accountability for macro processes; we will discuss the linkage for micro processes later.

Method

As with much process analysis, we find that task analysis is most valuable at lower levels, specifically Stratum 1 and Stratum 2. We have developed a method for determining if tasks can be completed at Stratum 1 or should be assigned to Stratum 2 (and possibly higher). This method involves applying the information processing requirement levels for strata of work. We have not found a method for differentiating Stratum 3 or above tasks. However, our experience is that the greatest value is at Stratum 1 and Stratum 2. This stratum differentiation of tasks is very powerful. However, our method goes beyond that to look at a number of additional variables.

There are several steps in this method to improve the alignment of tasks. The first is to determine the area in scope. What part of an organization will be focused on? We have worked with systems ranging from individual business units or functions within organizations to whole organizations. The positions in scope would generally be Stratum 1 and Stratum 2 positions, with occasional Stratum 3 positions. It is generally valuable to include the related managerial positions. It is important to also determine the strata of the positions. This is often done in advance of a task analysis review, but can be done simultaneously.

The next step is to determine what tasks are completed by individuals in these positions and develop a list of these tasks. Then we identify the key factors to assess. The list could be a long one, but we focus on the most important areas These could include the time requirement of tasks, their costs, their stratum, and whether they are core or noncore for the area in scope. Next, we survey the organization in scope to determine how much time is spent on the various tasks. The analysis and recommendations are then completed, and a meeting takes place with the accountable executive (and usually the management team) to understand the report, make decisions, and plan implementation.

The final step would be to implement the actions that have been decided. As with our broader organization design assessment, we are often but not always involved in implementation.

Outcomes

As with our organization design assessment, the outcomes vary considerably depending on the specifics of the situation. However, there are some recurring themes that are worth discussing.

Strata Comparisons   The strata of tasks compared to the strata of positions is one of the most powerful aspects of our method. There is an optimal situation for both Stratum 1 and Stratum 2 positions in relation to tasks.

Stratum 1 positions should not be accountable for any Stratum 2 tasks. These tasks require a higher-level capability. If Stratum 1 positions are properly designed and staffed, the incumbents do not have the capability to do Stratum 2 tasks. The inclusion of Stratum 2 tasks in Stratum 1 positions leads to suboptimal performance and likely to some dissatisfaction from internal and/or external customers. It will also likely lead to some dissatisfaction on the part of the employees. Our experience is that employees generally want to do their best and be successful. This situation does not support it.

Stratum 2 positions should be doing a significant majority of Stratum 2 tasks and a significant minority of Stratum 1 tasks. There are several reasons for this. First, they are being paid a premium relative to Stratum 1 positions. To the extent that they are doing Stratum 1 tasks, the organization is not getting full value. Second, they may be less satisfied if they have to spend a significant amount of time doing lower-level tasks that are not as challenging and consequently, they may not apply themselves properly. Third, they may not have sufficient skilled knowledge to do these tasks as well as individuals in Stratum 1 positions.

What percentage of Stratum 1 tasks is acceptable for Stratum 2 positions? It is generally unreasonable to expect that Stratum 2 positions will have no Stratum 1 tasks. A number of lower-level tasks (that are also important) are usually done by people in higher-level positions. However, we find that Stratum 2 positions spend an average of 50 percent of their time on Stratum 1 tasks—a percentage that we believe is far too high. Our view is that a range of 20–40 percent is generally manageable. For analysis purposes, to measure potential cost savings, we use 30 percent, which we consider to be quite doable. To the extent the number can be made lower, so much the better.

In studies of 14 organizations, Capelle Associates found that employees in Stratum 2 positions were spending about half of their time doing lower-level work (see the pie chart on the left in Figure 2.16). At the same time, our research reveals that frontline employees are spending 14.1 percent of their time attempting work that belongs in a higher-level position. Neither situation is likely to enhance organization performance. In addition, employee satisfaction may be compromised. Individuals with the capability to do higher-level work can become frustrated and bored if given too much lower-level work to do. When lower-level employees are given unrealistic expectations, they may not succeed and are also likely to become frustrated.

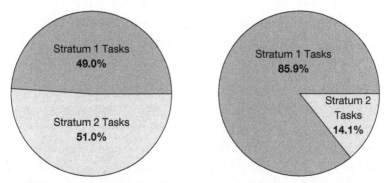

FIGURE 2.16.   Stratum of Work by Stratum 2 and Stratum 1 Positions

In short, the appropriate alignment of tasks is critical. When work is not properly aligned, very real issues emerge concerning employee satisfaction. And when employee satisfaction is compromised, customer satisfaction can decrease, which in turn negatively impacts overall financial performance.

Capelle Associates research shows that misaligned tasks (e.g., where professionals spend 50 percent of their time doing lower-level tasks that someone in a lower-level position could do as well for less money) provide average potential annual savings of about $10,951 per higher-level position. Relative to the investment required, this provides average potential annual return on investment (ROI) of 1,500 percent!

How are these situations resolved once they have been identified? When Stratum 2 tasks are being done by Stratum 1 positions, the optimal solution is to move the tasks to Stratum 2 positions. This is usually doable. While one might argue that this would be slightly more expensive (individuals in Stratum 2 are generally paid more than individuals in Stratum 1), we believe that this is a lower cost than suboptimal work output and the likelihood of rework, dissatisfied employees and dissatisfied customers.

When Stratum 1 tasks are being done by Stratum 2 positions, the solution is to move the tasks to Stratum 1 positions. Of course there are other possibilities: you could eliminate the tasks, automate them, or outsource them. However, if we start with the idea of moving them to Stratum 1 positions, we have to be sure there are sufficient Stratum 1 positions to take them on. Occasionally, this proves to be difficult. For example, there might be a situation where a single position that requires Stratum 2 capability must do the range of work at both Stratum 1 and Stratum 2 levels (e.g., a single Stratum 2 manager or professional in a remote location). However, there are usually Stratum 1 positions that the Stratum 1 tasks can be delegated to. If not, and if there is a lot of Stratum 1 work to be done, then it may be possible to add Stratum 1 positions and eliminate Stratum 2 positions. This can sometimes be a cost-effective solution. The review of Stratum 1 and Stratum 2 tasks can lead numerous improvement opportunities. We will discuss three of these.

The first is to determine if there are tasks currently at a Stratum 2 level that could be proceduralized and done at Stratum 1. This can provide a significant opportunity. An organization we worked with was developing a new product/service line that required a call center. Stratum 2 professionals were simultaneously developing the product/service line and working on the front line in the call center. As things moved along and they proceduralized the bulk of the work, they also became dissatisfied. There was not enough of the more challenging Stratum 2 work — it all was at a Stratum 1 level. This resulted in lower morale and greater absenteeism. They had been successful in proceduralizing Stratum 1 tasks but weren't interested in doing them. The solution was to first create Stratum 1 frontline positions and Stratum 2 manager positions to be accountable for them, and then staff all positions appropriately. Some of the original employees moved into the Stratum 2 manager positions, and others moved to Stratum 2 professional positions in other parts of the organization.

The second opportunity could be to determine if more Stratum 2 tasks should be developed. This may sound paradoxical. Shouldn't work be proceduralized as much as possible to reduce costs? The answer depends on determining what the work should be. For example, one client required sales at a Stratum 2 relationship management level. The analysis revealed that virtually all of the position's time was spent on Stratum 1 transactional sales. This was not in keeping with client requirements. Stratum 2 tasks were added to get the work up to the level that clients required.

The third opportunity could be to determine if Stratum 1 tasks can be changed. For example, it may be possible to centralize Stratum 1 tasks to provide greater efficiencies, eliminate Stratum 1 tasks that don't add value, automate them if suitable, or outsource them. It is interesting to note that organizations have multiple ways of adding tasks, but very few ways to eliminate them.

The Time and Costs of Tasks   The simplest analysis of tasks is how much time each task takes and how much it costs. Even this level of analysis can provide some interesting insights and improvement opportunities. Executives and managers tend not to understand their organizations at this level of detail. Since each organization is different, each review provides different insights. The following is a small sample from our experience.

One task that consumes considerable time and cost is meetings. This insight can lead to many opportunities. Who calls meetings? Who is compelled to attend? Are meetings efficient in terms of agendas, timeliness, and clear outputs? Issues with meetings often are also related to inappropriate committees being set up.

Responding to requests sometimes emerges as an issue. Organizations are often clear about accountabilities related to requests from outside the organization (e.g., requests from customers) but give no attention to requests from inside. Virtually everyone believes that they can request any amount of information from colleagues at any time. There is often no control! No consideration is given to the value of the information relative to the costs. Core delivery areas get bogged down by responding to requests that may duplicate other requests and be unclear. As with other cross functional issues discussed earlier, there should be clarity (and appropriate restriction) on these requests.

A third item that sometimes comes up is fixing problems. While we generally know that rework is an issue, this type of analysis can pinpoint it more specifically.

Fragmentation   A standard part of the analysis is fragmentation. Fragmentation occurs when many employees spend relatively small amounts of time on the same task. When this is happening, the question that arises is whether or not the task could or should be centralized. For example, if many employees are processing particular forms, it may be better to centralize this task and have fewer people focus on it for a greater percentage of their time. This would provide more specialization. It could allow for better training and management of individuals and possibly lead to the development of better work processes. It could provide for a better economy of scale. In the right circumstances it results in better work being done in a more cost efficient way.

Other Factors of Interest for Tasks   Different organizations choose other factors to focus on and better understand. These can include: tasks that are core to the work of the area as opposed to tasks that are not core; tasks that are customer related as opposed to tasks that are not customer related. Organizations are often surprised by the time and costs related to noncore and/or non-customer-focused tasks.

Getting Value from Contractors and Outsourcers   Contractors are often brought in to provide specialized skills. They often cost more. The assumption is that they provide unique added value. However, task analysis sometimes provides interesting additional information. First, the tasks in these positions often correlate highly with tasks in other positions. Second, a fair portion of the work is at a Stratum 1 level that may not require this higher level of expertise.

Another situation we believe should be reviewed is work that is outsourced. We have not done this type of analysis but anecdotal evidence suggests such an investigation could be valuable. In particular, there appear to be numerous issues in not differentiating Stratum 1 and Stratum 2 positions; Stratum 1– and Stratum 2–capable individuals; and Stratum 1 and Stratum 2 tasks. It is often simply assumed that the right work will be done by the right people at the right level. However, if executives and managers do not have this understanding in their own organizations, is it reasonable to expect that the organizations to which work is outsourced will have figured it out?

From Tasks to Processes   We often find that there is value in considering how tasks align into processes. While we tend not to get into this area in the same depth as many who specialize in it, the analysis can be valuable to better understand both tasks and positions and begin to make connections to processes.

Comparisons among Units   Sometimes in the task alignment work with an organization, there will be multiple units (sometimes with different geographic accountabilities) that are "doing the same work." Just as we find that it is difficult to know what someone does by their title (or even in many cases by their position description!), we generally find that units "doing the same work" are not. This discovery can provide some interesting insights and actions on areas that should be more similar and consistent. It can also provide valuable insight if some units are performing better than others.

Develop Position Descriptions   The task analysis and task alignment work provides significant opportunities to further develop and clarify position descriptions.

Conclusion

You can see that task alignment focuses at a more micro level than the other alignment areas that I have discussed. You should find that complements other alignment factors we have discussed and that you can derive numerous benefits from the process. You can further strengthen other work on position alignment and the alignment of people to positions. You can reduce costs. You can increase effectiveness and satisfaction by delegating tasks to the right level. Finally, you can use it as a foundation for further enhancing processes.

ORGANIZATION DESIGN PRINCIPLES

While it is difficult summarize all of the preceding discussion, we believe that underlying principles can serve as a foundation for this Optimizing Organization Design® approach. We would suggest the following.

- An organization should have the right number of layers or strata for the strategic positioning.
- Every position should be in the right layer or stratum.
- Position titles should be used in a consistent and stratum appropriate manner.
- Each layer or stratum should be divided into three substrata: low, medium, and high. The strata, each with three parts, should become a foundation for human resources management systems, such as position evaluation, succession planning, career planning and compensation.
- Every employee (with the exception of direct output support roles, e.g., executive assistants) should have a manager exactly one stratum above, both in terms of complexity of work done and capability to work at that level.
- Spans of control (number of direct reports) should be optimal for the required work.
- Functional alignment should be set up on a primary and secondary basis. Types of organizing could include function (e.g., marketing, sales, operations, etc.), geography, market/customer type, and product/service type.
- Employee, supervisor, manager, and manager once removed accountabilities and authorities should be clear and appropriate.
- Managers should be accountable for their direct reports, and all employees should be accountable for using their best efforts (doing their best).
- Managers once removed should be accountable for the future potential of their direct report once removed talent pool.

- Cross functional accountabilities and authorities should be clear and appropriate.
- Every employee should have only one manager, but may have multiple cross functional relationships.
- Cross over point managers should manage the "white space" between direct reports, provide appropriate context and prescribed limits, and provide context clarification and issue resolution mechanisms.
- The appropriate managerial and cross functional accountabilities and authorities should be established for all processes.
- The organization design framework, particularly related to accountabilities and authorities, should be used for all projects.
- Employees should be matched to positions in terms of information processing capability, skilled knowledge, and application.
- Employees should be working at the appropriate level of complexity for the stratum of their positions.
- Employees should be completing tasks that are appropriate for their level of work.

CONCLUSION

In this chapter, we have discussed organization design assessment or how organizations function. We have seen that organizations are stratified human systems. Our understanding of them is guided by three models: an organization systems functioning model, an organization systems change model, and an organization alignment model. We have shown that the organization alignment model involves the alignment of five factors:

- Vertical and functional alignment of positions: Vertical alignment uses time span analysis to determine the number of layers or strata and place each position in the proper stratum.

Every employee should have a manager exactly one stratum above. This manager–direct report alignment is the most important organization design factor. Functional alignment involves factors such as the role of a corporate office; business units; and within business units, core, and support functions.

- Alignment of accountabilities and authorities and related position descriptions: There are generic accountabilities and authorities for employees, managers, managers once removed, and supervisors. As well, there are cross functional accountabilities and authorities.
- Alignment of people to positions: Factors include information processing capability, skilled knowledge, and application. A talent pool process can be used for both current and future requirements.
- Alignment of deliverables: This would include vision, mission, values, strategic positioning, operational plan, and resources plan.
- Alignment of tasks: This is a more micro approach that can look at tasks relative to the strata of positions. It also looks at numerous other variables including the time and cost of tasks.

Finally, we listed a series of organization design principles.

These factors and principles together constitute a "toolkit" that can be used to improve organization performance. In the next section, we will look at organization design implementation or how organizations change. This becomes the companion piece for you in moving from understanding how your organization design should be improved to actually doing it.

CHAPTER 3

ORGANIZATION DESIGN IMPLEMENTATION

*The logic of the Capelle Associates approach to
organization design resulted in an unprecedented
level of support, at all levels, for a systemic change to
CP's organization.
The approach to change management was extremely
professional—highly detailed implementation plans
at every stage and strong support from leaders before
changes were implemented.*

—Bob MacIntyre, Assistant Vice President,
Human Resources, Canadian Pacific Railway,
June 2011

In this section I discuss organization design implementation. In other words, how does one implement the desired organization design improvements?

There is a rich history of thought on this topic, beginning with a body of work called organization development. It largely focused on the process of change, often working with smaller units (e.g., groups within organizations). One of the significant sets of writings was the Addison-Wesley Series in Organization Development, composed of 18 books published between 1969 and 1981, and edited by Schein, Bennis, and Beckhard. These books also included a number of related topics. There are other important books from this era, including *The Planning of Change*

(Bennis, Benne & Chin, 1969; Bennis et al., 1976). Additional books that I found to be of value include Conner (1993) and LaMarsh (1995). The term that is currently most commonly used for this area is change management. While we don't do generic change management, we have developed an approach to change management in the service of enhancing organization design. The foundation for us is understanding organizations as systems in environments.

It should be understood at the outset, in line with this organization development theory, that employee engagement is an important factor facilitating design implementation. There are several aspects to this. First, implementation is often easier in organizations that have higher levels of engagement and trust. Second, during an assessment phase, it is important to engage employees (e.g., we generally interview all managers and have a questionnaire that can be completed by all employees) and have strong communication with them. This communication could include objectives (e.g., in this approach, the objectives could include employee satisfaction, customer satisfaction, and financial performance, which can lead to a win-win-win situation). Communication could also include the approach to be used and the feedback process that will be utilized after the review. Finally, in the implementation, employees are involved in the design of their own areas. It is very much a hands-on implementation, involving learning, doing, and feedback.

The starting point is the organization systems change model (see Figure 2.1, page 24). The basic objective of this Optimizing Organization Design® approach is to improve performance. This requires an understanding of the current state of the organization, and the direction to move it to a future desired state. Our Optimizing Organization Design® approach requires a strong implementation approach in order to reach the desired future state. This chapter outlines the approach that we use.

OBJECTIVES OF AN ORGANIZATION DESIGN IMPLEMENTATION

While the specifics of each organization design implementation will vary, the general objectives tend to be consistent. The overarching objective is to improve organization performance. Our research and executive experience shows that this approach, as we describe it, leads to improved organization performance. Implementation should focus on both what should be changed and how it should be changed.

Our previous discussion of how organizations function shows us what should be changed. The implementation process generally focuses on some combination of the following factors:

- Align positions (vertically and functionally).
- Improve vertical alignment of positions (e.g., increase requisite alignment and decrease gaps and compression).
- Improve functional alignment of positions (e.g., have "like" functions better clustered together).
- Align accountabilities and authorities with positions (employee, supervisor, manager, manager once removed, and cross functional).
- Improve clarity of employee, supervisor, manager and manager once removed accountabilities and authorities (e.g., include in position descriptions and provision of education and training).
- Improve clarity of cross functional accountabilities and authorities (e.g., include in position descriptions and provision of education and training).
- Align people with positions.
- Improve matching of employees to positions (e.g., develop and implement talent pool process) to improve current fit and future requirements.
- Align deliverables with positions.
- Develop and implement organization planning and review system.

- Ensure that positions in each stratum are working at the right level of complexity and are in concert to move the organization in the desired direction.
- Align tasks with positions.
- Identify any areas in the organization where there is lack of differentiation between Stratum 1 and Stratum 2 positions.
- Analyze and optimize task configuration.

In parallel, a robust organization design implementation process should also do the following:

- Improve the level of organization design capability (e.g., transfer materials, methods, and skills to the internal team and the organization).
- Improve the functioning of critical related systems (e.g., human resources and organization planning and review systems).
- Implement organization design effectively and efficiently (utilizing appropriate project management and people change management best practices) resulting in a transformational change of the organization that can be sustained.

Successful implementation requires that a plan be developed to serve as the roadmap for the implementation process. In the development of this plan, the points in the next sections should be considered.

ORGANIZATION DESIGN IMPLEMENTATION COMPONENTS MODEL

We have developed a model of organization design implementation that includes components for both the what and the how of implementation. The model (Figure 3.1) includes the following four components:

- project scope, structure, and process
- organization design (the content of change)

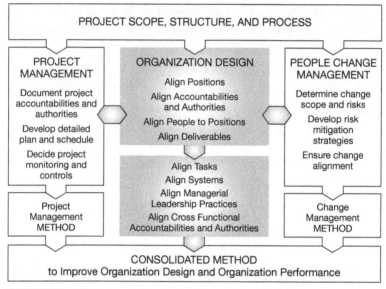

FIGURE 3.1.   Organization Design Implementation Model

- project management
- people change management

The effective combination of these four components can result in a consolidated method to improve both organization design and organization performance.

Project Scope, Structure, and Process

Fundamental to the success of any implementation process is having an appropriate project structure that is staffed by individuals who have the required information processing capability, skilled knowledge, and application. Positions should be established and filled. The head of the organization would be the accountable executive for the implementation. This individual would likely appoint a direct report as the internal project team executive to be accountable for the implementation project. This individual may directly lead the project team, or, in very large organizations, may appoint an internal project team director. Project team positions would be established and staffed. There is a requirement for clearly stated accountabilities and authorities for each position. Clear accountability for the overall change process, including the necessary management commitment, support, and visibility of that commitment and support, is vital.

The accountable executive must make it clear that all managers (defined generically as being accountable for the work of direct reports) become accountable for their parts of the change process. Within this context, managers (in both line and support functions) must then make the necessary macro decisions, provide the framework and issue resolution and context clarification process mechanisms necessary to move towards them, and demonstrate visible support for the change process.

The project executive would be accountable for monitoring and supporting each major change initiative. In larger organizations, the project executive would appoint a project director, and ensure the acquisition of the project team members, together with appropriate administrative support. Through cross functional support, the internal project team would support the managers accountable for various elements of the change process by providing the following support:

- developing the project plan and implementation processes
- developing the new or improved processes that arise from approved recommendations
- developing the support materials that are required for the natural work team implementation meetings
- facilitating education and training sessions
- providing advice to implementing managers
- coordinating the implementation work
- monitoring the implementation, resolving issues as they arise, and escalating those issues that cannot be resolved

It would also be necessary to ensure that sufficient capacity exists on the team to ensure the necessary activities in people change management and project management can be carried out.

The internal project team must be resourced appropriately. External expertise can provide specifics in terms of organization design and change management, but adapting these principles to the organizational context requires expertise within the organization, i.e., balancing the business with the change principles. Some of the important related points are outlined below:

- Because managers accountable for implementation in their organizations or functions are still accountable for maintaining their business operations, anything the project team can do in a cross functional way to support them will minimize disruption in the workplace during the change process.
- The best value-add for any organization is to obtain external expertise for the more highly specialized skills that typically do not exist within the organization and, while using the support of those with this expertise, do most of the work in house.
- In an implementation project of this sort, a great deal of external expertise, in the form of materials, methods, and skills, is naturally transferred to an internal project team and lessons learned from this transfer can then be used in the future to support managers and help maintain the integrity of the new organization design.

Organization Design

By carefully orchestrating the sequencing of several streams of work, the new organization design can be introduced in such a way that it does not overload managers in terms of the amount and sequencing of their work. These streams generally include aligning positions, accountabilities and authorities, people (to positions), and deliverables. Depending on the circumstances, other streams can include aligning tasks, systems, managerial leadership practices, and cross functional accountabilities and authorities.

It should be noted that this grouping is slightly different than the alignment factors discussed in the first part of the book, when I discussed alignment of positions, accountabilities and authorities, people, deliverables and tasks. In the organization design implementation model, we retain those five factors, although "align tasks" is dropped to a lower section because it tends to follow in a limited number of cases, and is not part of the comprehensive implementation. As well, we have added three new factors to align systems, managerial and leadership practices, and cross functional accountabilities and authorities. The three factors are as follows:

- Align systems: In order for the change to be transformational and sustainable, it is important to optimize related systems. This would generally include organization planning and review, human resources (including compensation), project management, and process management. While much of this work is done in the initial cascades (e.g., positions, accountabilities and authorities, people and deliverables), there are often additional opportunities for further enhancement that require a different focus.
- Align managerial leadership practices: This is leadership related to the accountabilities and authorities of a manager. Again, the focus is on the initial cascades, particularly with aligning accountabilities and authorities (and especially manager accountabilities and authorities). However, since this area requires significant skill building, additional focus is often desirable. As well, because most organizations do management training of some kind, this process can become the foundation for management training that would cover selection, setting context and prescribed limits, providing resources, delegating, development, managing performance, team building, and removal from position. An important part of this process,

aligning teams, creates an opportunity for the manager to set context for direct reports, and for them to develop expectations for their work together in the new organization design. By working together in this way, manager and direct reports establish a strong foundation for the team working relationship, an important part of building teams in a new organization design.

- Align cross functional accountabilities and authorities: This is an extension of "align accountabilities and authorities" but best left as a separate cascade at the end of the series. There are two reasons for this. First, we find that it is the most difficult cascade, and needs the other alignments in place to operate most effectively. Second, we generally work with natural work teams through the other cascades but, in order to do the cross functional work, we often need different configurations of people (e.g., those involved across the organization in major initiatives such as information technology or product development).

These streams are explored in more detail below:

- Aligning positions includes implementing the optimal alignment of positions from both vertical and functional perspectives; dealing with discrepancies of time span and compensation, including compression and gaps; and adding, removing, and modifying positions as required. Ideally, a master organization chart will be maintained on which all changes are recorded.
- Aligning accountabilities and authorities includes clarifying employee and managerial accountabilities and authorities (including generic ones) and initial work on cross functional accountabilities and authorities. These are documented in position descriptions.
- Aligning people to positions entails developing a talent pool process in which management is accountable for evaluating and

improving fit to position. Managers assess employees according to several criteria, including information processing capability, skilled knowledge, and application. The talent pool process is used for staffing both new and significantly changed positions. This further requires managers to determine current and future requirements and capabilities.

- Aligning deliverables entails developing and implementing a framework to ensure that positions in each stratum are working at the right level of complexity and in concert to move the organization in the desired direction. This usually involves enhancing organization planning and review.

- Aligning tasks can take place at a later point in parts of the organization where there is lack of clarity between Stratum 1 and Stratum 2 positions. To achieve this, managers are required to determine the tasks that are performed and look for opportunities for improvement.

- Aligning systems generally includes both organization planning and review and human resources. The systems are reviewed and adapted and strengthened to appropriately support the organization design implementation and to help ensure its sustainability.

- Aligning managerial leadership practices is often skill building in a real situation. One of the most important areas is building the new teams.

- Aligning cross functional accountabilities and authorities will help to break down silos by clarifying how work gets done across the organization and establishing a common understanding of integrating work across functions. This work begins at an earlier stage but generally benefits from more comprehensive work at a later stage.

- The organization design implementation model provides the planning, design, and development of the implementation of the organization design changes throughout the organization in an effective, efficient, and sustainable way.

Project Management

Project management is concerned with ensuring that the expected results are obtained on time and within budget and to a specified level of quality. In an organization design implementation ensuring that the implementation is carried out in an appropriate and effective way can be a complex business. Following are several activities that should be attended to in this stream of work:

- Describe in writing the key accountabilities of the accountable executive, and the key deliverables expected of that position.
- Describe in writing the key accountabilities of the line and functional managers that are accountable for the change, the key deliverables that are expected for each position, and the authority (mostly managerial) that is delegated to them by the accountable executive to implement this change.
- Describe in writing the key accountabilities of the internal project team executive and the internal project team director who are accountable for provision of the support for the change, the key deliverables that are expected of these positions, and the authority (mostly cross functional) that is delegated by the accountable executive to implement this change.
- Determine the number of and type of positions that will be required on the project implementation team.
- Describe in writing the key accountabilities of each project team position, the key deliverables that are expected of the position, and the authority (mostly cross functional) that is delegated to that position by the project team director to support the change.
- Recruit or assign individuals to each of the project team positions. Team members should be available for the duration of the project (on a full time or part time basis as required), and ideally migrate later to established positions within the organization in order to maintain the institutional learning.

- Design and put in place the main processes for the project team, e.g., meeting structure, reporting and monitoring requirements, etc.
- Determine the detailed project schedule for achieving the planning, design, and development deliverables.
- At the end of planning phase, develop the consolidated implementation plan.
- At the end of the project, conduct a review to determine lessons learned.

In totality, this approach as it is described becomes the project management method for the organization design implementation.

People Change Management

People change management refers to the application of a structured and disciplined change management methodology that can significantly increase the possibility of success of this project, reduce project time and cost, and at the same time mitigate the people risks associated with such a major change. These aspects of people change management are dealt with in implementation planning:

- education and training
- communications

The basic purpose of education and training is to equip employees, managers, managers once removed, and supervisors with the skilled knowledge they need to carry out their accountabilities in a way that is consistent with the new model of operating. It is important to provide education to managers in a macro way for implementation purposes. It is also important to provide training to employees (including managers) that will help them change their behavior and way of doing things over time. We are using training in the usual literal sense, as the provision of behavioral/change training and skill based training.

In keeping with the principles of implementation, related meetings constitute an opportunity to do the real work required in the cascading implementation process, for example, working through and clarifying cross functional accountabilities and authorities of the natural work team.

The second aspect, communications, does not need to be especially resource intensive, but it is an important component of the change process. Negative employee reactions generally do not result from decisions that have been made and communicated effectively and in a timely manner. Rather, negative employee reactions are more likely to come from indecision or poor communications that allow rumors to proliferate. Rumors tend to accentuate the negative spin on impending decisions, and in the absence of solid communication, people may assume the worst.

In totality, this approach as it is described becomes the people change management method for the organization design implementation.

Consolidated Method

The final box at the bottom of Figure 3.1 represents the consolidated method to improve organization design and organization performance. Each of the four components contributes critical aspects to the success of a project.

ORGANIZATION DESIGN IMPLEMENTATION PROCESS MODEL

We have discussed the components of the organization design implementation model. We now discuss the process. Implementation projects require the most significant investment of resources at the beginning. The time and energy spent in properly designing the project structure and processes will reap tangible benefits. The costs are generally much greater when an organization tries to implement change on the fly, because improvisation leads to rework and a confused (or at least less focused) work force.

The implementation process is largely concerned with pacing, which varies from project to project. We generally find that timelines range from 6 to 18 months, although full institutionalization may require longer. The underlying principles are usually the same:

- Implementation is always "front-end loaded": more of the work is done earlier than later.
- It is necessary to continue the timeline long enough to institutionalize the change. Resource requirements diminish significantly in the later stages of implementation. However, the objective is to "institutionalize" the change and avoid improvements that prove to be "a flash in the pan."
- The single biggest factor in the pacing of the cascading implementation is the quality and quantity of internal resources. Having the right resources in place early and for the duration can significantly improve the quality and pace of the process.
- Research shows that the single most important success factor is the accountable manager staying the course to complete the implementation.
- The pacing of the implementation will be affected by the judgment of the accountable manager as she balances the desire for faster pacing with other organization requirements. However, regardless of the exact pacing, the model shows the general factors and sequencing that we would find in most implementation projects.

The process method (shown in Figure 3.2) comprises four sequential phases: initiation, planning and design, implementation and monitoring, and sustainment. A brief discussion of each phase follows.

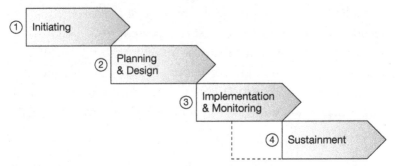

FIGURE 3.2.   Organization Design Process Methodology

Initiation

Project parameters are defined during the initiation phase. The project manager is appointed. He or she may be given some other title, but basically this position is accountable for the project and project team. The resources required for this phase of the project are identified and acquired.

A project charter is established, and typically includes the following information: scope, structure, roles of internal team and consulting team, processes, macro timeline, macro plan and deliverables, estimated resource requirements, and macro people change management plan. The project charter is approved by the accountable executive on the recommendation of the project executive. The initial communication plan is developed, including feedback loops, and the first few communications issued.

Concurrent to the project initiation work, macro decisions are made with respect to the organization design, which provides the framework for the rest of the organization design implementation work.

Planning and Design

During the planning phase, the desired future organization is further enhanced. The various project plans are crafted and integrated into the execution implementation plan.

The project structure and processes are finalized in this phase by the project manager. The project manager leads the process of designing the implementation of the new organization design. This includes: obtaining approval of the desired state organization design from the accountable manager, designing the materials necessary to support the cascading implementation, and ensuring the appropriate training of project team members that will facilitate the management meetings required for the implementation of the new organization design. The positions accountable for project management and people change management develop their respective plans in an iterative way. Issues are brought to the attention of the accountable manager, and decisions are made with respect to organization design, resourcing, and timing.

At the end of this phase, each of the three plans (organization design implementation, project management, and people change management) will have been approved and integrated into one project plan for the implementation. Ideally, all design and development work will be completed before the cascading implementation rollout begins. However, some design work for meetings that takes place later in the implementation can be undertaken later. It is also necessary to have a feedback loop to improve materials during the process. There will also generally be a need for additional design and development on related systems in preparation for the second round of implementation.

Implementation and Monitoring

The implementation is a series of cascading, iterative processes delivered within the context and prescribed limits set by the accountable manager. This would implement the new organization design, and at the same time deliver the education and training identified as core to the change during the planning phase. Line and support function managers would be accountable for implementation within their areas of accountability with support from the project team.

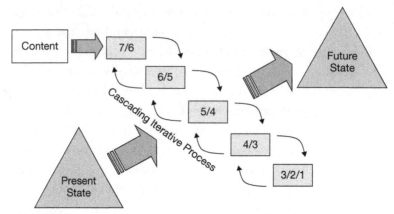

FIGURE 3.3.   Cascading, Iterative Implementation Process Model

Figure 3.3 shows the model of a cascading, iterative implementation process with a Stratum 7 organization. The first event of implementation once the rollout begins is the senior management team meeting. This meeting brings together the accountable manager with immediate direct reports according to the new organization design. This meeting would be replicated at each stratum with stratum-appropriate materials.

It is also important to review the various systems in the organization to ensure that they are properly aligned with the change process. To the extent that current systems (e.g., human resources, organization planning and review, etc.) do not support the changes (or in fact work counter to them), design work also has to be done to bring these systems in line with the changes. This work is not normally carried out by the project team directly, but the project manager would have an accountability to monitor the work and integrate it into the implementation.

Sustainment

The sustainment phase begins immediately after the first round of implementation meetings. This phase is concerned with integrating change support mechanisms into ongoing organization systems. For instance, the project team may have some specific accountability with regard to staffing during the implementation, with support from Human Resources. After the implementation, the Human Resources function would need to be equipped to support the new organization as a part of their ongoing accountabilities. Sustainment is listed as a separate stream because of the importance of identifying the organization systems that may need upgrading (or creation), and developing a plan with key milestones that would be integrated into the implementation plan.

At the end of the implementation, a project implementation review is conducted to identify the lessons learned and improve future organizational changes and projects.

ORGANIZATION DESIGN IMPLEMENTATION PRINCIPLES

We have found that the following principles are useful for organization design implementation:

Cascading, Iterative Process

Any process that will be rolled out throughout the organization should start at the top. The senior level then replicates the process with their direct reports. This process is repeated at the next level, until everyone in the organization that should participate has done so. This is the cascading element, as each person in the organization participates in the process under the direction of his immediate manager.

Each manager participates in the process twice: once as a participant and once as a manager. This is the iterative process, as a manager can provide feedback to her manager or peer group management team on how to improve the process. Any unforeseen difficulties or consequences can be dealt with at each level of the process. Each manager has the accountability of setting the context for each session in terms appropriate for the strata with which they are working.

Education and Training/Real Work/Feedback

Each cascading process should include three elements. One element is educational. This is the information portion, explaining to employees what is required—a new process, an improvement in a procedure, and so on. The second element is implementation. Each session must have an element of doing actual work, so participants begin to internalize the new approach. For instance, for a new planning system, the first part of the session would describe how planning is done. The second part would engage participants in doing actual planning in direct interaction with their immediate manager.

The third part is a feedback loop. Participants should be given feedback for their learning, as well as given the opportunity to provide feedback on the process they are learning so that it can be continually improved.

In summary, this process involves both a knowledge and a skill-building component.

Natural Work Teams

Each cascading process should be rolled out through natural work teams (i.e., a manager and his direct reports) as much as possible. This is important, for real learning and sustainable change best takes place through "doing." We find that individuals working with their managers in natural work teams have the benefit of doing real work as opposed to an artificial exercise. Making use of the natural work team also creates an environment where the manager can emphasize setting the context for the change that is being implemented. In an artificial training environment, participants are less likely to make the connection to their "real" work.

STRENGTHENING THE ORGANIZATION DESIGN IMPLEMENTATION

I have discussed the implementation approach, and the importance not only of what we want to change, but also how we go about changing it. As part of this, I have discussed project management and people change management. There is another dimension: strengthening the change process. The purpose of a change process is to move from a current state to an improved future state within a target completion time. Once the decision to change has been made, a process is initiated, by gathering information or assessing the current state. Figure 3.4 demonstrates desired and undesired change paths.

At Point 1, a review or assessment is announced. As there have been some issues or opportunities that led to the review, the announcement is often greeted by employees with optimism, along with some questions and concern. They may recognize the need for change, and most have ideas about what the changes should be. Particularly if the process is a participatory one, employee morale can actually improve during the review period.

This period of optimism has a tendency to peak at Point 2, when decisions are made as a result of the review. At that point, many employees realize that the changes they envisioned may not be implemented. There is also a general realization that the changes may have personal impact on them. When this idea takes hold, there may be a decline in morale. If care is not taken, this downturn can continue past the pre-change state, taking the organization along the undesired change path.

Management has its greatest opportunity to avoid the undesired change path at Point 2 by demonstrating effective and timely leadership. This means: making decisions early; announcing the decisions and providing compelling reasons for them that employees can relate to; supporting employees by listening to them; and

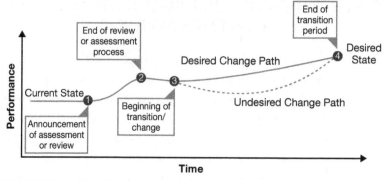

FIGURE 3.4.   The Change Path

by implementing feedback loops. The following points describe the key elements of Figure 3.4:

- Make decisions: At Point 2, the end of the review process, the faster that firm decisions are made, the better. Even an unpopular decision, that is firmly made, is better than a popular decision that is made after unseemly delays.
- Communicate: As soon as decisions are made, they should be communicated, together with the supporting rationale to obtain buy-in from employees. This includes communicating the process that will be followed to plan and execute the change.
- Celebrate early successes: Front-end load the change process so that early progress can be made in key areas. The moment some positive changes can be identified, communicate and celebrate them. The sooner the positive results from the changes can be seen and felt by the employees, the sooner they will support and promote the changes. Early wins and successes should come within three months. While the early successes may not be substantive in the long run, they are critical to build commitment and momentum.

- Build momentum: A change process needs to be maintained throughout at least one business cycle (often one year), and often more depending upon the scope of the change. The objective is to ensure that changes are institutionalized into the organization and its working systems and processes. The earlier in the process changes can be implemented and successes celebrated, the easier it will be to maintain the change process over time.
- Support employees: Management had an opportunity to review and discuss the recommendations of the organization design assessment and move personally, over a given period of time, through their personal change cycle. They need to support their employees going through the same process by explaining the need for the changes and by listening effectively to the feedback received from them to continually improve planned actions.

Point 3 marks the formal beginning of the change process. As noted above, the quality and timeliness of decisions made in Point 2 and the demonstration of visible managerial leadership will be helpful to build positive momentum early on in the change process.

With the objective of moving effectively and with the committed support of employees through the transition period (illustrated by the path from Point 3 to Point 4), the implementation project needs to be carefully planned. Project objectives and deliverables are to be determined and a realistic project plan should be formulated to achieve them. People factors are to be assessed and analyzed to create an appropriate people change management plan and ensure employee readiness. The payoff for planning and executing the change successfully will be substantial. In addition to getting the benefits from the organization design improvements, the process of changing will be more effective, efficient, take less time and be supported by employees. A well-executed change project also builds employee confidence and sets the tone for future organizational change projects.

INTERNAL-EXTERNAL TEAM APPROACH

*For others considering redesigning their
organizations, I think that a strong internal–external
partnership is critical. I am generally not a big
believer in external consultants, but there are certain
business issues and opportunities that require more
specialized and independent methodology or
perspective. I would put comprehensive organization
design in this category, and our relationship with
Capelle Associates as an example of a strong
internal–external partnership that has lasted for over
ten years. The strength of this partnership is based on
two main factors: 1) the quality of Capelle
Associates' research methodology and 2) the
experience, capability, reliability, and
trustworthiness of the members of their firm. Under
challenging timelines and resource constraints,
Capelle Associates have never missed a deadline or
commitment.*

—April Taggart, *Senior Vice President, Talent
Management and Diversity, BMO Financial
Group, April 2006*

Our experience shows that the best implementation comes from an internal–external team. External consultants can add value by providing

- organization design knowledge and experience
- knowledge about the organization gained from the assessment
- implementation experience, including project and people change management

The work should be done to provide the organization with the best results at the most reasonable cost. We have found that the internal team can generally do 80–90 percent of the work. The external team can provide the expertise that will support doing better work, doing it faster, and sustaining it better. The internal team doesn't have to "reinvent the wheel." The external team can bring in and adapt relevant methods and systems, work directly with the senior management team, train and qualify internal resources, and provide consultation as required (to both the internal consultants and senior managers).

The external consultant could provide direct higher level support to the accountable manager and project manager, and attend senior management meetings in which the accountable manager is personally involved. The external consultant could also deal with the more complex organization design issues, and could be accountable for

- helping to ensure "organization design integrity" of the implementation structures, processes, methods, and techniques from an organization design perspective
- provision and transfer of organization design expertise, including optimal deployment of external consultants and their work

The external consultant could also provide people change management and project management support. He would be the direct link to the project manager, and between the two of them they would oversee the implementation and would have coordinative and monitoring accountabilities.

The best value may be realized by combining the quality assurance from the external consultants, but having 80 to 90 percent of the work done inside the organization. This provides significant benefits at reduced costs.

Organization Design Managerial Leadership Keys to Success

The literature on organization change has consistently shown that a significant key to success is the leader (or, in our terminology, the manager or executive accountable for the organization in scope). Our experience has been consistent with that. We have generally found our client executives to have been highly capable and committed to improving performance.

These executives seek the input of others, but are prepared to make and back up important decisions. We once worked with a newly appointed executive who understood the value of better design. His team of direct reports had a full range of responses to a proposed organization design initiative. The most common appeared to be, "Keep your head down; this too shall pass." However, the executive stayed the course. His team started to get onboard when they read the assessment and recommendations, and were even more fully engaged when they became directly involved in the implementation and could experience it firsthand. One of the main critics at an early stage became one of the strongest supporters as matters evolved.

The head of the organization needs to "stay the course." The objective is to transform the organization in a sustainable manner. While much of the work is front-end loaded, staying the course (ideally through at least two business cycles) with continuous improvement adds considerably to the benefits.

While all leadership is critical in organization design, the other particularly important individual is usually the head of Human Resources. A significant aspect of organization design relates to people and human resources systems and practices. While the head of the organization in scope should lead the organization design initiative, the head of Human Resources is often accountable for the internal project team.

CONCLUSION

The literature consistently shows that many improvement initiatives (e.g., quality, re-engineering) fail to deliver the expected results. Analysis generally shows that the issues center on implementation or change management. Our research shows that improved organization design leads to better employee satisfaction, customer satisfaction, and financial performance. These are powerful outcomes. However, these outcomes require a strong implementation approach. This chapter provides it.

CHAPTER 4

AN OVERVIEW OF THE PROCESS

*More than two years have now elapsed since your
final presentation to me and other members of our
Management Committee of the analysis, conclusions
and recommendations arising from your review of
our Design and Procurement Department.
With the full benefit of hindsight I can only reiterate
the statement I made to you following your final
presentation: "This is the best value for money I
have ever experienced from any consultant."*

—Isadore Sharp, Chairman and Chief Executive
Officer, Four Seasons Hotels and Resorts,
December, 2003

We have discussed why organization design matters, and described organization design assessment and organization design implementation. In this chapter, we will provide an overview of the process for the Optimizing Organization Design® approach. This starts before an assessment is done, and ends after the implementation is over. The key steps are

- initial discussion, proposal, and contract
- assessment, report, and meetings
- implementation
- sustainment

This chapter is written from the perspective of an approach that Capelle Associates has developed over the past 25 years. I am not suggesting that this is the only possible approach, but I know it has proven value. These are steps that an executive could use with an external consultant. However, even if an executive decides to improve organization design from within the organization, the following steps provide a valuable checklist. This is not unlike project management. While projects of different complexities require approaches of different intensities, there are fundamental steps that should at least be thought through in these different situations.

INITIAL DISCUSSION, PROPOSAL, AND CONTRACT

The first contract may have been initiated by either the potential client (a manager or executive in an organization) or a consultant (either internal or external). In any event, the contract negotiation provides an opportunity for both parties to determine whether or not there is a good fit, and whether or not it is worthwhile to proceed.

Chemistry is a factor in this determination: Is there a sense of trust? Do the parties want to work with each other? In the initial discussions, the potential client outlines the perceived issues and opportunities. The consultant listens, learns, and discusses approaches to addressing the problems that have been identified and ways of enhancing performance.

From the potential client perspective, I believe that the following questions should be considered:

- Does the approach have research support? There are too many approaches that are someone's latest, greatest theory, with no research support.

- Does the approach have support from executives who have successfully used it? Are some of these individuals available for discussion? Reference checking is important.
- Is the consultant an expert? There is no singular definition for this, but the following will help to clarify this point. Does the consultant specialize (perhaps exclusively) in this area? How long has the consultant worked in this area? How many similar types of work has the consultant done? Will the consultant that you meet actually be doing the work (we have had numerous complaints from clients who, after an initial meeting with experienced senior staff, discovered that the work was actually done by inexperienced juniors). Malcolm Gladwell (2008) suggests that it takes 10,000 hours to become a world class expert.
- Can the consultant provide examples of reports or related materials (while of course maintaining all required confidentiality) that demonstrate the efficacy of the consulting?

From the consultant perspective, I believe that the following questions should be considered:

- Do I have the right client? The client should be the head of the total organization or head of the part of the organization that is in scope for the review.
- What is the scope of the review? Is it the whole organization or a part of an organization? If it is the latter, is it a pilot project?
- Can I help the client to be successful? Is this potential assignment within my expertise? Does the client appear to be committed to implementing the agreed outcomes? While we are proud of work we have completed, we are also proud of work that we have turned down when we concluded that it was not appropriate.

Assuming that these initial discussions are positive, the next steps would be developing a proposal and discussing it. Upon agreement, the proposal becomes the basis of a contract. This should cover the following points:

- What are the expected outcomes?
- What will be the method for doing the assessment?
- What will the report include?
- How will the meetings be conducted?
- Which consultants will be involved at each step?
- What are the requirements for the client in this process?
- What is the schedule?
- What is the cost or investment required?

ASSESSMENT, REPORT, AND MEETINGS

The next steps are: completing the assessment, completing the report, and conducting the related meetings. Again, I will discuss our approach, with the understanding that this is not the only way of proceeding.

Assessment

The objective of the assessment is to understand the current state and future direction of an organization, analyze the situation, and recommend improvements. This requires a thorough approach based upon a robust method. We generally find the following steps to be of value:

- Review organization documents: We want to learn about the organization before beginning the interviews. The documents would ideally include information about organization planning and review systems; practices including vision, mission, values, strategic positioning, operational plan, and resource plan; products and services; market and clients (ideally a customer satisfaction survey); and industry and competitors. It would also include information about human resources systems, including organization charts, compensation, titling, position descriptions, talent pool, and managerial leadership practices.

- Conduct a literature search: As part of due diligence we want to find any industry information on best organization design practices.
- Obtain employee information: We gather information on employee names, titles, reporting relationships, and compensation. We use this to create organization charts and conduct numerous analyses, including compensation relative to complexity of work.
- Conduct interviews: While those interviewed and the interview times will vary from project to project, we generally interview all managers (defined as anyone accountable for the work of others regardless of level or title) in interviews lasting up to one hour. In these interviews, we gather information on the work of the manager and all direct reports, the time spans of the direct reports (deliverable with longest target completion time, and the self span of the manager (what the manager thinks his time span is). We also ask managers about issues and opportunities; this provides some broader perspectives. This approach is a very effective and efficient way to gather considerable information in a relatively short period of time. It allows managers to participate in a significant way but requires very little of their time.
- Have employee satisfaction questionnaire completed: For example, we have developed an employee satisfaction questionnaire that has an organization design perspective. It requires only about 20 minutes to complete at our website. It provides a valuable complementary perspective on organization design and includes benchmarks we have developed. It can also be a method to involve all employees in the assessment. We have found information gleaned from this questionnaire is valuable when we move to implementation.

One final point should be made. We believe it is important to *not* assess people in this phase. The primary focus should be on the vertical and functional alignment of positions, and determining opportunities to improve critical systems (e.g., organization planning and review and human resources). We do have a method for matching people to positions, but this comes as part of our implementation approach that we have previously discussed.

Report

Our reports describe our analysis and recommendations for improvement. Before the report is written, it is important to first develop a comprehensive understanding of the current state of the organization. The strategy provides significant context for this. The major focus is on position alignment. We have three measures: the complexity of the position (time span provided by the manager of the position), what the incumbent in the position thinks the complexity of her position is (self span), and the level of compensation related to level of work or stratum (compensation span). We therefore have up to three pieces of converging data on a particular position. Ideally the three measures would be consistent; often they are not. When we understand the positions, we can also understand the position relationships, particularly those between manager and direct report. We can determine which manager–direct report alignments are appropriate, which are compressed (actually working at the same level), and which have gaps (too much distance between them). We also have a benchmarking database to provide comparison points.

A second way of understanding the current state is through our questionnaire. It measures employee satisfaction, with an organization design perspective. Again, a benchmarking database provides comparison points.

The next step is the most challenging. Given what the organization wants to accomplish (strategy, etc.), and given the current position alignment, how should positions be aligned to make the design more optimal? How many levels or strata of work should the organization have? What level or stratum should every position be in? How should functions be aligned, from the head of the organization on down? What positions are redundant and should be eliminated? What positions are missing and should be added?

We provide a full recommended organization structure (i.e., position alignment), along with detailed recommendations. We have done this with organizations ranging in size from fewer than 100 to more than 16,000. This Optimizing Organization Design® approach is both a science and an art. It is more common, and much easier, to do the analysis one piece at a time. This usually involves assessing the top few layers, and then the next few layers, etc. However, our view is that we can have a much stronger design if it encompasses the full organization system and combines the top down strategic view with the bottom up understanding of the real nature and levels of work.

The recommended organization design includes the types of positions, and numbers of them throughout the organization with one exception. We would not get so micro in our analysis that we could recommend numbers of positions at the first level of the organization (e.g., there should be seven accounts payable clerks instead of eight). Our task analysis approach, which we discussed earlier, does get down to that level of detail, but we usually do not complete that analysis at this early stage. Rather, we might recommend that a particular part of the organization could benefit from that analysis.

The report also includes other analyses and recommendations. For example, there are often recommendations on improving organization planning and review and human resources systems and practices. Further, because we ask some open-ended questions related to issues and opportunities, there often are additional analyses and recommendations that could not be fully predicted at the beginning. The report is a detailed and comprehensive document.

Meetings

We connect with our client during the assessment and report phases. The report is not simply dropped in at the end of these phases. It is important to ensure that our information is accurate and we were not making major errors of commission or omission.

However, we have a particular view of the respective roles of the client and consultant. Our client is accountable for making the final decisions on the organization design. The role of the consultant is to provide the best possible advice. We are not concerned if some of our recommendations are not accepted (although, because our approach is so robust, we generally find that 80–90 percent of our recommendations are accepted). Differences of opinion can be constructive, and we fully respect the accountability of our client to make these decisions.

It would appear that some consulting firms simply rewrite their reports to say what their clients say. We do not engage in this practice. We believe that the best results accrue when clients and consultants fulfill their roles collaboratively and respectfully.

Generally there are some preliminary discussions with the client, and the head of Human Resources is often included in these discussions. Before the client is sent a final report, we send a draft report for comments. At this stage we make any changes necessary to increase the accuracy or fairness of the report. The final report is then sent to the executive group (usually the head of the organization and direct reports). This is followed by a meeting at which the objective is to fully understand the report and make decisions on the recommendations. Decisions may be to accept or reject a recommendation (with or without modifications), or to defer the decision (with a date by which the decision should be made). The ideal of course is that all members of the executive group agree on particular points. However, failing that, the head of the organization should make a decision.

One of these decisions is how the report's recommendations are to be implemented. There is a chapter in the report on implementation and some clients choose to implement on their own. We discuss this in the next section.

IMPLEMENTATION

The first step in implementation is to develop an agreement on implementation scope, requirements, roles, timeline, etc. Explicit deliverables for implementation support are agreed on with the client. This agreement becomes the basis for an implementation contract.

Next, it is essential to establish the project roles, and accountabilities and authorities. The head of the organization should have overall accountability for the implementation. There is often a direct report executive (often the head of Human Resources) who is delegated more specific accountability for the implementation. Project plans, including schedules are developed. An internal project team is put in place, and the project manager is appointed. The external project team also is put in place.

In terms of the project team, our view (and the view of most of our clients) is that the best implementation comes from having an internal–external team combination. The external consulting team brings in the related organization design experience, skill sets, methods and materials, and works with the internal team. Consultant materials are adapted to the organization requirements and changes are made as appropriate to systems and practices (e.g., organization planning and review and human resources). Knowledge transfer from the external to the internal team is ensured. The internal team is trained and qualified and does 80 to 90 percent of the work.

The actual implementation is a cascading iterative process from the top of the organization on down. The work is done in natural teams. The first cascade is to align positions vertically and functionally. Aligning accountabilities and authorities and upgrading position descriptions can be part of this cascade or a separate one. So the head of the organization and direct reports make decisions about the next level down. The appropriate section of the report is used as an input document. A meeting of this nature involves pre work, education, decision making, and follow up. The human resources function is integrally involved.

Once the top-level meeting takes place and related actions are taken, meetings at the next level down can take place (e.g., direct reports of head of organization and their teams), and so on down the organization. The next cascade is usually aligning people (matching people to positions). There are often two aspects to this. The first is to upgrade existing systems and practices using our approach. The second is to actually use this upgraded approach to match people to positions throughout the organization.

The next cascade is usually aligning deliverables (i.e., what individuals produce). There are often two aspects to this too. The first is to upgrade existing organization planning and review approaches using our approach (including strategic planning, business planning, and performance management systems). The second is to actually use this upgraded approach to align deliverables to positions throughout the organization.

The following cascades do not occur in every implementation:

- Aligning tasks: This tends to take place in situations where there is a lack of clarity between first-level paraprofessional or support positions, and second-level professional or managerial positions.
- Team building: When there are new teams, potentially with new positions, accountabilities and authorities, people, and deliverables, time spent on developing the new teams can be valuable.
- Cross functional accountabilities and authorities: While this work can be started with position alignment, it is the most complex and difficult part of optimizing the organization design. It is often valuable to focus more intensively on this area. As well, it may be important to do some of this clarification with different groupings (e.g., teams accountable for major Information Systems projects or product development initiatives).

Finally, while this is not a cascade as are the above points, it is often important to provide one-on-one support to the head of the organization and other executives. A change such as this is significant, and additional support can be helpful.

SUSTAINMENT

The objective of this Optimizing Organization Design® approach is not to complete a project. It is to transform an organization in a sustainable manner. Among the features of the improved workplace are the following:

- improved organization planning and review and human resources management systems and practices
- improvements and alignment of related systems, processes, and materials
- employee participation in the change process, as they develop the necessary understanding and skilled knowledge
- trained and qualified internal teams with the capabilities necessary to facilitate the ongoing sustainment of the optimized organization design

Perhaps even more importantly, the head of the organization and other executives (especially the head of Human Resources) should be committed to continue to develop the organization. While organization design can be implemented in 6 to 18 months, it should really go through several years of continual improvement. For example, when the talent pool system is implemented, it will be better than the one that it replaced. However, it should continue to be improved each year, as people develop more experience with the approach.

CHAPTER 5

ADDITIONAL TOPICS OF IMPORTANCE

A number of related topics remain to be discussed: the role of the board, governance, project management, process management, and compensation.

THE ROLE OF THE BOARD

Organization design does not appear to be on the agendas of many Boards of Directors and CEOs. Since it has been shown to be a driver of organization performance, it deserves a higher profile. CEOs should be accountable for developing, implementing and maintaining superior organization designs. Boards of Directors should be accountable for ensuring that this happens.

—Claude Lamoureux, President and CEO,
Ontario Teachers' Pension Plan, October 2004

Most models of effective organization performance assume (a) a strong ownership function that (b) selects a strong governance function that (c) is accountable for a strong management function. It should be noted that each of these three roles should have a framework defining both appropriate and inappropriate behavior.

When owners (e.g., shareholders) are "absent" (e.g., dispersed, inactive shareholders), this model tends to significantly weaken.

We would suggest that this effort to improve governance could be further enhanced with a strong model of governance. We can look to many useful models for perspectives: one of the most popular has been developed by Carver (1990, 1997). However, we believe that our organization design model has the potential to provide additional specificity in a governance model that the existing models lack. We would see this as an attempt at further enhancement of the current models and effort. The governance framework presented in this section should guide practice. It also can be used diagnostically, and, to the extent it is not met, one would predict that there would be resulting issues.

The starting point for thinking about governance is an association. An association is a group of members that has joined together. The members may be shareholders of a company, members of a nonprofit organization, or citizens of a geographic area. The members of the association elect a governing body to represent them. This could be a Board of Directors for shareholders of a company or members of a nonprofit organization, or a government of a geographic area.

The governing body is accountable to the association for ensuring that the work for the association is done optimally. The governing body usually cannot do this work itself, so it creates an organization (we would say employment hierarchy) to do this work. For the purposes of this discussion, a Board of Directors is referred to as the governing body (a not infrequent use of the term). What is the work of the Board of Directors?

In a general sense, we would say governance. Unfortunately, this is a difficult word to define—the synonyms most often cited are "direct" and "control." Even the *Oxford English Dictionary* does not have a definition of "govern" or "governance" to adequately define the term for our purposes. (As a related aside, the language used in legal documents has the potential to be dysfunctional. A good example is the imputation that the Board of Directors should "supervise." But "supervise" is the word used for lower levels of an organization. Used in the context of a Board of Directors, it has the connotation of micromanagement, which boards can easily fall into.) I will return shortly to our governance model and definition. First let's consider the Board of Directors.

Selection of Members of the Board of Directors

The association should elect a Board of Directors and ensure that they work within an appropriate governance framework. This framework should include a mechanism for the selection and removal of members.

The selection of members of the Board of Directors should be based on exactly the same three criteria for matching employees to positions within an organization. The first is that members of the Board of Directors should have appropriate skilled knowledge. This often means ensuring that the individual members have different skilled knowledge so that collectively they have a broad skilled knowledge set. The second criterion is application. The members of the Board of Directors should value the work, so that they will fully apply themselves. The third criterion is that all members should have the level of information processing capability necessary for that level of work. Ideally this would be a level higher than that required by the CEO role. Minimally, it would be at the same level. Organizations of medium to high complexity and size could range between Stratum 4 and Stratum 8 (Stratum 5 is most common for a relatively large single industry business).

The information processing capability of the members of the Board of Directors is absolutely critical since the wrong level can lead to problems of gaps and compression that I will discuss.

An interesting question, for which we have no data, is, "Below what level of information processing capability would we hypothesize that board members would be significantly dysfunctional?" Stratum 4 is the first level of general management, and Stratum 5 is the first level of information processing at an abstract level. We would suggest that the minimal functional level would be somewhere in this range.

As an aside, in the Canadian federal government, it is not unusual for Deputy Ministers (who in our experience have higher levels of information processing capability than they are often given credit for) to deal with elected Ministers, who seem to have lower capability. Although we don't have direct research, we would hypothesize that this situation gets worse as one moves to lower levels of government (e.g., school boards, hospital boards, police commissions, etc.). And as another aside, anyone who has chaired meetings of one sort or another knows it can be quite draining to keep the discussion focused. One of the main reasons for this is that individuals often have different levels of information processing capability, and therefore process information and solve problems at quite different levels.

There are some situations in which it is likely, if not inevitable, that members of a Board of Directors will not have the information processing capability necessary to do the requisite level of work. Even in these cases, we would suggest that the model outlined here will be of value. Simply being aware of the issue presents an opportunity to deal with it more effectively. Conversely, being unaware of it simply increases that probability that any dysfunctional behavior will continue.

Governance: The Work of the Board of Directors

If the work of a Board of Directors is governance, what does this mean? We have developed the Governance Model shown in Figure 5.1.

The Board of Directors should be accountable to the association, and should establish mechanisms to communicate with the association. It should also identify other key stakeholders and make

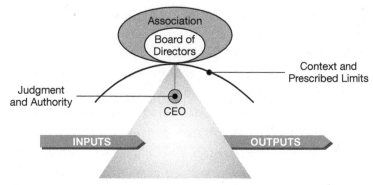

FIGURE 5.1. Governance Model

sure there are appropriate relationships with them. Alignment at this level is important.

The Board of Directors does not have a manager in the traditional sense. It therefore should establish self-management mechanisms, particularly a feedback system with information and reward components. It is also important to ensure that the Board has appropriate information for its decision making (independent as required), including audit information.

The members of the Board of Directors have a collective or joint accountability for the work of the Board. As a result, as much as possible, substantive work and decision making should take place at this level. Committees of the Board are important to alleviate workload and deal with specialized topics. However, as much as possible, their work should be directed to the Board decision making.

The Board of Directors should be accountable for the following four factors relative to the CEO:

- It should provide the appropriate context and prescribed limits to the CEO. The context would include factors such as the association framework, Board limits (e.g., legal, ethical, and policy requirements), and risk management limits. This third factor requires the Board to determine substantive risks, and develop appropriate frameworks to address them. The context and prescribed limits need to be right sized. If they are too narrow (or nonexistent), the Board will likely micromanage. We would expect this to happen if the Board members did not have sufficiently high information processing capability.

- It should make sure the CEO is clear about the outputs or results expected of her. This should include work quantity, quality, and timeliness, related to resources. It should include both doing the current work and finding ways to improve the work of the organization and ensuring a robust organization planning and review system (e.g., vision, mission, values, strategic positioning, operational plan, and resource plan). It also should include having the CEO working at the right stratum with the appropriate time span.

- It should ensure that the CEO has the appropriate resources required to do the work. The necessary resources include people (time and expertise), money (budget), and technology (especially information technology). The Board should ensure that the resources are deployed in an optimal way, which may also entail ensuring that there is an optimal organization design.

- Within this framework, the board should ensure that the CEO has appropriate authority to do the required work, and be prepared to support him in using his judgment and initiative.

If a Board of Directors is to have these accountabilities, it should also have the following commensurate authorities:

- To select the CEO.
- To decide performance appraisal and related consequences including compensation. (It should be noted that the time frame should be appropriate relative to the time span of the CEO role. Feedback and coaching are important.)
- To terminate the CEO.

Several additional points should be made. The Board as a whole is accountable for the CEO. It is not appropriate for individual members of the Board to give direction to the CEO. The Board is not accountable for employees below the level of CEO. It is inappropriate for the Board, and for any individual Board member, to give direction to employees below the level of the CEO. It should be noted that there are some dual roles that need to be carefully delineated (e.g., secretary to the Board, internal auditor, etc.).

Note that in research on the global pension fund industry (Ambachtsheer, Capelle & Scheibelhut, 1998), the governance items that were statistically significantly related to financial performance were the following: communicating with stakeholders; balancing overcontrol and undercontrol; the process for selecting, developing, and terminating governing fiduciaries; using time effectively; the high level of trust with the investment team; and clear allocation of responsibilities and accountabilities relative to the investment team.

Let's come back to where I started in this section: What is governance? We suggest the following definition: governance is a practice carried out by a governing body (e.g., Board of Directors), that is accountable to an association (e.g., owners or shareholders), and is accountable for an organization (e.g., employment hierarchy) through the head of the organization (e.g., CEO). The governing body accountability to the association should include setting up appropriate communication mechanisms, as well as setting up appropriate relationships with key stakeholders. The accountability to the association should also include having appropriate self-management practices, including ensuring the appropriate selection, evaluation, development, and termination of members of the governing body. Selection should be based upon skilled knowledge, application, and information processing capability. The governing body accountability for the CEO should include setting appropriate context and prescribed limits, being clear about outputs or results expected (including ensuring optimal organization planning and review), ensuring appropriate resources to do the work (including ensuring optimal organization design), and ensuring appropriate authority to do the work. The governing body authority for the CEO should include selection, appraisal, and (as required) termination.

Organization Design: A Missing Factor

There is an important governance accountability that Boards of Directors are not fulfilling. We would argue that a Board of Directors is not fulfilling its full accountability if it does not ensure that the CEO has an organization design that facilitates the optimal delegation and operationalization of accountability and authority throughout the organization. We would further argue that the same can be said of a CEO is who does not ensure an optimal organization design.

How does the Board of Directors ensure that an optimal organization design is in place? The fundamentals are simple. Positions are established in the organization. The positions are aligned both vertically (e.g., managers and direct reports) and functionally (different functions such as production, marketing, etc.). Employees are selected to fill the positions. Managerial and cross functional accountabilities and authorities are established and delegated throughout the organization. Deliverables and tasks are completed by employees in positions.

The following are governance/CEO organization design questions that can with respect to the current situation or some anticipated change (e.g., growth, downsizing, merger, acquisition, etc.):

- Does the organization have the right number of layers or strata in all parts of the organization? (Too many is a waste of money and too few can be fatal.)
- What percentages of manager–direct report alignments are requisite, compressed, or have gaps? (Compression leads to micromanagement and gaps to lack of direction.)
- What percentage of positions is redundant and should be eliminated? (Redundant positions are obviously costly, but also reduce effectiveness.)

- What percentage of positions is doing work with the appropriate level of complexity? (e.g., are more senior positions doing the required higher-level work?) Is the organization increasing or decreasing in higher value-added work? Some organizations are systemically compressed (i.e., virtually everyone is operating at too low a level; one sometimes finds this in organizations with an excessive cost orientation).
- What percentage of employees is optimally matched to positions in terms of skilled knowledge, application, and information processing capability?
- Are both managerial and cross functional accountabilities and authorities clear and appropriate?
- What is the current intellectual capital in the organization, and is it increasing or decreasing? Information processing capability provides an important measure to help answer this question. (There has been considerable discussion about intellectual capital, but little in the way of accurate measurement.)
- What is the level of intellectual capital required for the future of the organization, and is it increasing or decreasing?
- Are tasks assigned to the right levels in the organization? (E.g., professionals often spend about half of their time doing lower level work for which they are overpaid; employees at lower levels often try to complete more complex tasks of which they are not capable.)

It is important to be clear about the respective roles of a Board of Directors and a CEO in this regard. It is not appropriate for a Board of Directors to get involved in the micro details of organization design. It is important, however, for the Board to set context and prescribed limits related to optimal organization design, and expect a monitoring and reporting function from the CEO on the actions taken. Further, we would argue that a CEO should be accountable to ensure that there is an optimal organization design. This is virtually ignored by most CEOs, yet has been shown to be an important factor in organization performance.

PROJECT MANAGEMENT

We believe that projects often fail to produce the desired outcomes primarily because they lack the necessary organization design elements. The positions are misaligned, the accountabilities and authorities are inappropriate or unclear, and people are not properly selected for positions. This section deals with these issues and some possible solutions.

Managers choose to have some of their work done through project teams because it can be a focused and cost effective way to achieve results. The idea is to bring together a team of employees with varying skilled knowledge from across the organization that will contribute to the achievement of the desired project goal.

Projects should be planned and executed following generally accepted principles of project management for optimal results. When an accountable manager decides there is the need for a project team and recognizes that the project management skilled knowledge is not available or does not exist in her organization, the manager will proceed to acquire this essential skilled knowledge. The project team structure and project processes should be designed following appropriate organization design practices and principles for maximum efficiency and effectiveness. The project team needs to be properly aligned with the managerial accountability hierarchy, project accountabilities and authorities have to be clarified, and people matched appropriately to project positions.

Purpose of a Project Team

Project teams are created for three reasons:

- To analyze a particular issue or opportunity and make recommendations. This is direct output support to the accountable manager.
- To produce a specific deliverable. This is a situation of delegated direct output.

- To improve the organization. This is a situation that necessitates cross functional accountabilities and authorities (e.g., the work is organization-wide and the team coordinates the required work of the organization, similar to the cross functional accountabilities and authorities previously discussed).

Accountability and Authority to Establish a Project Team

The decision to establish a project team should be made by the cross over point manager (i.e., the accountable manager who controls most resources necessary for success). When an accountable manager decides that a project team is necessary, he should

- appoint the project manager
- set context and prescribed limits for the project
- clarify the project manager accountabilities and authorities
- ensure mechanisms to obtain team members
- ensure that the necessary resources are provided

The project manager could be the accountable manager if the project requires her direct leadership. It could also be another individual who could be selected from the direct reports of the manager, or from the once removed direct reports (direct report to one of the accountable manager's direct reports). In general, a project manager should not be more than once removed from an accountable manager. In order to successfully implement a project, the project manager needs to be able to understand the context set by the accountable manager, and to be able to use judgment and make decisions within that framework. If the project manager is more than two strata removed from the manager, he is generally too far removed from the manager to be effective.

If appointing another individual, the selection of the project manager must be at the right level relative to the complexity of the project. For example, a project with an appropriate time span (target completion time) of 18 months would be a Stratum 3 project, and would require a project manager with Stratum 3 information processing capability.

Project Structure, Accountabilities, and Authorities

Some of the factors to consider in deciding the appropriate project structure are: the purpose of a project, its level of complexity, and the skilled knowledge requirements. For example, the accountable manager might appoint a direct report as project manager and the project manager's peers as project team members for a direct output support project. In the latter situation, the accountable manager would delegate cross functional accountabilities and authorities to the project manager. Another example could be an eighteen month project to produce a direct output. The project manager could be a Stratum 3 individual accountable for the output of Stratum 2 project team members from across the organization. In this situation, the project manager would be delegated managerial accountabilities and authorities to manage the project team.

Project managers should be delegated clear and appropriate accountabilities and authorities. Consistent with the managerial accountability framework discussed earlier, the accountabilities of a manager also apply to a project manager's role relative to project direct reports (assuming managerial rather than cross functional accountability and authority). A project manager is accountable for

- the results of the project team's work and the team members' working behavior
- sustaining a team of direct reports capable of doing the work
- setting context and prescribed limits for direct reports
- holding regular manager–direct report meetings
- coaching direct reports
- contributing to performance appraisals

The project manager requires the following minimum authorities relative to direct reports:

- to veto the appointment of an individual to a project direct report position
- to decide types of work assignments for project direct reports
- to contribute to performance appraisal (home base manager is accountable for personal effectiveness review and base pay administration)
- to initiate removal of a project direct report from position
- to hold immediate project direct reports accountable for effective working relationships

When a project requires cross functional work, the cross over point manager needs to set context and prescribed limits to facilitate the process. She or he needs to delegate the necessary cross functional accountability and authority to the project manager and to clarify the accountability and authority of others (e.g., other direct reports and home based managers). The cross over point manager retains overall managerial accountability and authority.

Project Team Members

The project team member's role can be full time or part time. For projects longer than one year, the team members could be the direct reports of the project manager, who should be exactly one stratum above the direct reports and accountable for doing their performance effectiveness review. Team members are seconded to the team with the agreement of their home base managers. Agreements should be clear in terms of the work to be performed, the duration of the secondment, and other work requirements. This process is to be executed within the context and prescribed limits set by the accountable manager.

Projects by nature have a limited duration. Project team members generally return to their own positions after the completion of the project.

Project Team Members, Accountabilities

A project team is a group of individuals chosen for their particular skilled knowledge and capability brought together to produce a specified output. Team members are accountable for doing their best to achieve the level of effectiveness for which they are being compensated. They are accountable to inform the project manager when a deliverable that has been agreed on may not be delivered as agreed. They are also accountable to inform the project manager when resources are underutilized.

Project Manager Title

The project manager's title should be consistent with the titles in the organization, e.g., Project Executive at Stratum 4, Project Director at Stratum 3, and Project Manager at Stratum 2.

Project Life Cycle

Projects should be managed following the sequential phases of initiating; planning; doing and monitoring; and reviewing and closing or recycling. The project management process should be tailored by the project manager to the nature and purpose of the project and its degree of complexity. For example, a technology project might require the project phases of initiating, analyzing, designing, coding, testing, implementing, and post implementation. Other projects might necessitate a development phase. Each phase should conclude with the delivery of a specific output. Typically, the deliverables are respectively a project charter (initiating), a project plan (planning), achieved project outputs (doing and monitoring), and a post-implementation report (reviewing and closing).

People Change Management

When the implementation of a project will have impacts on employees, the project planning and execution is to be based upon fundamental change management principles. In such cases, one of the project's accountabilities is to assess and analyze people and organization change factors, including risks, and to develop an appropriate response plan. The extent of the people change management work depends on the purpose of the project and the related anticipated impact on employees. It is usually essential to do such work for cross functional projects and necessary, to varying degrees, for direct output support and direct output projects. The resulting people change management plan is integrated with the project plan for an optimal execution.

PROCESS MANAGEMENT

Process improvement efforts will fail to realize their potential unless the organization and its behaviors are fully aligned. The Capelle Associates approach squarely addresses this gap through standardizing structures and accountabilities within and across functions, followed by a critical evaluation of individual capabilities to perform these roles—all based on proven science.

—*Jeff Adams, General Manager, Continuous Improvement, Canadian Pacific Railway, February 2013*

Process management is part of organization design as we define it. We do not do the detailed process analysis that some process specialists might undertake. These more detailed methods can certainly complement our approach. However, we believe that our method adds value in three ways: at the macro process level, at the micro process level, and in terms of accountabilities and authorities.

You will recall that the Organizations Systems Functioning Model (Figure 2.1, p. 24) shows resources flow from providers/suppliers into the organization. There is a throughput function (the resources are changed in some ways) and an output (products/services) to a market with customers and recipients. There is a feedback loop. This is a process. Of course, organizations have many processes. Some go through the total organization as shown by the model. Others are smaller processes that are found in some parts of the organization. In this section, we will look at the accountability for process in general and at the macro and micro levels.

I have already discussed the accountability of a Board of Directors (governance). The Board can't do the work, so it delegates accountability to the head of the organization (CEO). Initially (at least theoretically) the CEO is accountable for everything. Of course the CEO cannot do all of the work, so she delegates to her direct reports and so on down the organization. We believe—and this is seldom understood—that the CEO delegates accountability for both function and process. These are two sides of the same coin. In order to illustrate this principle, I will describe a sample organization. Of course, not all organizations look like this, but I will use it for demonstration purposes.

Figure 5.2 shows a CEO position and nine direct report vice president positions. This would generally be viewed as a functional organization: each vice president is accountable for a function. The CEO delegates to each of these positions, but retains accountability for the interfaces among the positions.

Each position is also accountable for the process of its function. Depending upon the circumstances, this could be through managerial or cross functional accountabilities and authorities. Consider, for example, the position of Vice President, Product/Service Delivery. He is accountable for obtaining resources (input), transforming them (throughput), and delivering products/services (output) in the optimal quality and quantity, and in a timely and

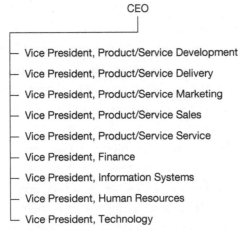

FIGURE 5.2.   CEO and Vice President Levels of an Organization

resource efficient manner, with a feedback loop for continuous improvement, and in a manner consistent with strategic positioning (providing better value to market/customers/recipients than alternatives/competitors). In our view, this is a macro process accountability that has the specificity necessary for measurement. Furthermore, the measurement can become time span specific.

This vice president position, as with all others, delegates accountability for parts of their function/process to direct reports and so on down the line. When we get down to delegating accountability for function/process to lower levels (e.g., Stratum 3, Stratum 2, and Stratum 1), we can use the task alignment method that was described earlier in the book. The tasks can be aligned into processes, and these processes can be further analyzed and improved.

Common current practice is to set up projects focused on rather narrow areas. The process is then "fixed" and another project is initiated. There is a lack of clarity about ongoing accountability. We believe that our model has the following advantages over conventional practice:

- The accountability for processes can be clearly specified from the top of the organization to the bottom. This is not about doing projects. It is about ongoing accountability for the continuous improvement of processes.

- It develops accountability for macro processes. The tendency to focus on micro processes limits impact. Broader perspectives are extraordinarily important but tend not to be addressed. They set the framework for the smaller processes and ensure that they will interact appropriately.
- It provides the tools to understand the differences between: Stratum 1 and Stratum 2 positions, Stratum 1 and Stratum 2 individual information processing capability, and Stratum 1 and Stratum 2 tasks. It provides additional task alignment methods to better understand lower-level tasks. We believe that these are invaluable for further enhancing micro process analysis.

COMPENSATION

We are clearer about what jobs are worth from a compensation perspective, and have improved our compensation systems and practices.

—Mike J. Donoghue, President and CEO,
Allstate Canada Group, February 2006

Time span, as a measure of the complexity of work, is a method of job evaluation, and can be used to determine the appropriate levels of compensation (Jaques, 1996). Research has shown that time span is closely related to felt fair pay, which is an employee judgment about the financial value of their level of work (Richardson, 1971). Further, there is a companion measure of the complexity of work, which is information processing requirement (the information processing capability that someone requires to work at that stratum).

We have completed six research studies related to compensation (see Appendix B). There are a few findings that are particularly important for this discussion. First, compensation is within the optimal range for only 63 percent of employees; therefore, there is significant opportunity for improvement (Capelle Associates Research Paper #16, July 10, 2012a). Second, time span is significantly related to actual compensation that would be paid on the basis of other job evaluation systems; directionally, they are both measuring complexity (Capelle Associates Research Paper #12, June 23, 2005a). Third, employees who are paid within the appropriate range have higher satisfaction in general and, more specifically, higher satisfaction with compensation. Note that those who are not paid within range include individuals paid both above and below the appropriate range.

The research would lead us to conclude that appropriate compensation matters, it is often not optimal, and there is a strong relationship between time span and compensation based on other job evaluation systems.

Why, then, would we use time span (or its companion measure of information processing requirement) as a job evaluation approach to determine compensation? We believe that there are several reasons:

- It provides a direct measure for the complexity of work; other systems seem to be specific and objective (for example, because they use a point system), but actually are quite subjective (because committees often sit around determining points).
- Other approaches are more time consuming, requiring committee work rather than direct measurement.
- Other approaches over-value the importance of size of the budget and number of reporting employees; this unduly penalizes individual contributors doing highly complex work (e.g., research). While career ladders are an attempt to deal with this, they are really a bandage solution required by weaknesses of the fundamental measurement.
- Other approaches are not clear about levels of work, and therefore have overlapping ranges. Our approach is quite clear that there are fundamental differences between types of work in

different strata. These boundaries between strata can be helpful in differentiating compensation.

In our experience, our clients are reluctant to use our approach as a job evaluation system. There is a significant industry promoting the existing approaches, and the switching costs can be seen as high. Several of our clients have switched, although they still supplement our approach with some other systems related to employment practices (e.g., physical requirements of position). They use a combination of time span and information processing requirement to determine the complexity of work. The majority of our clients have largely retained their existing systems, but used our approach in two ways. First, it can be useful in better differentiating boundaries between strata. We have found that existing job grades are sometimes entirely within one stratum, and sometimes overlap two strata. The other opportunity is to more appropriately assess the complexity of work of higher-level individual contributor positions.

Existing compensation practices could use significant improvement, and getting compensation right matters. Our measure of complexity of work, using some combination of time span and information processing requirement, can provide significant added value.

CHAPTER 6

A CALL TO ACTION

I thought I would provide an update as we are now in the eighth year from the time that you initially supported us with an organization design assessment and implementation. Over this period of time there have been a number of significant events, including a change in our distribution model, the retirement of four members of our senior leadership team, and two new Presidents. Even though these key events created significant changes within the organization, all of the key foundational organization design principles have remained intact within Allstate . . . in 2013, we have been selected by AON Hewitt as one of the Best Employers in Canada . . . In addition, over the last three years, we have outperformed the industry on all key performance metrics.

—Eric Pickering, Vice President, Human
Resources, Allstate Canada Group, May 2013

Our research and client experience shows that better organization design, as we define it, leads to better financial performance, customer satisfaction, and employee engagement. However, executives and their organizations tend not to optimize their organization designs and tend not to derive these benefits. Why is that? The following are the top 10 reasons that we have heard—and our response to them.

- "I don't really know what organization design is."

  While executives will seldom say this directly, there is some truth to the statement. Organization design is defined in many ways (we have gone to great lengths to provide our definition, including a glossary of terms). Education in organization design has been significantly lacking. Most business schools have courses on organization theory and organization behavior, but very few have courses on organization design. Human resources programs tend to be equally deficient. A human resources association of which I am a member recently came up with a list of about 15 knowledge areas. Organization design was not one of them. These curriculum omissions have adverse effects on organizations and their employees.

- "We already do it."

  There is some truth to this comment too: an executive cannot *not* do organization design. However, the objection misses the key point, which is whether the organization design is as optimal as it should be. Our research, with a database of over 59,000 manager–direct report relationships, shows that the manager–direct report alignment is the most important organization design factor. By itself, it directly leads to better organization performance. However, we find inappropriate alignment almost half of the time. This is a significant waste, one that makes it difficult to argue that "we already do it well."

- "I'm not sure that there are any benefits."

  In fairness, there is a requirement for (a) more research that (b) is better publicized. However, our research and client experience show that better organization design leads to better financial performance, customer satisfaction, and employee engagement. We have also made connections between our research and other research that support this relationship.

- "It will cost too much."

  It is certainly true that there is an investment required, in terms both of time and money. However the key issue is the return on investment. Our research shows that better organization design leads to better financial performance, which is a significant prize. It also shows potential average annual cost savings of about $2,500 per position (times the number of positions in the organization; e.g., $2,500,000 for a 1,000 person organization). Based on these points, our research shows a significant return on investment.

- "I'm afraid that it will disrupt our organization, client focus, etc."

  This is a legitimate concern. Many approaches focus only on the organization design itself. We have developed a robust implementation process, building in the best practices for project management and people change management (including communication and training). This is critical to bringing about positive change. As well, the leaders must lead: this is another critical success factor. Finally, since many aspects of existing organization designs are "broken," employees will be able to quickly experience these benefits.

- "It's not my job."

  This tends not be said explicitly, but is a reasonable conclusion when one observes behavior. CEOs tend not to consider organization design to be part of their job. We would suggest that it should be a critical part. Suboptimal strategy delivery is more often a function of the implementation rather than the plan. Organization design is the foundation of strategy implementation; a suboptimal organization design will lead to suboptimal strategy implementation. Similarly, heads of Human Resources tend not to put the focus on organization design that would be desirable even though it can provide the foundation for all human resources programs. Further, it allows Human

Resources functions to have a much more strategic, value-added impact on their organizations.

- "I don't know anyone that I trust to do it."

  This also is a legitimate concern. One would want someone who had a strong track record, and who was a good fit with the specific organization requirements.

- "I have a short time perspective. I'm afraid it will take too long to get results."

  It is possible to get cost savings results quite quickly. The speed of other financial results, employee engagement, and client satisfaction is related to both the nature of the organization design changes and the change management process. A strong implementation with a committed organization can deliver these outcomes quite quickly.

- "We are doing our strategy, and will consider organization design later."

  There are several issues with this perspective. First, strategic planning and organization design are integrally linked. While strategy certainly informs organization design decisions, the opposite is also true: the strategy is generally not a green field site with no limitations. Further, organization design is the foundation for strategy implementation, which should be considered in conjunction with strategic planning. Finally, our experience is that organizations with this perspective tend not to get around to optimizing organization design, and continue to have suboptimal strategy implementation.

- "Things are changing quickly, we need to be flexible, and the organization design would bog us down."

  This could be true if organization design was considered to be "carved in stone." However, if one learns the research-based principles, and can apply them, then having an optimal organization design supports changes that are more robust and quick, and less disruptive than would otherwise be the case.

Better organization design, as we define it, leads to better financial performance, customer satisfaction, and employee engagement. Many executives and organizations have not optimized their organization designs and have not achieved the commensurate benefits. We have listed, and responded to, a number of the reasons that we have heard for not doing so. Hopefully, more executives and their organizations will achieve these benefits in the future.

APPENDIX A

CLIENT EXPERIENCE

If an approach to improving organization performance is to be considered valid, we believe that it should meet two criteria. First, executives and their organizations should actually have success in using the approach and gaining the benefits. Second, there should be research substantiating the approach. This appendix deals with the first of these points. What follows are comments by more than 30 executives regarding their experience in utilizing our approach to improving organization design in order to improve organization performance. These comments are dated and some go back about 20 years.

While these remarks often express appreciation for the support that we have provided, that is not the reason they are reprinted here. They are valuable because of where they come from: these executives are accountable for improving the performance of their organizations. They are the ones who have to ensure that improvement takes place and is sustained. A consultant doesn't improve an organization—an executive does. They have been able to utilize our support and make something happen from it.

As I reread the commentaries I was struck by a couple of features. The first is the difference among the executives. While we have a comprehensive approach, not all parts are implemented all the time. Even when they are, there are differences in the organization priorities and emphasis. Our approach is not simply "one size fits all." While the underlying principles and practices are shared, the actual application has to be tailored to each organization. The second point is the variety of insights that are discussed. As a consultant, I have certain views of the world. What I find is that the executives with whom I work often have different insights and perspectives. I think that there is much to be learned from these perspectives.

These executive comments account for about half of the approximately 100 organization assessment and implementation projects that we have done over the past 20 years. I think that it would be fair to conclude that in these cases, executives have been able to improve organization design and achieve some of the benefits that one would expect. It should be noted that in many of these situations we also have client research (that will be covered in a separate appendix) demonstrating the changes and improvements.

However, one might reasonably ask, "Well, what about the other half of the projects? We know the research shows that a high percentage of projects fail to deliver the expected results. What about the other projects?" I will now address this point.

THE OTHER PROJECTS

The commentaries to this point in this book came from projects that we considered to be more substantive. This is some combination of our involvement in assessment, implementation, and research. Over the years, we have tended to limit our reaching out for comments to these situations. However, we have reviewed our other projects and have divided them into three categories. Government projects have accounted for about 25 percent of our projects, small companies and nonprofit organizations have accounted for about 10 percent of our projects, and larger, more substantive projects (without executive comments) have accounted for about 15 percent of our projects. I will review each of these.

Government Projects

We have made it a practice of not asking our government clients for letters on their experience. Our view has been that this could put them in what might appear to be a compromised situation, since the procurement process requires an "objectivity" and "perceived neutrality." In the private sector, on the other hand, an executive is accountable for the results, and tends to go where value can best be delivered. I will have more to say about government procurement shortly.

We have found that our assessment reports are very well received. In the meetings to discuss them, decisions are made on implementation and next steps are planned (our reports have information on both the recommendations for change and the implementation process). Our experience is that most of our government clients then choose to implement on their own. So, we generally have not had further direct involvement, and since many of these projects have been smaller, we have not followed up further in any formal way. Therefore, we do not have the same level of information here as we do on the larger, more substantive projects for which we have the comments in the previous section. However, we do have some observations and conclusions.

We believe that our work has been well received. Most recommendations have been accepted and implementation plans made. While we have not asked for commentary, with larger organizations we have asked to list the organization as a client and have never been refused. However, our general view is that improving organization design in any significant way is much more difficult in the government sector. There are two main reasons. The first is that there has been a tendency to rotate senior government executives quite frequently (some would say that this is planned strategy to prevent them from getting too much power). We have seen 18-month rotations at the highest levels. This is a short period of time to make substantive change that is properly institutionalized. One can make some smaller changes, but that's about it.

The second reason is that the central agencies are very powerful, with a multitude of rules and regulations. Even when our clients had decided on changes, it was often an uphill battle in this environment.

On the positive side, we have two outcomes to report. First, we have found more clear success in situations with a high need (e.g., a major government initiative that has to be done (unreasonably) quickly in a high-quality way with significant downside risk if not successful). We haven't found this to be as important in the private sector, but it sure helps in the government sector. Again, although not documented, we have had the privilege of being involved in both the assessment and implementation of several very successful initiatives of this nature. Second, we have also had more clear success on the quasigovernment side, that is, with the separate but related entities that have more independence and discretion. These would include organizations in investment, power generation, and health care.

There is an additional issue with government, and that is the procurement process. There has been a tendency to transfer the decision making away from the executives, who should be accountable, to the procurement function. While there is a need for clear and enforceable standards, we believe that this has often shifted too far. As a result the criteria have shifted more from value (the juxtaposition of benefits and costs) to low cost. Services tend to be treated as commodities, and the lowest cost is the best. We don't believe that this tends to provide the best value.

As a result of all of the above, we have pulled back from the government sector. We have not done any "pure" government projects in the past 10 years, although we have worked in related areas of investment, power generation, and health care. Quite frankly, we find this disappointing. Government is extremely important in our society. At one time it tended to attract many of the "best and brightest." This no longer seems to be the case. Enhancing organization design is no less important in government. In fact, our research would show that government organization design is not only worse than the private sector (not surprising) but also than the nonprofit sector. The upside potential is significant.

In summary, in the government sector, we generally (with some exceptions) have not had the known degree of success that we have had in the private sector. This is not in terms of clients not being pleased with our work or not agreeing to change—it is more in terms of not being in a position to clearly see the outcomes, and knowing that they would have been more difficult to obtain.

Small Company/Nonprofit Projects

This area has accounted for about 10 percent of our projects. We have been involved in some of the implementations. Again, we do not have the more robust information that we have with the larger projects. The feedback that we have received has been positive. We do not have a suspicion of these being suboptimal (as we have with the government sector), but we do not have the more specific documentation to back up this perception.

Other Larger Projects

This area has accounted for about 15 percent of our projects. These are substantive projects not unlike the ones that we have executive comments on, except that we don't have executive comments. Why not?

Half of these projects (seven) took place in one organization that had us do separate and successive assessment and implementation projects with virtually all parts of the company. The work was well regarded and led to significant change. They agreed to be listed as a client of ours. However, the executive accountable for this left the company quite suddenly before we got around to asking for comments. We didn't follow up further, although in hindsight we should have done so. One learning outcome is that it is more difficult to change a whole organization by successively changing each of its parts.

One of these other larger projects went well: the organization agreed that we could list them as a client (after much legal back and forth). However, because of their orientation, they did not allow for public executive comments on suppliers.

In two of the projects, the client used our report and recommendations, but decided to do it on their own. Because these were more substantive projects, we have followed up and have had positive reports about the change. However, since we were not involved it is more difficult for us to know about this.

Two of the projects were situations in which an executive group had received the assessment, agreed to recommendations, and were planning the implementation. In both cases, there was a change at the top of the organization that resulted in the implementation being abandoned. We would consider these to be failures.

In one project, we completed an assessment and were underway with the implementation when there was an executive change. A new implementation approach was formulated that, in our opinion, was not in keeping with the integrity of what we had agreed. After much discussion, it became clear that this new direction was fixed. At that point we resigned from the project. This is the only time that has happened, although we have turned down potential projects at an early stage in cases where we didn't think that there was a good fit. Although I think that they were far enough along to get some value, I would consider this to be a failure.

In one very early project, there was a mismatch between our perception of the deliverable and that of the client. It was somewhat ironic since we went to great lengths with the project and were quite pleased with the deliverable. However, the client perception is what is important. We would consider this to be a failure. However, we did learn from the experience, have been much more robust in clarifying expectations, and have not had a repeat of this experience.

Summary

Executives and their organizations have been able to use our approach to improve organization design and experience benefits from it. We have comments from executives representing about half of our approximately 100 projects.

Government and quasi government projects represent about 25 percent of our projects. We have generally not been involved in the implementations and don't have good information on the outcomes. We know that these would have been more difficult to implement. We have been involved in several successful implementations that were high profile and high risk, and therefore committed the necessary resources for success. Small company/nonprofit projects represent about 10 percent of our projects. Our sense is that they have a similar success rate to the more substantive projects for which we have comments. However, we do not have the same data to substantiate this.

Other larger projects, without executive comments, account for about 15 percent of our projects. Of these, we would consider four to be failures. In two cases, a new executive group came in as implementation was being initiated and did not follow through. In one early project we had a significant disconnect with a client around expectations (we learned from that and have not repeated it). In one case, we resigned from an implementation when a new executive entered and changes were made to the implementation that was not in keeping with our agreement or our view of the integrity of the implementation.

We would conclude that our approach has a high success rate and low failure rate. This is even truer with our elimination of pure government work. However, there are still projects in between that are not entirely clear in terms of outcomes.

EXECUTIVE COMMENTS

The following executive comments are in reverse chronological order. Immediately following the comment is the name, title, and organization of the sender at the time of sending the comment, and the date that the comment was sent.

I thought I would provide an update as we are now in the eighth year from the time that you initially supported us with an organization design assessment and implementation. Over this period of time there have been a number of significant events, including a change in our distribution model, the retirement of four members of our senior leadership team, and two new Presidents. Even though these key events created significant changes within the organization, all of the key foundational organization design principles have remained intact within Allstate. The project team that re-designed the new distribution model used the principles of cross functional accountability and authority utilizing project management rigor to clarify deliverables and roles. Three of the four leadership team roles were filled by internal employees who had been identified as high potential through our annual Talent Pool review process. In the last couple of years we have revisited our Vision/Mission and have engaged employees to develop a simplified and more meaningful Vision/Mission. We have also undertaken a significant strategic review that is identifying key strategies and tactics that will be employed over the next several years. A formal process has been established to help us assess and evaluate all current projects, align with key strategic deliverables and identify clear resource and cross functional accountabilities and authorities required to successfully deliver. Finally in 2013, we have been selected by AON Hewitt as one of the Best Employers in Canada. On debriefing us, they indicated that one of the key points of feedback from employees was identifying career development and career opportunities in the company. We attribute this success to the formal institutionalizing of the Talent Pool review process that was implemented as part of the organization design work.

As a testament to how sustainable some of this work is, and continues to be, is the continual use of common language such as stratum of work, valuing work, cross functional accountabilities and authorities, and information processing capability.

Clearly our employees understand how critical these concepts are to developing and sustaining a very successful organization.

In addition, over the last three years, we have outper-formed the industry on all key performance metrics.

—Eric Pickering, Vice President, Human Resources, Allstate Canada Group, May 2013

Our data now shows that we are the only company in all of Canada our size or larger to have grown revenues and net income on an uninterrupted basis for 12 years in a row. I am confident the work our teams have done on organization design contributed to our unparalleled success.

—Jim Baumgartner, President and CEO, Moneris Solutions, May 2013

We have recently been awarded the "Great Workplace Award" by the Gallup organization. The award positions LS as being one of the most engaging companies in the world. In 2013 only 32 companies globally received this special recognition, with LS being the sole retailer in the group. While we have worked hard on many fronts to achieve this level of performance, we believe that our organization design practices have provided an important foundation for the deployment of our employee-engagement initiatives and would like to thank Capelle Associates for their support in that regard.

—Gerry Savaria, President and CEO, LS travel retail North America, May 2013

Process improvement efforts will fail to realize their potential unless the organization and its behaviours are fully aligned. The Capelle Associates approach squarely addresses this gap through standardizing structures and accountabilities within and across functions, followed by a critical evaluation of indi-vidual capabilities to perform these roles—all based on proven science. The result reduces re-work and variability in communication, speeds decision-making and delivers increased value for the paying customer. Just like a lean manufacturing system attacks waste and cycle time, this methodology provides the same critical framework for effective leadership and strategy execution.

—Jeff Adams, General Manager, Continuous Improvement, Canadian Pacific Railway, February 2013

The organization assessment you carried out provided excellent insights, and your recommendations set a baseline for improvements that we have made to the organization. In addition, the implementation consulting support provided us with methods, materials and training, so we did not have to "reinvent the wheel". There is no question that you have helped us to achieve the significant improvements in our organization ... your firm's consulting expertise is world class. You and your team were always available, and we appreciated the quick turnaround time when it was required. We also appreciate your flexibility in providing guidance and support as and when we needed it.

—George Weber, President and CEO, Royal Ottawa Health Care Group, January 2012

Capelle Associates completed a review of our entire organization and then assisted us with implementing the improvements. We found their research based assessment method to be both thorough and practical. For our implementation, they brought in methods and materials that they had developed and worked with our internal team. The improvements were both significant and sustainable. We found that better aligning positions, clarifying accountabilities and authorities, matching people to positions, and developing business plans has resulted in improved employee performance and customer satisfaction.

—Naseem Somani, President and CEO, Gamma-Dynacare, Medical Laboratories, October 2011

The organizational design support Ron Capelle and his team provided us helped create role clarity and accountability across the organization. The methodology paved the way for a more transparent and productive organizational structure allowing managers more time to focus on operational excellence.

—Robert Petryk, Senior Vice President, Human Resources, EPCOR Utilities Inc., August 2011

Ever struggled with often daunting questions like

- How many layers should my organization have to be most efficient?
- How can I be sure that I have the right people in the right seats and promote them from within?
- How can I reduce micromanagement and improve cross functional efficiencies?
- How can I trust that the organizational design and everyone's work is supporting the deployment of the strategy?

Capelle Associates Inc. provides surprisingly clear answers to all these questions, and a robust methodology of deployment. The result is a stronger, leaner and clearer organization, where everyone can focus on moving the business forward.

—Vadim Motlik, Chief Administrative and Chief Financial Officer, LS Travel Retail North America, July 2011

While the theory behind organization design is not new, the benefits of its implementation to our business are certainly in with the times. For starters, we gained from our managers being provided with greater clarity, increased consistency and overall better discipline. Second, with a strong commitment from the top, our organization design initiative provided our people, from senior management to front-line, with more arsenal in their toolbox and helped them make better decisions as managers. The icing on the cake is that, although organization design did not start for us as a cost-cutting exercise, it ended up paying for itself within the first year of implementation and that's a recurring benefit.

—Gerry Savaria, President and CEO, LS Travel Retail North America, July 2011

The application of Capelle's approach focused our efforts to address some longstanding opportunities for improvement. The decision making model, delineation of roles and responsibilities provides clarity and a framework for our team. Capelle Associates provided a high level of consistent, professional support for our efforts; we were pleased with their accessibility and availability.

—Jim Oosterbaan, Senior Vice President, Operations and Commodity Portfolio Management, Capital Power Corporation, June 2011

The logic of the Capelle Associates' approach to organization design resulted in an unprecedented level of support, at all levels, for a systemic change to CP's organization.

The approach to change management was extremely professional—highly detailed implementation plans at every stage and strong support from leaders before changes were implemented. Although the organization design model is time tested over many years and across numerous businesses and organizations, Capelle Associates were very mindful in their approach that management judgment must prevail.

—Bob MacIntyre, Assistant Vice President, Human Resources, Canadian Pacific Railway, June 2011

After Capital Power's IPO, we were at a point where we needed to ensure our organization structure was efficient and our employees were provided the right level of authorities and accountabilities to do their work. Capelle Associates' organizational design model and implementation have made a significant contribution to the alignment of our people to the business results.

—Brian Vaasjo, President and CEO, and Peter Arnold,
Senior Vice President, Human Resources and EH&S,
Capital Power Corporation, June 2011

For the past 8 years, Ron Capelle and Capelle Associates have provided advice on a number of corporate reorganizations to the Ontario Teachers' Pension Fund investment division. He has provided advice to senior management at the divisional level on organization structures and assisted in individual departments such as fixed income and finance. The advice came at significant turning points in our history and helped to keep the fund competitive and focused on identifying unexpected risks while remaining at the top of our game.

—Bob Bertram, Executive Vice President, Investments,
Ontario Teachers' Pension Plan, November 2007

The implementation of better role alignment and related leadership processes, enterprise wide, lead to newfound organizational capabilities and opportunities. One of the major benefits we gained is higher level of contribution from managers. We reframed the expected contribution and are now having managers think, talk, and act with broader and longer term perspectives than we had before. This is to me a key foundation in ensuring that we deliver, by the appropriate roles and in a coordinated way, the right mix of short- and long-term results we require to materialize our strategic plan.

Another improvement we benefitted from is more effective cross functional work. The combined effect of having better clarified the alignment of roles, accountabilities, authorities, and business plans, provides our national organization with a system and process enabling leaders and employees to work better together.

I also think that achieving significant progress, in a relatively short period of time, was made possible by working with Capelle Associates.

—*Christianne Dostie, Vice President, Allstate Brand,*
November 2006

Capelle Associates has provided organization design support to us for over ten years. They have conducted four major organization assessments. Each assessment has been rich in insight, thorough, comprehensive, very well documented, and focused in terms of recommendations.

For others considering redesigning their organizations, I think that a strong internal—external partnership is critical. I am generally not a big believer in external consultants, but there are certain business issues and opportunities that require more specialized and independent methodology or perspective. I would put comprehensive organization design in this category, and our relationship with Capelle Associates as an example of a strong internal—external partnership that has lasted for over ten years. The strength of this partnership is based on two main factors: 1) the quality of Capelle Associates' research methodology and 2) the experience, capability, reliability, and trustworthiness of the members of their firm. Under challenging timelines and resource constraints, Capelle Associates have never missed a deadline or commitment.

—*April Taggart, Senior Vice President, Talent*
Management and Diversity, BMO Financial Group,
April 2006

I have been using the Capelle Associates approach to organization design for more than 10 years and wanted to provide an overview of my experience.

We have accomplished much over the years. Accountabilities are clearer. Administration is appropriately centralized. We created a new Product Development function to deal with the increasing complexity of this area. This separate focus helped us to accomplish much more than would otherwise have been the case. Similarly, we created a new function to deal with our fastest growing business line, which further enhanced its growth. In summary, we designed our organization to better achieve our strategy. In fact, I believe that organization is part of strategy, and is divorced from it to the peril of both.

The benefits to our organization are multiple. First, we are clearer about our objectives. We have a cascading business planning and review process and measure our performance carefully. Employee opinion surveys, which are conducted by an independent third party, have shown excellent improvements in employee satisfaction, particularly with regard to knowing what's expected. In this regard, our results far exceed industry benchmarks. The satisfaction of external stakeholders is also surveyed annually and we have consistently achieved high scores on an international benchmark.

—Derek Fry, President, Visa Canada Association,
March 2006

I recommend the Capelle Associates approach to IT senior executives that are looking to improve organizational performance. Their approach is powerful as it provides senior executives with a more comprehensive framework for aligning strategy, roles, accountabilities, and tasks in complex situations. This approach is helping us execute our IT plan, improve efficiencies, make better staffing choices, and is having management and IT professionals do work at a higher level than we had prior to this assignment.

—Ted Carter, Vice President, Information Technology,
Allstate, March 2006

Our role descriptions and jobs are clearer, with more-clearly articulated accountabilities and authorities. We are clearer about what jobs are worth from a compensation perspective, and have improved our compensation systems and practices. We have become more objective and disciplined in matching people to positions, particularly when it comes to promotions.

One of our biggest improvements has been in business planning. Because we had taken the time to properly align the organization, we have been able to create and overlay a cascading business planning and review system in which employees have clearer deliverables with more appropriate complexity at each level. This is extremely powerful.

In summary, improving the organization design brings clarity to so many different areas. I believe that we have increased our effectiveness while also achieving efficiency gains.

> —*Mike J. Donoghue, President and CEO, Allstate Canada Group, February 2006*

We have reorganized significant parts of our business, improved role clarity, created "deeper" jobs, reduced "white space" between positions, improved succession planning, and strengthened cross functional relationships.

While cost savings were not a significant driver of wanting to improve our organization design, improving our organization alignment has produced significant cost savings. Being in a growth business, we have chosen to reinvest much of these savings into positions that can further enhance our return on these investments.

I would encourage CEOs to review and refresh their organization designs. I would strongly recommend Capelle Associates for their unique research-based approach and excellent support. They have certainly helped us to further improve our business.

> —*Jim Baumgartner, President and CEO, Moneris Solutions, February 2006*

We have accomplished a lot. Interestingly, one of the important outcomes was better understanding why we weren't able to accomplish some things. This understanding was critical in our change process. For example, we understood that being caught up in silos was related to misaligned roles and unclear cross functional accountabilities and authorities. Roles are now clearer, and jobs are deeper and more robust. I believe that we can better match people to positions and have better succession planning. We have eliminated some jobs, and invested in other higher-value-added jobs. We can better coach employees in this system, and this is related to lower turnover. Breaking down silos results in better customer focus and leads to better retention and satisfaction of customers.

Capelle Associates gave us a thorough and insightful assessment of our organization. This cannot be done from within an organization.

Joan Mitchell, Vice President, Human Resources,
Moneris Solutions, February 2006

With Capelle's help we have been able to move further and faster as we create role clarity, align deliverables with our business plans, and most importantly, clarify cross functional accountabilities, reducing inefficiencies and silo thinking.

We have been able to utilize these principles to strategically realign several critical Human Resources' systems and practices. Of greatest significance is the impact they have had in the areas of Talent Management, Talent Pool Assessment, Compensation, and Job Evaluation.

There is already tangible, measurable evidence of significant returns driven primarily by the principles and methods inherent in our investment in organization design.

—Eric Pickering, Vice President, Human Resources,
Allstate Canada Group, February 2006

Organization design does not appear to be on the agendas of many Boards of Directors and CEOs. Since it has been shown to be a driver of organization performance, it deserves a higher profile. CEO's should be accountable for developing, implementing and maintaining superior organization designs. Boards of Directors should be accountable for ensuring that this happens.

The Capelle Associates approach to organization design has been shown through research and client experience to be related to better financial performance, better customer satisfaction, and better employee satisfaction.

Ontario Teachers' Pension Plan has benefited from the Capelle Associates approach to organization design through both being a sponsor and participant in a global research project. We have benefited from high-value organization design work that they have done for us—they have certainly added value to our business.

> —*Claude Lamoureux, President and CEO, Ontario Teachers' Pension Plan, October 2004*

More than two years have now elapsed since your final presentation to me and other members of our Management Committee of the analysis, conclusions, and recommendations arising from your review of our Design and Procurement Department.

With the full benefit of hindsight I can only reiterate the statement I made to you following your final presentation: "This is the best value for money I have ever experienced from any consultant."

> —*Isadore Sharp, Chairman and Chief Executive Officer, Four Seasons Hotels and Resorts, December 2003*

Everything that we measure has improved markedly. Our financial performance is up. Our customer service scores are up. Our employee morale and the general attitude around all of this are up ... I can say with just absolute conviction that getting the organization design right ... has been fundamental to the improvements around this place.

—Robert W. Pearce, President and Chief Executive Officer, Personal and Commercial Client Group, BMO Financial Group, September 2002

Your research methodology was extremely thorough and detailed, enabling all our stakeholders to understand our existing difficulties and many of their causes. The proposed organisational design had immediate face validity, as a result of which it was quickly accepted by all members of senior management and key leaders in the procurement area. The assistance you personally provided at individual and group level in the process of change management was truly invaluable.

Productivity in the department has improved, and user satisfaction has increased remarkably while employee morale and team work have shown exceptional gains.

—John W. Young, Executive Vice President, Human Resources, Four Seasons Hotels and Resorts, April 2002

We want to thank you for your organization design work related to our recent merger. Your work gave us a clear and understandable framework for our new organization, facilitated our decision making about people and positions, and helped us avoid much of the politics often found in these situations (creation of Moneris Solutions).

—Frank G. Moore, Vice President, Merchant Services and Point of Sales, Royal Bank, November 2000

—Wendy K. Porter, Senior Vice President, Merchant Services, Bank of Montreal, Electronic Banking Services, November 2000

Canadian Tire was recently selected as the Number 1 Company in the Best Companies to Work For in Canada published by *The Globe and Mail Report on Business*. Organization design has been an important part of our success. I want to thank you for your significant contributions in this area.

—Dale Reeson, Divisional Vice President, Human Resources Services, Canadian Tire, April 2000

Ron Capelle has worked with Visa Canada Association since June 1996 helping to optimize organization design. The following defines his major contributions and the beneficial impacts of his studies and recommendations:

- Ten recommendations for organization and process change were accepted and implemented over a two year period.
- Customer satisfaction with our performance, as measured by three annual surveys, has shown improvement every year.
- Employee satisfaction, again, as measured by three annual surveys, has shown improvement each year.
- The clarity of organization responsibilities makes objectives setting and measuring a straightforward and believable process.

I would recommend Ron to any organization wishing to evaluate the way it is organized. His analytical framework and his extensive research in the subject convince you that his recommendations are not just "flavour of the month" but are well anchored in practical experience.

—Derek Fry, President, Visa Canada Association,
December 1999

Overall, provided helpful insight and thought-provoking advice and counsel that advanced our work on organizational effectiveness "to the greatest extent possible".

Your availability/access has always amazed me with your busy schedule—very much appreciated.

In most instances you exceeded my expectations (were always met). Stimulating, fresh ideas were always anchored in a disciplined (but flexible) approach.

Given our ongoing challenges (as an HR Division), I do not believe that our team would have been as successful as we have been without your consultations. You provided us with the frameworks we needed and the confidence to move forward.

—Peter J. Tate, Vice President, Human Resources, Bank of Montreal, November 1999

The work Ron Capelle did for Canadian Tire Corporation was highly valuable to our organization. In particular, his advice on the following areas was critical:

- organizational design (structure)
- role clarity
- scope of roles (size and level of work of teams)
- reporting relationships of noncore areas
- connect/link people in key roles

Many of the changes Ron recommended were implemented and in all cases, our operations have benefited. Employee satisfaction in both distribution centers is on the upswing. Employee Opinion Survey results indicates a steady improvement over the time span we have worked with Ron. In addition, operating results have also steadily improved over the same time period.

—Dale Reeson, Divisional Vice President, Organizational Development, Supply Chain, Canadian Tire, November 1999

It has been my pleasure to work with you on a major project designed to understand the relationship between organization design and performance in the global pension fund sector. The project was sponsored by 8 major funds.

We were indeed able to establish a statistically positive relationship between organization design and performance using our performance data and your organization design framework. We found that Capelle Associates' approach to better organization design is related to better financial performance in the global pension fund industry. This includes governance, layering, and delegation.

The project and its findings have had a significant impact on organization development within the 8 sponsoring pension funds.

—*Keith P. Ambachtsheer, President, K.P.A. Advisory Services, and co-author,* **Pension Fund Excellence: Creating Value for Stakeholders,** *October 1999*

I would like to thank you for the organization design work that you did for the Federation in 1994. The groundwork that your work and your report laid out for us has served us very well over the years.

In particular, the recommendations you made on the vertical and functional alignment in the Secretariat including our country and regional delegations have stood the test of time. The way we operate has improved significantly because of a clearer understanding of the relationships amongst these critical operating areas.

I might add that the planning system we initiated with your advice is still thriving, and cascading, iterative work plans are a normal part of every manager's working life.

—*George Weber, Secretary General, International Federation of Red Cross and Red Crescent Societies, October 1999*

I recently won a prestigious award, Canada's Call Centre Manager of the Year. I'm confident in saying that we would be struggling today if we had not implemented your suggestions. Getting the right organization design enabled us to do all the other things that were necessary to become successful.

—John Carver, Senior Manager, Customer Service, Bank of Montreal, September 1999

I specifically requested that you conduct an independent "health check" on how our corporate staff was organized and how their commitment to service levels was viewed by their various internal customers. The quality of the report you produced was outstanding in its method of analysis, completeness and organization. However, you also did a remarkable job in your follow-up to ensure that key management staff were sufficiently conversant with all sections of the report to enable them to review relevant findings with their staff.

The results of your work have provided a rich source of information and ideas which we are now committed to address over the next several months.

—Keith Willard, Chairman, Zeneca Inc., October 1996

Now, two years or so after your project, I have had the opportunity to reread your recommendations. Although not all were consciously acted upon, many were and those have proven to be wise decisions. Even some that we did not act on formally have in fact "evolved" to your solution; this is most encouraging.

I have found your work always to be well planned and executed and your research timely and complete. What was most interesting was that, although to my knowledge you had not had a client in the software industry before, you were able to learn quickly to a sufficient degree to make your work relevant to our challenges. This was most helpful.

—Peter C. Reid, Chief Financial Officer, Fulcrum Technologies, Inc., June 1996

By now you will have read the 'Change' page of Tuesday's *Globe and Mail*.

As you know, over the past few years the Passport Office management team has worked very hard to place the organization on a sound business footing. It is nice to see recognition of our efforts to date, particularly by a newspaper of the stature of the *Globe and Mail*.

I would be remiss if I did not recognize the contribution you personally have made to our success. Your leadership, advice, and encouragement in the areas of empowerment of our Employees, delayering of our organization, and Business Process Reengineering of the passport issuance process have been key factors in influencing the path we have chosen and the success we have had to date.

—**R. J. MacPhee, *Chief Executive Officer, Passport Office, December 1993***

RESEARCH

OVERVIEW OF CAPELLE ASSOCIATES RESEARCH

Capelle Associates has been conducting research on organization design for over 20 years. This has been a collaborative effort involving several people. Chris Becker was critical to the initial setting up of the research focus, and its early days. The most significant person in our research over the years has been Bob Lavery. He has led our research function, has done most of the analysis, and has taken a lead in much of the research writing. Dwight Mihalicz oversaw our research function for many years. In this role, he oversaw much of the analysis and was a significant contributor to the writing.

We are presenting these papers here to demonstrate that our Optimizing Organization Design® approach is supported both by successful executive experience and by research substantiating it. In addition, we believe that this research adds value to the organization design field.

Our practice is primarily a consulting practice but we have always had a strong interest in research, and have created opportunities where possible to do more. This research includes one previously published paper (Ambachtsheer, Capelle & Scheibelhut, 1998) and 23 that have not been published before. The previously unpublished papers are presented following this overview. We have updated papers to provide more consistency and continuity. For example, we now use the term "information processing capability" instead of "mental processing capability." We have added references from one research paper to another in the chronological order that they were written. However, the essence of each paper remains as it was originally written. It should be noted that there is some repetition among the papers (e.g., similar references are cited); however, this is done so that each research paper can be read on its own.

This research builds on an extensive body of literature. Craddock (2009) has put together an astounding annotated bibliography that lists 6,927 items. Research papers accounted for 4,074 items, of which 2,472 are direct research and 1,602 are supplementary research. Of these 4,074 research papers, 1,506 of which were published in peer-reviewed journals. There are 90 PhD dissertations.

We consider management and organization studies in general, and organization design studies in particular, to be part of the broader social sciences field (concerned with society and human behavior). While the social sciences are distinct from the natural sciences (biology, chemistry, physics, etc.), in both fields one of the research objectives is to determine causality. The ideal way to do this is to conduct robust experiments (e.g., randomly assign subjects to an experimental group that receives a treatment and a control group that does not).

This experimental approach is more difficult to apply in social sciences than in the natural sciences. Controlled experiments can be conducted on individuals in laboratory settings but it is less easy to design comparable tests for broad concepts. For example, we are interested in the impact of design on the functioning of organizations. This is a broad concept that cannot be tested in a laboratory setting (although parts of it may be). As a result, much of our research is what is termed "quasiexperimental" (Campbell & Stanley, 1969; Cook & Campbell, 1979; Shadish, Cook & Campbell, 2001). It lacks the rigor of experimental research.

Our research is mainly concerned with the impact of two factors, organization design and manager–direct report alignment. Although we have not conducted experimental research with control groups and randomized selection, we have conducted numerous types of research over many years. Among the varieties of research we have engaged in are the following:

- nonequivalent control group design (there is a control group, but members are not assigned on a random basis)
- one group pretest posttest design (measurement before and after organization design has been implemented)
- a survey of the top 2,000 companies in Canada
- a measurement and survey within the global pension fund industry
- analysis from the Capelle Associates Benchmarking Database of more than 59,000 manager–direct report relationships from 76 organizations
- numerous other studies showing relationships among variables

We provide support to clients in numerous ways, ranging from short consultations to comprehensive organization design assessment and implementation projects. This research is largely based, directly or indirectly, on our comprehensive organization design assessment and implementation projects.

As part of our assessment process, we collect client organization information on a confidential basis and provide clients with feedback from our benchmarking database. As a result of this process over many years, we have developed the extensive Capelle Associates Benchmarking Database. It includes more than 59,000 manager–direct report relationships from 76 organizations, and over 13,000 employee satisfaction responses from 38 organizations. The database has evolved to the stage where it can be used to look at relationships across a range of organizations.

Our research covers two broad areas. The first is what we would call "outcome measures." The second is other research which contains a number of inter-related pieces.

Outcome Measures

We are primarily interested in the relationships between

- organization design and manager–direct report alignment
- organization design and relationship with manager (relationship perceived by employee, often based on employee satisfaction survey), employee satisfaction, customer satisfaction, and financial performance
- manager–direct report relationship and relationship with manager, employee satisfaction, customer satisfaction, and financial performance

We have a secondary interest in the following relationships between

- relationship with manager and employee satisfaction
- employee satisfaction and customer satisfaction
- relationship with manager, employee satisfaction, and customer satisfaction; and financial performance

The reason that these are of secondary interest is that they are generally not a direct part of our research. Others, whom we shall cite, have done significant work on these relationships. They are obviously important in general and enhance our work in particular.

These 14 relationships are shown in Figure B.1, which we call the "Organization Design–Organization Performance Model." This model, along with the correlations shown, was developed from our study of the top 2,000 Canadian companies (Capelle Associates Research Paper #9, 2003b). This involved surveying CEOs and Heads of Human Resources. One can see that each of the 14 relationships is statistically significant.

For this model, we would use the following definitions:

- Organization design: the relationship of an organization to its environment and the inter-relationships of its parts. This would include the alignment of positions, accountabilities and authorities, people, deliverables and tasks.

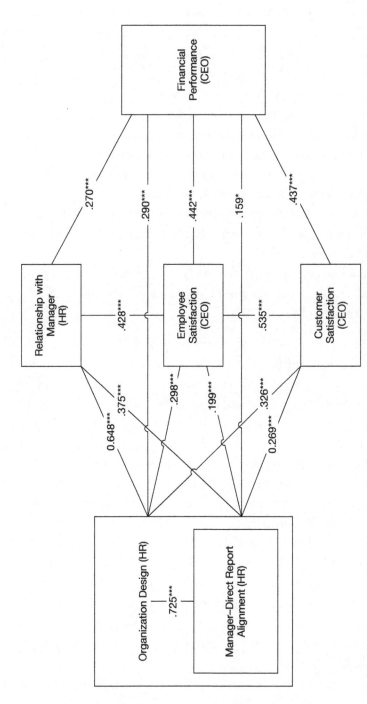

FIGURE B.1. Organization Design–Organization Performance Model (* P < 0.05, *** P < 0.001)

- Manager–direct report alignment: every employee should have a manager exactly one level or stratum above. This builds on the work of Jaques (1996) and his colleagues.
- Relationship with manager: the perception of an employee of her relationship with the immediate manager.
- Employee satisfaction: the perception of an employee with her/his relationship with an organization. This includes a number of factors, the most important of which is usually relationship with manager. It is also related to other factors such as engagement, absenteeism and turnover.
- Customer satisfaction: the satisfaction of a customer with the relationship to the organization. It is related to perceived value and customer loyalty.
- Financial performance: this can be determined on both a profit and loss and a balance sheet basis. It includes the interplay of revenues and costs.

We will first briefly address the relationships that our research will not pursue further, but are important to us. Other researchers have done extensive work in these areas. Buckingham and Coffman (1999) have conducted significant research showing the importance of the manager–direct report relationship. They have shown it to be related to productivity, profitability, retention, and customer satisfaction. Heskett and his colleagues have developed the service profit chain (Heskett, Jones, Loveman, Sasser & Schlesinger, 1994; Heskett, Sasser & Schlesinger, 1997; Heskett, Sasser & Schlesinger, 2003; Heskett, Sasser & Wheeler, 2008). They have shown that there is a relationship between the employee (including satisfaction and loyalty), the customer (including value equation, satisfaction and loyalty), and financial performance (including revenue growth and profitability). We believe that these streams of research provide further support to the importance of the relationships that we have researched and will discuss.

We will provide a brief overview of the research related to the relationships in which we are interested. They are as follows:

- organization design and manager–direct report alignment
- organization design and employee satisfaction
- organization design and relationship with manager
- organization design and customer satisfaction
- organization design and financial performance
- organization design and organization performance (not in Figure B.1, but a composite measure worth mentioning)
- manager–direct report alignment and employee satisfaction
- manager–direct report alignment and relationship with manager
- manager–direct report alignment and customer satisfaction
- manager–direct report alignment and financial performance
- employee satisfaction and relationship with manager

We believe that both better organization design and better manager–direct report alignment lead to better employee satisfaction, relationship with manager, customer satisfaction, and financial performance. There are several reasons for this:

- We would expect these outcomes from a theoretical perspective, and can specify the factors that influence these outcomes.
- We have research results that support the relationships among these factors.
- In most cases, these research results have been replicated through many types of research over an extended period of time.
- The research results are consistent with executive comments about their success in using this approach to achieve these benefits.
- The research is consistent with related case studies (Appendix C).

- There is considerable supporting research on many of the organization design variables that we use (Craddock, 2009).
- There is complementary research by Buckingham and Coffman (1999) on the importance of the manager–direct report relationship. They have shown it to be related to productivity, profitability, retention, and customer satisfaction.
- There is complementary research on the service profit chain (Heskett et al., 1994; Heskett, Sasser & Schlesinger, 1997; Heskett, Sasser & Schlesinger, 2003; Heskett, Sasser & Wheeler, 2008). They have shown that there is a relationship between the employee (including satisfaction and loyalty), the customer (including value equation, satisfaction, and loyalty), and financial performance (including revenue growth and profitability).

From a "purist" research perspective, we do acknowledge that we do not have the stronger research designs found in the natural sciences. However, we generally do not find this type of research in the management/organization field related to the sorts of relationships we are considering. We believe that the combination of theoretical underpinnings, replicated research of many types over many years, related evidence, and research (Craddock, 2009; Buckingham & Coffman, 1999; Heskett et al., 2003) provide a strong foundation. Therefore, we believe that both better organization design and better manager–direct report alignment lead to better employee satisfaction, relationship with manager, customer satisfaction, and financial performance.

With this context, we will now review these 11 relationships.

Organization Design and Manager–Direct Report Alignment We define organization design as the relationship of an organization to its environment and the inter-relationship of its parts (including positions, accountabilities and authorities, people, deliverables and tasks). Since manager–direct report alignment is the alignment of manager and direct report positions, it is a part of organization design. Therefore we would expect these two factors to be related.

This relationship is shown in Figure B.9.1 from the survey of top 2000 Canadian companies (Capelle Associates Research Paper #9, 2003b). This relationship is also shown in six studies in which we completed a comprehensive organization design assessment and implementation (Capelle Associates Research Paper #1, 1999; Capelle Associates Research Paper #3, 2000b; Capelle Associates Research Paper #4, 2000c; Capelle Associates Research Paper #5, 2000d; Capelle Associates Research Paper #13, 2005b; Capelle Associates Research Paper #15, 2011). In five of the six cases, pre and post measures showed an improvement of manager–direct report alignment following the implementation. In the sixth (Capelle Associates Research Paper #5, 2000d), this change was reported but not measured. These changes would be expected.

Capelle Associates Research Paper #13, 2005b, is particularly interesting. It shows the expected improvements in manager–direct report alignment related to organization design assessment and implementation. However, it shows that, at a later stage, when the organization became more complex and new organization design improvements were not implemented, there was a decline in manager–direct report alignment.

Organization Design and Employee Satisfaction We would expect that better organization design would lead to better employee satisfaction. Organization design provides better manager–direct report alignment (as well as overall better position alignment); better clarity of accountabilities and authorities; better matching of people to positions; and better alignment of deliverables. Any one of these alone might have a positive impact on employee satisfaction. The combination of all or most of them would seem to significantly improve that probability.

The relationship between organization design and employee satisfaction is shown in Figure B.9.1 from the Survey of Top 2000 Canadian companies (Capelle Associates Research

Paper #9, 2003b). As well, all seven of our pre-post studies show that, following an organization design assessment and implementation, employee satisfaction improved significantly (Capelle Associates Research Paper #1, 1999; Capelle Associates Research Paper #2, 2000a; Capelle Associates Research Paper #3, 2000b; Capelle Associates Research Paper #4, 2000c; Capelle Associates Research Paper #5, 2000d; Capelle Associates Research Paper #13, 2005b; Capelle Associates Research Paper #15, 2011). In all but one case (Capelle Associates Research Paper #13, 2005b), the employee satisfaction information was provided by the organization—it was a part of their ongoing measurement process. In the one exception, the Capelle Associates Employee Satisfaction Questionnaire was used. In one of the studies, benchmark data was also used (Capelle Associates Research Paper #1, 1999), and in another (Capelle Associates Research Paper #2, 2000a), more general comparators were used. In one study, absenteeism was also measured, and was shown to decrease in three of four business units (Capelle Associates Research Paper #15, 2011). In one study, employee satisfaction was shown to decline after a recommended organization design improvement was not implemented (Capelle Associates Research Paper #13, 2005b).

Organization Design and Relationship with Manager   We would hypothesize that better organization design would lead to better relationship with manager. As with employee satisfaction, the inclusion of several improvement factors would seem to increase the probability of this happening. The relationship between organization design and relationship with manager is shown in Figure B.9.1 from the survey of top 2000 Canadian companies (Capelle Associates Research Paper #9, 2003b). We have one additional study showing this relationship (Capelle Associates Research Paper #15, 2011). Following an organization design assessment and implementation, a measure called "relationship with supervisor" improved. This was a pretest posttest design. The information was provided by the organization as part of their ongoing measurement program. We have two studies, one correlational and one pre-post, which demonstrate the relationship between organization design and relationship with manager. We believe that better organization design leads to better relationship with manager.

Organization Design and Customer Satisfaction   We would hypothesize that better organization design would lead to better customer satisfaction. Improvements in alignment of positions, accountabilities and authorities, people, and deliverables should provide a better clarity and foundation to focus on customers. The relationship between organization design and customer satisfaction is shown in Figure B.9.1 from the survey of top 2000 Canadian companies (Capelle Associates Research Paper #9, 2003b).

We have one additional study showing this relationship (Capelle Associates Research Paper #3, June 23, 2003b). In this study, customer satisfaction significantly improved following an organization design intervention. The information was provided by the organization as part of their ongoing measurement. Note that customer satisfaction showed continuous improvement over a three-year period following the organization design assessment and implementation.

We have two studies, one correlational and one pre-post, which demonstrate the relationship between organization design and customer satisfaction.

Organization Design and Financial Performance   We would hypothesize that better organization design would lead to better financial performance. There are three factors related to this. The first is that improvements in the alignment of positions, account-abilities and authorities, people and deliverables should lead to better financial performance. These are foundations for perfor-mance, and should be factors that should support better financial performance. The relationship between organization design and financial performance is shown in Figure B.9.1 from the survey of top 2000 Canadian companies (Capelle Associates Research Paper #9, 2003b). In addition there are two other studies showing this relationship. The first is a research study showing that financial performance improved, compared to a benchmark, after an organization design assessment and implementation (Capelle Associates Research Paper #1, 1999). The related information was provided by the organization. The second additional supporting study was in the global pension fund industry (Ambachtsheer, Capelle & Scheibelhut, 1998). Organization design, as measured by 80 CEOs of pension funds, was significantly related to pension fund financial performance (in this case risk-adjusted net value added (RANVA).

The second factor relating organization design to financial performance is that organization design assessments can produce cost savings. The Capelle Associates Benchmarking Database shows average potential annual cost savings of $2,505 per position (Capelle Associates Research Paper #23, 2012). The total in each case would be found by multiplying this number by the number of positions in the review (e.g., in a 1,000-employee organization, the number would be $2,505,000).

The third factor is the related research that was previously cited. Buckingham and Coffman (1999) show a relationship between the manager–direct report relationship and profitability. Heskett and his colleagues (Heskett et al., 1997) have developed the service profit chain showing the relationship between employee satisfaction, customer satisfaction and financial performance (revenue growth and profitability). So, not only do we show a direct relationship between organization design and financial performance, we would expect that improvements in relationship with manager, employee satisfaction, and customer satisfaction would further drive financial performance. This hypothesis is further supported by the statistically significant relationships found in our survey of top 2000 Canadian companies (Capelle Associates Research Paper #9, 2003b).

In conclusion, we have three streams of support for the relationship between organization design and financial performance: three studies showing direct relationships; one study showing cost savings; and the citation of related studies showing the relationship of relationship with manager, employee satisfaction, and customer satisfaction with financial performance.

Organization Design and Organization Performance While this relationship is not a direct part of our model in Figure B.1, it is worth mentioning. We define organization performance at a macro level as providing better value to stakeholders than alternatives. This would include employee satisfaction, customer satisfaction, and financial performance. In our survey of Canadian private sector companies (Capelle Associates Research Paper #9, 2003b) we found a significant relationship between organization design as reported by the head of Human Resources and organization performance as reported by the CEO. This more macro relationship would seem consistent with the more specific relationships that we have been discussing.

Manager–Direct Report Alignment and Employee Satisfaction We will now shift from the broader concept of organization design to the more focused concept of manager–direct report alignment.

By using the concept of "time span" we can determine how many strata an organization should have, and place every position in the correct stratum. More specifically, we can develop optimal manager–direct report alignment. This is a situation in which a manager is exactly one stratum above a direct report.

While there is this one optimal situation, there are two that are suboptimal. The first is when a manager and direct report are operating at the same level or stratum (called "compression"). We would expect that the manager would be micromanaging and not adding sufficient value and that the direct report could not use her full capability. The second suboptimal situation is when a manager and direct report are operating more than one level or stratum apart (called "gap"). We would expect the manager to see the direct report as having no "initiative" and the direct report to see the manager as providing inappropriate direction. This manager–direct report alignment is fundamental to the relationship with manager and employee satisfaction. We can see how it could be related to customer satisfaction and financial performance. There are relationships with all of these factors. Quite frankly, we have been surprised at the robustness of manager–direct report alignment. While we would have expected that organization design would be related to these outcome measures, we would not have expected that any of the sub factors would be robust enough to do so. Manager–direct report alignment has proved us wrong.

The relationship between manager–direct report alignment and employee satisfaction is shown in Figure B.9.1 from the survey of top 2000 Canadian companies (Capelle Associates Research Paper #9, 2003b).

We have nine other studies showing this relationship. The first six are organization design assessment and implementation projects (Capelle Associates Research Paper #1, January 1, 1999; Capelle Associates Research Paper #3, 2000b; Capelle Associates Research Paper #4, 2000c; Capelle Associates Research Paper #5, 2000d; Capelle Associates Research Paper #13, 2005b; Capelle Associates Research Paper #15, 2011). In each of the studies both the manager–direct report relationship and employee satisfaction improved following the organization design intervention.

In all but one case (Capelle Associates Research Paper #13, 2005b), the employee satisfaction information was provided by the organization as part of their ongoing measurement process. In the one exception, the Capelle Associates Employee Satisfaction Questionnaire was used. In one of the studies, benchmark data was also used (Capelle Associates Research Paper #1, 1999), and in another (Capelle Associates Research Paper #3, 2000b), more general comparators were used. In one study, absenteeism was also measured, and was shown to decrease in three of four business units (Capelle Associates Research Paper #15, 2011). In one study, employee satisfaction was shown to decline after a recommended organization design improvement was not implemented (Capelle Associates Research Paper #13, 2005b). It should be pointed out that these are the same six studies that we previously cited to demonstrate the relationship between organization design and employee satisfaction. A critic might argue that the relationship between manager–direct report relationship and employee satisfaction is "contaminated" by the broader relationship between organization design and employee satisfaction. We would reply that, while there is more going on, the relationship between manager–direct report relationship and employee satisfaction is clearly demonstrated.

In addition to these studies, we also have three more studies in which there was no organization design intervention. The first is a study of 30 organizations from the Capelle Associates Benchmarking Database (Capelle Associates Research Paper #14, 2005c). It shows a significant relationship between manager–direct report alignment and employee satisfaction. The second is an interesting study from one organization that looks at one role—analyst (Capelle Associates Research Paper #21, 2012). It shows that individuals in analyst positions who have requisite or optimal alignment with their managers (exactly one stratum below) have higher satisfaction than those who are in gap or compression situations. The third study (Capelle Associates Research Paper #22, 2012) shows a significant relationship between manager–direct report alignment and employee satisfaction in three interrelated organizations.

Manager–Direct Report Alignment and Relationship with Manager We believe that better manager–direct report alignment leads to a better relationship with manager. It is not the only relevant factor. However, we have shown that gaps and compression in this alignment lead to suboptimal behaviors that one would surmise would weaken the relationship with manager.

The relationship between manager–direct report alignment and relationship with manager is shown in Figure B.9.1 from the survey of top 2000 Canadian companies (Capelle Associates Research Paper #9, 2003b). There are three additional studies demonstrating this relationship. In each, the manager–direct report alignment is determined by time span information, while the relationship with manager is determined by employee satisfaction questionnaires. The first study is a review of 30 organizations from the Capelle Associates Benchmarking Database (Capelle Associates Research Paper #14, 2005c). It shows a significant relationship between manager–direct report alignment and relationship with manager. The second is an organization design intervention in one organization that showed improvement in both manager–direct report alignment and relationship with supervisor (Capelle Associates Research Paper #15, 2011). The third is a review of the analyst role in one organization (Capelle Associates Research Paper #21, 2012). It shows that analysts who were in an optimal manager–direct report alignment with their managers had a stronger relationship with manager.

Manager–Direct Report Alignment and Customer Satisfaction The relationship between manager–direct report alignment and customer satisfaction is shown in Figure B.9.1 from the survey of top 2000 Canadian companies (Capelle Associates Research Paper #9, 2003b).

There are two additional pieces of research. The first is an organization design intervention that showed improvement in manager–direct report relationship and customer satisfaction (Capelle Associates Research Paper #3, 2000b). The latter was measured three times over three years. The second is a review of 30 organizations from the Capelle Associates Benchmarking Database

(Capelle Associates Research Paper #14, 2005c). It shows a relationship between manager–direct report relationship and customer and recipient satisfaction. It should be noted that the latter is the perception of employees, is not the direct measure of customers as was found in the first study.

Manager–Direct Report Alignment and Financial Performance

We would hypothesize that better manager–direct report alignment would lead to better financial performance. There are three factors related to this. The first is that the absence of optimal or requisite manager–direct report alignment leads to problems such as gaps or compression. These are fundamental to the operation of an organization. It is not unreasonable to hypothesize that these would have an impact on financial performance. The relationship between manager–direct report alignment and financial performance is shown in Figure B.9.1 from the survey of top 2000 Canadian companies (Capelle Associates Research Paper #9, 2003b). In addition, there are two other studies showing this relationship. The first is a research study showing that both manager–direct report alignment and financial performance improved (the latter compared to a benchmark) after organization design assessment and implementation (Capelle Associates Research Paper #1, 1999). The related financial performance information was provided by the organization. The second additional supporting study was in the global pension fund industry (Ambachtsheer, Capelle & Scheibelhut, 1998). Manager–direct report alignment and delegation were shown to be significantly related to pension fund financial performance; in this case risk-adjusted net value added (RANVA).

The second factor supporting the relationship between manager–direct report alignment and financial performance is that organization design assessments can produce cost savings. The Capelle Associates Benchmarking Database shows average potential annual cost savings of $2,505 per position (Capelle

Associates Research Paper #23, 2012). These are all directly related to the manager–direct report alignment. The total savings in each case would be found by multiplying $2,505 by the number of positions in the review (e.g., in a 1,000-employee organization, the number would be $2,505,000).

The third factor is the related research that was previously cited. Buckingham and Coffman (1999) show a relationship between the manager–direct report relationship and profitability. Heskett and his colleagues (Heskett et al., 1997) have developed the service-profit chain showing the relationship between employee satisfaction, customer satisfaction, and financial performance (revenue growth and profitability). So, not only do we show a direct relationship between manager–direct report alignment and financial performance, we would expect that relationship with manager, employee satisfaction, and customer satisfaction would further drive financial performance.

In conclusion, we have three streams of support for the relationship between manager–direct report alignment and financial performance: three studies showing direct relationships; one study showing cost savings; and the citation of related studies showing the relationship of relationship with manager, employee satisfaction, and customer satisfaction with financial performance.

Employee Satisfaction and Relationship with Manager   The final relationship to be discussed is that between employee satisfaction and relationship with manager.

We would consider relationship with manager to be the strongest factor affecting employee satisfaction. That is true of the Capelle Associates Employee Satisfaction Questionnaire, and would seem to be true of most questionnaires of this nature. The relationship between employee satisfaction and relationship with manager is shown in Figure B.9.1 from the survey of top 2000 Canadian companies (Capelle Associates Research Paper #9, 2003b).

There are two other studies showing this relationship. The first is a review of 30 organizations from the Capelle Associates Benchmarking Database (Capelle Associates Research Paper #14, 2005c). It shows that manager–direct alignment (based on time span) is significantly related to both overall employee satisfaction and the more specific relationship with manager (both from an employee satisfaction questionnaire). The second is an organization design intervention in one organization (Capelle Associates Research Paper #15, 2011). It shows that improvement in manager–direct alignment (based on time span) is related to improvement in both overall employee satisfaction and the more specific relationship with manager (both from an employee satisfaction questionnaire).

Other Research

This concludes the discussion of outcome measures. We will now move on to other research. We have seven additional categories of research as follows:

- manager–direct report alignment
- compensation
- delegation
- information processing capability
- task alignment
- Capelle Associates Employee Satisfaction Questionnaire
- span of control

Manager–Direct Report Alignment   We have one study related to manager–direct report alignment. Information is presented from the Capelle Associates Benchmarking Database of over 59,000 manager–direct report relationships from 76 organizations (Capelle Associates Research Paper #16, 2012a). It shows the numbers and percentages that are optimal or requisite (manager exactly one level or stratum above a direct report), are compressed (manager and direct report are at some level or stratum), and have gaps (manager is more than one level or stratum above a direct report).

Compensation We have six studies related to compensation. The first is information from the Capelle Associates Benchmarking Database of over 59,000 manager–direct report relationships from 76 organizations (Capelle Associates Research Paper #16, 2012a). It shows the numbers and percentages that are paid within, above, and below range. The second study provides analysis showing that the equitable differential pay scale for the Canadian market is somewhat different than the original (U.S.-based) scale (Capelle Associates Research Paper #11, 2004b). The third study, from 57 organizations with over 30,000 employees, shows that both actual compensation and compensation span (our determination of what the level or stratum of compensation should be) are significantly related to time span (measure of complexity of work) (Capelle Associates Research Paper #12, 2005a). The actual compensation and compensation span are also significantly related to each other. The fourth study, from the Capelle Associates Benchmarking Database, shows that compensation span is significantly related to time span (Capelle Associates Research Paper #18, 2012c). The fifth study, based on 20 organizations, shows that employees that are paid within range have higher overall satisfaction and also greater satisfaction with compensation than employees who are paid either above or below the range (Capelle Associates Research Paper #8, 2003a). The sixth and final study, from the Capelle Associates Benchmarking Database, shows that better manager–direct report alignment is significantly related to more appropriate compensation (i.e., being paid within range) (Capelle Associates Research Paper #19, 2012d).

In conclusion, there is evidence of a relationship between appropriateness of compensation and several other factors including time span, manager–direct report alignment, employee satisfaction in general, and satisfaction with compensation in particular.

Delegation   We have three studies related to delegation. To determine delegation, we ask managers to provide the deliverable of a direct report with the longest target completion time (time span). We also ask managers to state what they think that their own deliverable is that has the longest target completion time (self span). To determine delegation, we compare for a given individual the time span provided by the manager and the self span estimated by the direct report. If they are in the same level or stratum, we call this clear context. If the time span is greater than the self span, we call this broad context. If the time span is less than the self span, we call this narrow context.

The first study provides information from the Capelle Associates Benchmarking Database of over 59,000 manager–direct report relationships from 76 organizations (Capelle Associates Research Paper #16, 2012a). It shows the numbers and percentages that are clear, broad, and narrow context. The second study, from the Capelle Associates Benchmarking Database, shows that self span is significantly related to time span (Capelle Associates Research Paper #18, 2012c). The third and final study, from the Capelle Associates Benchmarking Database, shows that better manager–direct report alignment is significantly related to better (i.e., clear context) delegation (Capelle Associates Research Paper #19, 2012d).

In conclusion, there is some evidence that there is a relationship between time span and self span, and that better manager–direct report alignment is related to better delegation.

Information Processing Capability   There are two studies related to information processing capability. In the first, the information processing capability of about 400 executives was assessed. The actual job grades of the individuals were obtained. There was a statistically significant relationship between the two variables (Capelle Associates Research Paper #6, 2012e). The second study involved organization design improvement over time (Capelle

Associates Research Paper #7, 2012). Numerous relationships were found to be statistically significant. Information processing capability (determined by talent pool) was significantly related to both time span and information processing capability (determined by outside assessors). Information processing capability (talent pool) was shown to be reliable over two years, and information processing capability (assessors) was shown to be reliable between two assessor ratings. Job grade was significantly related to both time span and information processing capability (talent pool).

These studies support previous work that has been done on information processing capability (Jaques & Cason, 1994).

Task Alignment   There is one study on task alignment (Capelle Associates Research Paper #10, 2004a). This is a method to optimally align tasks within an organization. The study shows potential annual cost savings and return on investment based on work with 19 organizations.

Capelle Associates Employee Satisfaction Questionnaire   There is one study on the Capelle Associates Employee Satisfaction Questionnaire (Capelle Associates Research Paper #17, 2012b). It describes the questionnaire, the related factor analysis, and the resulting 10 factors. It also provides benchmark data from more than 13,000 employees from 38 organizations.

Span of Control   There is one study on span of control (Capelle Associates Research Paper #20, 2012e). There is a general perception that there is an ideal span of control. Our view is that span of control needs to be determined based on the uniqueness of work in every situation. This study looked at three large organizations and found no relationship between span of control and employee satisfaction.

RESEARCH PAPERS

Capelle Associates Research Paper #1, **Optimizing Organization Design: Improvements in Manager–Direct Report Alignment, Financial Performance and Employee Satisfaction (January 1, 1999)**

There is research suggesting that both better organization design and better manager–direct report alignment are related to better organization performance (Ambachtsheer, Capelle & Scheibelhut, 1998). In this study, we measure changes in manager–direct report alignment, employee satisfaction, and financial performance related to an organization design assessment and implementation.

Since manager–direct report alignment is a critical part of organization design, we would hypothesize that this would improve. We would also hypothesize that better organization design and better manager–report alignment would result in better employee satisfaction and better financial performance.

Method   An organization review of a financial services business unit with more than 1,000 employees was conducted in 1995. Following this review, a two-year change process was initiated to implement the recommended organization design and related changes. The implementation included aligning positions, accountabilities and authorities, people, and deliverables. This included improving the manager–direct report alignment. In early 1998, a second organization review was initiated to measure progress in a rapidly changing competitive environment. In both reviews, we assessed the manager–direct report alignment using time span analysis, a measure of the complexity of work developed by Jaques (1996) and his colleagues.

The information on financial results and employee satisfaction was provided by the financial institution. This information was part of ongoing measurements that the broader organization collected.

This included both internal information and benchmark data. We used information that had been collected over a period from 1992 to 1998.

Results   The results show that manager–direct report alignment, employee satisfaction, and financial performance all improved. The percentage of manager–direct report relationships that were correctly aligned increased significantly from the time of the initial assessment to the time of the second assessment (1995; Figure B.1.1; $X2=115$, $P<0.001$) (analysis shows that result is statistically significant). We define correct alignment as the manager being exactly one level or stratum above a direct report based upon time span analysis.

Financial performance consistently improved in the target business unit. The benchmark, which was originally much higher,

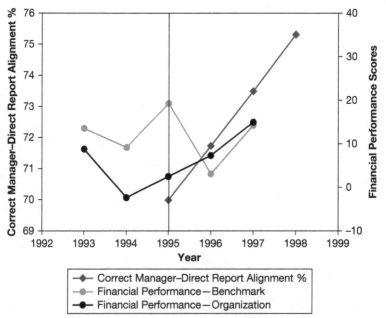

FIGURE B.1.1. Percentage of Correctly Aligned Manager–Direct Report Relationships and Financial Performance in a Financial Services Business Unit

FIGURE B.1.2. Improvements in Percentage of Correct Manager–Direct Report Alignment and Employee Satisfaction in a Financial Services Business Unit

ended up being about the same as the target business unit (Figure B.1.1).

Furthermore, employee satisfaction improved in the target business unit that underwent an organization design assessment and implementation (Figure B.1.2). This is consistent with the improvement in manager–direct report alignment. Employee satisfaction in the benchmark did not improve.

Discussion   This study shows improvements in manager–direct report alignment, financial performance, and employee satisfaction following an organization design intervention (assessment and implementation). These factors were measured both before and after the organization design intervention.

We would expect that the manager–direct report alignment would have improved. This is a significant part of our Optimizing Organization Design® approach, and was one of the significant activities in the implementation. We also hypothesized that an organization design implementation would result in better employee satisfaction and financial performance.

This research study has some particular strengths and weaknesses. The strengths include having independent employee satisfaction and financial performance information that preceded the organization design implementation and the pre and post assessment measures. Both showed improvement. As, well, for both the employee satisfaction and financial performance measures, there was a benchmark that did not show similar improvement over the same period of time. A weakness is that since we received only summary data at points in time from the organization, we could not do any statistical analysis. However, the trajectory of the lines would strongly indicate improvement in performance that is better than a benchmark.

It should also be noted that the improvements began in 1994 before the intervention. In the case of financial performance, this improvement was less than the benchmark, and it continued while the benchmark dropped. In the case of employee satisfaction, this was likely due to the new leadership had decided to address the existing issues. This provided some initial motivation. This continued and grew due to strong communication, and the demonstration of early success from both employee and financial perspectives. The benchmark conversely stayed flat. There is a common view that an organization has to go through a decline in performance to subsequently improve. We do not believe that to be the case, and this research would tend to support this opinion.

These results are consistent with the prior cited study (Ambachtsheer, Capelle & Scheibelhut, 1998).

References

Ambachtsheer, K., Capelle, R. & Scheibelhut, T. (1998a) "Improving Pension Fund Performance." *Financial Analysts Journal* 54(5), 15–20.

Jaques, E. (1996a). *Requisite Organization: A Total System for Effective Managerial Organization and Managerial Leadership for the 21st Century* (2nd ed.). Arlington, VA: Cason Hall & Co.

Capelle Associates Research Paper #2, Optimizing Organization Design: Improvement in Employee Satisfaction (March 1, 2000a)

There is research suggesting that both better organization design and better manager–direct report alignment are related to better employee satisfaction, customer satisfaction, and financial performance (Ambachtsheer, Capelle & Scheibelhut, 1998; Capelle Associates, 1999). Buckingham and Coffman (1999) concluded from employee satisfaction surveys that one of the most important factors in organization performance is the manager–direct report relationship. In this study, we measure changes in employee satisfaction both before and after an organization design assessment and implementation.

Since manager–direct report alignment is a critical part of organization design, we would hypothesize that this would improve. We would also hypothesize that better organization design and better manager–report alignment would result in better employee satisfaction.

Method   Employees in a call center completed an employee opinion survey. Following that, we supported the call center with organization assessment and implementation. This included alignment of positions, accountabilities and authorities, people, and deliverables. A significant part of the implementation was manager–direct report alignment (Jaques, 1996). The following year after these changes were made, another survey was conducted by the call center using the same six categories and 70 questions. The surveys were part of ongoing internal organization measurement, and we were not involved in either survey.

Results Employee satisfaction increased dramatically after the organization design changes; all six categories showed improvement in employee commitment scores (Figure B.2.1). The overall employee commitment index (six categories combined) improved to 10th best out of 700 groups. The call center was ranked number one of all groups with more than 100 employees.

FIGURE B.2.1. Employee Commitment Scores before and after Organization Design Change

Discussion   The results suggest that organization design improvements can have positive effects on employee satisfaction and commitment. The call center showed improvements in all six dimensions of the employee questionnaire after the organization design changes. As well, these improvements were relative to other groups, which further supports the notion that the organization design implementation made a difference.

Leadership and fair treatment all improved. We would expect that improving position alignment, increasing clarity of accountabilities and authorities, and matching people to positions and deliverables would positively impact these areas. Customer service scores also improved. We would hypothesize that the former improvements would lead to improved customer service. There is evidence that employee satisfaction can have positive effects on customer satisfaction and consequently financial performance (Heskett et al., 1994; Halloway et al., 1996).

References

Ambachtsheer, K., Capelle, R. & Scheibelhut, T. (1998b) "Improving Pension Fund Performance." *Financial Analysts Journal* 54(5), 15–20.

Buckingham, M., & Coffman, C. (1999). *First, Break All the Rules: What the World's Greatest Managers Do Differently*. New York: Simon & Schuster.

Capelle Associates (1999). Optimizing Organization Design: Improvements in Manager–Direct Report Alignment, Financial Performance and Employee Satisfaction. Research Paper #1.

Hallowell, R., Schlesinger, L. A., & Zornitsky, J. (1996). "Internal Service Quality, Customer and Job Satisfaction: Linkages and Implications for Management." *Human Resource Planning* 19(2), 20.

Heskett, J. L., Jones, T. O., Loveman, G. W., Sasser, W. E. & Schlesinger, L. A. (1994). "Putting the Service Profit Chain to Work." *Harvard Business Review* 72(2), 164–174.

Jaques, E. (1996). *Requisite Organization: A Total System for Effective Managerial Organization and Managerial Leadership for the 21st Century* (2nd ed.). Arlington, VA: Cason Hall & Co.

Capelle Associates Research Paper #3, **Optimizing Organization Design: Improvements in Manager–Direct Report Alignment, Employee Satisfaction and Customer Satisfaction (June 23, 2000b)**

There is research suggesting that both better organization design and better manager–direct report alignment are related to better employee satisfaction, customer satisfaction and financial performance (Ambachtsheer, Capelle & Scheibelhut, 1998; Capelle Associates 1999; Capelle Associates, 2000a). Buckingham and Coffman (1999) concluded from employee satisfaction surveys that one of the most important factors in organization performance is the manager direct-report relationship.

There is considerable research documenting the positive relationship between employee and customer satisfaction (Heskett et al., 1994). Furthermore, customer satisfaction is positively related to financial performance (Heskett et al., 1997). It is believed that employee satisfaction and loyalty result in good customer service. In turn, good customer service leads to customer satisfaction and loyalty (Ulrich et al., 1991) which ultimately results in profit and growth for the organization (Dresner & Xu, 1995). A key to the service-profit chain is obtaining and maintaining high employee satisfaction, as it is a key driver of the system.

In this study, we measure changes in employee satisfaction and customer satisfaction following an organization assessment and implementation. Since manager–direct report alignment is a critical part of organization design, we would hypothesize that this would improve. We would also hypothesize that better organization design and better manager–direct report alignment would result in better employee satisfaction. Further, based partially on the work of Heskett and his colleagues, we would hypothesize that customer satisfaction would also increase.

Method   An organization design review was initially conducted in 1996 at a financial institution. The suggested changes were implemented, which included aligning positions, accountabilities and authorities, people, and deliverables. After suggested changes were implemented, a second review was conducted in 2000. In each review, time span analysis was used to assess manager–direct report alignment. Every employee should have a manager exactly one level or stratum above; this would be called "requisite manager–direct report alignment" (Jaques, 1996).

As well, employee satisfaction and customer satisfaction were measured for three consecutive years by an external human resources consulting firm, independent of this work.

Results   The results show that the requisite manager–direct report alignment improved from 37 percent to 76 percent in the four years (P<0.001); this is a significant increase in the number of managers who are exactly one stratum above their direct reports (18/48 in 1996 to 41/54 in 1999; Figure B.3.1). Comparative information

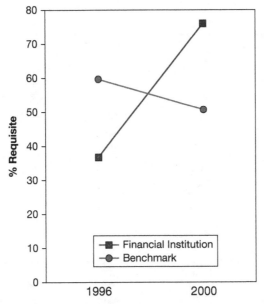

FIGURE B.3.1. Percentage of Requisite Manager–Direct Report Alignment in Financial Institution and Capelle Associates Benchmark Database in 1996 and 2000

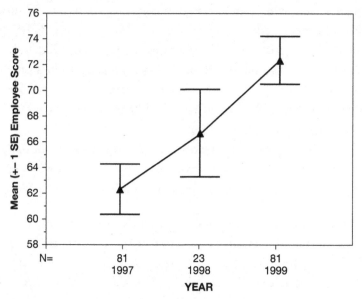

FIGURE B.3.2.   Employee Satisfaction over 3 Years

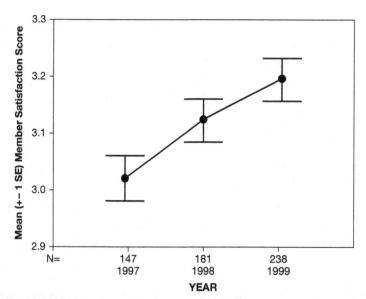

FIGURE B.3.3.   Customer Satisfaction over 3 Years

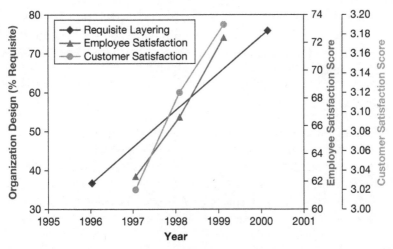

FIGURE B.3.4. Improvements in Manager–Direct Report Alignment, Employee Satisfaction, and Customer Satisfaction

is provided from our organization design–benchmarking database. At the latter time (2000), it included over 8,000 manager–direct report relationships from 27 different organizations.

Within the period between our initial assessment and the follow-up assessment (1997–1999), employee and customer satisfaction both improved significantly (P<0.01, Figures B.3.2 and B.3.3).

In Figure B.3.4, we combine the previous figures to illustrate the strong relationships among manager–direct report alignment, employee satisfaction, and customer satisfaction.

Discussion These results show that there were significant improvements in manager–direct report alignment, employee satisfaction, and customer satisfaction. This followed an organization design assessment and implementation. We would expect the improvement in manager–direct report alignment—this is an important part of organization design. We would also hypothesize improvements in employee satisfaction and customer satisfaction. This is consistent with other reviews (Ambachtsheer,

Capelle & Scheibelhut, 1998; Capelle Associates 1999; Capelle Associates, 2000a), as well as related research on the relationship between employee satisfaction and customer satisfaction (Heskett et al., 1997).

References

Ambachtsheer, K., Capelle, R. & Scheibelhut, T. (1998c) "Improving Pension Fund Performance." *Financial Analysts Journal* 54(5), 15–20.

Buckingham, M., & Coffman, C. (1999). *First, Break All the Rules: What the World's Greatest Managers Do Differently*. New York: Simon & Schuster.

Capelle Associates (1999). Optimizing Organization Design: Improvements in Manager–Direct Report Alignment, Financial Performance and Employee Satisfaction. (Research Paper #1).

Capelle Associates (2000a). Optimizing Organization Design: Improvements in Organization Design and Employee Satisfaction. Research Paper #2.

Dresner, M., & Xu, K. (1995). "Customer Service, Customer Satisfaction, and Corporate Performance." *Journal of Business Logistics* 16(1), 23–41.

Heskett, J. L., Jones, T. O., Loveman, G. W., Sasser, W. E., & Schlesinger, L. A. (1994). "Putting the Service Profit Chain to Work." *Harvard Business Review* 72(2), 164–174.

Heskett, J. L., Sasser, W. E. & Schlesinger, L. A. (1997). *The Service Profit Chain: How Leading Companies Link Profit and Growth to Loyalty, Satisfaction, and Value*. New York: Free Press.

Jaques, E. (1996). *Requisite Organization: A Total System for Effective Managerial Organization and Managerial Leadership for the 21st Century* (2nd ed.). Arlington, VA: Cason Hall & Co.

Ulrich, D., Halbrook, R., Meder, D., Stuchlik, M., & Thorpe, S. (1991). "Employee and Customer Attachment: Synergies for Competitive HR." *Human Resource Planning* 14(2), 89–103.

Capelle Associates Research Paper #4, **Optimizing Organization Design: Improvements in Manager–Direct Report Alignment and Employee Satisfaction (March 1, 2000c)**

There is research suggesting that both better organization design and better manager–direct report alignment are related to better employee satisfaction, customer satisfaction, and financial performance (Ambachtsheer, Capelle & Scheibelhut, 1998; Capelle

Associates 1999; Capelle Associates, 2000a; Capelle Associates, 2000b). Every employee should have a manager exactly one level or stratum above. This is called requisite alignment (Jaques, 1996). Buckingham and Coffman (1999) concluded from employee satisfaction surveys that one of the most important factors in organization performance is the manager direct-report relationship. There is also considerable research documenting the positive relationship between employee and customer satisfaction (Heskett et al., 1994). Furthermore, customer satisfaction is positively related to financial performance (Heskett et al., 1997).

In this study we measure changes in manager–direct report alignment and employee satisfaction following an organization design assessment and implementation. Since manager–direct report alignment is a critical part of organization design, we would hypothesize that this would improve. We would also hypothesize that better organization design and better manager–report alignment would result in better employee satisfaction.

Method   A distribution division of a major organization underwent an organization review in 1996. The review consisted of interviewing about 50 individuals and a review of over 1,000 positions. At this time, employees completed a questionnaire that measured employee satisfaction. This was part of regular surveys that the larger organization conducts. The survey measures the current level of employee engagement.

An implementation of organization design improvements was completed. This included alignment of positions, accountabilities and authorities, people, and deliverables. After 18 months in 1998, the distribution division had a second organization review. As well, the same employee opinion survey was again completed by employees.

Results   There was a significantly higher percentage of requisite manager–direct report relationships (manager exactly one level or stratum above direct report) relative to our comparative benchmark

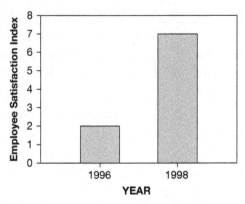

FIGURE B.4.1. Employee Satisfaction Index before (1996) and after (1998) Organization Design Changes

(91.5 percent vs. 48.5 percent). At the time, this was the highest result that we have encountered. There was less compression (manager and direct report in same layer or stratum) than we normally find (5.5 percent vs. 27.1 percent). The proportion of gaps (manager more than one layer or stratum above direct report) was also lower relative to the comparative benchmark (3.1 percent vs. 24.4 percent). The results show a significant improvement in manager–direct report alignment. This conclusion was reinforced by many comments in the second organization review.

Employee opinion survey results improved significantly after the organization design changes (Figure B.4.1). The overall score was significantly higher in 1998 than in 1996 (t-test, $P<0.01$).

Discussion   The results show that manager–direct report alignment can be significantly improved as a result of an organization design assessment and implementation process. This is not surprising since improvement of manager–direct report alignment is a significant part of an organization design implementation. Further, the results show that employee satisfaction improved significantly after the organization design implementation. Again, this is not surprising. One would expect that greater clarity would result in better employee satisfaction.

These results are consistent with other research (Ambachtsheer, Capelle & Scheibelhut, 1998; Capelle Associates, 1999; Capelle Associates, 2000a; Capelle Associates, 2000b).

There is considerable evidence that the manager–direct report relationship and employee satisfaction are important to performance (Buckingham & Coffman, 1999); Heskett et al., 1994; Heskett et al., 1997). There is growing evidence that improving the manager–direct report alignment can improve both of these variables.

References

Ambachtsheer, K., Capelle, R. & Scheibelhut, T. (1998d) "Improving Pension Fund Performance." *Financial Analysts Journal* 54(5), 15–20.

Buckingham, M., & Coffman, C. (1999). *First, Break All the Rules: What the World's Greatest Managers Do Differently*. New York: Simon & Schuster.

Capelle Associates (1999). Optimizing Organization Design: Improvements in Manager–Direct Report Alignment, Financial Performance and Employee Satisfaction. Research Paper #1.

Capelle Associates (2000a). Optimizing Organization Design: Improvements in Organization Design and Employee Satisfaction. Research Paper #2.

Capelle Associates (2000b). Optimizing Organization Design: Improvements in Manager–Direct Report Alignment, Employee Satisfaction and Customer Satisfaction. Research Paper #3.

Jaques, E. (1996). *Requisite Organization: A Total System for Effective Managerial Organization and Managerial Leadership for the 21st Century* (2nd ed.). Arlington, VA: Cason Hall & Co.

Heskett, J. L., Jones, T. O., Loveman, G. W., Sasser, W. E., & Schlesinger, L. A. (1994c). "Putting the Service Profit Chain to Work." *Harvard Business Review* 72(2), 164–174.

Heskett, J. L., Sasser, W. E. & Schlesinger, L. A. (1997). *The Service Profit Chain: How Leading Companies Link Profit and Growth to Loyalty, Satisfaction, and Value*. New York: Free Press.

Capelle Associates Research Paper #5, **Optimizing Organization Design: Improvements in Manager–Direct Report Alignment, Leadership and Direction, and Employee Commitment (March 1, 2000d)**

There is research suggesting that both better organization design and better manager–direct report alignment are related to better employee satisfaction, customer satisfaction, and financial performance (Ambachtsheer, Capelle & Scheibelhut, 1998; Capelle Associates 1999; Capelle Associates, 2000a; Capelle Associates, 2000b; Capelle Associates, 2000c). Every employee should have a manager exactly one level or stratum above. This is called "requisite alignment" (Jaques, 1996).

Buckingham and Coffman (1999) concluded from employee satisfaction surveys that one of the most important factors in organization performance is the manager–direct report relationship. There is also considerable research documenting the positive relationship between employee and customer satisfaction (Heskett et al., 1994). Furthermore, customer satisfaction is positively related to financial performance (Heskett et al., 1997).

In this study we measure changes in manager–direct report alignment, leadership and direction, and employee commitment following an organization design assessment and implementation. Since manager–direct report alignment is a critical part of organization design, we would hypothesize that this would improve. We would also hypothesize that better organization design and better manager–report alignment would result in better leadership and direction and employee commitment. We would consider both of these to be subsets of employee satisfaction.

Method The manager–direct report alignment of over 200 employees in a transportation division of a major organization was assessed in 1997. In what should have been a Stratum 4 (four-level) organization, there was only one level of management and most of the positions (91 percent) were at the first level (Stratum 1–level).

This resulted in less than 7 percent of the manager–direct report positions being requisite (properly aligned). It also resulted in gaps occurring (manager positions too distant from direct report positions) in over 92 percent of the cases. Furthermore, less than 4 percent of the total positions were manager positions and the average span of control (number of direct reports) was 29 employees per manager. This was a significant issue and was related to the lack of a sufficient management infrastructure. The organization design assessment recommended the clarification of two levels of management (Stratum 2 and 3) between the Stratum 1 employees and the Stratum 4 manager. These suggested changes were implemented by 1998.

An organization design implementation was completed. Employee opinion surveys were conducted before (1996) and after (1999) the implementation (1997–98) by the organization. One would expect that this change would have a major impact on manager–direct report relationships and employee satisfaction.

Results Manager–direct report relationships, as measured by leadership and direction, improved after the organization design improvement, which included the manager–direct report alignment (Figure B.5.1). This index measures the degree of satisfaction

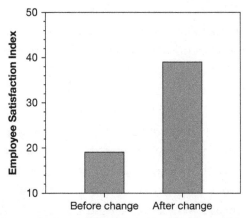

FIGURE B.5.1. Leadership and Direction Scores before and after an Organization Design Implementation That Included Manager–Direct Report Alignment

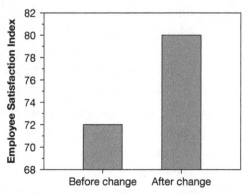

FIGURE B.5.2.   Organization Commitment Scores before and after an Organization Design Implementation That Included Manager–Direct Report Alignment

and sense of motivation employees derive from the leadership of their immediate supervisors. This index also reflects employee well-being and their motivation for greater productivity.

Organization commitment also improved following the organization implementation (Figure B.5.2). This index measures the degree to which employees are committed to their organization and the degree to which they perceive being valued by their organization. Employee loyalty can have beneficial effects on organization performance.

Discussion   The results suggest that improvements in organization design, including manager–direct report alignment, are related to improvements in leadership and direction and employee commitment. We would consider these both to be measures of employee satisfaction.

This research underlines the importance of appropriate manager–direct report alignment. When this was improved, there was a dramatic improvement in the leadership and direction score. However, the impact did not stop here. it carried over to organization commitment, which is critical to employee satisfaction, engagement, and retention.

These results are consistent with other research (Ambachtsheer, Capelle & Scheibelhut, 1998; Capelle Associates 1999; Capelle Associates, 2000a; Capelle Associates, 2000b; Capelle Associates, 2000c).

There is considerable evidence that the manager–direct report relationship and employee satisfaction are important to performance (Buckingham & Coffman, 1999); Heskett et al., 1994; Heskett et al., 1997). There is growing evidence that improving the manager–direct report alignment can improve both of these variables.

References

Ambachtsheer, K., Capelle, R. & Scheibelhut, T. (1998) "Improving Pension Fund Performance." *Financial Analysts Journal* 54(5), 15–20.

Buckingham, M., & Coffman, C. (1999). *First, Break All the Rules: What the World's Greatest Managers Do Differently*. New York: Simon & Schuster.

Capelle Associates (1999). Optimizing Organization Design: Improvements in Manager–Direct Report Alignment, Financial Performance and Employee Satisfaction. Research Paper #1.

Capelle Associates (2000a). Optimizing Organization Design: Improvements in Organization Design and Employee Satisfaction. Research Paper #2.

Capelle Associates (2000b). Optimizing Organization Design: Improvements in Manager–Direct Report Alignment, Employee Satisfaction and Customer Satisfaction. Research Paper #3.

Capelle Associates (2000c). Optimizing Organization Design: Improvements in Manager–Direct Report Alignment and Employee Satisfaction. Research Paper #4.

Heskett, J. L., Jones, T. O., Loveman, G. W., Sasser, W. E. & Schlesinger, L. A. (1994). "Putting the Service Profit Chain to Work." *Harvard Business Review* 72(2), 164–174.

Heskett, J. L., Sasser, W. E. & Schlesinger, L. A. (1997). *The Service Profit Chain: How Leading Companies Link Profit and Growth to Loyalty, Satisfaction, and Value*. New York: Free Press.

Jaques, E. (1996). *Requisite Organization: A Total System for Effective Managerial Organization and Managerial Leadership for the 21st Century* (2nd ed.). Arlington, VA: Cason Hall & Co.

Capelle Associates Research Paper #6, The Information Processing Capability of an Employee and the Job Grade of a Position: Is There a Relationship? (Oct 16, 2000e)

We would expect that, if job evaluation systems were reasonably accurate, higher job grades within an organization would have more complex work than lower job grades. We would also expect that, if promotion systems were reasonably accurate, those in higher job grades would have high levels of information processing capability than those in lower job grades.

Jaques and Cason (1994), in a landmark study, demonstrated that the information processing capability of an individual could be assessed, and that each level or stratum of an organization required a different type of information processing capability. Higher levels of work, which are more complex, require higher levels of information processing capability.

Method   We assessed the information processing capability of over 400 executives and senior managers in a large organization using the approach developed by Jaques and Cason (1994). Each individual selected and discussed two complex topics. The responses were tape recorded and transcribed. The transcripts were independently assessed by two trained assessors, and a conclusion was drawn about the information processing capability of each candidate. The assessors did not have any prior knowledge on the job grade, title or salary of the interviewee (single-blind method). After the assessments were completed, job grades for individuals were provided by organization. These were used for the analysis.

Results   The hypothesis was supported in that individuals in higher job grades had higher levels of information processing capability (ANOVA, $F=4.9$, $P=0.008$, Figure B.6.1). The information processing capability averages on shown in terms of strata (i.e., the averages ranged from mid Stratum 3 (between 3.5 and 3.6) to high Stratum 3 (close to 3.9).

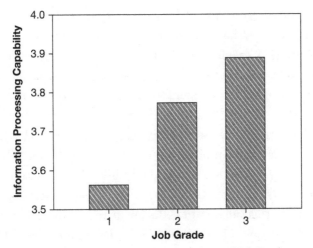

FIGURE B.6.1.   Information Processing Capability and Job Grade

Discussion   These results support the hypothesis that one can measure information processing capability through an independent interview process, and that higher levels of individual information processing capability are related to being in more complex positions as measured by job grade. They further support the original work completed by Jaques and Cason (1994).

Reference

Jaques, E. & Cason, K. 1994. *Human Capability*. Cason Hall & Co: Fall Church, VA.

Capelle Associates Research Paper #7, Information Processing Capability, Time Span, and Job Grade (Sept 14, 2000f)

The matching of people to positions is a critical step in organization design. It is often best done after positions have been optimally aligned (organization structure), and accountabilities and authorities have been clarified. There are three key factors to matching people to positions. First, employees should have the skilled knowledge required by the position. The second is that employees should have application (i.e., value the work), which is important if employees are going to fully apply themselves. For example, some technical and professional individual contributors move into management positions, but do not perform as well in this area because they do not value management work (e.g., delegating work and supervising employees). The third is having the required information processing capability. While the first two factors are more commonly used in organizations, the last factor, the evaluation of information processing capability, is unique to this organization design method, which is based on the work of Jaques (1964, 1968, 1996), Jaques and Cason (1994), and others.

Complexity of information processing can be evaluated by observing the categories of information processing that an individual uses (see Jaques & Cason 1994). This results in an evaluation of an individual's information processing capability. This is a measure of the stratum of work that an individual is currently capable of doing, assuming skilled knowledge and application (i.e., valuing the work) for the particular position. Information processing capability is an expression of the person's raw native ability—the individual's current maximum complexity of information processing (Jaques & Cason, 1994).

Mismatches between complexity of work in a position and the information processing capability of an individual should be avoided. There are two possible mismatches. One is that the individual is working below his level of capability (i.e., being "underemployed"), which often results in low employee satisfaction and turnover issues. The second possible mismatch is that the individual is over promoted, and is in a position with greater complexity than the individual is capable of handling. This process of climbing up the hierarchical ladder can go on until the employee reaches a position where he or she is no longer competent—the Peter Principle (Peter & Hull, 1969). The result is that the required work of the position is not satisfactorily completed because the individual does not have the right level of capability.

There can be an additional benefit of evaluating complexity of information processing in an organization. Information processing capability matures over time in relatively predictable patterns (Jaques & Cason, 1994). Determination of future information processing capability (highest level, or stratum, in the future, which an individual could work) can be extrapolated through the use of progression curves (Jaques, 1968). This can provide valuable information on the "bench strength" of the organization. This is particularly important because demographic research shows that there will be a shortage of employees in senior positions (e.g., baby boomers begin to retire—see Fusaro, 2001; Brock, 2003). Talent pool development can be used in organizations to plan current and future human resources requirements. Detailed information on the distribution of talent across functions and strata within the organization can be obtained with this empirical method.

There are two main methods for assessing the information processing capability of an individual using this approach (Jaques and Cason 1994). One method uses an external consultant; the other is conducted internally by the individual's manager and manager once removed. In the external evaluation methodology, a trained consultant interviews the individual. The interview is taped and then transcribed. The transcription is then analyzed and categorized according to Jaques modes of information processing capability. The second method is to have a judgment made by the manager and manager once removed of the individual. Ideally, the organization should be properly stratified before this method is used.

There is considerable research that a talent pool process conducted in an organization can reliably judge employees' information processing capability. The employees are evaluated by their managers in a meeting of peer managers. The manager once removed (MoR—the employee's manager's manager (Jaques & Cason, 1994)) chairs the meeting where the rating takes place.

This serves to apply a self-leveling dynamic to the evaluations, as managers hear the evaluations of their peers and can comment. At the end of the meeting, the manager once removed signs off on the evaluations based on the recommendations of the employee's manager. This process, together with the applied methodology, establishes a common language that aids in managerial judgment.

Participating in a talent pool review process also greatly assists managers in coming to grips with the concepts of complexity of work and patterns of information processing. This understanding is invaluable in designing an organization and in placing people into positions.

Jaques (1964, 1996) has developed a method for measuring the complexity of work in a position (time span analysis). The time span of a position is determined by the deliverable within the position that has the longest target completion time. This method can be used to determine how many layers or strata an organization should have and the placement of every position in the correct layer (vertical alignment). A position with a longer time span is more complex than a position with a shorter time span. Also, positions in higher strata should have longer time spans than positions in lower strata.

We would predict that time span and information processing capability would be positively related in an organization that properly matches individual capability with position requirements. We tested this hypothesis by comparing scores obtained from a financial institution.

Method Information processing capability judgments were obtained from two talent pool meetings. In these meetings, managers evaluated information processing capability of direct reports, with comments from peer managers and approval from their immediate manager. In total, 197 individuals were evaluated in 1997 and 240 individuals were evaluated in 1998. The correlation, for individuals assessed in the two meetings, was 0.81 ($P < 0.05$).

To obtain information processing capability scores from the interview method, individuals at the financial institution were interviewed for 30 minutes. Those interviewed volunteered to do so, with the understanding that they would receive feedback but their results would be kept confidential. The discussions were tape recorded and later transcribed. Individuals were asked to discuss two of six possible big topics (e.g., "How would you solve the drug problem?" or "How would you improve the performance of your financial institution?"). In total, 51 individuals were interviewed. Two raters independently assigned information processing scores to each participant from the transcribed tapes. Any differences were resolved.

Time span information was collected by interviewing all 110 managers and supervisors within the organization. The interviews were scheduled so that each manager could discuss her work for up to 25 minutes and that of each immediate direct report for up to 5 minutes. In situations in which a manager had more than four sub-ordinates, each with an identical position and doing identical work, no more than 20 minutes would be taken to focus on the position.

Each manager was asked to state the deliverable with the longest target completion time that was delegated to each direct report. This provides the time span for each position. Each manager was also asked for a perception of his time span. This provides a check on clarity of delegation. Time span analysis is a measure of the complexity of work, and can be used to determine how many layers an organization should have and the correct layer or stratum for every position.

Results   We found that the time span of a position was significantly related to the incumbent's information processing capability (as measured through the talent pool process) ($r=0.792$, $P<0.001$, $n=43$). This is shown in Figure B.7.1.

There was a statistically significant relationship between the information processing capability measured by the talent pool process and that measured by the interview method ($r=0.334$,

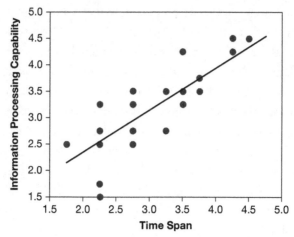

FIGURE B.7.1.   Time Span of Position and Information Processing Capability of Incumbent in a Position

P<0.05, n=49). Both assessment methods should not be affected by the gender of the employee; our research shows that the gender of the employee has no effect on the measurement of current processing capability (t-test: interview process: P=0.795; talent pool process: P=0.127).

We further found evidence that both methods of assessing an individual's information processing capability are reliable. Two annual Talent Pool processes showed a significant relationship (r=0.911, P<0.001, n=29), and the interview assessments by two independent judges also showed a significant relationship (r=0.521, P<0.001, n=50).

We also found that the organization's internal job grade system (a measure of complexity of work) was positively related to both time span (a measure of complexity of work) (r=0.781, P<0.001, n=43) and talent pool score (a measure of an individual's information processing capability) (r=0.827, P<0.001, n=49).

Discussion   As predicted, time span and information processing capability (talent pool score) are positively related in an organization that properly matches individual capability with position requirements. Furthermore, talent pool scores were positively related to scores obtained through an interview process. The internal evaluation method (talent pool) is preferred because it keeps the accountability for the evaluation and development of the talent pool where it belongs—inside the organization and with the managers of the employees.

We also found that the company's job-grade system was positively correlated with both time span and talent pool scores. In another study (Capelle Associates 2000), we found that information processing capability as measured by an independent interview process was related to job grade. These results support a number of hypotheses on information processing capability and its relationship to complexity of work.

References

Brock, F. (2003). "Who'll Sit at the Boomers' Desks?" *New York Times*. October 12.

Capelle Associates (2000). The Information Processing Capability of an Employee and the Job Grade of a Position: Is There A Relationship? Research Paper #6.

Fusaro, R. (2001). "Needed: Experienced Workers." *Harvard Business Review* 79, 20–21.

Jaques, E. (1964). *Time-Span Handbook: The Use of Time-Span of Discretion to Measure the Level of Work in Employment Roles and to Arrange an Equitable Payment Structure*. London: Heinemann.

Jaques, E. (1968). *Progression Handbook: How to Use Earnings Progression Data Sheets for Assessing Individual Capacity, for Progression, and for Manpower Planning and Development*. Carbondale, IL: Southern Illinois University Press.

Jaques, E. & Cason, K. (1994). *Human Capability: A Study of Individual Potential and Its Application*. Falls Church, VA: Cason Hall.

Jaques, E. (1996). *Requisite Organization: A Total System for Effective Managerial Organization and Managerial Leadership for the 21st Century* (2nd ed.). Arlington, VA: Cason Hall.

Peter, L.J. & Hull, R. (1969). *The Peter Principle*. New York: Bantam Books.

Capelle Associates Research Paper #8, Appropriateness of Compensation, Overall Employee Satisfaction, and Employee Satisfaction with Compensation: Review of 20 Organizations (March 28, 2003a)

Felt fair pay is the employee's judgment of perceived financial value of their level of work. Felt fair pay is a hypothetical concept while actual pay is the compensation an employee is paid. It has been shown that felt fair pay is positively correlated with Jaques' time span measure (Richardson, 1971). Given this relationship between time span and felt fair pay, one would predict that employees whose actual pay corresponds to their time span would be more satisfied than employees who are not appropriately compensated.

Method   To test this notion, we looked at 20 organizations in which we had collected time span information, compensation information, and employee satisfaction information. Time span information on individuals was provided by their immediate managers. Compensation information was provided by the organization. Employee satisfaction was determined by employee completion of a questionnaire that consisted of 74 questions. Employees were asked to respond on a six-point Likert scale to statements concerning factors such as the organization, workload, skills, and their relationship with manager. External compensation survey data from the Toronto Board of Trade was used to determine appropriate compensation for each stratum or level of the organization.

Results   Organizations that have a larger percentage of employees that are appropriately paid for their level of work have higher employee satisfaction scores than organizations that have a lower percentage of appropriately paid employees ($r=0.466$, $P < 0.05$, $n = 20$; Figure B.8.1).

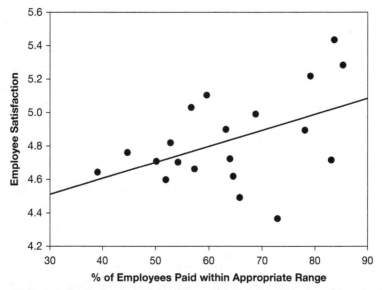

FIGURE B.8.1. Relationship between Overall Employee Satisfaction and Percentage of Employees Paid within Appropriate Range

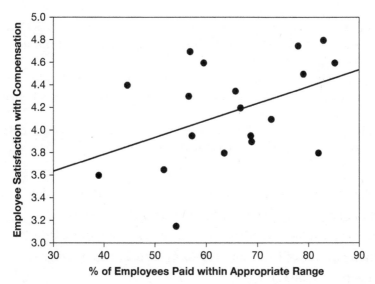

FIGURE B.8.2. Relationship between Employee Satisfaction with Compensation and Percentage Employees Paid within Appropriate Range

On a specific question related to compensation (my compensation is fair for the work that I do), organizations that have a higher percentage of employees that are appropriately paid for their level of work have higher scores on satisfaction with compensation than organizations that have a lower percentage of equitably paid employees ($r = 0.446$, $P < 0.05$, $n = 19$; Figure B.8.2).

Discussion   Our results suggest a strong relationship between an organization's compensation system and its employee satisfaction. Organizations that pay their employees appropriately (i.e., time span equals compensation span) have higher employee satisfaction scores than organizations that compensate their employees outside of the expected range.

Given that employee satisfaction is positively correlated with customer satisfaction and financial performance (Heskett et al., 1997), the effects could be more broadly beneficial.

References

Heskett, J. L., Sasser, W. E. & Schlesinger, L. A. (1997). *The Service Profit Chain: How Leading Companies Link Profit and Growth to Loyalty, Satisfaction, and Value.* New York: Free Press.

Jaques, E. (1996). *Requisite Organization: A Total System for Effective Managerial Organization and Managerial Leadership for the 21st Century* (2nd ed.). Arlington, VA: Cason Hall.

Richardson, R. (1971). *Fair Pay and Work: An Empirical Study of Fair Pay Perception and Time Span of Discretion.* London: Heinemann.

Capelle Associates Research Paper #9, Organization Design, Manager–Direct Report Alignment, and Organization Performance in Canadian Private Sector Companies: Results from Surveys of CEOs and Heads of Human Resources (March 28, 2003a)

There is research that suggests that the organization design in general and manager–direct report alignment in particular are important factors related to employee satisfaction, customer satisfaction, and financial performance (Ambachtsheer, Capelle & Scheibel-hut, 1998; Capelle Associates 1999; Capelle Associates, 2000a; Capelle Associates, 2000b; Capelle Associates, 2000c; Capelle Associates 2000d). Every employee should have a manager exactly one level or stratum above. This is called "requisite alignment" (Jaques, 1996). Buckingham and Coffman (1999) concluded from employee satisfaction surveys that one of the most important factors in organization performance is the manager–direct report relationship. There is also considerable research documenting the positive relationship between employee and customer satisfaction (Heskett et al., 1994). Furthermore, customer satisfaction is positively related to financial performance (Heskett et al., 1997).

This paper presents a survey of CEOs and heads of Human Resources on their evaluations of these variables.

Method   Two surveys were developed to assess the state of organization design and organization performance of Canada's largest 2,000 private sector companies. One was designed for the CEO while the other was designed for the head of Human Resources. We asked both executives to evaluate their organization on a six-point scale relative to comparable organizations. CEOs were asked to evaluate organization performance (financial performance, employee satisfaction, and customer satisfaction). Heads of Human Resources were asked to evaluate organization design, manager–direct report alignment, and manager–direct report relationships. Each respondent was given their own envelope and asked to return their questionnaire directly to us.

The surveys were conducted in the springs of 2000 and 2001. In total, 210 organizations responded in 2000, for a response rate of 10.5 percent. This response rate is comparable to prior work involving executives (Capron, 1999). A variety of industries across Canada were represented with an average workforce of 2,331 per organization. In 2001, 170 organizations responded (response rate of 8.5 percent). The average workforce was 2,663 employees per organization. The average number of layers from the CEO to the frontline employees was 5.4.

We found no significant differences between years on the responses to the survey questions. If we restrict our analysis to only the 53 organizations that completed the survey both years, we also found no significant differences between survey years (repeated measures t-test). Also, the correlation values did not differ significantly between years for any of the comparisons presented in this report (Hays, 1988).

Results   These results show that there is a positive relationship between organization design and organization performance. Companies that have better organization design as perceived by head of Human Resources had significantly better performance as perceived by the CEO (Figure B.9.1; year 2000: Pearson r=0.344, P<0.001, n=162 companies; year 2001: Pearson r = 0.368, P<0.001, n=122).

Other relationships in the survey are of interest. These include the following.

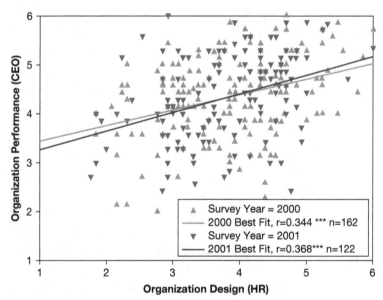

FIGURE B.9.1.   Positive Relationship between Organization Design and Organization Performance (*** P < 0.001)

- There was a positive correlation between the manager–direct report relationship (provided by head of Human Resources) and the employee satisfaction (provided by the CEO) ($r=0.199$, $P<0.001$).
- There was a positive correlation between employee satisfaction and customer satisfaction (both provided by the CEO) ($r=0.535$, $P<0.001$).
- There was a positive correlation between customer satisfaction and financial performance (both provided by CEO) ($r=0.437$, $P<0.001$).

Organization Design–Organization Performance Model We have developed an Organization Design–Organization Performance Model that summarizes our survey findings (Figure B.9.2). These show the following. First, organization design and manager–direct report alignment are positively related to each other. Second, both organization design and manager–direct report alignment are positively related to relationship with manager, employee satisfaction, and customer satisfaction, which in turn are positively related to financial performance. Third, organization design and manager–direct report alignment are directly and positively related to financial performance. Fourth, relationship with manager is positively related to employee satisfaction; employee satisfaction is positively related to customer satisfaction; and all three are related to financial performance.

Validity A measuring instrument is considered valid if it measures what it is supposed to measure.

To demonstrate the validity of our survey, we will compare its findings to an external data source, our benchmark database. We will also present some research on validity comparing the financial component of the survey to data obtained from an external source (Dun & Bradstreet).

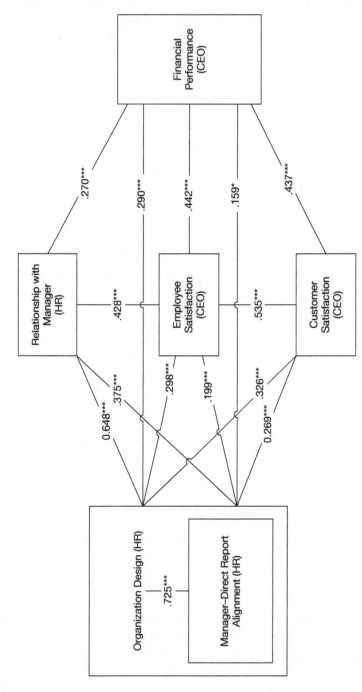

FIGURE B.9.2. Organization Design–Organization Performance Model (* P < 0.05, *** P < 0.001)

Survey 2000, Survey 2001, and Capelle Associates Benchmark Database   Capelle Associates has a database of over 59,000 manager–direct report relationships from 76 organizations. In this database, the manager–direct report relationship (question 72 in the surveys) is considered optimal if the manager is exactly one layer (stratum) above a direct report (a person who reports directly to the manager), both in terms of the complexity of work that the manager does, and the manager's capability to do that complexity of work. If the manager and the direct report are in the same layer (stratum), the manager will likely micromanage and the direct report will likely not be able to use her full capability. If the manager and the manager's direct report are more than one layer (stratum) apart, the manager will likely not provide sufficient direction, and the work of the direct report will likely be suboptimal (see Jaques 1996). This is a direct measure of the related factors, and is therefore a more objective measure of organization design than the perceptions of individuals in surveys.

Table B.9.1 compares layering, delegation, and compensation scores from three sources: Survey 2000, Survey 2001, and the Capelle Associates Benchmark Database.

On average in Survey 2001, the heads of HR estimated that 53.5 percent of manager–direct report relationships (layering) are optimally aligned (does not over or undermanage; not micromanaging or too distant). There was no significant difference in layering scores between Survey 2001 and the previous year's survey, Survey 2000 (t-test, t=0.51, P=0.613).

Table B.9.1.   Organization Design Surveys Compared to Capelle Associates Benchmark

Percentage of situations where:	Data Source		
	Survey 2000	Survey 2001	Capelle Benchmark
Layering is optimal	54.8%	53.5%	55.2%
Delegation is optimal	60.6%	61.7%	64.0%
Compensation is optimal	70.9%	71.3%	63.1%

The Capelle Associates Benchmark has 55.2 percent of manager–direct report relationships that are optimally aligned (the employee and manager are one layer apart). On average, the heads of HR in 2001 estimated that 61.7 percent of manager–direct report relationships have appropriate delegation by managers (Table B.9.1). Survey 2001 did not differ significantly from Survey 2000 (t-test, t=0.56, P=0.579). The Capelle Associates Benchmark has found that 64 percent of manager–direct report relationships have appropriate delegation by managers. Finally in Survey 2001, the heads of HR estimated that 71.3 percent of manager–direct report relationships have appropriate compensation. This number is similar to the Survey 2000 number of 70.9 percent (t-test, t=0.23, P=818). The Capelle Associates Benchmark has found that 63.1 percent of manager–direct report relationships have appropriate compensation in their organization.

This is a strong validation of the accuracy of the assessments of the heads of Human Resources. In terms of both the manager–direct report alignment (layering) and clarity of delegation, there are no major differences between their assessments and the Capelle Associates comparative database of manager–direct report relationships. There is roughly a 7 to 8 percent difference between the Capelle Benchmark and survey compensation numbers, but this is not surprising given the nature of the data and the wide variety of compensation systems that exist. In our experience, most compensation systems place too much emphasis on the size of a budget and number of employees supervised, while our measurement approach avoids these issues. As well, we often find differences between what job descriptions specify for individuals (and therefore what they are paid), and the real complexity of work that they do. It is not surprising to us, therefore, that there is some difference in assessing the appropriateness of compensation between the assessments of the heads of Human Resources and our benchmark database.

Table B.9.2. Comparison between Survey 2000 CEO Financial Performance Measures and Dun & Bradstreet's Industrial Sector Financial Performance Measures

		Dun and Bradstreet Financial Measures	
		Return on Assets	Return on Net Worth
Survey 2000 Financial Performance Measures	Profitability	0.379**	0.226*
	Return on Investment	0.379**	0.231*

Survey 2000 Financial Performance Measures Compared to Dun & Bradstreet Financial Measures As another test of validity, financial information was obtained from Dun & Bradstreet for participating organizations. This data provided the positioning of the company for return on assets and return on net worth. The survey questionnaire asked the CEO to rank the profitability and the return on investment of their organization against comparable organizations. If the CEO was accurate in representing her company, one would expect a correlation amongst these measures from different sources. The results show a significant correlation between Survey 2000 and the Dun & Bradstreet financial measures (Table B.9.2).

Based on the combined results of all of these tests, we are confident that Survey 2001 is measuring what it was intended to measure: the state of organization design in Canadian private sector corporations.

Discussion These surveys provide a different perspective on organization design and organization performance variables. However, they are consistent with prior research.

First, we would consider manager–direct alignment to be the most powerful organization design factor related to organization performance. Both factors have been shown to be related to employee satisfaction, customer satisfaction and financial performance (Ambachtsheer, Capelle & Scheibelhut, 1998; Capelle

Associates, 1999; Capelle Associates, 2000a; Capelle Associates, 2000b; Capelle Associates, 2000c; Capelle Associates, 2000d).

Second, Buckingham and Coffman (1999) concluded from employee satisfaction surveys that one of the most important factors in organization performance is the manager direct-report relationship. The manager–direct report alignment is a significant underlying factor driving this relationship.

Third, there is also considerable research documenting the positive relationship between employee and customer satisfaction (Heskett et al., 1994) and financial performance (Heskett et al., 1997). This study also shows these positive relationships.

We would have one caution. Surveys of this nature that rely on only two roles (CEO and head of Human Resources) run the risk of same source bias. However, this risk has been mitigated in several ways. Many of the ratings between the two roles did not overlap (e.g., organization design and financial performance); the survey was repeated over two years; independent information was also used (e.g., Dun & Bradstreet financials and Capelle Associates Benchmarking Database). In addition to this, the results are quite consistent with other results that we have found with other research methods.

References

Ambachtsheer, K., Capelle, R. & Scheibelhut, T. (1998) "Improving Pension Fund Performance." *Financial Analysts Journal* 54(5), 15–20.

Buckingham, M. & Coffman, C. (1999). *First, Break All the Rules: What the World's Greatest Managers Do Differently*. New York: Simon & Schuster.

Capelle Associates (1999). Optimizing Organization Design: Improvements in Manager–Direct Report Alignment, Financial Performance and Employee Satisfaction. Research Paper #1.

Capelle Associates (2000a). Optimizing Organization Design: Improvements in Organization Design and Employee Satisfaction. Research Paper #2.

Capelle Associates (2000b). Optimizing Organization Design: Improvements in Manager–Direct Report Alignment, Employee Satisfaction and Customer Satisfaction. Research Paper #3.

Capelle Associates (2000c). Optimizing Organization Design: Improvements in Manager–Direct Report Alignment and Employee Satisfaction. Research Paper #4.

Capelle Associates (2000d). Optimizing Organization Design: Improvements in Manager–Direct Report Alignment, Leadership and Direction, and Employee Commitment. Research Paper #5.

Capron, L. (1999). "The Long-Term Performance of Horizontal Acquisitions." *Strategic Management Journal* 20, 987–1018.

Jaques, E. (1996). *Requisite Organization: A Total System for Effective Managerial Organization and Managerial Leadership for the 21st Century* (2nd ed.). Arlington, VA: Cason Hall.

Hays, W. L. (1988). *Statistics* (4th ed.). New York: Holt, Rinehart, and Winston.

Heskett, J. L., Jones, T. O., Loveman, G. W., Sasser, W. E. & Schlesinger, L. A. (1994). "Putting the Service Profit Chain to Work." *Harvard Business Review* 72(2), 164–174.

Heskett, J. L., Sasser, W. E. & Schlesinger, L. A. (1997). *The Service Profit Chain: How Leading Companies Link Profit and Growth to Loyalty, Satisfaction, and Value.* New York: Free Press.

Capelle Associates Research Paper #10, Task Alignment: A More Micro Organization Alignment Approach (Dec 16, 2004a)

The major focus of our approach to improving organization performance through enhancing organization design would be the alignment of four factors. The first is the alignment of positions vertically and functionally. This provides the spine of the organization and the all-important manager–direct report alignment. The second is the alignment of accountabilities and authorities. This would include employee, supervisor, manager, manager once removed, and cross functional accountabilities and authorities. The third is the alignment of employees to positions. The fourth is the alignment of deliverables to positions.

These factors provide the broader framework that we would consider to be critical to successful organization design. A key to alignment of positions is a measure of the complexity of work called "time span" (Jaques, 1996). A key to the alignment of people to positions is individual information processing capability (Jaques & Cason, 1994). However, it is also possible to move to a more micro analysis and alignment. This would be a focus on tasks.

We would define a task as an activity carried out by an individual. A task would generally have input (receiving something), throughput (doing something), and output (delivering something). In defining tasks, it is necessary to decide how micro or macro to be. We generally find that an individual would have 10 to 12 tasks on average, with a range of 5 tasks to 20 tasks.

There are numerous opportunities to improve tasks. One can improve the amount of time they take, their cost, the percentage of tasks that are core to the mission of the organization, etc. However, one of the most interesting is determining whether or not they are appropriate for the level or stratum of a position.

We find that task analysis is most valuable at lower levels in the organization, specifically at Stratum 1 (first-level employee) and Stratum 2 levels (professional or manager). We have developed a method for determining if tasks can be completed at Stratum 1 levels or should be completed at Stratum 2 (and possibly higher) levels. The fundamental difference is that Stratum 1 tasks are proceduralized and can be completed by Stratum 1 positions staffed by Stratum 1 capable individuals. Stratum 2 tasks require a diagnostic capability and therefore should be assigned to Stratum 2 or above positions. We have not found a method for differentiating Stratum 3 or above tasks. However, our experience is that the greatest value is at the Stratum 1 and Stratum 2 levels.

Method   We have completed 15 task alignment reviews and all are included in this study. For each of these reviews, a task list was gathered from a cross section of Stratum 1 and 2 employees in the various positions in the organization. The tasks were categorized by a number of variables, including whether they could be completed at a Stratum 1 level or whether they needed to be completed at a Stratum 2 or above level. For this purpose Stratum 1 tasks were considered to be those that either were currently or could be proceduralized and did not require diagnostic capability. Stratum 2 tasks were those that required diagnostic capability to complete.

A final review by the managers of the task list, definitions, and task differentiation was undertaken, which resulted in final enhancements to the task list. The task list was completed by the employees in Stratum 1 and 2 positions, who recorded the amount of time that they spent on each task.

Results   We found that on average employees in Stratum 2 positions are spending 49 percent of their time doing Stratum 1 tasks and only 51 percent doing Stratum 2 tasks (see Figure B.10.1).

If we conservatively say that employees in Stratum 2 positions could spend up to 30 percent of their time doing Stratum 1 tasks, we have found that 66.3 percent of Stratum 2 employees spend more time than this. Only 33.7 percent of employees in Stratum 2 positions spend at least 70 percent of their time on Stratum 2 tasks (Figure B.10.2).

We also found that employees in Stratum 1 positions are spending 85.9 percent of their time on Stratum 1 tasks, and

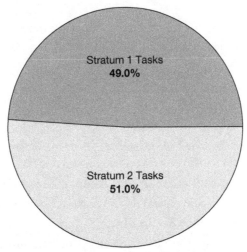

FIGURE B.10.1.   Type of Tasks Performed by Employees in Stratum 2 Positions

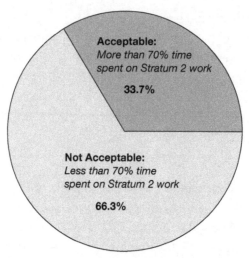

FIGURE B.10.2.   Percentage of Employees in Stratum 2 Positions Performing More and Less than 70 Percent of Their Time on Stratum 2 Tasks

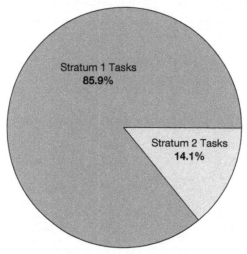

FIGURE B.10.3.   Types of Tasks Performed by Employees in Stratum 1 Positions

14.1 percent of their time trying to complete Stratum 2 tasks (Figure B.10.3). Our view would be that 100 percent of the time should be spent on Stratum 1 tasks.

In terms of inappropriate task focus for Stratum 2 positions, this translates into potential annual cost savings of approximately

$10,951 for each higher-level position included in the task align-
ment study (n=12,154 employees, 15 organizations). This results
from simply reducing time spent on Stratum 1 tasks to less than 30
percent. The potential annual savings identified for clients of task
alignment reviews ranges from $60,000 to $7.5 million per annum
(Figure B.10.4). One organization (#7) compensated employees
only at Stratum 2 and above and hence could not save money by
delegating level 1 tasks from Stratum 2 employees to Stratum 1
employees.

Potential annual savings for task alignment projects average 15
times the investment in the project. The return on investment
(ROI, blue dots; Figure B.10.4) is based solely on the cost savings
associated with optimally aligning work and not having higher-
level (and higher-paid) employees doing excessive amounts of
lower-lever work (>30 percent Stratum 1 work), thus reducing the
premium pay for the lower-level work .

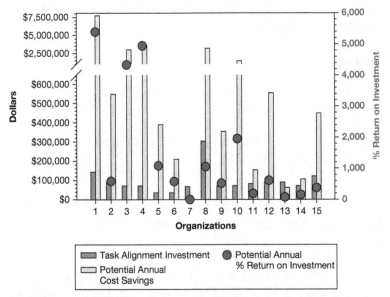

FIGURE B.10.4.   Task Alignment Potential Annual Cost Savings, Task Alignment Investment, and Potential Annual Percent Return on Investment (ROI)

Discussion   Capelle Associates has developed a method to differentiate tasks that can be completed at a Stratum 1 level from those that should be completed at a Stratum 2 or above level. The research shows that the potential annual cost savings and return on investment are significant. However, consistent with our research and client experience at a broader level, we believe that better organization design is related to better employee satisfaction, customer satisfaction, and financial performance. Task alignment is no exception.

Individuals who have Stratum 2 capability and are in Stratum 2 positions should primarily focus on Stratum 2 tasks. Similarly, individuals who have Stratum 1 capability and are in Stratum 1 positions should focus on Stratum 1 tasks. When tasks are not aligned with capability, the likely result is decreased employee satisfaction, less satisfactory customer outcomes, and reduced financial performance.

While aligning the more macro areas (positions, accountabilities and authorities, people, and deliverables) is foundational, further enhancement to performance can be derived from also improving task alignment.

References

Jaques, E. (1996). *Requisite Organization: A Total System for Effective Managerial Organization and Managerial Leadership for the 21st Century* (2nd ed.). Arlington, VA: Cason Hall.

Jaques, E. & Cason, K. (1994). *Human Capability: A Study of Individual Potential and Its Application*. Falls Church, VA: Cason Hall.

Capelle Associates Research Paper #11, Equitable Differential Pay Scale for the Canadian Market (Mar 9, 2004b)

Capelle Associates has developed for the Canadian market an equitable differential pay scale. This scale shows increasing levels of pay for increasing levels of work, that is, pay differentials and discrete pay ranges are linked to organization levels or strata. The scale builds upon Jaques' equitable differential scale (1961). This scale was developed sometime after his discovery of time span as a means of measuring the level of work. By using time span, it is possible to determine the optimal number of strata an organization should have, the level of complexity of work specific to each level, and the placement of every role in the correct stratum.

The Jaques' scale, which uses "felt fair pay" (the employees' view of what constitutes fair pay rather than actual pay), and manager-assigned time spans, provides a useful framework for developing and maintaining equitable pay structures and pay practices in the workplace. The high correlations observed between time span and felt fair pay indicates that both are measuring a similar entity: measured level of work in a role (Richardson, 1971).

The Jaques scale is constructed on universally applicable concepts but uses U.S. salary data and is therefore U.S.-centric. Canadian market data show salary levels are compressed compared to U.S. levels at the higher organization levels or strata, and slightly higher than U.S pay at the lowest organization level of stratum. A "realistic" differential scale for a region should reflect the pay practices of that region.

Method   Capelle Associates developed a Canadian scale based on compensation data from a widely used and well-known Toronto compensation survey. This survey was chosen because it represents positions (or roles), ranging from chief executive officers to administrative assistants in small, medium, and large organizations in a wide variety of industrial sectors. To develop the pay scale, two key pieces of information are needed: the values of the roles and the rates of pay. The Capelle Associates scale is based on market rates of pay and rater-estimated time spans. Time spans for all positions in the compensation survey were independently estimated and assigned by two raters (X axis). The raters' scores were highly correlated ($r=0.971$, $P<0.001$, $n=637$). Furthermore, the high correlation between the rater-estimated time spans and pay levels strongly indicates that both look at a similar entity: measured level of work in a role (r=0.925, P<0.001, n=474).

Results   A comparison of the Capelle Associates' scale and the Jaques' felt fair pay ratio scale confirms our experience that there is compression in Canadian salaries relative to U.S. salaries at the higher organization stratum. Table B.11.1 highlights the

Table B.11.1.   Comparison between Pay Differentials

		Jaques (2002)	Cappelle Associates Scale (2003)
Stratum	I	.31	.37
	II	.55	.54
	III	1.00	1.00
	IV	2.00	2.02
	V	4.00	3.44
	VI	8.00	6.37

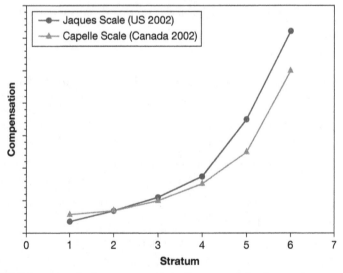

FIGURE B.11.1.   A Comparison of the Bottom of the Ranges between the United States and Canada for Each Stratum

differences between the two scales with respect to pay differentials while Figure B.11.1 highlights the differences in terms of compensation.

Table B.11.1 shows the ratios for each stratum of work. The Jaques scale, for example, shows that pay levels for Stratum 6 should be eight times that of Stratum 3, whereas the Capelle Associates scale shows Canadian salaries at Stratum 6 are actually slightly more than six times those at Stratum 3.

The Canadian scale is based on 2002 survey data of 637 positions from 316 organizations.

Figure B.11.1 shows that Jaques' U.S. compensation is higher than Capelle's Canadian compensation for all strata except Stratum 1.

Discussion The Capelle Associates approach can be adapted to fit the unique needs and constraints of different organizations and regions. For example, the economy of a region, industry, or company impacts its ability to pay. The design of the company's pay scale should reflect the affordability issue within which any relative and differential inequities among its roles would be resolved. This can mean expanding or compressing the pay differentials. Lack of appropriate and equitable compensation for any level of work can hurt an organization in terms of employee morale, turnover, and productivity.

References

Jaques, E. (1961). *Equitable Payment*. Hoboken, NJ: Wiley.

Jaques, E. (2002). *The Life and Behavior of Living Organisms: A General Theory*. Westport, CT: Praeger.

Richardson, R. (1971). *Fair Pay and Work: An Empirical Study of Fair Pay Perception and Time Span of Discretion*. London: Heinemann.

Capelle Associates Research Paper #12, **Relationship between Time Span, Compensation Span, and Actual Compensation: Review from 57 Organizations (June 23, 2005a)**

The construct "felt fair pay" refers to a stated level of pay that is considered fair by the employee for the work that he has been assigned by his manager (Jaques, 1961).When evaluating their pay, employees take into account the market rate for the role, the differential pay relationships within their organization, and the complexity of the work (Richardson, 1971).

Jaques' theory of equitable payment states that employees have an intuitive knowledge of their capacity for work and the appropriateness of their pay. If their pay is either too high or too low (by more than 20 percent either way), Jaques believed psychological disequilibrium would result. This cognitive dissonance can be measured with employee satisfaction surveys (Carraher & Chait, 1999) or through face to face interviews (Jaques, 1996). Jaques (1961) also believed that an individual's perception of being paid fairly can be indirectly measured through time span or an individual's current capacity for work (information processing capability). Richardson (1971) observed high correlations between time span and felt fair pay. He suggested that both constructs were actually measuring the same thing: level of work in a role (Richardson, 1971).

In this study, we looked at the relationship between an employee's time span, compensation span, and actual compensation.

Method   We examined the relationship between time span, compensation span, and actual compensation using our benchmarking database of over 30,000 employees from 57 organizations.

Compensation is defined as actual salary and expected bonus. Compensation span translates compensation into the appropriate stratum based upon analysis of entry-level compensation and expected ratios in each stratum (Jaques, 1996). Time span is the deliverable with the longest target completion time. The time span is provided by the manager of each direct report.

Results   We found that time span is highly correlated with actual compensation (r=0.668, P<0.001) and compensation span (r=0.662, P<0.001). Furthermore, compensation span and actual compensation were highly correlated (r=0.867, P<0.001). These results are shown in Table B.12.1.

Table B.12.1.   Relationship between Time Span, Compensation Span, and Compensation

		Time Span	Compensation Span	Compensation
Time Span	Pearson Correlation		.662**	.668**
	Sig. (2-tailed)		.000	.000
	N		30,510	30,510
Compensation Span	Pearson Correlation	.662**		.867**
	Sig. (2-tailed)	.000		.000
	N	30,510		32,685
Compensation	Pearson Correlation	.668**	.867**	
	Sig. (2-tailed)	.000	.000	
	N	30,510	32,685	

** Correlation is significant at the 0.01 level (2-tailed).

Discussion   There is considerable research to show that time span analysis can be used to determine compensation. In fact, the research shows that this system correlates more highly with felt fair pay than traditional job evaluation systems (Jaques, 1961). With the time span method, each stratum is different in terms of the nature of the work, including the information processing capability requirement. Therefore, each stratum has a distinct, and nonoverlapping, range of compensation. For example, employees in Stratum 1 positions would always be in a compensation range that would be lower than employees in Stratum 2 positions. Within each stratum, substratum compensation can be established.

If we assume that higher compensation is related to higher complexity of work, time span is shown to be a valid measure of this. Further, compensation span would also be a useful way to relate compensation to strata.

References

Carraher, S. M. & Chait, H. (1999). "Level of Work and Felt Fair Pay: An Examination of Two of Jaques' Constructs of Equitable Payment." *Psychological Reports* 84(2), 654–656.

Jaques, E. (1961). *Equitable Payment*. Hoboken, NJ: Wiley.

Jaques, E. (1996). *Requisite Organization: A Total System for Effective Managerial Organization and Managerial Leadership for the 21st Century* (2nd ed.). Arlington, VA: Cason Hall.

Richardson, R. (1971). *Fair Pay and Work: An Empirical Study of Fair Pay Perception and Time Span of Discretion*. London: Heinemann.

Capelle Associates Research Paper #13, Organization Design: From Improvement to Decline (Sept 27, 2005b)

There is considerable research that suggests that the organization design in general, and manager–direct report alignment in particular, are important factors related to employee satisfaction, customer satisfaction and financial performance (Ambachtsheer, Capelle, & Scheibelhut, 1998; Capelle Associates, 1999; Capelle Associates, 2000a; Capelle Associates, 2000b; Capelle Associates, 2000c; Capelle Associates, 2000d; Capelle Associates, 2003b). Every employee should have a manager exactly one level or stratum above. This is called requisite alignment (Jaques, 1996).

Buckingham and Coffman (1999) concluded from employee satisfaction surveys that one of the most important factors in organization performance is the manager–direct report relationship. There is also considerable research documenting the positive relationship between employee and customer satisfaction (Heskett et al., 1994). Furthermore, customer satisfaction is positively related to financial performance (Heskett et al., 1997).

However, there is also evidence that organization change efforts fail.

An important outcome of any redesign effort is to improve financial performance and the related drivers of employee satisfaction and customer satisfaction. However, most redesign attempts fail to achieve their goals. A 1994 report revealed that 67 percent of restructuring attempts produced marginal or failed results (Davenport, 1995). Furthermore, a 2003 study found that 66 percent of mergers fail to add value; if there is a strategic fit, the study concluded that implementation and integration are crucial to a successful merger (McNaught, 2004).

We believe the reason most redesign activities fail is twofold: an inadequate redesign method to begin with, and an inadequate implementation process to implement and sustain the new design.

We believe that one of the key components in an organization's design is the manager–direct report alignment. It is important not only because managers and direct reports work closely with one another, but also because managers are accountable for the work of their direct reports. They set the context and prescribed limits for the work. Managers should be exactly one level or stratum above their direct reports, both in terms of the complexity of the work done, and the capability of the individual to work at that level or stratum. Any redesign effort should ensure that positions are properly aligned both vertically and functionally; employee, managerial, and cross functional accountabilities and authorities are clear; people are properly aligned to positions; and deliverables are appropriate.

In this study we had an opportunity to review an organization over an extended period. During this time, there was both an improvement in organization design and employee satisfaction, and a subsequent decline.

Method   An organization assessment was conducted at four different points in time with an organization over an extended period.

Four assessment points were as follows:

- initial assessment of organization
- reassessment after implementing organization design improvements (including manager–direct report alignment)
- assessment of organization and second organization at point of merger
- reassessment after merger

The four different assessments included an organization design review (manager–direct report alignment) and the completion of an employee satisfaction questionnaire.

An assessment or reassessment included interviewing all of the managers to determine the time spans of their direct reports. During the interview, the manager identified the deliverable with the longest completion time of each direct report. These deliverables were then classified into strata (Jaques, 1996). Manager–direct report alignments were determined. The alignment is considered requisite if a manager is exactly one stratum above a direct report (Jaques, 1996).

An employee satisfaction questionnaire consisted of 74 questions. Employees were asked to respond on a six-point Likert scale (strongly disagree to strongly agree) to statements pertaining to factors such as organization, employee skills, workload, compensation, and relationship with their manager.

Results   The results show that both manager–direct report alignment and employee satisfaction both increased from Point 1 to 2 (Figure B.13.1). This resulted from a successful implementation of organization design improvements.

At Point 3, the organization merged with another organization that had not gone through a prior redesign effort. After the assessment at Point 3, the recommendations were not implemented. This was primarily due to many transitional activities, including a significant time lag in getting new executives.

FIGURE B.13.1. Manager–Direct Report Alignment and Employee Satisfaction Improvement from Point 1 to 2 after a Successful Organization Design Implementation

To the credit of the merged organization, when they had new executives well established in their new roles, and had moved through many of the transitional activities, they decided to focus on organization design. We did another assessment (Point 4) which not surprisingly showed deterioration in both manager–direct report alignment and employee satisfaction (Figure B.13.2).

A closer look at the organization design reveals that compression increased from Point 3 to 4 (Figure B.13.3): there were too many managers in the same layer as their direct reports. In other words, there were too many redundant managerial positions; consequently, span of control decreased significantly. Managers were micromanaging employees. In such situations, employees often report that managers are "breathing down their necks." Organizations with such symptoms experience lower employee satisfaction scores and higher employee costs due to the redundant managerial positions. These latter factors ultimately impact customer satisfaction and organization performance.

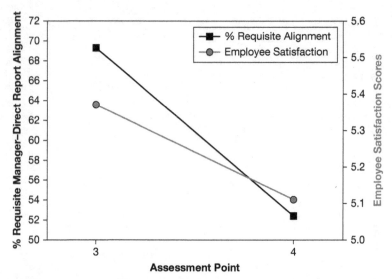

FIGURE B.13.2. Manager–Direct Report Alignment and Employee Satisfaction Decline from Point 3 to 4 after Not Attending to Organization Design Following a Merger

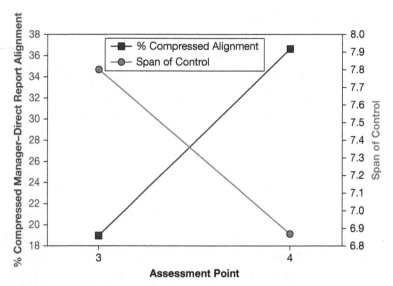

FIGURE B.13.3. Compression Increased and Consequently Span of Control Decreased from Point 3 to 4 after Not Attending to Organization Design Following a Merger

The executive team was able to use the reassessment to assist the managers in enhancing the organization design. We had some involvement in the implementation process. While we were not able to collect any further data, all indications are that they have been successful in improving both manager–direct report alignment and employee satisfaction.

Discussion   These results highlight the importance of organizations having a clear plan for implementing their redesign efforts and sustaining their efforts over time. Organization design must be sustained to achieve and maintain organization performance gains. It is precisely this commitment that makes it hard for competitors to copy a successful organization design initiative. However, should an organization design regress, a committed executive team can enhance the design and the related employee satisfaction.

References

Ambachtsheer, K., Capelle, R. & Scheibelhut, T. (1998) "Improving Pension Fund Performance." *Financial Analysts Journal* 54(5), 15–20.

Buckingham, M. & Coffman, C. (1999). *First, Break All the Rules: What the World's Greatest Managers Do Differently.* New York: Simon & Schuster.

Capelle Associates (1999). Optimizing Organization Design: Improvements in Manager–Direct Report Alignment, Financial Performance and Employee Satisfaction. Research Paper #1.

Capelle Associates (2000). Optimizing Organization Design: Improvements in Organization Design and Employee Satisfaction. Research Paper #2.

Capelle Associates (2000). Optimizing Organization Design: Improvements in Manager–Direct Report Alignment, Employee Satisfaction and Customer Satisfaction. Research Paper #3.

Capelle Associates (2000). Optimizing Organization Design: Improvements in Manager–Direct Report Alignment and Employee Satisfaction. Research Paper #4.

Capelle Associates (2000). Optimizing Organization Design: Improvements in Manager–Direct Report Alignment, Leadership and Direction, and Employee Commitment. Research Paper #5.

Capelle Associates (2003). Organization Design, Manager–Direct Report Alignment and Organization Performance in Canadian Private Sector Companies:

Results from Surveys of CEOs and Heads of Human Resources. Research Paper #9.

Davenport, T. H. (1996). "The Fad That Forgot People." *Fast Company* 1(1), 70–74.

Heskett, J. L., Jones, T. O., Loveman, G. W., Sasser, W. E. & Schlesinger, L. A. (1994). "Putting the Service Profit Chain to Work." *Harvard Business Review* 72(2), 164–174.

Heskett, J. L., Sasser, W. E. & Schlesinger, L. A. (1997). *The Service Profit Chain: How Leading Companies Link Profit and Growth to Loyalty, Satisfaction, and Value.* New York: Free Press.

Jaques, E. (1996). *Requisite Organization: A Total System for Effective Managerial Organization and Managerial Leadership for the 21st Century* (2nd ed.). Arlington, VA: Cason Hall.

McNaught, T. (2004). "Managing: Most M&As Fail!" *New Zealand Management*, 41–42.

Capelle Associates Research Paper #14, Manager–Direct Report Alignment Is Directly Related to Employee Satisfaction: A Review of 30 Organizations (March 15, 2005c)

There is considerable research that suggests that the organization design in general, and manager–direct report alignment in particular, are important factors related to employee satisfaction, customer satisfaction, and financial performance (Ambachtsheer, Capelle and Scheibelhut, 1998; Capelle Associates, 1999; Capelle Associates, 2000a; Capelle Associates, 2000b; Capelle Associates, 2000c; Capelle Associates, 2000d; Capelle Associates, 2003b).

Jaques (1996) and his colleagues have developed a measure of the complexity of work called "time span." With it, one can determine how many layers or strata an organization should have, and place every position in the correct layer or stratum. More specifically, one can develop an optimal manager–direct report alignment. This is a situation in which a manager is exactly one layer or stratum above a direct report.

Buckingham and Coffman (1999) concluded from employee satisfaction surveys that one of the most important factors in organization performance is the manager–direct report relationship. It would appear that manager–direct report alignment is a driver of the manager direct report relationship (Capelle Associates, 2003b).

There is also considerable research documenting the positive relationship between employee and customer satisfaction (Heskett et al., 1994). Furthermore, customer satisfaction is positively related to financial performance (Heskett et al., 1997). It would appear that organization design and manager–direct report alignment are drivers of these variables, and that they are positively related (Capelle Associates, 2003b).

In this paper we will use the Capelle Associates benchmarking database to review the relationship between manager–direct report alignment and employee satisfaction.

Method We collected time spans and employee satisfaction scores from 30 organizations from 1996 to 2003. For each organization, time spans and employee satisfaction scores were obtained within two months of each other. This results in 21,251 manager–direct report relationships and 6,155 employee satisfaction scores from the private, public and nonprofit sectors.

Time Span Measurement Time spans were obtained by interviewing managers who were accountable for the work of direct reports. The duration of each interview was between 30 and 60 minutes depending on the number of direct reports. Managers were asked to describe the deliverables of each of the positions they were accountable for. During the interview, the deliverable with the longest completion time of each direct report was identified and classified according to Jaques (1996) stratum framework.

The manager–direct report alignment is considered requisite if the manager is exactly one stratum above a direct report.

To obtain the manager–direct report score for an organization, the number of requisite alignments was divided by the total number of manager–direct report alignments in the organization. Higher percent scores are better. For example, a score of 60 percent means that 60 out of 100 manager–direct report relationships are requisite within the organization. The other 40 relationships are suboptimal. Either the manager and direct report are in the same layer or stratum (compressed situation), or are separated by more than one layer or stratum (gap situation).

Employee Satisfaction Measurement   Employees from each of the 30 organizations were asked to complete a questionnaire. The questionnaire was identical for each organization and was administered by the authors. The questionnaire consisted of 74 questions that measured employee satisfaction. Employees were asked to respond on a six-point Likert scale (strongly disagree to strongly agree) to statements concerning the organization, employee skills, workload, compensation, and relationship with their manager. The questionnaire is oriented to organization design, but covers many of the same factors that one would find in other employee satisfaction surveys.

We have performed a factor analysis and found that the 74 questions grouped into 10 factors. The scores were compiled for each organization and the mean score for the organization was used as the employee satisfaction score. As we were interested in the general relationship between manager–direct report alignment and employee satisfaction for an organization, we aggregated the scores for all employees.

The questionnaire score is independent from the time span measurement; the questionnaire was completed by the employee while the time span measurement was provided by an employee's manager.

Data Analysis   To demonstrate the relationship between manager–direct report alignment and employee satisfaction, we aggregated the scores within each organization for each of the two variables. This procedure resulted in two data points for each organization, one for the percent requisite manager–direct report alignment and one for the employee satisfaction score. We used Pearson's correlation coefficient to describe the relationship between the percent requisite manager–direct report alignment and the employee satisfaction score (Zar, 1999).

Results   In this study, the average requisite manager–direct report alignment score for the 30 organizations was 45.9 percent. Less than half of the manager–direct report alignments were appropriate. The average number of instances where a manager and direct report were separated by more than one layer or stratum (gap) was 23 percent, while the average number of instances where a manager and direct report were in the same layer or stratum (compression) was 31.1 percent. It should be noted that we measure these factors when we do an assessment upon entry into an organization. This is done before any work takes place to optimize the organization design. These numbers are not aspirational!

We found that organizations with a higher percentage of requisite manager–direct report alignments have higher overall employee satisfaction scores than organizations with a lower percentage of requisite manager–direct report alignments ($r=0.450$, $P<0.013$, $n=30$ organizations; Figure B.14.1).

In Table B.14.1, we show the 10 factors from the employee satisfaction survey. Four of the 10 factors were significantly correlated with manager–direct report alignment: workload ($r=0.550$, $P=0002$), work improvement ($r=0.527$, $P=0.003$), customer and recipient satisfaction ($r=0.406$, $P=0.029$), and relationship with manager ($r=0.388$, $P=0.037$). All of the employee satisfaction factors were positively related to alignment scores, but 6 of the 10 factors were non-significant (Table B.14.1).

When we move from the 10 factors to the 74 questions, we can look at the 10 questions that were most highly correlated with manager–direct report alignment. We find that 4 of these 10 questions come from the factor of "relationship with manager."

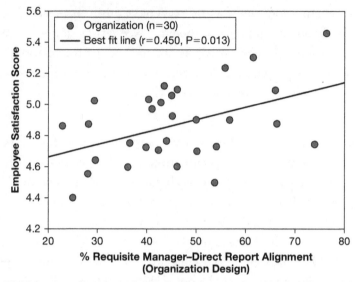

FIGURE B.14.1.   Positive Relationship Between Manager–Direct Report Alignment (Organization Design) and Employee Satisfaction

Table B.14.1.   Results of a Correlation Analysis Examining the Relationship Between Manager–Direct Report Alignment (Organization Design) and 10 Employee Satisfaction Factors

Factor	r-value	P-value
Workload	0.550	0.002
Work Improvement	0.527	0.003
Customer & Recipient Satisfaction	0.406	0.029
Relationship with Manager	0.388	0.037
Previous Change Projects	0.361	0.055
Collaboration	0.302	0.104
Suitability of Skills	0.280	0.141
Compensation & Benefits	0.225	0.241
Organization & Resources	0.223	0.236
Business Planning	0.211	0.262

Table B.14.2. The Ten Employee Satisfaction Questions with Highest
Correlation to Manager–Direct Report Alignment (Organization Design)

Question	r-value	P value
Employees have the necessary time to further improve the work of our organization.	0.592	0.001
I am clear about the expectations of the recipients or customers of my work.	0.535	0.003
My manager is good at delegating work to me (i.e., is clear about what needs to be done, why it needs to be done and what results are expected).*	0.514	0.005
My manager is concerned about my personal well-being.*	0.510	0.018
My work load is appropriate.	0.504	0.005
I receive adequate feedback on my work.*	0.469	0.010
I am clear about what is expected of me.	0.467	0.033
I feel in my work that I have enough time for the big picture and am not constantly being pulled down by too many minor details (i.e., pulled down into the weeds).	0.462	0.013
I have reasonable work goals.	0.411	0.027
I receive good support from my manager.*	0.211	0.032

* Questions are from the factor "relationship with manager."

All 10 questions are shown in Table B.14.2, and those from the "relationship with manager" factor are shown with an asterisk (*).

Discussion   There are several levels of discussion that are of value. We will begin with the manager–direct report alignment itself, and then move on to discussing its relationship to employee satisfaction.

This review includes manager–direct report alignment information from 30 organizations. We found that the average requisite manager–direct report alignment was 45.9 percent. Less than half of the manager–direct report alignments were appropriate. The average number of instances where a manager and direct report were separated by more than one layer or stratum (gap) was 23 percent, while the average number of instances where a manager and direct report were in the same layer or stratum (compression) was 31.1 percent.

In this study, we found that managers and direct reports were separated by more than one layer or stratum in 23 percent of the situations. A gap between a manager and direct report often results in poor delegation. Employees in such a situation often feel they are not receiving sufficient direction. Managers in such situations often feel that they are being "pulled down into the weeds" and/or the direct report has no initiative. Besides lower employee satisfaction scores, gaps can be a serious risk to an organization. For example, a 27-year-old futures trader, working without sufficient supervision, caused the financial collapse of Barings Bank (Leeson & Whitley, 1996). While nothing in organizations has single causality, the gap, and hence lack of supervision, was a significant factor in the demise of the bank.

In this study, we found that managers and direct reports operated in the same layer or stratum in 31 percent of the situations. If a manager and direct report are in the same layer or stratum (compression), the manager tends to micromanage and does not provide the added value for which they are bring paid (reduced financial performance). The direct report tends not to be able to use her full capability. In both cases, one would expect employee satisfaction to be negatively impacted. Employees in such situations often report that managers are breathing down their neck.

Given the accumulating research showing the important relationship of manager–direct report alignment to organization performance (employee satisfaction, customer satisfaction, and financial performance), this is a horrendous waste of human resources! When we began the research, we would have expected that organization design in general would be related to organization performance. However, we would not have expected that one factor by itself would be robust enough to show a direct relationship to organization performance. We were wrong. This one factor is extremely powerful!

In thinking about why, employee satisfaction surveys inevitably show that the most powerful factor is "relationship with manager." This was also the conclusion from Buckingham and Coffman (1999). We would assert that the manager–direct report alignment is a necessary but not sufficient condition for a strong and positive manager–direct report relationship. The relationship will be suboptimal if they are working at the same level (compression) or if there is too much distance between them (gap).

We will now move from looking specifically at manager–direct report alignment to looking at its relationship with employee satisfaction.

Our results show that there is a significant relationship between manager–direct report alignment and employee satisfaction. This is not surprising. It is consistent with the growing body of research that was cited in the introduction. What is interesting about this study is that it looked at 30 organizations within the Capelle Associates benchmarking database. The other studies have tended, with some exceptions, to focus on one organization.

When we look at the 10 factors within the questionnaire, we find significant relationships between manager–direct report alignment and four of the factors: relationship with manager, work improvement, workload, and customer and recipient satisfaction.

The relationship that we would have most strongly predicted is relationship with manager. Our view is that manager–direct report alignment is a necessary but not sufficient condition for a strong relationship with manager. In this study, we found that the employee satisfaction factor that focused on the manager–direct report relationship (relationship with manager) was significantly correlated with requisite manager–direct report alignment ($r=0.388$, $p=0.037$; Table B.14.1).

The employee satisfaction factors of "work improvement" and "workload" were also significantly correlated with requisite manager–direct report alignment (r=0.527, p=0.003 and r=0.550, P=0.003 respectively; Table B.14.1). Work improvement deals with how employees look for ways to improve their work, spend more time on work that adds value and to spend less time on work that provides little value. Workload is a factor that aggregates questions regarding the amount of work, work goals and the balance between work and personal time. These findings are interesting. Not only does the manager–direct report relationship improve, but there is improvement in the work itself. This is at least partially related to better delegation.

The employee satisfaction factor of "customer and recipient satisfaction" was also significantly correlated with requisite manager–direct report alignment (r=0.406, p=0.029; Table B.14.1). This factor encompasses questions that are concerned with how well a direct report feels he or she understands customer expectations in terms of quality, quantity and timeliness. If a manager is clear with direct reports about the work that must be provided to others, and the framework within which that happens, a direct report is more likely to be able to make decisions that are consistent with those expectations. Managers that are exactly one stratum above the direct report are more likely to be knowledgeable about the required framing of the work for the direct reports. This is a key factor in findings that better manager–direct report alignment is related to better customer satisfaction.

Although all employee satisfaction factors were positively related to requisite manager–direct report alignment, the relationship was not significant for all factors (see Table B.14.1). Some of the questions in our employee questionnaire involve issues that could be considered more independent of the manager–direct report relationship. Factors such as resources, compensation, and business planning, while important, tend to go beyond the manager–direct report alignment and relationship.

When we look at the individual questions that correlate most highly with the manager–direct report alignment, four of the questions are part of the relationship with manager factor. It is interesting to see that on the other six questions, while not part of this factor, are variables that would be affected by the nature of the relationship with manager.

In conclusion, we have two comments. First, manager–direct report alignment is a powerful organization design factor that is appropriate less than half of the time. Second, manager–direct report alignment is directly related to employee satisfaction in general and the relationship with the manager in particular.

References

Ambachtsheer, K., Capelle, R. & Scheibelhut, T. (1998) "Improving Pension Fund Performance." *Financial Analysts Journal* 54(5), 15–20.

Buckingham, M. & Coffman, C. (1999). *First, Break All the Rules: What the World's Greatest Managers Do Differently*. New York: Simon & Schuster.

Capelle Associates (1999). Optimizing Organization Design: Improvements in Manager–Direct Report Alignment, Financial Performance and Employee Satisfaction. Capelle Associates Research Paper #1.

Capelle Associates (2000a). Optimizing Organization Design: Improvements in Organization Design and Employee Satisfaction. Research Paper #2.

Capelle Associates (2000b). Optimizing Organization Design: Improvements in Manager–Direct Report Alignment, Employee Satisfaction and Customer Satisfaction. Research Paper #3.

Capelle Associates (2000c). Optimizing Organization Design: Improvements in Manager–Direct Report Alignment and Employee Satisfaction. Research Paper #4.

Capelle Associates (2000d). Optimizing Organization Design: Improvements in Manager–Direct Report Alignment, Leadership and Direction, and Employee Commitment. Research Paper #5.

Capelle Associates (2003). Organization Design, Manager–Direct Report Alignment and Organization Performance in Canadian Private Sector Companies: Results from Surveys of CEOs and Heads of Human Resources. Research Paper #9.

Heskett, J. L., Jones, T. O., Loveman, G. W., Sasser, W. E. & Schlesinger, L. A. (1994). "Putting the Service Profit Chain to Work." *Harvard Business Review* 72(2), 164–174.

Heskett, J. L., Sasser, W. E. & Schlesinger, L. A. (1997). *The Service Profit Chain: How Leading Companies Link Profit and Growth to Loyalty, Satisfaction, and Value.* New York: Free Press.

Jaques, E. (1996). *Requisite Organization: A Total System for Effective Managerial Organization and Managerial Leadership for the 21st Century* (2nd ed.). Arlington, VA: Cason Hall.

Leeson, N. W. & Whitley, E. (1996). *Rogue Trader* (1st ed.). London: Little, Brown and Company.

Zar, J. H. (1984). *Biostatistical Analysis* (2nd ed.). Englewood Cliffs, NJ: Prentice-Hall.

Capelle Associates Research Paper #15, Organization Design, Manager–Direct Report Alignment, and Employee Satisfaction (Oct 26, 2011)

There is considerable research that suggests that the organization design in general, and manager–direct report alignment in particular, are important factors related to employee satisfaction, customer satisfaction and financial performance (Ambachtsheer, Capelle & Scheibelhut, 1998; Capelle Associates, 1999; Capelle Associates, 2000a; Capelle Associates, 2000b; Capelle Associates, 2000c; Capelle Associates, 2000d; Capelle Associates, 2003b; Capelle Associates, 2005c).

Jaques (1996) and his colleagues have developed a measure of the complexity of work called "time span." With it, one can determine how many layers or strata an organization should have, and place every position in the correct layer or stratum. More specifically, one can develop optimal manager–direct report alignment. This is a situation in which a manager is exactly one layer or stratum above a direct report.

Buckingham and Coffman (1999) concluded from employee satisfaction surveys that one of the most important factors in organization performance is the manager–direct report relationship. It would appear that manager–direct report alignment is a driver of the manager–direct report relationship (Capelle Associates, 2003b).

There is also considerable research documenting the positive relationship between employee and customer satisfaction (Heskett et al., 1994). Furthermore, customer satisfaction is positively related to financial performance (Heskett et al., 1997). It would appear that organization design and manager–direct report alignment are drivers of these variables, and that they are positively related (Capelle Associates, 2003b).

In this study we will look at the relationship between improved organization design and employee satisfaction.

Method   An organization design assessment and subsequently an implementation were completed with an organization with four business units in 2008. Both were supported by Capelle Associates. Six months before the assessment and implementation, an employee satisfaction survey was conducted by an independent consulting company. The same survey was administered to the employees of the four business units two years after the assessment and implementation in 2010.

The organization design assessment recommended 30 actions to improve the functioning of the organization. Key organization design implementation work included:

- vertical alignment of positions in the organization, starting with the vice president level
- Improvement of the managerial accountability and authority framework (documented in position descriptions)
- Development of the cross functional accountabilities and authorities framework, and commencement of its implementation in high conflict areas
- A talent pool review of the vice president direct reports;
- internal project team training on organization design methods, processes, and materials for adaptation and use by managers throughout the organization

One of the important initiatives was to correct the vertical alignment within the organization. Each manager should be exactly one stratum above a direct report in a requisite alignment (Jaques, 1996). At the time of the assessment in the spring of 2008, only 20 percent of the Stratum 3 and 4 roles were in a requisite situation. By January 2010, the top three strata (Stratum 5, 4, and 3) of the organization had been realigned. By 2011, implementation work had started on all 30 suggested actions with 20 percent of them "virtually complete" and 86.7 percent of them more than half complete. In the spring of 2011 when we reevaluated the vertical alignment of the Stratum 3, 4, and 5 roles implemented in January 2010, we found 97.5 percent of them to be in an appropriate situation.

Results   The organization showed a significant improvement in employee satisfaction from the time before the organization design improvement to the time after the organization design improvement. We aggregated the 11 work environment questions for brevity as each exhibited the same pattern. Comparing the survey scores of 2008 and 2010, employees were significantly more satisfied with their work environment after the organizational changes ($X2 = 42.1$, $P < 0.001$; Figure B.15.1).

Looking at four of the individual questions within the aggregate, we found that employee trust shifted from negative to positive after the changes (Figure B.15.2). They were also more positive about their relationship with their supervisor (Figure B.15.3).

Furthermore when asked about the organization as a whole at the end of the survey, 60 percent of employees said they were satisfied with the organization after the organization changes compared to only 38 percent of the employees before the changes (Figure B.15.4; we combined "agree" and "strongly agree" in the graph below to calculate the percentages).

These positive changes in employee satisfaction scores are evident in each of the four business units of the organization.

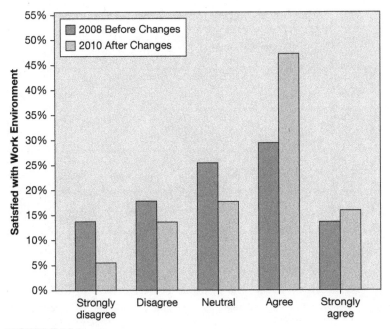

FIGURE B.15.1.

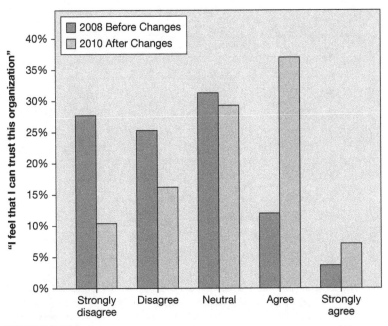

FIGURE B.15.2.

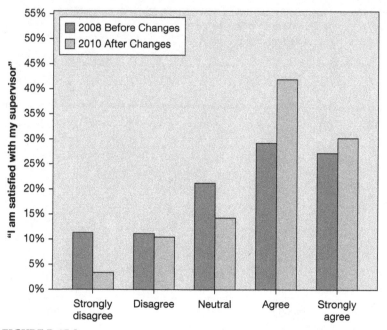

FIGURE B.15.3.

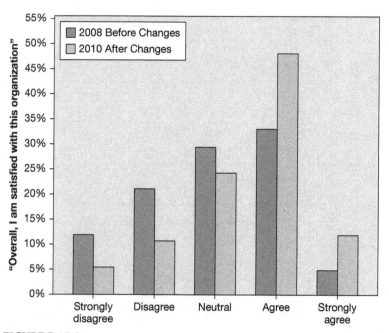

FIGURE B.15.4.

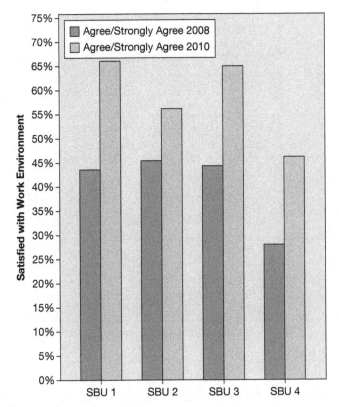

FIGURE B.15.5.

Employees in all four business units were more likely to agree or strongly agree that their work environment was satisfactory in 2010 than in 2008 (Figure B.15.5).

Furthermore, employee absenteeism was also reduced after the changes to the organization in three of the four units (Figure B.15.6).

Discussion   Employee satisfaction increased significantly following an organization design assessment and implementation. This organization design improvement included an improvement in the manager–direct report alignment. These results are not surprising. As shown in the introduction to this study, there is a growing

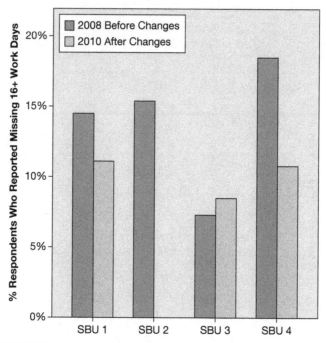

FIGURE B.15.6.

body of research showing the relationship of organization design to employee satisfaction.

We also found that employee absenteeism was reduced after the organization changes in three of the four units. We tend not to look at this factor. However, the result is not surprising since employee satisfaction and absenteeism appear to be linked. Satisfied employees are more productive and have lower absence rates than unsatisfied employees (Brooks, 1998; Robbins & Davidhizar, 2007). Employee productivity is also known to be positively related to customer satisfaction and financial performance (Grant, 1998).

References

Ambachtsheer, K., Capelle, R. & Scheibelhut, T. (1998) "Improving Pension Fund Performance." *Financial Analysts Journal* 54(5), 15–20.

Brooks, E. R. (1998). *Loyal Customers, Enthusiastic Employees and Corporate Performance: Understanding the Linkages*. Ottawa: Conference Board of Canada.

Buckingham, M. & Coffman, C. (1999). *First, Break All the Rules: What the World's Greatest Managers Do Differently*. New York: Simon & Schuster.

Capelle Associates (1999). Optimizing Organization Design: Improvements in Manager–Direct Report Alignment, Financial Performance and Employee Satisfaction. Capelle Associates Research Paper #1.

Capelle Associates (2000a). Optimizing Organization Design: Improvements in Organization Design and Employee Satisfaction. Research Paper #2.

Capelle Associates (2000b). Improvements in Manager–Direct Report Alignment, Employee Satisfaction and Customer Satisfaction. Research Paper #3.

Capelle Associates (2000c). Optimizing Organization Design: Improvements in Manager–Direct Report Alignment and Employee Satisfaction. Research Paper #4.

Capelle Associates (2000d). Optimizing Organization Design: Improvements in Manager–Direct Report Alignment, Leadership and Direction, and Employee Commitment. Research Paper #5.

Capelle Associates (2003b). Organization Design, Manager–Direct Report Alignment and Organization Performance in Canadian Private Sector Companies: Results from Surveys of CEOs and Heads of Human Resources. Research Paper #9.

Capelle Associates (2005c). Manager–Direct Report Alignment is directly related to Employee Satisfaction: A Review of 30 Organizations. Research Paper #14.

Grant, L. (1998). "Happy Workers, High Returns." *Fortune* 137, 81.

Heskett, J. L., Jones, T. O., Loveman, G. W., Sasser, W. E. & Schlesinger, L. A. (1994). "Putting the Service Profit Chain to Work." *Harvard Business Review* 72(2), 164–174.

Heskett, J. L., Sasser, W. E. & Schlesinger, L. A. (1997). *The Service Profit Chain: How Leading Companies Link Profit and Growth to Loyalty, Satisfaction, and Value*. New York: Free Press.

Jaques, E. (1996). *Requisite Organization: A Total System for Effective Managerial Organization and Managerial Leadership for the 21st Century* (2nd ed.). Arlington, VA: Cason Hall.

Robbins, B. & Davidhizar, R. (2007). "Transformational Leadership in Health Care Today." *The Health Care Manager* 26(3), 234–239.

Capelle Associates Research Paper #16, Manager–Direct Report Alignment, Delegation, and Compensation from Capelle Associates Benchmarking Database (July 10, 2012a)

There is considerable research that suggests that the organization design in general, and manager–direct report alignment in particular, are important factors related to employee satisfaction, customer satisfaction and financial performance (Ambachtsheer, Capelle & Scheibelhut, 1998; Capelle Associates, 1999; Capelle Associates, 2000a; Capelle Associates, 2000b; Capelle Associates, 2000c; Capelle Associates, 2000d; Capelle Associates, 2003b; Capelle Associates, 2005c; Capelle Associates, 2011).

Jaques (1996) and his colleagues have developed a measure of the complexity of work called "time span." With it, one can determine how many layers or strata an organization should have, and place every position in the correct layer or stratum. More specifically, one can develop optimal manager–direct report alignment. This is a situation in which a manager is exactly one layer or stratum above a direct report.

Buckingham and Coffman (1999) concluded from employee satisfaction surveys that one of the most important factors in organization performance is the manager–direct report relationship. It would appear that manager–direct report alignment is a driver of the manager–direct report relationship (Capelle Associates, 2003b).

There is also considerable research documenting the positive relationship between employee and customer satisfaction (Heskett et al., 1994). Furthermore, customer satisfaction is positively related to financial performance (Heskett et al., 1997). It would appear that organization design and manager–direct report alignment are drivers of these variables, and that they are positively related (Capelle Associates, 2003b).

We have a benchmarking database of over 59,000 manager–direct report relationships from 76 organizations. In terms of manager–direct report alignment, there are three possibilities. The

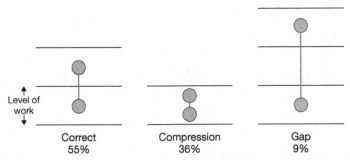

FIGURE B.16.1.   Percentage of Manager–Direct Report Alignments That Are Correct (Requisite) and Suboptimal (Compression and Gaps) in the Capelle Associates Benchmarking Database

manager could be exactly one level or stratum above a direct report. This would be an optimal or requisite situation. Our benchmarking database shows that the optimal or requisite manager–direct report alignment occurs 55 percent of the time (Figure B.16.1).

There are two suboptimal alignments. The first is when a manager and direct report are in the same level or stratum. We call this "compression" and it occurs in 36 percent of all situations in our database (Figure B.16.1). The symptoms include the manager micromanaging and not adding value, and the direct report not being able to use his full capability.

The second suboptimal alignment is when a manager and direct report are more than one stratum apart. These situations, which we call a gap, occur 9 percent of the time (Figure B.16.1). The symptoms can include the managers not providing sufficient direction or feeling that in order to do so they are "pulled down into the weeds" and doing lower-level work. The direct report is not getting sufficient direction and is usually feeling frustrated. This situation is seldom discussed. However, it is an effectiveness issue and can kill an organization. A good example is the collapse of Barings Bank. This was due of course to many interconnected and changing variables, but one important variable was lack of adequate management of the rogue trader Nick Leeson (Leeson & Whitley, 1996).

Poor alignment is a significant barrier to optimal performance. The alignment of manager–direct report relationships is the spine of the organization, upon which other factors are overlaid. If it is not properly aligned, other factors will be suboptimal. This is a horrendous waste of human resources. Many organizations unintentionally create barriers to employees doing optimal work.

A closer look at the layering within each stratum reveals that the distribution of these three types of manager–direct report alignment varies significantly among strata (X2 = 5209, P < 0.001; Table B.16.1).

The manager–direct report alignment of positions in Stratum 1 is consistently better than that of the higher strata (Table B.16.1). This is not surprising as it is the easiest to get right. The time span of Stratum 1 positions is relatively short (i.e., one day to three months). This is generally understood. Therefore if the Stratum 2 manager position is operating at the right level (which is not always the case), the manager–direct report alignment will be appropriate.

Table B.16.1. Manager–Direct Report Alignment by Stratum

Stratum and Time Span			Manager–Direct Report Alignment			Total
			Gap	Requisite	Compression	
Stratum	1: 0–3 Months	Count	3,153	27,908	13,229	44,290
		%	7.1	63.0%	29.9%	100.0%
	2: 3–12 Months	Count	2,083	3,422	6,111	11,616
		%	17.9%	29.5%	52.6%	100.0%
	3: 1–2 Years	Count	129	1,005	883	2,017
		%	6.4%	49.8	43.8%	100.0%
	4: 2–5 Years	Count	22	252	781	1055
		%	2.1%	23.9%	74.0%	100.0%
	5: 5–10 Years	Count	0	8	34	42
		%	.0%	19.0%	81.0%	100.0%
	6: 10–20 Years	Count	0	0	5	5
		%	.0%	.0%	100.0%	100.0%
Total		Count	5,387	32,595	21,043	59,025
		%	9.1%	55.2%	35.7%	100.0%

Because of the large sample size of Stratum 1 positions, it makes our requisite benchmark number (55 percent in Figure B.16.1) look much better than it actually is at other strata.

At Stratum 2 we observe an increase in compression; employees with a time span of Stratum 2 have a manager who also has a time span of Stratum 2. Business planning is typically a one-year process. Employees in Stratum 3 positions appear to be following the annual plan similar to employees in Stratum 2 positions, and not doing higher-value-added work. This is evident by the high compression observed at Stratum 2 and 3 (52.6 percent and 43.8 percent respectively; Table B.16.1).

Compression among strata is also a serious issue in Stratum 4, 5, and 6. For instance, all five employees in Stratum 6 positions were compressed with a manager also having a time span of Stratum 6.

To understand a position within the organization, we also look at other quantifiable measures such as delegation and compensation.

We will start with delegation. When we do an assessment, we interview managers. Managers provide the time spans for their direct reports. However, we also ask the manager what they think that their own time span is. We call this "self span." The clarity of delegation of work is determined by the concurrence between a manager's time span rating, and the perception by the direct report of her time span (self span). In other words for a clear context, both the time span as determined by the manager and the self span as provided by the direct report would be in the same stratum. Delegation is clear about two-thirds of the time. We find that 64 percent of positions show clear context; that is, the time span given by the manager is equal to the self span given by the direct report. Broad context (where time span is greater than self span) occurs in 17.6 percent of the cases while narrow context (where time span is less than self span) occurs in 18.4 percent of the cases (Figure B.16.2).

We will now look at compensation. We would expect that people who do more complex work (as measured by time span and shown by higher strata) would receive higher compensation (Jaques, 1961; Richardson, 1971). Our research on our

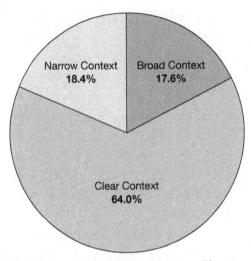

FIGURE B.16.2. Percentage of Delegation Situations That Are Correct (Clear Context) and Suboptimal (Narrow or Broad Context) in the Capelle Benchmarking Database

benchmarking database has shown that time span and compensation levels are highly correlated (Capelle Associates 2005a).

In the assessments, we receive compensation information from the organization. We use a compensation scale (Jaques, 1961; Jaques, 1996; Capelle Associates, 2004b) to determine the stratum that the compensation would be in. We call this "compensation span." We then compare the time span of a position with the compensation span of the same position. We would expect that they would be consistent. For example, we would expect that a position with a time span of Stratum 2 would have a compensation span of Stratum 2.

Our analysis of over 59,000 employees in 76 organizations reveals that 63.1 percent of them are paid within range (i.e., compensation span equals time span). We find that 21 percent are paid above range, and 15.9 percent are paid below range (Figure B.16.3).

For positions that are paid above the range, there are several possible reasons for this, which include the following. First, it may simply be a fact and an inappropriate level of compensation.

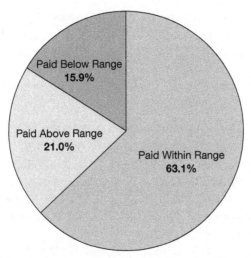

FIGURE B.16.3. Percentage of Compensation Situations That Are Paid within Range and Suboptimal (Paid Either Below or Above Range) in the Capelle Benchmarking Database

Second, the market may require higher compensation due to employee scarcity situations. For example, there is an ebb and flow in the demand for computer programmers and various types of engineers. At the extremes, this can impact compensation levels.

Another possibility is that traditional job evaluation systems often underestimate the value of high-level individual contributor positions in which the work is complex but the numbers of direct reports or budget is relatively low (e.g., senior research, development or policy positions). Dual career ladders have been an attempt to overcome this deficiency. However, this is a band-aid approach since the underlying problem is neither understood nor remedied. Since the fundamental cause is the inadequate measurement of the complexity of work, the solution should be to use a more precise measure. Time span is such a measure.

We would have several summary comments. First, manager–direct report alignment is correct only slightly more than half the time. Given the importance of this factor, there is a horrendous waste of human resources. Second, using our self span measure of delegation, we find that delegation is clear less than two-thirds of the time. Third, we find that compensation is appropriate less than two-thirds of the time. Clearly, with respect to all three findings, there are significant opportunities for improvement.

References

Ambachtsheer, K., Capelle, R. & Scheibelhut, T. (1998) "Improving Pension Fund Performance." *Financial Analysts Journal* 54(5), 15–20.

Buckingham, M. & Coffman, C. (1999). *First, Break All the Rules: What the World's Greatest Managers Do Differently*. New York: Simon & Schuster.

Capelle Associates (1999). Optimizing Organization Design: Improvements in Manager–Direct Report Alignment, Financial Performance and Employee Satisfaction. Research Paper #1.

Capelle Associates (2000a). Optimizing Organization Design: Improvements in Organization Design and Employee Satisfaction. Research Paper #2.

Capelle Associates (2000b). Optimizing Organization Design: Improvements in Manager–Direct Report Alignment, Employee Satisfaction and Customer Satisfaction. Research Paper #3.

Capelle Associates (2000c). Optimizing Organization Design: Improvements in Manager–Direct Report Alignment and Employee Satisfaction. Research Paper #4.

Capelle Associates (2000d). Optimizing Organization Design: Improvements in Manager–Direct Report Alignment, Leadership and Direction, and Employee Commitment. Research Paper #5.

Capelle Associates (2003b). Organization Design, Manager–Direct Report Alignment and Organization Performance in Canadian Private Sector Companies: Results from Surveys of CEOs and Heads of Human Resources. Research Paper #9.

Capelle Associates (2004b). Equitable Differential Pay Scale for the Canadian Market. Research Paper #11.

Capelle Associates (2005c). Manager–Direct Report Alignment is Directly Related to Employee Satisfaction: A Review of 30 Organizations. Research Paper #14.

Heskett, J. L., Jones, T. O., Loveman, G. W., Sasser, W. E. & Schlesinger, L. A. (1994). "Putting the Service Profit Chain to Work." *Harvard Business Review* 72(2), 164–174.

Heskett, J. L., Sasser, W. E. & Schlesinger, L. A. (1997). *The Service Profit Chain: How Leading Companies Link Profit and Growth to Loyalty, Satisfaction, and Value*. New York: Free Press.

Jaques, E. (1961). *Equitable Payment.* Hoboken, NJ: Wiley.

Jaques, E. (1996). *Requisite Organization: A Total System for Effective Managerial Organization and Managerial Leadership for the 21st Century* (2nd ed.). Arlington, VA: Cason Hall.

Leeson, N. W. & Whitley, E. (1996). *Rogue Trader* (1st ed.). London: Little, Brown and Company.

Capelle Associates Research Paper #17, Capelle Associates Employee Satisfaction Questionnaire (July 5, 2012b)

Capelle Associates has developed a questionnaire on employee satisfaction. This questionnaire has more of a focus on organization design variables. We have responses from 13,861 employees from 38 organizations. This includes employees from a broad range of organizations in the private, public and nonprofit sectors. The questionnaire was identical for each organization. The questionnaire was usually administered online but if access was not available a paper version was provided.

The questionnaire consists of 74 questions that are phrased in positive terms. Employees are asked to respond on a 10-point Likert scale (strongly disagree to strongly agree) to statements related to a range of factors.

We have completed a factor analysis and found that the 74 questions were represented best by 10 factors (little explained variance was gained by adding additional factors). A factor is a group of questions that "hang together" (i.e., are statistically interrelated). Each of these 10 factors has been named to represent the nature of the questions that are grouped within the factor. The average score and sample sizes for each of the factors are presented in Table B.17.1.

The 10 factors are described below:

Factor 1: Relationship with manager

Eleven questions clustered together to create this factor. Buckingham and Coffman (1999) consider this factor to be

Table B.17.1. Questionnaire Scores and Sample Size for the Ten Factors That Comprise the Capelle Associates Employee Satisfaction Questionnaire Benchmark

Average of 74 Questions and 10 Factors	Questionnaire Scores	
	Mean	n
Total Average	**7.59**	**13,681**
Factor 1. Relationship with Manager	7.61	13,428
Factor 2. Clarity, Recipients, and Customers	8.26	13,424
Factor 3. Previous Change Projects	6.72	12,110
Factor 4. Organization and Resources	7.76	13,677
Factor 5. Suitability of Skills	8.21	13,420
Factor 6. Workload	7.11	13,425
Factor 7. Compensation, Benefits, and Career Outlook	6.95	13,405
Factor 8. Collaboration	7.28	13,672
Factor 9. Work Improvement	8.11	13,419
Factor 10. Manager Planning	7.33	4,617

one of the most important in influencing employee satisfaction. Our own research supports this conclusion, although we would also say that appropriate manager–direct report alignment is a necessary but not sufficient condition for a strong relationship with a manager. In general, the questions that comprise this factor focus on how a direct report perceives his manager. More specifically, the questions are concerned with how a manager delegates, supports, treats, and encourages a direct report.

Factor 2: Clarity, recipients, and customers

Ten questions make up this factor. This factor encompasses questions that focus on employees' perceptions of the work they do. Four of the ten questions involve employees' expectations regarding the quality, quantity, and timeliness of their own work. The other questions focus on the employee's perception of how customers and recipients view their work.

Factor 3: Previous change projects

The seven questions that comprise this factor focus on the success of various elements of previous change management projects. Issues such as management support, necessary resources, communication, and training are covered in these project questions. This factor is important for implementing organization design improvements.

Factor 4: Organization and resources

Seven questions fall into this factor that focuses on the employees' perceptions of their organization and department. The quality of resources, technology, and information is also covered within this factor.

Factor 5: Suitability of skills

The employee's perception of the suitability of their own skills is assessed by the seven questions within this factor. The questions include areas such as skills, knowledge, judgment, development, and learning.

Factor 6: Workload

Six questions dealing with the employee's perception of their workload are grouped into this factor. Time, work goals, workload, work scheduling, and sufficient family time are covered by questions within this factor.

Factor 7: Compensation, benefits, and career outlook

Four questions on compensation and career issues are grouped into this factor. Questions focus on compensation, benefits, career opportunities, and job security.

Factor 8: Collaboration

Six of the eight questions within this factor involve the employees' perception of coworkers. Do fellow employees have the necessary skill, motivation, time, and authority to do quality work? The other two questions deal with the effectiveness, efficiency, and number of meetings.

Factor 9: Work improvement

Six questions are grouped within this factor that assesses the employees' perception of how they try to improve their work.

It also asks employees how they perceive that customers or recipients view their work.

Factor 10: Manager planning

Only managers with direct reports were asked to complete these eight questions. They ask managers if they can describe the company's vision, mission, values, strategic positioning, operational, and resource plans. There is also a question that asks if managers have access to written documents describing the organization's business plan. The final question concerns the manager's opinion on whether her direct reports understand the above documents. In combination, these questions reflect how well an organization uses its business plan with its employees.

We find the questionnaire to be valuable in both our work with clients and our research. Employee satisfaction is an important performance factor. Capelle Associates has considerable research showing the better organization design in general, and better manager–direct report alignment in particular, are related to employee satisfaction (Capelle Associates, 2005c). Further, there is considerable research on the profit service chain showing that employee satisfaction is linked to and core to customer satisfaction and financial performance (Heskett et al., 1997).

References

Buckingham, M. & Coffman, C. (1999). *First, Break All the Rules: What the World's Greatest Managers Do Differently.* New York: Simon & Schuster.

Capelle Associates (2005c). Manager–Direct Report Alignment is Directly Related to Employee Satisfaction: A Review of 30 Organizations. Research Paper #14.

Heskett, J. L., Sasser, W. E. & Schlesinger, L. A. (1997). *The Service Profit Chain: How Leading Companies Link Profit and Growth to Loyalty, Satisfaction, and Value.* New York: Free Press.

Pett, M. A., Lackey, N. R. & Sullivan, J. S. (2003). *Making Sense of Factor Analysis: The Use of Factor Analysis for Instrument Development in Health Care Research.* Thousand Oaks, CA: Sage.

Capelle Associates Research Paper #18, Relationship among Time Span, Self Span, and Compensation Span from Capelle Associates Benchmarking Database (July 30, 2012c)

Time span analysis is a method for directly measuring the complexity of a position. The time span of a position is determined by the deliverable within the position that has the longest target completion time. This is a measure of the complexity of work in the position; a position with a longer time span is more complex than a position with a shorter time span. Therefore, as one goes up the organization, the longer one would expect the time span of the position to be. Time span analysis can help us determine how many strata an organization should have and place each position in the correct layer or stratum.

The research has shown that there is a universal pattern of organization strata that transcends organization types, countries, and cultures (Jaques, 1996). Each stratum is discrete and discontinuous from the adjoining one, and the nature of work in each stratum is different. The research indicates that a reason for this is that people have different information processing capabilities that are discontinuous. In other words, there are state transitions in moving from one to another (e.g., ice to water to steam). Therefore, work at each stratum of the organization requires a different level of individual information processing capability (Jaques & Cason, 1994). The strata and time span boundaries in the model are presented in Table B.18.1.

It should also be noted that work at each level varies to some extent in complexity. For example, individuals at Stratum 3 will do some work requiring information processing capability no higher than that at Stratum 2 and Stratum 1 levels. However, their work outputs will nonetheless reflect the perspective requisite at Stratum 3. The important issue for measuring level of work and complexity of information processing is that it defines the maximum levels and not the minimum levels.

Table B.18.1.   Organization Strata
and Time Span Ranges

Strata	Time Span
8	50 years or greater
7	20 to 50 years
6	10 to 20 years
5	5 to 10 years
4	2 to 5 years
3	1 to 2 years
2	3 to 12 months
1	Less than 3 months

The time span of a position is determined by the manager of the direct report. In our assessment of an organization design we often ask the direct report what they think their time span is. We call this the "self span." The relationship between time span and self span score is a measure of the clarity of delegation.

There is also considerable research to show that time span analysis can be used to determine compensation. In fact, the research shows that this system correlates more highly with felt fair pay than traditional job evaluation systems (Jaques, 1961; Richards, 1971; Capelle Associates, 2003a). In our assessment of an organization design, we often determine what the stratum of compensation is for a position. We call this compensation span. In this report, we document the relationship among time span, self span, and compensation span.

Method   In this analysis, the manager of a direct report provides the time span of the position by identifying the deliverable with the longest target completion time. Self span scores were obtained by asking direct reports what they perceived their time span to be (i.e., their perception of their deliverable with the longest target completion time).

We also quantify time span and self span scores within a stratum as either low, medium or high (1.25, 1.50, and 1.75, respectively). Because we usually only interview managers, we only have self span scores for managers in our benchmarking database.

Compensation is defined as actual salary and expected bonus. Compensation span translates compensation into appropriate stratum based upon analysis of entry-level compensation and expected ratios in each stratum (Jaques 1996, Capelle Associates 2004b). Time span, self span, and compensation span scores were obtained from individuals in 76 organizations.

Results   The results are shown in Figures B.18.1, B.18.2, and B.18.3 and summarized in Table B.18.2.

It should be noted that the three figures use sunflower graphs (symbols), which show the overlap of occurrences. The higher the

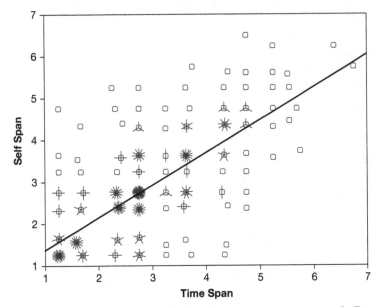

FIGURE B.18.1. Relationship between a Manager's Determination of a Direct Report's Time Span and the Direct Report's Own Perception of Time Span (Self Span)

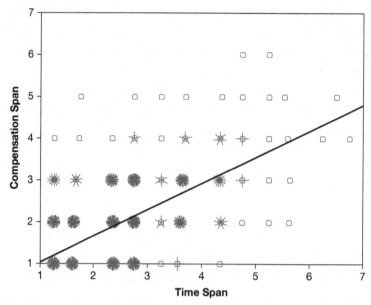

FIGURE B.18.2.   Relationship between a Manager's Determination of a Direct Report's Time Span and the Compensation Span of the Direct Report

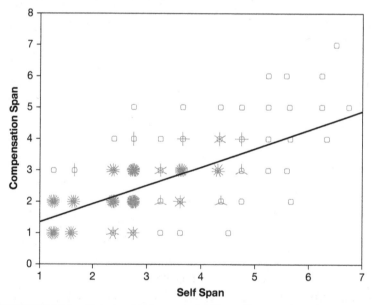

FIGURE B.18.3.   Relationship between the Direct Report's Own Perception of Time Span (Self Span) and the Compensation Span of the Direct Report

Table B.18.2. Correlations among Time Span, Self Span, and Compensation Span

		Time Span	Self Span	Compensation Span
Time Span	Pearson Correlation		.755**	.672**
	Sig. (2-tailed)		.000	.000
	N		7,134	58,806
Self Span	Pearson Correlation	.755**		.669**
	Sig. (2-tailed)	.000		.000
	N	7,134		7,137
Compensation Span	Pearson Correlation	.672**	.669**	
	Sig. (2-tailed)	.000	.000	
	N	58,806	7,137	

** Correlation is significant at the 0.01 level (2-tailed).

number of cases that occur in a given space the more petals are drawn on the graph. Each line or petal through the data point represents one case (i.e., an open dot with one line through it represents two cases).

If we look at the relationship between the time span and the self span of an employee, we find that these measures of complexity of work are positively correlated ($r=0.755$, $P<0.001$, $n=7134$; Figure B.18.1).

Larger sunflowers represent more cases, each petal represents 25 cases. Compensation span is positively correlated with both time span ($r=0.672$, $P<0.001$, $n=58,806$; Figure B.18.2) and self span ($r=0.669$, $P<0.001$, $n = 7137$; Figure B.18.3).

The correlations among these variables are shown in Table B.18.2.

Discussion Time span, self span, and compensation span are all positively correlated. The relationship among these variables is one indicator of the health of an organization. The relationship between time span and self span scores is an indication of the clarity of delegation in the organization. Similarly, the relationship between time span or self span and compensation span is an indication of the appropriateness of compensation.

References

Capelle Associates (2004b). Equitable Differential Pay Scale for the Canadian Market. Research Paper #11.

Jaques, E. (1961). *Equitable Payment*. Hoboken, NJ: Wiley.

Jaques, E. (1996). *Requisite Organization: A Total System for Effective Managerial Organization and Managerial Leadership for the 21st Century* (2nd ed.). Arlington, VA: Cason Hall.

Jaques, E. & Cason, K. (1994). *Human Capability: A Study of Individual Potential and Its Application*. Falls Church, VA: Cason Hall.

Richardson, R. (1971). *Fair Pay and Work: An Empirical Study of Fair Pay Perception and Time Span of Discretion*. London: Heinemann.

Capelle Associates Research Paper #19, Relationship among Manager–Direct Report Alignment, Delegation, and Compensation from Capelle Associates Benchmarking Database (Aug 1, 2012d)

Time span analysis is a method for measuring complexity of work. It can be used to determine how many strata an organization should have and place each position in the correct stratum.

Time span analysis provides a framework for manager–direct report alignment. The optimal manager–direct report alignment occurs when the manager is exactly one stratum above a direct report. We call this requisite alignment, it occurs in 55 percent of the cases in our benchmarking database of over 59,000 employees in 76 organizations (Capelle Associates 2012a).

The clarity of delegation of work is determined by the concurrence between a manager's time span rating, and the perception by the direct report of his time span (self span). If time span equals self span, we call this "clear context." Clear context occurs in 64 percent of the cases in our database (Capelle Associates 2012a).

Compensation span translates compensation (salary and any expected benefits) into appropriate strata based upon analysis of entry-level compensation and expected ratios in each stratum (Jaques, 1996; Capelle Associates, 2004b). A congruence between time span and compensation span shows that employees are being paid within range. We find that 63.1 percent of employees in our database are paid within range (Capelle Associates, 2012a).

In this study, we look at the relationship among these three organization design measures. We show that organizations with better manager–direct alignment had clearer delegation and more employees that were paid appropriately (i.e., within range).

Method   We compared the manager–direct alignment, delegation, and compensation scores of 71 organizations for which we had all three types of information. Time spans were provided by managers for direct reports during an interview that lasted between 30 and 60 minutes depending on the number of direct reports. Self spans were obtained from managers during the same interviews, consequently we only have delegation scores for managers.

Compensation span translates compensation (salary and any expected benefits) into appropriate strata based upon analysis of entry-level compensation and expected ratios in each stratum (Jaques 1996; Capelle Associates, 2004b).

Results   We found a positive relationship between the manager–direct report alignment of an organization and the delegation score of an organization ($r=0.319$, $P<0.01$, $n=71$; Figure B.19.1), that is organizations with more requisite manager–direct report alignment also had more clear context (time span = self span). Each dot in the figure below represents an organization.

We found a positive relationship between manager–direct report alignment in an organization and appropriate compensation (i.e. employees paid within range) ($r=0.339$, $P<0.005$, $n=71$; Figure B.19.2).

Although there is a slight upward trend, there is no statistically significant relationship between delegation and compensation across organizations ($r=0.099$, $P=0.427$, $n=66$; Figure B.19.3).

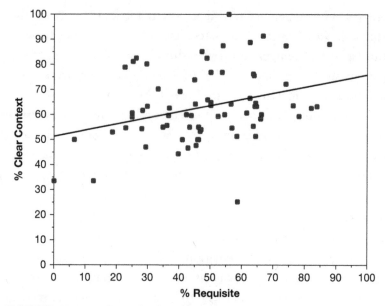

FIGURE B.19.1. Relationship between Manager–Direct Report Alignment and Delegation Scores for Each Organization

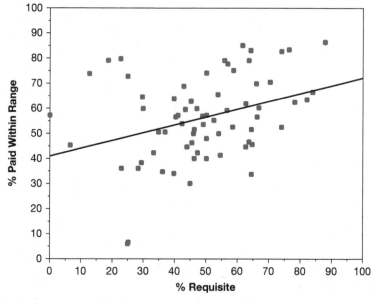

FIGURE B.19.2. Relationship between Manager–Direct Report Alignment and Compensation Scores for Each Organization

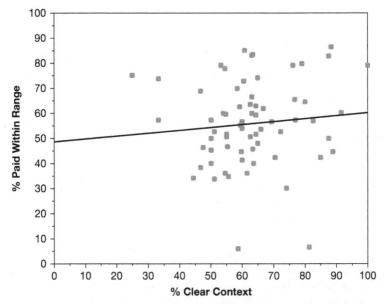

FIGURE B.19.3. Relationship between the Delegation and Compensation Scores for Each Organization

The correlations for these relationships are shown in Table B.19.1.

Table B.19.1. Correlations Among Requisite Manager–Direct Report Alignment, Clear Context (Delegation), and Paid Within Range (Compensation)

		% Requisite	% Clear Context	% Paid Within Range
% Requisite	Pearson Correlation		.319**	.339**
	Sig. (2-tailed)		.007	.005
	N		71	68
% Clear Context	Pearson Correlation	.319**		.099
	Sig. (2-tailed)	.007		.427
	N	71		66
% Paid Within Range	Pearson Correlation	.339**	.099	
	Sig. (2-tailed)	.005	.427	
	N	68	66	

** Correlation is significant at the 0.01 level (2-tailed).

Discussion   Organizations that are strong in one aspect of organization design tend to be strong on other measures of organization design. The results suggest that these three organization design measures are inter-related. More specifically, organizations that have better manager–direct report alignment also are more likely to have clearer delegation and employees that are paid in a range that is consistent with their strata.

References

Capelle Associates (2004c). Equitable Differential Pay Scale for the Canadian Market. Research Paper #11.

Capelle Associates (2012a). Manager–Direct Report Alignment, Delegation, and Compensation from Capelle Associates Benchmarking Database. Research Paper #16.

Jaques, E. (1961). *Equitable Payment*. Hoboken, NJ: Wiley.

Jaques, E. (1996). *Requisite Organization: A Total System for Effective Managerial Organization and Managerial Leadership for the 21st Century* (2nd ed.). Arlington, VA: Cason Hall.

Richardson, R. (1971). *Fair Pay and Work: An Empirical Study of Fair Pay Perception and Time Span of Discretion*. London: Heinemann.

Capelle Associates Research Paper #20, Span of Control and Employee Satisfaction from Capelle Associates Benchmarking Database (Aug 9, 2012e)

Span of control refers to the number of direct reports that a manager is accountable for. It is widely believed there is a single optimal span of control. The range of 4 to 8 is often suggested. Some consulting firms even propose that the number should be 7. Our view is that the span of control will vary from situation to situation. It starts with understanding the nature of work. The optimal span of control will depend on a number of factors, including nature of the work being done, how measureable it is, the experience and capability of the manager and direct reports, the amount of change, etc. On the one hand, it should have a degree of cost efficiency. On the other hand, it should be such that the manager can be effective in doing the required work.

There do appear to be some variations in the span of control related to the level or stratum of the work. For example, managers of first-level employees tend to have larger spans of control than managers of professionals in professional functions of organizations. If there was an ideal span of control, we would hypothesize that it would be related to higher levels of employee satisfaction.

In this study, we examine span of control from our benchmark database of over 59,000 manager–direct report relationships from 76 different organizations (Capelle Associates 2012a). We look at span of control relative to organizational layers or strata. We also examine the relationship between span of control and employee satisfaction.

Method   We have obtained employee data from 76 different organizations over a 20-year period. It consists of 67,315 employees of which 8,009 are managers (11.9 percent). We have manager–direct report alignment data for 59,025 of these employees.

Time span is a measure of the complexity of work used to determine the number of layers or strata that an organization should have and place each role in the correct stratum (Jaques 1996). The time span of each position was provided by managers for their direct reports in interviews ranging from 30 to 60 minutes.

The Capelle Associates Employee Satisfaction Questionnaire consists of 74 questions that are phrased in positive terms. Employees were asked to respond on a Likert scale (strongly disagree to strongly agree) to statements related to a range of organization factors. There are responses from 13,861 employees from 38 organizations (Capelle Associates, 2012b).

Results   We will first look at the span of control by organization level or stratum. The average span of control of 7913 managers in our database is 8.5 with a median of 5.

This number of managers is slightly lower than the number above (in method) because some direct reports of certain managers were out of scope so we eliminated these managers from the analysis.

The span of control varies significantly by the manager's level or stratum (ANOVA, F=17.5, P<0.0001; Figure B.20.1).

It should be noted that our database consists of information that we find when we initially go in to assess organizations. These are not situations in which the organization design has been improved.

Figure B.20.1 shows that spans of control tend to be higher at the lower levels (Stratum 1 and 2 managers) and the higher levels (Stratum 5 and 6 managers). There is an interesting anomaly here. Managers are shown at Stratum 1. In an optimal design, there would be no managers at Stratum 1. This situation is a result of supervisors inappropriately being used as a layer of management. In resolving these situations, the spans of control may be higher.

The Stratum 5 and Stratum 6 levels would be up at a president or CEO level. It is interesting the spans of control seem to move up at these levels. So, we find some variation in the number of direct

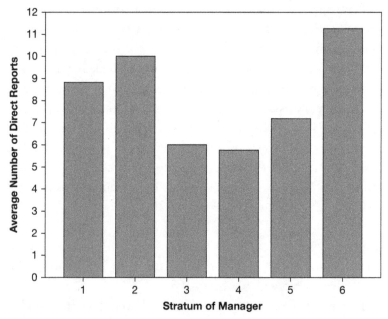

FIGURE B.20.1. The Average Number of Direct Reports per Manager by Stratum in Capelle Associates Benchmarking Database

reports by stratum. This is not surprising since this is one indicator of the nature of work being done.

Employee Satisfaction and Span of Control   If we look at the relationship between the span of control of the manager and the employee satisfaction scores of their direct reports, we find that there is no significant relationship in a large organization (Organization A). Figure B.20.2 shows that very little variation in employee satisfaction is explained by the span of control of the manager ($r^2 < 0.0001$; $r=0.004$, $P=0.840$, $n=2537$).

We performed this analysis on the three largest organizations in our database. The other two organizations showed the same lack of relationship between the span of control of the manager and the employee satisfaction scores of their direct reports (Organization B: $r^2=0.0098$, $n=1758$; Organization C: $r^2=0.0001$, $n=326$). The three organizations were in three different industries.

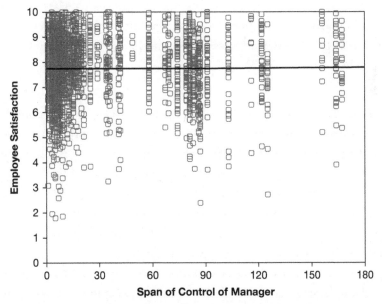

FIGURE B.20.2.   The Overall Employee Satisfaction Score of Direct Reports by the Span of Control of Managers in a Large Organization

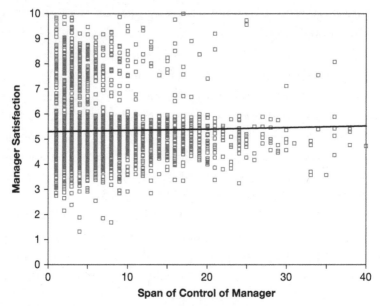

FIGURE B.20.3. The Overall Satisfaction Score of Managers by Their Spans of Control

Similarly, the number of direct reports of the manager is not related to manager's overall satisfaction (overall, $r^2 = 0.0026$; $n = 3347$; Figure B.20.3).

Discussion We did find a relationship between span of control and organization level or stratum. This is not surprising. The starting point is understanding the nature of the work, and the level or stratum in the organization is one indicator of this.

It should be noted that we have used analysis of variance (ANOVA) in a situation in which parametric assumptions may not have been met. However, the high level of significance makes acceptable the conclusion of probable differences across strata.

We found no evidence of a relationship between span of control and employee satisfaction. This would be in keeping with our view that span of control does and should vary depending on the nature of the work. For example, a span of control of 6 may be ideal in some situations and totally inappropriate in others. If there was an ideal span of control, it would be reasonable to expect that it would be reflected in differences in employee satisfaction. We found no such relationship in these analyses, although we have found such a relationship with other variables. For example, we find that better manager–direct report alignment (i.e., manager exactly one level or stratum above a direct report) is related to better employee satisfaction.

In conclusion, this paper raises serious questions for those who claim that there is a universal ideal span of control.

References

Capelle Associates (2012a). Manager–Direct Report Alignment, Delegation and Compensation from Capelle Associates Benchmarking Database. Research Paper #16.

Capelle Associates (2012b). Capelle Associates Employee Satisfaction Questionnaire. Research Paper #17.

Jaques, E. (1996). *Requisite Organization: A Total System for Effective Managerial Organization and Managerial Leadership for the 21st Century* (2nd ed.). Arlington, VA: Cason Hall.

Capelle Associates Research Paper #21, Manager–Direct Report Alignment and Employee Satisfaction for an Analyst Role (Aug 7, 2012f)

There is considerable research that suggests that the organization design in general, and manager–direct report alignment in particular, are important factors related to employee satisfaction, customer satisfaction and financial performance (Ambachtsheer, Capelle & Scheibelhut, 1998; Capelle Associates, 1999; Capelle Associates, 2000a; Capelle Associates, 2000b; Capelle Associates, 2000c; Capelle Associates, 2000d; Capelle Associates, 2003b; Capelle Associates, 2005c).

Jaques (1996) and his colleagues have developed a measure of the complexity of work called "time span." With it, one can determine how many layers or strata an organization should have, and place every position in the correct layer or stratum. More specifically, one can develop optimal manager–direct report alignment. This is a situation in which a manager is exactly one layer or stratum above a direct report.

Buckingham and Coffman (1999) concluded from employee satisfaction surveys that one of the most important factors in organization performance is the manager direct-report relationship. It would appear that manager–direct report alignment is a driver of the manager–direct report relationship (Capelle Associates, 2003b).

There is also considerable research documenting the positive relationship between employee and customer satisfaction (Heskett et al., 1994). Furthermore, customer satisfaction is positively related to financial performance (Heskett et al., 1997). It would appear that organization design and manager–direct report alignment are drivers of these variables, and that they are positively related (Capelle Associates, 2003b).

In this study, we review manager–direct report alignment and employee satisfaction for an analyst role.

Method   We looked at one role (analyst) within an organization to examine how the manager–direct report alignment affects employee satisfaction. This was the second most frequent position in the organization (n=774). The role with the greatest frequency (1681) could not be used since there were very few requisite and compressed situations between an employee and manager (thereby making a valid comparison among the three situations impossible).

There are several advantages to this approach of examining just one role: variation among roles is eliminated, the role is at stratum level where all three alignment scenarios occur, and the role accounts for well over 10 percent of the workforce of the organization.

Time span information was obtained by interviewing all the managers within the organization. The interviews typically lasted between 30 and 60 minutes depending on the number of direct reports (Capelle Associates 2012a). Employee satisfaction data was obtained by administering the Capelle Associates Employee Satisfaction Questionnaire to each employee within the organization. Employees were asked to respond on a 10-point Likert scale to statements related to their manager, workload, compensation, and the organization (Capelle Associates, 2012b).

Results   We found that analysts who were in a requisite situation (manager exactly one stratum above) had higher employee satisfaction than analysts who had a manager in the same stratum (compression) or had a manager separated by more than one stratum (gap, ANOVA, $P=0.025$; Figure B.21.1). This is true for the overall average as well as 9 of the 10 factors that comprise our questionnaire. One of the most important factors, relationship with manager, is presented in Figure B.21.2.

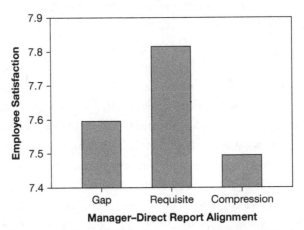

FIGURE B.21.1.   Analysts in Requisite Situations Had Higher Employee Satisfaction Than Analysts in Suboptimal Situations (Gaps and Compression)

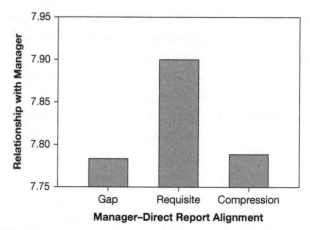

FIGURE B.21.2. Analysts in Requisite Situations Scored Higher on the Factor Relationship with Manager Than Analysts in Suboptimal Situations (Gaps and Compression)

Discussion Analysts in requisite situations, where their manager is exactly one stratum above them, had higher employee satisfaction scores than analysts in suboptimal situations (gap or compression). This is consistent with other research cited in the introduction that there is a strong relationship between manager–direct report alignment and employee satisfaction.

Analysts in requisite situations, where their manager is one stratum above them, had a stronger relationship with manager than analysts in suboptimal situations (gap or compression). This is also consistent with other research cited in the introduction. It is important since Buckingham and Coffman (1999) consider it to be one of the most important factors in organization performance. Our view, that manager–direct report alignment is a driver of stronger relationship with manager, would be supported by this outcome. Employee satisfaction is important in its own right, but it also has broader importance. It has been shown to be linked to customer satisfaction and financial performance (Heskett et al., 1997; Capelle Associates, 2003).

While this study is consistent with other research, it adds unique value by focusing on only one role (analyst).

References

Ambachtsheer, K., Capelle, R. & Scheibelhut, T. (1998) "Improving Pension Fund Performance." *Financial Analysts Journal* 54(5), 15–20.

Buckingham, M. & Coffman, C. (1999). *First, Break All the Rules: What the World's Greatest Managers Do Differently*. New York: Simon & Schuster.

Capelle Associates (1999). Optimizing Organization Design: Improvements in Manager–Direct Report Alignment, Financial Performance and Employee Satisfaction. Research Paper #1.

Capelle Associates (2000a). Optimizing Organization Design: Improvements in Organization Design and Employee Satisfaction. Research Paper #2.

Capelle Associates (2000b). Optimizing Organization Design: Improvements in Manager–Direct Report Alignment, Employee Satisfaction and Customer Satisfaction. Research Paper #3.

Capelle Associates (2000c). Optimizing Organization Design: Improvements in Manager–Direct Report Alignment and Employee Satisfaction. Research Paper #4.

Capelle Associates (2000d). Optimizing Organization Design: Improvements in Manager–Direct Report Alignment, Leadership and Direction, and Employee Commitment. Research Paper #5.

Capelle Associates (2003b). Organization Design, Manager–Direct Report Alignment and Organization Performance in Canadian Private Sector Companies: Results from Surveys of CEOs and Heads of Human Resources. Research Paper #9.

Capelle Associates (2005c). Manager–Direct Report Alignment Is Directly Related to Employee Satisfaction: A Review of 30 Organizations. Research Paper #14.

Heskett, J. L., Jones, T. O., Loveman, G. W., Sasser, W. E. & Schlesinger, L. A. (1994). "Putting the Service Profit Chain to Work." *Harvard Business Review* 72(2), 164–174.

Heskett, J. L., Sasser, W. E. & Schlesinger, L. A. (1997). *The Service Profit Chain: How Leading Companies Link Profit and Growth to Loyalty, Satisfaction, and Value*. New York: Free Press.

Jaques, E. (1996). *Requisite Organization: A Total System for Effective Managerial Organization and Managerial Leadership for the 21st Century* (2nd ed.). Arlington, VA: Cason Hall.

Capelle Associates Research Paper #22, Manager–Direct Report Alignment and Employee Satisfaction in Three Organizations (Aug 9, 2012g)

There is considerable research that suggests that the organization design in general, and manager–direct report alignment in particular, are important factors related to employee satisfaction, customer satisfaction and financial performance (Ambachtsheer, Capelle and Scheibelhut, 1998; Capelle Associates 1999; Capelle Associates, 2000a; Capelle Associates, 2000b; Capelle Associates, 2000c; Capelle Associates, 2000d; Capelle Associates, 2003b; Capelle Associates, 2005c).

Jaques (1996) and his colleagues have developed a measure of the complexity of work called "time span." With it, one can determine how many layers or strata an organization should have, and place every position in the correct layer or stratum. More specifically, one can develop optimal manager–direct report alignment. This is a situation in which a manager is exactly one layer or stratum above a direct report.

Buckingham and Coffman (1999) concluded from employee satisfaction surveys that one of the most important factors in organization performance is the manager direct-report relationship. It would appear that manager–direct report alignment is a driver of the manager–direct report relationship (Capelle Associates, 2003b).

There is also considerable research documenting the positive relationship between employee and customer satisfaction (Heskett et al., 1994). Furthermore, customer satisfaction is positively related to financial performance (Heskett et al., 1997). It would appear that organization design and manager–direct report alignment are drivers of these variables, and that they are positively related (Capelle Associates, 2003b).

In this study, we review the relationship between manager–direct report alignment and employee satisfaction in three organizations within the same business line.

Method We compared employee satisfaction and the manager–direct report alignment in three organizations. Each organization was assessed within the same time frame with respect to manager–direct report alignment and employee satisfaction.

Employees from each organization were asked to complete a questionnaire; and their responses to 74 questions were averaged (Capelle Associates, 2012a). We also assessed the vertical alignment of the organization by obtaining time spans for each employee. Time spans were used to determine the percentage of manager–direct report relationships that were properly aligned (Capelle Associates, 2012b).

Results Each organization differed significantly with respect to manager–direct report alignment ($X2=62.4$, $P<0.001$). The percentage of correctly aligned positions varied from 55.8 percent to 61.5 percent to 76.8 percent. Employee satisfaction was positively related to manager–direct report alignment ($r=0.992$, $P<0.04$; Figure B.22.1). Organizations with a higher percentage

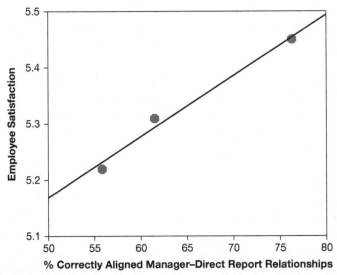

FIGURE   B.22.1. Relationship between Employee Satisfaction and Manager–Direct Report Alignment

of correctly aligned manager–direct report relationships also had higher employee satisfaction scores.

Discussion The result that better manager–direct report alignment is positively related to better employee satisfaction is consistent with previous research cited in the introduction of this paper. It should be noted that there can be problems of significance testing with extreme values of r and N. However, a visual inspection of Figure B.22.1 would seem to substantiate this conclusion.

While employee satisfaction is important in its own right, it also has broader importance. It has been shown to be linked to customer satisfaction and financial performance (Heskett et al., 1997; Capelle Associates, 2003).

References

Ambachtsheer, K., Capelle, R. & Scheibelhut, T. (1998) "Improving Pension Fund Performance." *Financial Analysts Journal* 54(5), 15–20.

Buckingham, M. & Coffman, C. (1999). *First, Break All the Rules: What the World's Greatest Managers Do Differently*. New York: Simon & Schuster.

Capelle Associates (1999). Optimizing Organization Design: Improvements in Manager–Direct Report Alignment, Financial Performance and Employee Satisfaction. Research Paper #1.

Capelle Associates 2000a. Optimizing Organization Design: Improvements in Organization Design and Employee Satisfaction. Research Paper #2.

Capelle Associates (2000b). Optimizing Organization Design: Improvements in Manager–Direct Report Alignment, Employee Satisfaction and Customer Satisfaction. Research Paper #3.

Capelle Associates (2000c). Optimizing Organization Design: Improvements in Manager–Direct Report Alignment and Employee Satisfaction. Research Paper #4.

Capelle Associates (2000d). Optimizing Organization Design: Improvements in Manager–Direct Report Alignment, Leadership and Direction, and Employee Commitment. Research Paper #5.

Capelle Associates (2003b). Organization Design, Manager–Direct Report Alignment and Organization Performance in Canadian Private Sector Companies:

Results from Surveys of CEOs and Heads of Human Resources. Research Paper #9.

Capelle Associates (2005c). Manager–Direct Report Alignment Is Directly Related to Employee Satisfaction: A Review of 30 Organizations. Research Paper #14.

Heskett, J. L., Jones, T. O., Loveman, G. W., Sasser, W. E. & Schlesinger, L. A. (1994). "Putting the Service Profit Chain to Work." *Harvard Business Review* 72(2), 164–174.

Heskett, J. L., Sasser, W. E. & Schlesinger, L. A. (1997). *The Service Profit Chain: How Leading Companies Link Profit and Growth to Loyalty, Satisfaction, and Value*. New York: Free Press.

Jaques, E. (1996). *Requisite Organization: A Total System for Effective Managerial Organization and Managerial Leadership for the 21st Century* (2nd ed.). Arlington, VA: Cason Hall.

Capelle Associates Research Paper #23, Potential Annual Cost Savings from Organization Design Assessments (August 22, 2012h)

There is considerable research that suggests that the organization design in general, and manager–direct report alignment in particular, are important factors related to employee satisfaction, customer satisfaction and financial performance (Ambachtsheer, Capelle and Scheibelhut, 1998; Capelle Associates 1999; Capelle Associates, 2000a; Capelle Associates, 2000b; Capelle Associates, 2000c; Capelle Associates, 2000d; Capelle Associates, 2003b; Capelle Associates, 2005c).

Jaques (1996) and his colleagues have developed a measure of the complexity of work called "time span." With it, one can determine how many layers or strata an organization should have, and place every position in the correct layer or stratum. More specifically, one can develop optimal manager–direct report alignment. This is a situation in which a manager is exactly one layer or stratum above a direct report.

Buckingham and Coffman (1999) concluded from employee satisfaction surveys that one of the most important factors in organization performance is the manager–direct report relationship.

It would appear that manager–direct report alignment is a driver of the manager–direct report relationship (Capelle Associates, 2003b).

There is also considerable research documenting the positive relationship between employee and customer satisfaction (Heskett et al., 1994). Furthermore, customer satisfaction is positively related to financial performance (Heskett et al., 1997). It would appear that organization design and manager–direct report alignment are drivers of these variables, and that they are positively related (Capelle Associates, 2003b).

While manager–direct report alignment is a critical factor, our benchmarking database shows that only 55 percent of the manager–direct report alignments are optimal (Capelle Associates, 2012c). While improving the alignment is critical for longer-term performance, one can also attain shorter-term cost savings.

Shorter-term cost savings can result from removing positions that are redundant in terms of vertical alignment. These cost savings come from situations in which there is compression. This means that a manager and direct report are actually operating at the same stratum or level. Compression occurs in about 36 percent of the manager–direct report alignments in our benchmarking database (Capelle Associates, 2012c).

It should be noted that not all compressed positions are caused by having a redundant position that should be removed. It can also be caused by positions not being set up properly and not having the optimal level of work delegated. It can also be caused by individuals in positions not working at the level that they should (and in some cases, not having the capability to do so).

Therefore, one needs to be cautious in identifying and removing redundant positions. These can be identified with some assessment of the position alignment. As well, it will be necessary to ensure that work done by the redundant position is dealt with appropriately.

As part of an assessment, we identify such positions, and determine the cost of the positions. We call this "potential annual cost savings." We determine the cost to be salary and expected bonus. This is a conservative number since it does not include benefits and other costs of employment. On the other hand it does not include any potential severance costs.

We find that executives make different choices with these savings. Some reinvest in new positions that provide better value. Some take the savings. With the difficulty of finding top employees, employees often end up in different positions that provide better value.

It should be noted that our clients consider these cost savings to be a bonus on the path to better performance. The most significant payoff is better performance, not the cost savings. Removing redundant positions can not only provide cost savings, it can also enhance employee satisfaction. Compression results in managers not adding value and direct reports not being able to use their full capability. This has impact on employee satisfaction as well as financial performance (Capelle Associates, 2005c).

In this paper we review potential annual cost savings.

Method   We calculated the potential annual cost savings of 19 organization assessments that we have completed. An organization assessment consists of interview with managers to obtain time spans of their direct reports. The time spans are used to analyze the manager–direct report alignments in the organization. Out of all of the compression, redundant positions are determined, as are their annual costs (salary and expected benefits only).

Results   A review of 19 organizations found significant potential annual cost savings. These savings result from the elimination of redundant managerial positions (i.e., positions that are in the same stratum or layer as their immediate manager). The average potential annual cost savings was $2,994,298 per organization. The average investment in the assessment was significantly lower at $454,779. The average potential annual return on investment (ROI) was 589 percent. These variables are presented in Figure B.23.1 for each of the 19 organizations.

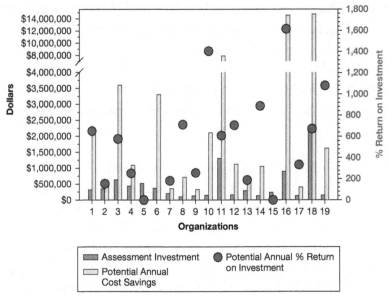

FIGURE B.23.1. Potential Annual Cost Savings, Assessment Investment, and Potential Annual Percent Return on Investment for 19 Organizations

It should be noted that while the investment is one time, the savings recur on an annual basis (e.g., if there is savings in a position being eliminated, that savings recur each year).

The average potential annual cost savings per employee was $2,505 (n=19). This number is calculated by dividing the annual cost savings by the number of employees in the organization.

It should be noted that two of the organizations had no potential annual cost savings. It is important that these numbers have integrity, and be based on the best interest of the organization. In these two cases, the organizations were in a significant growth mode. Not only were there no redundant positions, but there were requirements to add positions. We have included these numbers in our averages since these are also actual situations that one might encounter.

There is a slight positive relationship between the number of compressed positions in an organization and the average savings per

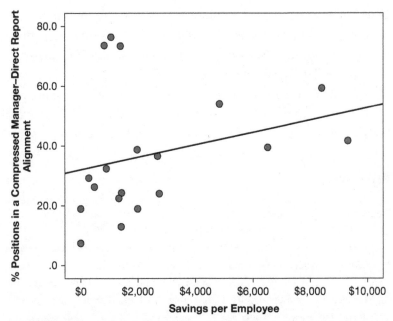

FIGURE B.23.2.   Relationship between the Percentage of Compressed Positions and the Potential Annual Cost Savings per Employee

Each point represents an organization (n=19)

employee (Spearman's r=0.319, P=0.184, n=19; Figure B.23.2). However, it does not reach statistical significance. This also provides a caution.

Compression in itself does not mean that there is a redundant position. Further review is necessary to make this determination. As well, the potential annual cost savings is also related to the compensation in the positions. A few more highly compensated positions can provide a better return that numerous lower level positions.

We believe that the number of redundant positions that we identify is quite conservative (i.e., quite low). The average percentage of compressed situations in this study was 37.1 percent while the average number of redundant positions was only 2.2 percent per organization. If one used more aggressive criterion, it would be possible to further elevate this number.

Discussion The most substantive benefit from improving manager–direct report alignment is improving organization performance (employee satisfaction, customer satisfaction, and financial performance) (Capelle Associates, 2005, 2012c). However, it is also possible to achieve shorter-term cost savings by removing redundant positions. Care must be taken in doing so. However, both the savings and the return on investment can be significant.

References

Ambachtsheer, K., Capelle, R. & Scheibelhut, T. (1998) "Improving Pension Fund Performance." *Financial Analysts Journal* 54(5), 15–20.

Buckingham, M. & Coffman, C. (1999). *First, Break All the Rules: What the World's Greatest Managers Do Differently.* New York: Simon & Schuster.

Capelle Associates (1999). Optimizing Organization Design: Improvements in Manager–Direct Report Alignment, Financial Performance and Employee Satisfaction. Research Paper #1.

Capelle Associates (2000a). Optimizing Organization Design: Improvements in Organization Design and Employee Satisfaction. Research Paper #2.

Capelle Associates (2000b). Optimizing Organization Design: Improvements in Manager–Direct Report Alignment, Employee Satisfaction and Customer Satisfaction. Research Paper #3.

Capelle Associates (2000c). Optimizing Organization Design: Improvements in Manager–Direct Report Alignment and Employee Satisfaction. Research Paper #4.

Capelle Associates (2000d). Optimizing Organization Design: Improvements in Manager–Direct Report Alignment, Leadership and Direction, and Employee Commitment. Research Paper #5.

Capelle Associates (2003b). Organization Design, Manager–Direct Report Alignment and Organization Performance in Canadian Private Sector Companies: Results from Surveys of CEOs and Heads of Human Resources. Research Paper #9.

Capelle Associates (2005c). Manager–Direct Report Alignment Is Directly Related to Employee Satisfaction: A Review of 30 Organizations. Research Paper #14.

Capelle Associates (2012c). Manager–Direct Report Alignment, Delegation and Compensation from Capelle Associates Benchmarking Database. Research Paper #16.

Heskett, J. L., Jones, T. O., Loveman, G. W., Sasser, W. E. & Schlesinger, L. A. (1994). "Putting the Service Profit Chain to Work." *Harvard Business Review* 72(2), 164–174.

Heskett, J. L., Sasser, W. E. & Schlesinger, L. A. (1997). *The Service Profit Chain: How Leading Companies Link Profit and Growth to Loyalty, Satisfaction, and Value.* New York: Free Press.

Jaques, E. (1996). *Requisite Organization: A Total System for Effective Managerial Organization and Managerial Leadership for the 21st Century* (2nd ed.). Arlington, VA: Cason Hall.

Conclusion

We have presented 23 previously unpublished Capelle Associates Research Papers, as well as referred to one previously published paper (Ambachtsheer, Capelle & Scheibelhut, 1998).

Our research shows that there are statistically significant relationships between each of the following pairs of factors:

- organization design and manager–direct report alignment
- organization design and employee satisfaction
- organization design and relationship with manager
- organization design and customer satisfaction
- organization design and financial performance
- organization design and organization performance
- manager–direct report alignment and employee satisfaction
- manager–direct report alignment and relationship with manager
- manager–direct report alignment and customer satisfaction
- manager–direct report alignment and financial performance
- employee satisfaction and relationship with manager

Our research also provides information on the following factors:

- manager–direct report alignment
- compensation
- delegation
- information processing capability

- task alignment
- Capelle Associates Employee Satisfaction Questionnaire
- span of control

We believe that better organization design and better manager–direct report alignment lead to improvements in employee satisfaction, relationship with manager, customer satisfaction and financial performance. There are several reasons for this:

- We would expect these outcomes from a theoretical perspective, and can specify the factors that are related to this.
- We have research results that support the relationships among these factors.
- In most cases, these research results have been replicated through many types of research over an extended period of time.
- The research results are consistent with executive comments about their success in using this approach to achieve these benefits.
- The research is consistent with related case studies (Appendix C).
- There is considerable supporting research on many of the organization design variables that we use (Craddock, 2009).
- There is complementary research by Buckingham and Coffman (1999) on the importance of the manager–direct report relationship. They have shown it to be related to productivity, profitability, retention and customer satisfaction.
- There is complementary research on the service profit chain (Heskett, Jones, Loveman, Sasser & Schlesinger, 1994; Heskett, Sasser & Schlesinger, 1997; Heskett, Sasser & Schlesinger, 2003; Heskett, Sasser & Wheeler, 2008). They have shown that there is a relationship between the employee (including satisfaction and loyalty), the customer (including value equation, satisfaction, and loyalty), and financial performance (including revenue growth and profitability).

From a "purist" research perspective, we do acknowledge that we do not have the stronger research designs found in the natural sciences. However, this type of research in the management/organization field related to the sorts of relationships we are considering is rarely found. We believe that the combination of theoretical underpinnings, replicated research of many types over many years, related evidence (executive comments and case studies), and related research (Craddock, 2009; Buckingham & Coffman, 1999; Heskett et al., 2003) provide a strong foundation. Therefore, we believe that both better organization design and better manager–direct report alignment lead to better employee satisfaction, relationship with manager, customer satisfaction, and financial performance.

APPENDIX C

CASE STUDIES

In this section we will provide four case studies on improving organization performance with our optimizing organization design approach. These real life examples provide a better sense of what actually happens in this approach. The case studies have been provided by Allstate Insurance, Canadian Pacific, Capital Power, and Royal Ottawa Health Care Group. Each one comes from a different industry (financial services, railway, power generation and health care), and each is different in the nature of its challenges and outcomes. As much as possible, these are in the words of the clients, and present the uniqueness of each of the situations.

I appreciate the support of my colleagues, Raymond Daigneault and Dwight Mihalicz, and our clients on these case studies. For Allstate Insurance, Raymond Daigneault took the lead for us, and Eric Pickering and Jim Allin of Allstate both made significant contributions. For Canadian Pacific, Raymond Daigneault took the lead for us, and Peter Edwards, Bob MacIntyre, and Mary-Ellen Selby of Canadian Pacific made significant contributions. For Capital Power, Dwight Mihalicz took the lead for us, and Peter Arnold of Capital Power made significant contributions. For Royal Ottawa Health Care Group, Dwight Mihalicz took the lead for us, and George Weber of Royal Ottawa Health Care Group made significant contributions.

In addition to these four case studies, there is one previously published case study on the work of our firm. This was an assessment and implementation with the International Federation of Red Cross and Red Crescent Societies (Weber & Mihalicz, 2007).

ALLSTATE INSURANCE CASE STUDY

Introduction

Allstate Insurance Company of Canada (Allstate Canada) is a Canadian Property and Casualty insurer.

Allstate Canada management wanted to better align people and systems to meet its strategic goals and decided to go about this by improving its organization design. Capelle Associates was selected to provide support, and the organization design work was initiated in the early part of 2004.

This case study is significant for two main reasons:

- The organization design was comprehensive. It included an organization review and the implementation of agreed actions; task alignment work for the Information Technology and Claims functions; the design and implementation of an integrated business planning and review system; and the alignment of the compensation system;
- The sustainment has been excellent, and the organization has continued to enhance its design to this day (2012).

Organization

Allstate Insurance Company of Canada (Allstate Canada) is a subsidiary of Allstate Corporation. It has been operating since 1953 and had approximately 1,500 employees.

The Property & Casualty industry in Canada had difficult years in the early part of the 2000s and the company was no exception. In 2002 and 2003, there was a sense that the industry was finally improving, and Allstate more strongly focused on longer term strategic goals and actions that were necessary to improve company profits in this competitive industry.

The President and CEO and the management team had aggressive goals and wanted to improve profits significantly in the upcoming 5 years. It was determined that there were some systemic enablers that would help to successfully execute the strategy. These included:

- Aligning the organizational structure to the strategy
- Clarifying roles and accountabilities
- Developing a stronger, more disciplined business planning and review approach
- Improving and fostering teamwork within the organization, including breaking down silos
- Creating a more formal management development talent pool and succession planning process to ensure that the company had the right people in the right roles at the right time.

The President and CEO and the management team were looking for an approach that would help produce these deliverables. The Head of Human Resources recommended an organization design intervention as he believed that improving organization design would lay the necessary foundation, including improved systems to execute the strategy and improve performance.

Method

Initial Discussion, Proposal, and Contract Discussions between the President and CEO, the Vice President of Human Resources, the Chief Financial Officer and Capelle Associates took place and a decision to proceed was made in February 2004. Due to other initiatives that were taking place, it was decided not to include the Claims department at this point.

Approximately 1,000 Canada-wide positions were in scope for this phase of the work. To ensure appropriate employee involvement, it was decided to give all employees access to the Capelle Associates employee satisfaction/organization design questionnaire.

Assessment   The objectives of the organization review were as follows:

- Develop an accurate picture of the current organization design of Allstate Canada, including the complexity of work (as measured by time span), compensation (relative to complexity of work), and (for managers) clarity of delegation.
- Complete an organization review of Allstate Canada to determine opportunities for current improvement and future evolution.
- Recommend an overall optimal organization design for Allstate Canada, including vertical and functional alignment.
- Recommend an overall implementation plan for the new organization design, including the major issues that should be addressed.

The review method included the following:

- a document review and literature search;
- interviews with about 120 individuals, all of whom are in management roles;
- interviews with five stakeholders who could provide context for the review;
- completion of the Capelle Associates Organization Design/Employee Satisfaction Questionnaire by about 780 employees; and,
- a compilation and review of information on employee roles and their reporting relationships.

Through this process, slightly more than 1,000 employee roles were reviewed.

Report   The full report detailed 50 suggested actions and associated analysis.

One of the major findings went back to strategy. Allstate Canada had more than one brand, and it was not clear whether these brands were strategic business units or distribution channels.

It was recommended that Allstate Canada should be a Stratum 5 (5 level) organization.

There were significant opportunities to improve the vertical alignment of positions. This included manager–direct report alignments in which managers and direct reports were actually working at the same level (compression), and situations in which they were too far apart (gaps).

There were opportunities to combine and centralize some lower level transactional work and also better differentiate tasks at the Stratum 1 first level and Stratum 2 professional level in the Information Technology (IT) Department. In the latter case, one of the findings was that some professionals were spending significant time doing lower level work. A suggested action was to conduct a task alignment analysis to improve the alignment of tasks and improve overall effectiveness and efficiency.

One key finding of the assessment phase was that the company was not capitalizing on the full potential of Stratum 3 roles (roles that manage professionals and first level managers). They tended to operate at too low a level, and were not doing the higher level, unique added value work for which they were paid.

Other selected opportunities included:

- better integrate the Underwriting work;
- elevate the technology project manager role to make it commensurate with the associated project complexity (and ensure that it was staffed at that level);
- introduce an Accountability and Authority framework and clarify managerial and cross functional accountabilities and authorities;

- improve the business planning and review; and
- ensure the consistent use of position titles.

Meeting   The President and CEO and his direct reports met to review the report, and to discuss and decide the suggested actions and next steps. It was decided to proceed with a full implementation.

Other decisions included:

- Executives and managers would be accountable for the implementation within their area of accountability.
- Executives and managers would be supported by an implementation team that would comprise internal resources (individuals from the Human Resources department) and external resources (Capelle Associates).
- The focus of the implementation would be on aligning positions; aligning accountabilities and authorities; and aligning people to positions in the new design.
- The Claims Department would be out of scope for this implementation but would be covered at a later point.

In parallel, discussions were held regarding the possibility of performing a task alignment engagement for the Information Technology Function, as recommended in the report.

Implementation: Content

Aligning Positions   A first major implementation deliverable was to align positions (vertically and functionally) and ensure the appropriate manager–direct report alignment. There were significant compression and gap situations to address. The proposed design for each department from the organization design review report was the baseline for the implementation changes.

Vice Presidents were asked to review the design of their respective organization within the context and prescribed limits set for the implementation and present their proposed blueprints. These were reviewed in terms of alignment to the strategy; integrity to the organization design principles; and net resulting impact of their final recommendations (e.g., adding new positions and/or eliminating redundant positions). This was a winning buy-in approach for executives. The Vice Presidents presented and discussed their proposed designs with the President and CEO, and the desired state blueprints were decided. The President and CEO was very involved in understanding the logic of the proposed designs and did challenge the proposed changes to ensure the best possible end result.

The organization design framework had very good face validity for executives and managers, making its implementation much easier than otherwise would þe the case.

Aligning Accountabilities and Authorities   The second major deliverable was to align accountabilities and authorities. This included:

- Generic employee, manager, and manager once removed accountabilities and authorities;
- Position specific accountabilities and authorities, including managerial accountabilities and authorities when appropriate; and
- Cross functional accountabilities and authorities.

A company position description template was decided. Company-wide generic employee, manager, and manager once removed accountabilities and authorities were decided to ensure a consistent approach throughout Allstate Canada. The latter accountabilities and authorities were documented on the position description template to ensure a consistent distribution and serve as a handy reminder of what is expected.

Position descriptions were developed for the President and CEO and the Vice President positions. The President and CEO position description provided context for Vice President's position description development, and so on down the organization. A manager's guide was developed to help managers develop position descriptions in a consistent way and ensure sustainment over time.

The position descriptions were very helpful in clarifying what was expected from each position and what the requirements were to fill the positions.

The alignment of cross functional accountabilities and authorities began at the Stratum 4 Vice President level and cascaded down from there. A manager's guide was developed to help managers understand the cross functional accountability and authority framework and how to apply this approach. A context clarification and issues resolution process was also developed and communicated throughout the organization. A process guide for the implementation of cross functional role relationships was developed.

As part of the process of clarifying accountabilities and authorities, a managerial leadership framework was introduced and managerial leadership practices and expectations were communicated through the cascading natural team implementation meetings.

Aligning People to Positions   The third major deliverable was to align people through a Talent Pool Review process. Four review criteria were decided and included: information processing capability, skilled knowledge, valuing the work, and required behaviours. A manager's guide was developed including a Talent Pool Review worksheet to document the review of the employees in scope. A facilitator's guide was developed to help qualified individuals facilitate Talent Pool Review preparation tasks and meetings. Timely education meetings were held before the Talent Pool Review meetings. Manager once removed and direct reports meetings were held to review direct reports once removed.

Two key outcomes of the meetings were to have the information necessary to make decisions related to matching people to positions, and to have the information to assist with the longer-term development of the talent pool. The Talent Pool Review process has been, since its inception, a yearly process at Allstate Canada.

Implementation: Process

The President and CEO was determined to see the implementation process succeed and provided constant managerial leadership during the implementation. This included providing opening remarks to many cascading meetings where he would stress the importance of improving Allstate Canada organization design and share his vision of the desired state.

An Internal–External team approach was used. The external team provided materials and processes and these were adapted for this specific implementation while the internal team provided knowledge and skills related to the organization. Members of the Human Resources function were selected for the implementation team, as well as the company's Corporate Relations Director to support the communication requirements. This was a particularly strong team in terms of capability and commitment, which contributed to a smooth implementation, a faster knowledge transfer than typical, excellent people change management, and valuable contribution in improving the materials.

In terms of project management, the implementation planning was effective taking into account the experience of the external consultants in organization design implementations and the diligent work of the internal team members in pacing the implementation commensurate to management's readiness. Another consideration for planning was to ensure the translation of the materials into French. The translation work was done by the company's translation unit.

People change management was a key consideration. A comprehensive communication program was developed for the duration of the implementation. Regular educational communications were issued to involve all employees and provide knowledge transfer progressively about the organization design framework and the new terminology. It was anticipated that changing the 'language' would strengthen the message of change and would help communicate new expectations. Education and training was provided in a timely fashion to natural teams (e.g., position alignment principles; accountability and authority framework including position description development; talent pool review criteria and approach).

The implementation process was cascading and iterative, in natural work teams, starting with the President and CEO and his Vice President direct reports. Executives and managers would be accountable for the implementation within their area of accountability and would participate twice:

- The first as a participant to their immediate manager meetings;
- The second, as the accountable manager for the meetings held with their direct reports.

Each event included education and training (e.g., how to develop a position description); real work (e.g., starting to develop direct reports position descriptions); and feedback.

Selected members of the internal team were trained and qualified for facilitating the cascading and iterative team meetings. This qualification process was essential to ensure a consistent implementation, at the highest level of quality, and to ensure the integrity of the organization design principles. These qualified resources ensured the cascading and iterative implementation for the assigned teams and gained considerable experience and skills to help sustain the improvements over time.

Additional Organization Design Enhancement

Management decided to proceed with four additional interventions. These were task alignment in the Information Technology (IT) department; Business Planning and Review; the Organization Design Review and Task Alignment Review of the Claims Department; and Compensation.

Task Alignment in the Information Technology (IT) Department The consultant facilitated the process of identifying key IT tasks; classifying the key tasks; determining the key factors that one wanted to assess; and ensuring the data gathering for the analysis. The consultant analyzed the data collected and prepared a report with suggested actions. The Vice President, Information Technology and his direct reports met to review the report, and to discuss and decide the suggested actions and next steps.

Some of the major findings included:

- Some roles compensated at Stratum 2 and above levels were spending a high percentage of time carrying out Stratum 1 tasks. This provided the opportunity to realign the tasks to positions at the right level and reduce task execution costs.
- The ratio of Business Advancement work and Non Business Advancement work (e.g., 'keeping the lights on') from time spent, cost and FTE perspectives should be improved to better support strategic plan achievement.

Given the opportunities identified as a result of the task alignment assessment, a task alignment implementation project was agreed. This comprised better aligning tasks by moving some tasks to the appropriate level and specific positions, eliminating some positions resulting from task's movement, and creating other positions at a lower level and lower cost for doing these tasks.

In terms of implementation of the suggested actions, the work was performed by a small internal–external team that included two IT Directors and the Allstate Canada Compensation and Benefits Director.

Business Planning and Review A company-wide Business Planning and Review system was developed and documented. This included integrating and synchronizing the strategic planning and the budgeting systems. The Business planning and review design and development work was performed by a small internal–external team that included the CFO and two Finance Directors. The implementation process was cascading and iterative, in natural work teams. A guide and materials were provided to managers. Sessions were facilitated by qualified individuals.

The President and CEOs organization plan was developed using the new framework (mission, vision, values, strategic positioning, operational plan and resource plan) and the appropriate level of complexity in terms of the longest deliverables. The President and CEOs organization plan and delegation of executive deliverables provided the foundation for the development of Vice President plans. This approach of plan development from the immediate manager to direct reports repeated itself throughout the organization, ensuring appropriate alignment and deliverables. Meetings were also held to understand plans of functional colleagues and ensure cross functional coherence. At the conclusion of this implementation, the President and CEO commented:

> One of our biggest improvements has been in business planning. Because we had taken the time to properly align the organization, we have been able to create and overlay a cascading business planning and review system in which employees have clearer deliverables with more appropriate complexity at each level. This is extremely powerful.

Organization Design Review and Task Alignment Review of the Claims Department   An organization design review and a task alignment review of the Claims Department were performed using the same process as described earlier for the Allstate Canada review and the IT task alignment. This work was contained within the Claims Department. Implementation was planned and executed by the internal team members that were qualified as part of the core implementation. This allowed addressing compression and gaps for an improved position alignment and aligning claims positions in a consistent way than the rest of the organization. The task alignment work was helpful in identifying opportunities to better align Stratum 2 vs. Stratum 1 tasks, better differentiate risk man-agement vs. internal control tasks, and provide critical information for ensuring the appropriate development of the Claims technology system.

Compensation   The compensation system was reviewed, aligned and enhanced with the organization design method. The system design and development work was performed by a small internal–external team that included the Vice President of Human Resources and Director of Compensation and Benefits. A guide "Measurement of Role Complexity: Information Processing Requirement and Time Span" was developed. This provided additional tools, for managers and Human Resources individuals, to better evaluate the position complexity and grading and align compensation appropriately.

Sustainment

In this case, not only was the original work sustained to this day (2004 to 2012), but because of constant attention and commitment particularly by the Human Resources individuals, including the Vice President of Human Resources and Director of Corporate Learning, the systems and practices have continued to improve over time. This is particularly remarkable since there were many fundamental changes in the organization since then, e.g., changes of CEO, changes to the distribution channels, etc.

Some aspects of the implementation were conducive to facilitate sustainment over time. These included:

- Knowledge was transferred to the internal resources, including the specific training and qualification of selected individuals.
- Systems and processes (e.g., Talent Pool Review system) were documented. Manager's guides were developed, distributed and explained.

- Relevant systems were aligned and improved during the implementation (position descriptions; talent pool review; business planning and review; and compensation).
- Managers were directly involved throughout the implementation.
- The Vice President of Human Resources was determined to continue to align HR systems, including aligning recruitment system and training and development.
- Introducing terms that had operational definitions provided a more precise and consistent 'language' to all employees.

Results

Two major improvements included business planning and review (i.e. production of appropriate individual deliverables; clearer organization goals; and better organization-wide resources allocation) and better people selection (i.e. matching people to positions system). There was also an improvement in eliminating compression and gaps and optimizing the position alignment. There was a reduction, and in many cases the elimination, of needless work that was not prioritized. There was some very strong positive feedback related to employee satisfaction regarding teamwork and career development. Teamwork improved. Some individuals were demoted to appropriate strata of work for their level of capability. There was more formal recognition of sole contributor roles to put people into roles where they do value the work. The job evaluation system was aligned and enhanced to reflect the complexity of the work tied to variables.

On the financial side, while it is hard to articulate some of the financial and expense aspects due to the radical change that the company made in their distribution model in 2007, Allstate Canada, for the last three years, has had increasingly better performance where in many cases has outperformed the industry both in terms of growth and profitability. These years also experienced improvements in overall employee satisfaction.

Other results from the organization design work included improvement of IT and Claims task alignment; improved clarity of accountabilities and authorities; and excellent knowledge transfer to HR individuals as demonstrated by their capability to continue the implementation at lower levels and do the claims implementation on their own.

Conclusion

This case study demonstrates that improving organization design is related to improving financial performance and employee satisfaction. It also demonstrates that improvements can be sustained and systems further improved with continued focus and commitment.

Management felt that they learned a lot in terms of how to create an aligned organization with clarity around roles, accountabilities, deliverables, and tasks. A significant achievement was the implementation of the Talent Pool Review Process as it completely reinforced putting the right people in the right position, and matching position's requirements with individual's capability.

Other key lessons learned through the process were the following:

- The President's support, leadership and commitment are critical to successfully improve the organization;
- The duration and pace of the implementation should be adapted to the requirements of the organization;
- It is important to use a detailed, cascading and iterative implementation process so that everyone is involved, at the right time, in the right conditions;
- This approach is not a quick fix, however, when done right, it provides significant pay back;
- It is critical that the implementation process provides sound education for all employees, e.g., organization design principles, expected changes and behaviours, and new 'language';

- It is important to celebrate implementation successes and communicate, appropriately, in a timely and effective fashion;
- It is key to provide training and education to new managers when they join the organization since both the 'language' and how the company goes about doing work is different than other organizations.

Organization design improvements were key contributors for Allstate Canada being selected as a Top 50 Employer by *Maclean*'s magazine and AON Hewitt for 2013.

CANADIAN PACIFIC CASE STUDY

Introduction

In early 2009, Canadian Pacific (CP) senior management decided that improving organization design would provide major opportunities to further enhance performance. Capelle Associates was engaged to support this initiative.

It was decided to start with two pilot projects. These were in Information Technology and Locomotive Reliability Centres. This work was completed from June to August 2009. The results were positive, and a decision was made to complete an organization design assessment of all of CP. The assessment and draft report were completed between August 2009 and the end of the year. A final report and related decision making were completed by April 2010. An implementation was initiated in May 2010. The primary implementation was completed by June 2011. Some additional cross functional support was completed by October 2011.

This case study is interesting in that it involved large scale change (approximately 16,000 employees) that required an aggressive schedule but also maintained high quality standards. It was also somewhat different in that the implementation started with one function (Operations) in order to meet CP operational requirements. All other areas in the company were subsequently completed. The Capelle Associates implementation process is usually done one level or stratum at a time and cascades down across the whole organization. This implementation approach created some integration challenges across the whole organization, but met its objective of aligning Operations (over 13,000 positions) quickly and in a high quality way. A major contributing factor to this achievement was the very high level of commitment of the Head of Operations, as well as other Operations executives and managers. They put in long hours over and above their "day job", and with changing schedules and short lead times, managed to produce high quality, on-time deliverables. High quality implementation was also completed in all other areas of the company, but without as aggressive a schedule.

Organization

Canadian Pacific is a Class I Railway, with operations in Canada and the United States. CP is a public company. It provides rail, transload and intermodal transportation services. There were approximately 16,000 employees. A significant number of positions, particularly in Operations, were unionized.

There was a perceived opportunity for improvement. Improvement areas developing a robust and flexible organization design approach that would provide alignment with strategy, consistency across the organization, and adaptability to changing priorities; removing redundant positions; increased clarity of accountability and authority; better cross functional work (reduction of stovepipes/silos); lower cost; more engaged workforce; increased productivity; and improved career planning.

Method

Initial Discussion, Proposal, and Contract   The CP Senior Vice President of Human Resources and Labour Relations attended a Conference Board presentation by Ron Capelle and one of his clients, EPCOR/Capital Power. The presentation was on recent organization design improvements. Ron Capelle was invited to present to the CP Senior Leadership Team. The Senior Vice President of Human Resources and Labour Relations, and the Assistant Vice President, Human Resources became strong advocates for an organization design initiative.

The President and CEO decided to initially only proceed with two pilot projects. One was Information Technology and the other was Locomotive Reliability Centres. CP was cautious and wanted to do pilot projects first to test the method and see the results. The assessments for these two areas were completed in July 2009, and some implementation of the recommendations took place in both areas. The results were positive and it was decided to review the full company. The main objectives of the review were to understand the current design and to determine opportunities for improvement.

Assessment   The assessment phase included a document review (e.g., business plans, position descriptions, etc.), a review of related employee information, a computerized literature search, and interviews.

Interviews were completed with approximately 1,200 individuals. This included virtually all managers (defined as being accountable for the work of others regardless of title). Interviews were up to one hour in length, and focused on the work of the manager and her/his direct reports, as well as related issues and opportunities. In this way it is possible, without requiring much time from the organization, to develop an understanding of the work of all employees.

The assessment was particularly difficult to conduct. There was considerable change in the organization. There was a major initiative (integration of DM&E (Dakota, Minnesota and Eastern Railroad) that had recently been acquired) and numerous smaller and unrelated initiatives throughout the organization.

Report   The information was obtained through company documents; employee information; and during the interviews was analyzed and a comprehensive draft report was completed by December 2009. The final report and related decision making was completed by April 2010.

The starting point for the report was understanding the strategy and designing the organization to best deliver it. There were two keys. The first was that CP was one business. The implication was that CP needed to be one single, large, complex organization in which cross functional work was critical to success. The second is that every organization design has an entry point—the most fundamental building block of the design. For CP, this was the physical plant (Operations). This included physical infrastructure (tracks and terminals); rolling stock (locomotives and cars); and the movement of the rolling stock across the infrastructure and beyond.

The report had eleven chapters. The current accountability hierarchy (current state organization charts as determined during the interviews) was provided in an appendix on a CD. The report included ninety (90) suggested actions and their supporting analyses; CP business drivers for Organization Design; specific organization design principles used to help determine an optimal design; and a proposed organization design.

The report contained detailed recommendations for vertical and functional alignment of positions. The framework would be a Stratum 7 (seven layers or strata) organization. There had previously been up to 10 layers. The recommended functional alignment included core functions (Operations, Logistics and Marketing/Sales) and support functions (Finance, Human Resources, Information Technology, etc.). Secondary alignments (and related cross functional accountabilities and authorities) were required for Operations (this would be geography) and for Marketing/Sales (this would be customer type).

There were also many specific recommendations related to various areas or practices. These included improving manager–direct report alignment (there was considerable compression in which managers and their direct reports operate at the same level); improving the nature of managerial work (often weak or nonexistent); improving delegation of accountabilities and authorities (there was considerable micro management); improving spans of control (often far too large but in some cases too small); developing a consistent titling protocol; using strata and sub strata as a framework for Human Resources practices (e.g., job evaluation; organization planning and review); further enhancing the Talent Pool system with practices related to information processing capability, skilled knowledge and application.

Meetings   Meetings took place with the President and CEO and selected senior executives. The analysis and most of the recommended actions resonated with these individuals. It was decided that an organization design implementation should be planned and executed.

The organization design implementation was to focus on three main deliverables:

- aligning positions (vertically and functionally);
- clarifying accountabilities and authorities including the development of position descriptions to replace existing job descriptions;
- matching people to positions in the new design through an enhanced Talent Pool Review process.

In terms of the organization design implementation process, it was decided that the initial focus would be on Operations. This area would be completed first and as quickly as reasonable to produce the expected deliverables before the winter season. The

Operations group was also prioritized as this group was by far the largest and had some of the best opportunities for improvement. Implementation in all other areas of the company followed this.

It should be noted that there were two significant changes to the executive ranks. Both individuals came from a major competitor, Canadian National (CN) and therefore brought in different perspectives. One was a new Vice President of Human Resources who joined in late 2009. He assumed overall accountability for the organization design implementation, and subsequently became the Vice President of Human Resources and Industrial Relations. The other was a new Chief Operations Officer. His capability and commitment were significant factors in the operations implementation proceeding very quickly and in a high quality manner. Both of these individuals could see the value of this organization design initiative, and became critical to the successful implementation.

In the next sections, we will discuss the implementation that took place from process and content perspectives.

Implementation: Process

Throughout the implementation, the process was cascading and iterative, in natural work teams, with provision of education and training, real work and feedback. However, instead of implementing simultaneously across company functions, implementation within Operations was prioritized, and completed at an accelerated pace taking into account the upcoming winter conditions and related operational requirements. Implementation for all other CP functions was completed by April 2011.

An Internal–External team was created to support the implementation. Some of the major implementation project team deliverables included the development and monitoring of the project plan using generally accepted project management and people change management principles and practices; the design and development of the necessary materials and processes; the facilitation of education and training sessions; and the provision of advice and services to implementing managers.

Internal–External Team   An Internal–External team was set up shortly after a decision to proceed. This is the ideal approach as the CP individuals know the organization and the employees while the external team brings organization design expertise, materials, processes, and implementation skills to speed up the process and help ensure high quality outcomes.

The core team was kept small. Capelle Associates provided the external team. The Assistant Vice President, Human Resources became a full time project director. He was supported by a very small and very capable internal team. One of these team members was the General Manager of the Human Resources Business Partners. She was not only a key part of the internal team, but also directed the broader implementation team that was created when facilitation requirements increased, as per the implementation plan. This was staffed primarily by more senior Human Resources Business Partners. Capelle Associates brought in implementation materials and worked with the internal team to adapt them to CP. When appropriate, senior Human Resources Business Partners also supported their internal clients (e.g., helping with the development of position descriptions and preparing employee information for the Talent Pool Review process). As well, the larger internal team was trained and qualified, the latter process involving having them observe sessions and actually facilitate sessions under supervision.

However, due to the required speed of the implementation for Operations, it began before the materials were fully adapted and the team was fully trained and qualified. Capelle Associates therefore facilitated more of the initial sessions than would be typical. However, the internal team did develop organization design capabilities that were not only valuable to the implementation, but also to subsequent support and sustainment.

Another difference in this organization design implementation was the decision to start with Operations. As a result, there was less work with the entire CP senior management team than would normally be the case. This decision did provide the desired benefit, but also had some cost in making integration across the top of the organization more difficult.

Project Management   Project plans were developed. However, their execution required a great deal of flexibility. Changes in Operations requirements due to field work and frequent changes requested by other groups resulted in numerous planning and scheduling changes. Nonetheless, these were manageable and kept the priority on Operations requirements.

People Change Management   People change management plans were developed and included education and training, and communication.

Education and training was a natural part of the cascading program. Education and training was provided to senior Human Resources Business Partners to help them support managers in doing the implementation work expected of them.

The implementation project team did not have access to a communication resource as much as would have been desirable. However, communication support was obtained for critical communications.

Implementation: Content

As mentioned earlier, the organization design implementation was to focus on three main deliverables: aligning positions (vertically and functionally); clarifying accountabilities and authorities including the development of position descriptions; and matching people to positions.

Aligning positions   Considering that CP had a significant number of compressed positions, and some position alignment gaps, there was considerable work to be done by managers, supported by the organization design implementation team, in aligning positions (vertical and functional), in aligning manager–direct report relationships, and in applying a new consistent titling protocol. Most gaps and compression were eliminated, providing CP with improved strategic execution capability.

One of the most significant changes, particularly in Operations, was eliminating compression at a Stratum 3 level (senior manager/director level), and creating Stratum 4 General Manager (first level of executive work) positions that had been missing. The fact that Stratum 4 general manager positions were missing resulted in important Stratum 4 work (longer term planning and execution work) not being done. As well as creating these positions, later work was done on judging individual capability and matching people to these positions.

Clarifying Accountabilities and Authorities   In terms of better clarifying and aligning accountabilities and authorities, there was extensive work that resulted in considerable improvement.

A company wide framework was decided, which aligned accountabilities and authorities for all employee, manager, manager once removed, and supervisor positions. This provided a foundation for developing more consistent managerial behaviour and for clarifying managerial expectations. Among other things, this framework provided much needed clarity about the differentiation between Stratum 2 managerial accountabilities and authorities and Stratum 1 supervisor accountabilities and authorities.

A framework to align company wide cross functional accountabilities and authorities was decided. Given that CP is one business, cross functional accountabilities and authorities are critical. One of the most helpful ideas was about the role of the cross over point manager.

There was significant improvement, in Operations particularly, in the clarity of accountabilities and authorities between those accountable for field execution and those accountable for "goodness of function" (e.g., quality assurance).

Position descriptions were developed by managers. This provided opportunities for clarifying what employees were accountable for, what authorities they had, and the position requirements (what an individual requires to fill the position). The latter was also helpful during the Talent Pool Review process.

One of the most impactful ideas was about the role of a Stratum 2 Manager in knowing the employees, knowing the work, and continually improving both.

Capelle Associates recommended the review and potential discontinuance of many Committees. Committees are often dysfunctional and not required when managerial accountabilities and authorities are clear. While there was some movement in this area, there was also some resistance in changing the status quo.

Aligning People to Positions   In terms of aligning people to positions, including new and significantly changed positions, there was considerable work. CP adopted and managers used the Talent Pool Review system. CP had already a very good succession planning system with meetings involving two managerial levels (e.g., a manager and her/his direct report managers would review the next level down). The overall process was enhanced by the introduction of new criteria (information processing capability, skilled knowledge, and application) and by aligning the related accountabilities and authorities, materials, skills and process.

The greatest added value, and most difficult part to understand, was information processing capability. There were some significant changes in perception of the capability of some employees in many instances, either higher or lower than the original perception.

Other Organization Design Implementation Content Areas
Capelle Associates organization design implementation content often also includes the alignment of deliverables; tasks; systems

(Human Resources (including Compensation); Organization Planning and Review; Project Management; Process Management); managerial leadership practices; and further work on cross functional accountabilities and authorities.

In this implementation, the following additional steps were taken.

- Align deliverables: The main idea is to ensure that managers have properly stratified business plans (vision, mission, values, strategic positioning, operational plan and resource plan) that are appropriate for the level of their positions and aligned with the business plan of their immediate managers. There was little work done in this area. There were some minor improvements to existing systems (e.g., Performance Management System).
- Align tasks: There was no significant requirement to align tasks and work was not done in this area at CP.
- Align systems (Human Resources (including Compensation), Organization Planning and Review, Project Management, and Process Management). There was enhancement to some systems, including position descriptions, Talent Pool, project management, process management, compensation, titling of positions, and position evaluation.
- A framework was developed for project management. It was implemented in some areas but not universally. The most significant application was in a major IT project. We believe that major IT projects often fail due to unclear accountabilities and authorities. We were able to provide some enhancement in this important area. Some senior CP people involved mentioned that the framework resonated with them and that they now knew why they had project issues before.
- Connections were made to process management. CP had a significant Lean area. We consider this to be complimentary to, and added value to, what we do. We provided some training for them, and they were able to use this framework to further enhance their Lean work.

- Position Evaluation and Compensation systems were reviewed and enhanced with better alignment with the strata. This work was done by CP and an external consultant. Capelle Associates was not involved in this process.
- A position titling protocol was developed and applied from both vertical and functional alignment perspectives. The number of different titles was reduced and titles made consistent across CP. Some industry Railroad titles were implemented, e.g., Trainmaster and Superintendent.
- Align managerial leadership practices: There was considerable work done on the underlying accountabilities and authorities. There was broad education and understanding about this. This was built into individual position descriptions. However, there was no direct skill training.
- Align cross functional accountabilities and authorities: This was done as part of the implementation cascade on aligning accountabilities and authorities. However, it was not further enhanced across the organization, although, there was further work done in some specific areas (e.g., SAP intervention and some work efforts requiring coordination across the organization.

The potential organization design implementation content was not as fully implemented as it might have been. However, the core areas were successfully implemented in a high quality way.

Sustainment

There were a number of steps that supported sustainment:

- Organization design principles were established by CP. These were discussed and applied with managers during the organization design education and training.
- Relevant systems were changed and enhanced, particularly related to position descriptions, Talent Pool, projected

management, process management, compensation, titling of positions, and position evaluation system. One of the most critical was position evaluation. This "hard wiring" and related policies are critical to sustainment.

- New materials and company wide processes were created and integrated into the new systems.
- All managers participated in the implementation. There was education, real work and feedback. Organization design education and training materials were provided to all managers.
- The team members on the larger internal team were trained in facilitation and qualified.

Results

- Position alignment was improved. Gaps and compression were (largely) eliminated.
- Position descriptions were created. Accountabilities and authorities (employee, supervisor, manager and manager once removed) were clarified. Cross functional, project and process accountabilities and authorities were improved.
- People were better matched to positions.
- Cost savings were produced. Some were invested back into the organization and some were taken.
- CP position titling was improved, and railroad titles were introduced, when appropriate (e.g., Trainmaster).
- Organization design model and principles provide a pragmatic foundation for managers in making future re-organizations, re-alignments or changes to positions in a consistent, disciplined, and appropriate fashion.

Conclusion

Organization design can be implemented quickly with a large organization (16,000 employees) and still maintain a high quality level.

Those in Operations in particular were quite amazing in the commitment and quality that they were able to maintain in the face of extraordinarily demanding time lines (e.g., "You have to be in Calgary for a two day meeting in one week, and before the meeting use this manager's guide to prepare 15 position descriptions"). Individuals in other parts of the company also produced high quality outcomes, although with less aggressive timelines.

While the typical organization design implementation content was not completely used at CP, the implementation focusing on the three main deliverables of aligning positions (vertically and functionally); clarifying accountabilities and authorities including the development of position descriptions; and matching people to positions demonstrated that significant organization improvement is possible with a focus on these core areas.

Implementation work provided CP with a stronger organization design and the knowledge required for reviewing and modifying the design when needed. it also provided a foundation for strategic implementation and human resources policies, procedures and processes.

CAPITAL POWER CASE STUDY

Introduction

In a unique situation, the Capital Power Corporation organization design process began before the company was even formed. In 2008, EPCOR Utilities Inc. (EPCOR) initiated a comprehensive organization design assessment of all of its operations, including its power generation business. However, in parallel, and with appropriate secrecy, strategic decisions were being made to spin out its power generation business lines and have an IPO (initial public offering) which led to a demerger.

In 2008, when the comprehensive assessment was conducted, EPCOR had about 3,000 employees. It was a growing and evolving company with a long history. It was formed in 1996 from the

Edmonton Electric Lighting and Power Company, founded in 1891. At that time, the company operated five power and water plants. In 2008 EPCOR operated more than 50 power and water plants across North America, including more than 3,400 MW of power generation and drinking water services for more than one million people. Over the next five years, EPCOR planned to invest significantly in new power generation, infrastructure and water and wastewater facilities.

EPCOR recognized that optimal organization design is fundamental to achieving optimal organization performance. This was particularly important to integrate the growth that had occurred, and develop an infrastructure that would be robust and flexible enough to provide the foundation for future growth. Some of the perceived opportunities included too many job levels, job titles that were not consistent or clear, opportunities to be better in a "hot market" at attracting and retaining top talent, and a sense of not getting optimal performance (e.g., lack of clarity of accountabilities, and a proliferation of silo mentalities).

EPCOR had been through an intensive process improvement project, and while there were some successes, the results were not getting the intended traction. It was believed that optimizing the organization alignment could help to deliver the intended results.

The search for organization design expertise was led by Human Resources. There was a desire to increase the impact of HR and make it more strategic, so Peter Arnold, Senior VP, Human Resources & Corp Health & Safety, and Robert (Bob) Petryk, Director, Talent Management devoted significant resources to— and were advocates for—an organization design assessment and implementation.

Method

Initial Discussion, Proposal, and Contract Capelle Associates was first approached in late 2006 by Peter and Bob to explore the Capelle Associates organization design methodology. This was followed by a meeting in January 2007, when Peter, Bob and the core process improvement leader traveled to Toronto for due diligence. Following a meeting with Capelle Associates, they met with Capelle Associates' clients to understand how the process worked in their situations, and the potential benefits.

This was followed by initial discussions with EPCOR executives in Edmonton. While there was agreement that optimizing the EPCOR organization design would lead to improvements in organization performance, there was not enough support to initiate a comprehensive review across the whole organization.

As a result, a discrete organizational unit, which was a significant part of the EPCOR business and was led by a strong executive, volunteered to be a pilot project. This pilot project consisted of an assessment conducted in 2007, followed by an implementation process in early 2008. The implementation could not be as comprehensive as would typically be the case since the pilot project was in only one part of the organization. However, significant improvements in alignment were made, and the pilot project was considered a success.

Following this successful pilot project, another organizational area volunteered to go through an organization design assessment and implementation. This second pilot project was also successful.

In the summer of 2008 it was then decided to do a review of the entire organization.

Assessment   Following the decision to proceed with a comprehensive assessment, a project plan was put in place to complete the assessment in calendar year 2008, and produce the report in early 2009.

The objectives of the assessment were to:

• Develop an accurate picture of the current organization design of EPCOR.

- Complete an organization review of EPCOR, to determine opportunities for current improvement and future evolution.
- Recommend an overall optimal organization design for EPCOR, including vertical and functional alignment.
- Recommend an overall implementation plan for the new organization design, including the major issues that will have to be addressed.

The assessment included the following:

- A document review and literature search.
- Collecting employee information, including compensation information.
- Completing interviews with all managers (about 500).
- Conducting the Capelle Associates Employee Satisfaction Questionnaire, which was completed by 1,800 employees, for a response rate of about 60%.

Report The interviews, together with the other sources of information, provided the data for the analysis of the current state of EPCOR and the recommendations for potential change.

The report included:

- a description of the methodology used and an educational component to assist the reader with the review of the report;
- a detailed analysis of the current situation and recommendations for improvements;
- information on each position in the organization;
- comparisons with the Capelle Associates benchmarking database;
- questionnaire analysis relative to the benchmarking database;
- recommendations on the vertical and functional realignment of positions (adding, deleting and modifying);
- recommendations on other improvements identified during the assessment process; and

- a chapter on implementation with recommendations on macro implementation directions.

The report was completed in January 2009. Major findings included:

- EPCOR had a higher percentage of managers than the Capelle Associates Benchmarking Database.
- The manager–direct report alignment showed considerable opportunity for improvement.
- The questionnaire results were slightly lower than the Capelle Associates Benchmarking Database.
- It was recommended that EPCOR be a Stratum 7 organization. There were five business units, only one of which (Power Generation) was a Stratum 6 organization.

Meetings   After the report was completed and submitted, a series of meetings resulted in a big surprise. A strategic decision had been made to spin off the power generation business, through an IPO. Further work was necessary to assist in the creation of two organizations instead of one.

It was decided to create two Stratum 6 organizations. The Power Generation business had been identified as a Stratum 6 organization, and ultimately became Capital Power Corporation. The demerger of the Power Generation business reduced the complexity of EPCOR, so it could be designed as a Stratum 6 organization instead of a Stratum 7 organization. The results of the assessment were particularly helpful with this new requirement. Since the assessment had looked at every single position in EPCOR, the entire system was very well understood, and the implications of the IPO to the organization design could be applied to this very different situation.

The separation of the business units for each of the organizations did not require significant additional work. Power Generation operations were grouped together. The remaining operations stayed within EPCOR. However, considerable work was necessary on the support services side (e.g., Finance, Human Resources, Information Technology, etc.). The challenge was to provide the required support that each company required, without adding undue additional overhead cost. Because of economies of scale, it was not simply a matter of splitting the support service functions in half. In the two new organizations, for example, two heads of HR, two CFOs, two heads of IT, and so on, were required. Once those individuals were appointed, it was necessary to work with them to design appropriate support services that would meet the needs of each of the two companies within an appropriate cost structure.

Implementation: Process

Implementation of a new organization design can be complex in even a moderately sized organization. It was realized going into the assessment that there were likely to be significant changes, and as a result implementation planning started in parallel with the assessment process. As a result, a complete implementation plan was developed in the fall of 2008, and was completely in place ready for initiation in January 2009. This was fortuitous, as once the intention to file an IPO for Capital Power became known it was much easier to amend the plan than it would have been to start from scratch.

In early 2009, the core executive team informed the Capelle Associates project team of the intent to file an IPO. Of course it was not possible to make this information public, and only a very small team within EPCOR was aware of the requirement for this work. This had two significant implications for the implementation:

- The timeframe for the implementation of two organizations needed to be reduced considerably to comply with the IPO target date. The front end of the implementation process that could typically take nine months was compressed to five months.

- Since the intent to file the IPO was on a need-to-know basis, work at the top of the organization (the design of positions, determination of accountabilities and authorities, and assignment of people to positions) had to be done in confidence and with extremely limited support.

Once the executive teams were in place, it was then possible to start the organization design implementation rollout. In fact, there were two implementation processes, completed in parallel, one for each company. This included splitting the support functions into the two companies.

The implementation involved a series of cascading, iterative processes from the top of the organization to the bottom. This was done in natural work teams. Each manager participated twice, first as a participant, and then as the head of his or her team. Managers were expected to lead part of the sessions; this both reinforces learning and models commitment. Facilitation support was provided by project team members.

Internal–External Team   The internal project team was formed in late 2008 as part of the implementation planning process. The CEO of EPCOR initially had overall accountability for the change process. Subsequently the CEO's of each of the two companies had this accountability. In both cases, Human Resources took a strong lead in the implementation, with the head of Human Resources having been delegated accountability for the project. The Human Resources Coordinator positions (HRCs) comprised the project team. As the team was in place by early 2009, initial project team training was conducted even before the final assessment report was prepared.

During the first part of 2009, once the IPO was publicly known, separate project teams were formed for EPCOR and Capital Power, even though there was ostensibly only one company at the time.

This was necessary so that the Human Resources personnel that would be accountable for the sustainment of the organization design practices principles would have received the proper training in both companies.

The organization design implementation was carried out by cohesive internal and external teams. The Internal Project Team knew the organization in a different way than the Consulting Team, and added unique value in this way. The Consulting Team brought the experience, methods and materials resulting from having done this type of work many times before.

This approach provided good value for EPCOR and Capital Power, as the Internal Project Teams carried out and completed the majority of the Project work, while gaining from the oversight and expertise of the Consulting Team. In this way it was possible to avoid falling into many of the potential traps of major organization change that can result in wasted resources, rework, or worse, generation of a negative dynamic in the workforce.

The role of the Consulting Team was to contribute methods, materials and expertise, work directly at senior levels, transfer capability to the Internal Project Team, and monitor the implementation process.

Project Management   Project management was developed for each company. As much as possible, the implementation steps were run in parallel and concurrently. The fact that a comprehensive project plan had been put in place before the beginning of the implementation project was a large part of the success of the extremely shortened time frame for implementation.

People Change Management   The people change management program was put in place at the beginning of the implementation in early 2009. This comprised an education and training component and a communication component.

The overall change management process was based on best practices in this area, and as a result supported the implementation in a strong way.

Once Capital Power was separated from EPCOR, the resources were not available to maintain the change management program at its same level of sophistication.

Implementation: Content

As described in the previous section, the first part of the implementation process was run in parallel with that of EPCOR. As a result, the overall implementation process was more complex. However the initial materials and methods were used for both companies, so this provided some efficiency. The content was organized into five streams of work which included the alignment of positions (including accountabilities and authorities), the alignment of people to positions, the alignment of teams, the alignment of deliverables, and the alignment of cross functional accountabilities and authorities.

Align Positions and Align Accountabilities and Authorities   The first stream of work was to align positions (vertical and functional) in the organization. The organization design assessment report provided the template for the functional alignment of positions. It also provided a great deal of information in terms of compression (overlapping layers of management) and in some cases missing layers of management. At the same time this work was done, the accountabilities and authorities for each position were determined, and captured in position description templates that had been developed for the two organizations. The accountabilities and authorities included specifics for employees, managers, managers once removed, and front line supervisors. It also looked at the high level cross functional relationships that would be necessary for success.

Align People   Once the positions had been determined and approved, the second stream of work was to align people to positions. A Talent Pool review process was adapted for the organizations and implemented. The main elements of the assessment were information processing capability, skilled knowledge, and application. A series of natural team meetings were held to review the talent one level down, i.e., the manager and direct reports assessing the next layer down. In the operations parts of Capital Power, this was relatively straightforward, but in support services it was quite complex as the same talent pool was being assigned to two different companies.

The availability of a sophisticated talent pool review process proved to be very helpful during the demerger process. Capital Power was envisioned to be a smaller, more entrepreneurial organization, while EPCOR, with its regulatory environment, would continue with a different sort of operating culture. The talent pool process was able to take this into account to help match people to positions in companies where they would have a greater chance of success.

Align Teams In parallel with the talent pool review meetings, work was started to align the teams. This was particularly important for the Support Services units as they had been split amongst the two companies. In a typical implementation, this work would be done as a separate stream. However, time was very short, and all employees were very engaged not only with the organization design implementation, but with all of the background work required to prepare for the IPO. It was therefore decided that there simply wasn't sufficient manager capacity to implement this as a separate stream of work.

All of this work was completed by the end of June 2009, at which time Capital Power was formally split off as its own company.

It was decided not to proceed with further implementation at Capital Power in the fall of 2009, as the foundation had been laid, and the CEO was concerned that managers would not have sufficient time and energy at this point to do the high quality work that would be necessary.

Align Deliverables   In early 2010, a new stream of work was launched to develop and implement a business planning and review system for Capital Power. This combined the functions of strategic planning, budgeting, and performance management into one unified system. By the end of the process, each manager had her or his own business plan which included vision, mission, values, strategic positioning, operational plan and resource plan. The plans were stratified, in that the appropriate complexity of work was focused in the appropriate stratum of the organization. In addition, each plan was nested within that person's manager's plan, with links all the way back to the organization's strategic plan.

This work was considered to be vital to the CEO to further developing a disciplined, high performance organization, and the work received a high priority.

Align Cross Functional Accountabilities and Authorities   In early 2010, a stream of work was also launched to focus on the cross functional accountabilities and authorities in the organization. The preliminary work undertaken at the time of the demerger was not comprehensive, and the CEO felt it extremely important to have systems in place to break down silos and encourage the flow of work across the organization.

These last two streams of work were completed by mid-2010.

Sustainment

The implementation project was designed from the beginning to facilitate long-term sustainment. One of the key mandates of the external consulting team was to transfer skills, methods and materials to Capital Power so that the new organization design could be supported over the long term.

Sustainment was supported by the following:

- Systems were enhanced. This included both the Human Resources system and the development of an integrated Organization Planning and Review system.

- Managers were provided with the tools necessary to do the work and in the process developed the necessary skills.
- The internal team developed the necessary facilitation skills.

Properly embedding the knowledge and skills in the organization is very important. Experience has shown that in the first year of the implementation of a new process, the results are not perfect. However, the organization attains further enhanced results in each year that the process is repeated. At Capital Power they are now starting the third year of their business planning and review process, and managers believe that the organization is really hitting its stride in terms of getting excellent results from the process.

As well, Capital Power has initiated several additional steps.

In early 2012, Capital Power began working with Capelle Associates to put in place some processes to re-energize the organization design principles, and to support managers with respect to the organization design.

At the heart of this program is the development of a manager's handbook, which will be written in a user-friendly, how-to way so that managers have a solid tool for supporting them in their work.

Capital Power has also invested in its orientation and training programs to support Managing the Capital Power Way. This begins with Strong Start, a new hire orientation which is delivered in several steps. It is augmented for all managers with the iLead Journey, which is a series of intense training sessions for managers to give them the basic information they need, with increasing sophistication throughout the modules.

Acquisitions are an important part of this business. Specific methods have been developed for assessing the organization design of acquisitions, and integrating them seamlessly into Capital Power.

Finally, a policy for guiding and monitoring the organization design of Capital Power is being put into place.

Results

The major result is the successful creation of a well-designed new organization. Position alignment was significantly improved, and, more importantly, managers have a language for discussing their organizations and ensuring the appropriate alignment of their direct reports. Because of this awareness, managers are much less likely to attempt to create redundant manager positions within their organizations.

Capital Power is better able to deliver its business strategy. Deliverables are appropriately delegated at the right level of complexity for the people assigned to do the work. There is better attention to the more complex, added- value work, and it all aligns better with the strategy of the organization.

Results include

- Improved vertical alignment of positions (e.g., increase requisite alignment and decrease gaps and compression).
- Improved functional alignment of positions (e.g., have "like" functions better clustered together).
- Improved clarity of positions (e.g., improved position descriptions together with education and training in natural work teams).
- Improved clarity of employee and managerial accountabilities and authorities (e.g., included in position descriptions and supported by education and training).
- Improved clarity of cross functional accountabilities and authorities (e.g., included in position descriptions and supported by education and training).
- Improved fit of employees to positions (e.g., develop and implement Talent Pool process and measure fit of employees to positions) to improve current fit and determine future requirements (e.g., talent shortages).

- Improved level of organization design capability (e.g., transfer of materials, methods and skills).
- Improved functioning of critical related systems (e.g., Human Resources and Organization Planning and Review).

Conclusion

As a first learning, a pilot project can provide the credibility necessary to move on to a comprehensive organization review. For larger organizations, it can be a large leap of faith to launch an organization design review of the entire organization. By focusing in on a pilot project, it is possible to begin the process, achieve some benefits in the shorter term, demonstrate the results and success, and develop internal support.

This case study also shows that it is possible to emerge from a demerger situation as a strong, well designed new organization. One of the biggest challenges is to ensure that the support services costs are reasonably sized for the new organization.

A strong organization design provides the foundation for better integration of acquisitions, as this provides the benchmark against which potential acquisitions can be measured. Even when an acquired company does not have a good organization design, understanding the fundamentals of organization design, and working from the base of an organization that is well-designed, makes it much easier to integrate the acquired company.

The single most significant learning was the introduction of the concepts and language of strata. Managers throughout the organization understand in a much better way the complexity of work. More importantly, they understand the nature of individual capability and how to better match the capabilities of individuals to the complexity of output that is required. Managers also have the language for discussing this and it creates the foundation for success in many other ways: getting the right people to meetings, properly structuring project teams, delegating the right work to the right people, and creating positions in the correct stratum. It creates an opportunity for discipline in the way work is done that would not otherwise be possible.

Capital Power benefited from a strong and enthusiastic Human Resources team to lead the project. More importantly, the CEO understood the importance of organization design, and saw it as a means of attaining his strategic objectives as quickly and efficiently as possible. The excellent results for Capital Power demonstrate the importance of a fully engaged and committed CEO, with full support from the HR team, over an extended period of time.

ROYAL OTTAWA HEALTH CARE GROUP CASE STUDY

Introduction

One of the most difficult types of organizations to change is a hospital. One of the main reasons is that many of the main health care providers are medical doctors who are not employees of a hospital. Therefore, there are usually two groupings: one of the medical doctors, headed by a Chief Medical Officer (or in this case study, a Chief of Staff/Chief Psychiatrist), and one for the rest of the employees, generally headed by a President and CEO. This makes for a more complex set of working relationships. The second reason change is difficult is that these systems tend to be conservative, which is not surprising given that they are dealing with life and death matters.

The following is an interesting case study about change in a hospital.

Organization

In 2008, at the time of the organization design assessment, The Royal Ottawa Health Care Group (ROHCG) was made up of the Royal Ottawa Mental Health Care Centre (a new 188 bed state-of-the-art mental health facility located in Ottawa), the Brockville

Mental Health Centre (a specialized 219 bed psychiatric facility located in Brockville), a large number of community operations, the University of Ottawa Institute of Mental Health Research (home of leading-edge multidisciplinary programs), Royal Ottawa Place (96 bed long-term residential care centre located in Ottawa), and the Royal Ottawa Foundation for Mental Health (the fundraising organization supporting mental health research, capital projects and equipment purchases). The organization design considered the whole organization, with the primary focus on the three mental health facilities and related community operations. There were approximately 2,000 employees.

George Weber had been newly appointed as President and CEO after a period as interim CEO, and wanted to make significant changes. The presenting problems included the following:

- There was conflict and turnover at senior levels.
- There was no strategic plan and a lack of focus.
- There were major financial issues (e.g., running major deficits).
- They had just moved into a new building in Ottawa, which was the first P3 (Public-Private Partnership) hospital to open in Canada, and there were some significant issues.
- There was significant union dissatisfaction.
- There were inconsistent management layers and unreasonable spans of control.

Mr. Weber had used organization design improvement success-fully in two previous organizations, and understood the impact that a properly aligned organization design could have. He approached Capelle Associates, who had supported him previously at The International Federation of Red Cross and Red Crescent Societies in Geneva, Switzerland, and at the Canadian Dental Association.

It should be noted that Mr. Weber not only initiated an organization design process, but also initiated a strategy process in parallel. While most would see these as sequential (i.e., do strategy first and then organization design), he had shown in a previous role that doing the two simultaneously, in an iterative way, results in a high quality outcome with a much shorter time frame.

Method

Initial Discussion, Proposal and Contract   After preliminary discussions, a decision was made to primarily focus on the three mental health facilities and related community operations. The Psychiatry group was not a direct part of the review, although senior members such as the Chief of Staff/Chief Psychiatrist and Clinical Directors were interviewed and part of ongoing discussions and implementation. It was also decided that the Foundation and Research Institute would not be a direct part of the review, although the Presidents were interviewed for context.

Assessment   Following the decision to proceed with a comprehensive assessment, a project plan was put in place to complete the assessment in the summer of 2008, and produced the report in September 2008.

The objectives of the assessment were to:

- Develop an accurate picture of the current organization design of ROHCG.
- Complete an organization review of ROHCG, to determine opportunities for current improvement and future evolution.
- Recommend an overall optimal organization design for ROHCG, including vertical and functional alignment.
- Recommend an overall implementation plan for the new organization design, including the major issues that will have to be addressed.

The assessment included the following:

- A literature review to identify best practices was conducted.

- Internal documents were reviewed to understand the organization.
- Interviews were completed with some 50 managers and another 20 key stakeholders.
- An online survey was made available to every ROHCG employee, to which some 450 responded.
- Employee information was reviewed, including compensation information.

Report   The interviews, together with the other sources of information, provided the data for the analysis of the current state of ROHCG and the recommendations for potential change. The report included:

- a description of the methodology used and an educational component to assist the reader with the review of the report;
- a detailed analysis of the current situation and recommendations for improvements;
- information on each position in the organization;
- comparisons with the Capelle Associates benchmarking database;
- questionnaire analysis relative to the benchmarking database;
- recommendations on the vertical and functional realignment of positions (adding, deleting and modifying);
- recommendations on other improvements identified during the assessment process;
- a chapter on implementation with recommendations on macro implementation directions.

The results of the assessment were compared to the Capelle Associates Benchmarking Database. The report was completed in September 2008. Major findings included:

- There was a significantly lower percentage of managers and corresponding higher span of control.

- Employees in general tended to operate at too low a level.
- Employee satisfaction was significantly lower, including on the key factor of Relationship with Manager.
- One of the lowest scores was on success of previous change projects, which was an ominous sign for this implementation.

There were 30 suggested actions arising from the report findings. The major ones included:

- ROHCG should be a Stratum 5 (5 level) organization.
- Positions should be realigned so that spans of control are significantly reduced, and manager–direct report alignment would be improved.
- Appropriate managerial and cross functional accountabilities and authorities should be established.
- Titles should be appropriate and consistent.
- There should be an improved process for matching people to positions.

Two of the key roles at ROHCG were the then called Directors of Service Delivery Units and Directors of Professional Practice. The spans of control for the Directors of Service Delivery Units were very large, and needed to be improved. In addition, the managerial and cross functional accountabilities and authorities between the two roles needed to be clarified. There was also an opportunity to further differentiate Stratum 2 and Stratum 1 nursing roles, incumbents and tasks.

Meetings Meetings were held with the Senior Leadership Team. It was decided to proceed with implementation of the 30 recommendations of the report.

It should be noted that implementation of these suggested actions would have to be within the existing financial envelope, while at the same time implementing the strategic plan and undergoing a major restructuring to deal with a financial operating deficit. It was necessary to close some beds at the Brockville site, and transform 32 of 96 long term beds at the Ottawa site to recovery beds.

Implementation: Process

Once the decision to proceed was made, the organization design implementation rollout began.

Resource allocation was a particular challenge facing ROHCG. As a health care institution, budgets were under intense scrutiny, so identifying additional resources to support the implementation was difficult. This was further exacerbated by the fact that the day-to-day requirements of staff in a healthcare organization are pressing, and cannot be delayed. It was therefore very difficult to reprioritize duties in order to support the implementation process.

The strategic planning process was intended to provide additional focus for employees. While this can happen over time, at the time the implementation was started the strategic planning process was also ramping up. Finally, ROHCG was mandated to embark on a major restructuring program to close beds. So, in the short term there was very significant demand on management time, and organization design implementation, while fundamental, was one priority amongst many.

Internal–External Team   A project team manager was appointed in September 2008, and the internal project team was formed from a cross section of managers in the organization. The accountable executive for the change process was the CEO.

The organization design implementation was carried out by cohesive internal and external teams. The Internal Project Team knew the organization in a different way than the Consulting Team, and added unique value in this way. The Consulting Team brought the experience, methods and materials resulting from having done this type of work many times before.

This approach provided good value for ROHCG, as the internal project team carried out and completed the majority of the project work, while gaining from the oversight and expertise of the consulting team. In this way it was possible to avoid falling into many of the potential traps of major organization change that can result in wasted resources, rework, or worse, generation of a negative dynamic in the workforce.

The role of the Consulting Team was to contribute methods, materials and expertise, work directly at senior levels, transfer capability to the Internal Project Team, and monitor the implementation process.

Project Management   Project management was relatively straight forward because of the size of the organization. For each of the 30 suggested actions, the manager accountable for the change, together with a target time frame for completion was identified. This was used as a tool by the project team to gauge the progress of the implementation.

People Change Management   The people change management program was put in place at the beginning of the implementation in late 2008. This comprised an education and training component, and a communication component.

Uniquely at ROHCG, an Advisory Panel was created from front-line employees to provide feedback to the implementation team. Members were recruited, and asked to attend focus group sessions to provide feedback and advice on various matters with respect to the organization design implementation, including review of selected communications and materials.

Implementation: Content

The content was organized according to the Suggested Actions from the assessment report. However, the content could be described in five categories, which included the alignment of positions (including accountabilities and authorities), the alignment of people to positions, the alignment of teams, the alignment of deliverables, and the alignment of cross functional accountabilities and authorities.

Align Positions   The first category of work was to align positions (vertical and functional) in the organization. For ROHCG to become a Stratum 5 (5 level) organization, a considerable realignment of positions was required.

The organization design assessment report provided the template for the functional alignment of positions. It also provided a great deal of information in terms of compression (overlapping layers of management) and in some cases missing layers of management.

In this category of work, the most significant challenge was in Patient Care services. Directors had spans of control that were too large for effective management. Because of budget constraints, the realignment had to be carried out within the current head count. Through determined effort, and using organization design principles, it was possible through program realignment and vertical realignment to reduce the spans to more manageable levels.

Align People   Once the positions had been determined and approved, the second category of work was to align people to positions. A talent pool review process was adapted for the organizations and implemented with a meeting of the CEO and the VPs to review and align people to Stratum 3 positions. The main elements of the assessment were information processing capability, skilled knowledge, and application.

Align Accountabilities and Authorities   A process was developed and initiated for managers to document the accountabilities and authorities for each position for which they were accountable.

This information was captured in position description templates that had been developed. The accountabilities and authorities included specifics for employees, managers, and managers once removed. Accountabilities and authorities were clarified and position descriptions were developed/enhanced.

Particular effort was put into cross functional accountabilities and authorities, as this had been identified as a significant issue. The most significant area of concern, which was causing a lot of churn in the organization, was the cross functional relationship between the Directors of Patient Care Services and the Chiefs of Professional Practice with respect to staffing in patient care units. The cross functional accountabilities and authorities framework was adapted for ROHCG, and this was used to document the respective cross functional accountabilities and authorities of Directors and Chiefs with respect to hiring, performance management, and dismissal of employees.

Align Deliverables   Alignment of deliverables was enhanced and linked closely with the newly developed strategic plan. Corporate objectives were delegated into position appropriate objectives, starting with the CEO delegating objectives to VPs. VPs were then accountable for rolling out the strategic plan and stratum appropriate deliverables throughout their departments.

Because the internal expertise existed, this work was done in parallel to the organization design implementation and was not supported by the project team directly.

Align Tasks   One of the more significant challenges was in the patient care services units. Of course, patient care is of paramount importance. The assessment had identified a significant opportunity to further differentiate Stratum 2 and Stratum 1 nursing roles, incumbents and tasks. It appeared that an inordinate amount of Stratum 2 nursing time was used for Stratum 1 tasks that could notionally be carried out by Stratum 1 employees that would be trained specifically to do this work, and could therefore free Stratum 2 nursing time for professional level tasks. While there was general agreement that this offered potential to ROHCG to improve its patient care services, it was necessary to do this in a way that was not disruptive to patient care.

After trying various approaches, it was decided that support would be provided to the Directors of Patient Care for them to determine optimal staffing mixes for their programs. Because of the uniqueness of each program, while general principles could be put in place, it was not possible, and probably would not be appropriate, to mandate staffing mixes across programs. The accountability for the staff within a program rests with the Director of Patient Care, with support from the Chief of Professional Practice. By clarifying these respective accountabilities, and making it clear that the Director of Patient Care was accountable for identifying and implementing, over time, the optimal skill mix for staff within the program, it became possible for ROHCG to move in this direction.

Align Systems   There were significant changes to Human Resources systems, including position descriptions and Talent Pool. A new Strategic Planning System was developed and linked to individual deliverables, and the second planning cycle has been launched.

Align Managerial Leadership Practices   The primary focus in this category of work was through the clarity of accountabilities and authorities. In addition, a series of workshop themes were developed which could be implemented by managers and their immediate direct reports. There was limited "take up" on this material, but it does serve as a resource to the organization.

Sustainment

When asked how he was able to keep the organization focused on organization design with the limited budgets and the competing priorities of a hospital, George Weber responded that it was necessary to: "Overcome resistance with persistence". He felt strongly that significant new initiatives require a significant amount of time to "imbed the change into the corporate DNA". The organization design project at ROHCG is an excellent example of persistence, over time.

Most organizations, when faced with conflicting priorities, will engage external consultants to provide the extra resources to kick-start and supplement the process. While this happened to some extent, the internal project team and the managers at ROHCG were required to carry a much more significant load in developing and implementing the change processes. Capelle Associates was able to provide the methodology and assist with the adaptation of materials, but ROHCG took the initiative exclusively for lower levels in the organization. It is a tribute to the CEO and the project team that they were able to persevere over time with this implementation. The CEO put a priority on constantly re-energizing the focus.

Following the primary implementation, the CEO also undertook initiatives to revitalize the process. For strategic planning, a consulting firm was engaged on a pro bono basis to do an interim assessment of the status of the strategic plan. For the organization design implementation, an evaluation was conducted at the three year mark, both to understand the status of the implementation of the suggested actions, and to revitalize the organization design principles with ROHCG managers.

Results

A follow up organization design review showed that at senior levels, vertical alignment was appropriate in all but one case. Delegation had significantly improved. Work on all 30 recommendations had started; 20% were virtually completed; and 86.7% were more than half complete.

In the three year period (2008 to 2010), from before the initiative to after the major part of the implementation, there was significant improvement. A work life study (independent from this review) showed significant improvements in satisfaction with work environment. Significant improvement was shown on percentage of employees who trusted the organization; were satisfied with the organization; and felt that the work environment was safe.

Results include

- Improved vertical alignment of positions (e.g., increase requisite alignment and decrease gaps and compression).
- Improved functional alignment of positions (e.g., have "like" functions better clustered together).
- Improved clarity of positions (e.g., improved position descriptions together with education and training in natural work teams).
- Improved clarity of employee and managerial accountabilities and authorities (e.g., included in position descriptions and supported by education and training).
- Improved clarity of cross functional accountabilities and authorities (e.g., included in position descriptions and supported by education and training).
- Improved fit of employees to positions (e.g., develop and implement Talent Pool Process and measure fit of employees to positions) to improve current fit and determine future requirements (e.g., talent shortages).
- Improved level of organization design capability (e.g., transfer of materials, methods and skills).
- Improved functioning of critical related systems (e.g., Human Resources and Strategic Planning).

Strategic plan implementation was successful, and financial performance improved significantly.

Conclusion

The primary conclusion is that it is possible to significantly improve a hospital. Key success factors include a strong President & CEO; a strong internal Project Team Leader and Team; a strong External

Team; and a strong Internal–External Team working relationship. One of the keys to success was communication and transparency, particularly from the President & CEO.

It is also possible to improve strategy and organization design simultaneously in an iterative process. This goes against conventional wisdom. However, the relationship between the two is not one way; each informs the other. The quality in this process can be at least as good, and the timelines are considerably shortened.

Transparency was a critical element of the work at ROHCG. One of the CEO's first initiatives was to demonstrate transparency at staff forums. He also encouraged emails from any staff person to him at any time, and maintained an open door policy. All of the information for the change process was made available, except for personnel records. Through weekly senior management team meetings the senior team was able to keep each other in the loop on all of the initiatives. Further, in terms of transparency, ROHCG initiated 360 reviews of the CEO and the vice presidents. This provided a forum for feedback to help with our management practices.

Cross functional work is fundamental for successful work in a health care organization. While work is still ongoing to break down silos, significant progress has been made in understanding and using cross functional accountabilities and authorities.

In the words of the CEO:

> The role of the leader is to read the environment, interpret it to the organization, and prepare the organization for the new reality. The leader interprets the future as it unfolds, ensures transparency to the organization, establishes appropriate accountabilities and authorities, and monitors the results in terms of outcomes, safety and quality. This kind of positive transformation is the essence of our work at the Royal—a commitment that we carry forward with pride, respect and well-founded optimism into our next century of service.

GLOSSARY

Accountability   A situation in which an individual can be called to account by another individual or body authorized to do so.

Accountability hierarchy   The alignment of positions (vertical and functional) within an organization.

Accountable manager   The term applied to a specified manager position with accountability (and the necessary managerial authority) for a specified deliverable (including a project). *See also* manager

Application   There are three criteria in matching employees with positions. They are information processing capability, skilled knowledge and application. Application is individuals fully applying their capabilities to the requirements of the position. This is a function of valuing the work, being motivated, being committed, and putting energy into the work.

Assignment   A deliverable that fulfills one or more of the following criteria:
- a general accountability (e.g., provide a specified service to specified recipients)
- a direct assignment from a manager to a direct report

- a self-assigned deliverable that the direct report undertakes as deemed appropriate within the context and prescribed limits established by the manager

Authority   Legitimate power vested in individuals or bodies because of their positions.

Broad context   The situation when the time span of a position (as established by the manager) is greater than the self span of the position (as reported by the incumbent). *See also* clear context; narrow context

Capability   The full capability of a person to do work. This is related to information processing capability, skilled knowledge, and application.

Change management   The structure and process of change and implementation, as contrasted with the content of change (e.g., organization design). Significant parts of change management methods have come from the earlier established field of organization development.

Clear context   The situation when the time span of a position (as established by the manager) is the same as the self span of the position (as reported by the incumbent). *See also* broad context; narrow context

Compensation (actual)   Compensation is the total monetary and nonmonetary pay given to an employee. This can be measured in different ways. In our analyses, we only use salary and expected bonus, and not other items such as benefits and longer-term incentive payments.

Compensation span   Compensation span translates compensation into appropriate stratum based upon analysis of entry level compensation and expected ratios in each stratum.

Competencies   *See* skilled knowledge.

Complexity of work   Work is the use of discretion and judgment in making decisions and providing deliverables. Work can have varying levels of complexity related to time span and information processing requirement.

Compression   A characteristic of the vertical alignment of positions in which the manager and direct report occupy the same stratum within the organization

Context   The framework provided by a manager to a direct report that can be used as a basis for the direct report to use judgment in decision making. Examples of context include the organization strategic plan, the department business plan, delegated accountability and authority, the direct report position description, ongoing discussion, and communications between the manager and the direct report with respect to the direct report's accountabilities and deliverables. Context is too broad if the direct report does not have a sufficiently clear framework. Context is too narrow if the direct report does not have enough scope to use appropriate judgment in making decisions.

Context and prescribed limits   The framework provided by a manager to the manager's direct report(s) to provide guidance to the direct report for the use of judgment in making decisions so that outputs are consistent with the manager's intent. *See also* context; prescribed limits.

Cross functional accountability and authority   Accountabilities and authorities among positions across functions. These include advising, service providing, coordinating, monitoring, stopping and prescribing. There is a related concept of recommending policy, standards, procedures, and objectives. While this is actually direct output support work (DOS), it provides, in conjunction with monitoring, a "quasi governance" function within an organization. The essence of this is that a function head (e.g., CFO) recommends policy and, once approved, monitors compliance. Recommending policy is direct output support to the CEO. Once the policy is approved, the CEO provides the function head (e.g., CFO) with monitoring (cross functional) accountability and authority across the organization to ensure compliance with the policy. It should be noted that there are specific accountabilities and commensurate authorities.

Cross over point manager   The lowest level manager position in the organization that has the accountability and authority for virtually all of the resources required to be successful in resolving an issue or achieving an opportunity. This position is accountable for setting the context and prescribed limits for the interactions and for establishing an issues resolution and context clarification mechanism. The cross over point manager will differ for different issues and opportunities. This position is usually critical for successful cross functional work.

Customer satisfaction   A critical driver of organization performance. Can be measured in numerous ways from surveys to actual behavior.

Delegated direct output (DDO)   A type of output resulting from deliverables being delegated by a manager to a direct report in which the output is created at the level of the direct report.

Delegation   The assignment of a deliverable to a direct report.

Delegation, clarity of   We measure clarity of delegation by looking at the time span of a position (as established by the manager) and the self span of a position (as reported by the incumbent). This could result in clear context, broad context, or narrow context.

Deliverable   A deliverable is an output produced by an employee. It should have a target completion time. Other parameters can include quality and quantity. It should be within context and prescribed limits of the manager, and have clarity about required resources. Deliverables may be recurring, project related, and/or achieving a specific target. *See also* stratum specific deliverable; interim deliverable

Direct output (within context)   Output that is not delegated but is completed by an individual with understood context and prescribed limits.

Direct output support (DOS)   A situation in which an individual in a lower level position provides support to an individual in a higher level position to support the output of the individual in the higher level position.

Direct report   A person who is the direct report of a manager, who is delegated work by the manager with the objective of producing output, and for whom the manager is accountable.

Direct report once removed (DRoR)   If there is a direct report (A) of a manager position (B) that is a direct report of a manager position (C), then A is a direct report once removed of C. *See also* manager once removed

Employee   An individual who has an employment contract with an organization to perform work. An employee may or may not have managerial accountabilities.

Employee satisfaction   An important measure of organization performance. Usually measured by an employee satisfaction questionnaire such as Capelle Associates Employee Satisfaction Questionnaire. Shows a strong relationship with organization design, manager–direct report alignment, customer satisfaction, and financial performance. Can also be measured by other factors such as absenteeism and turnover.

Financial performance   Financial performance can be determined on both a profit and loss basis and a balance sheet basis. It is important to have the appropriate time frames for meaningful measures; time frames are often too short.

Functional alignment   The process of aligning core (developing, delivering, and marketing/selling/communicating products and services) and support (e.g., finance, human resources, and information technology) functions of an organization. For a larger organization, it may also include corporate and business unit functions.

Gap   The situation of a manager–direct report relationship in which the manager and direct report are more than one stratum apart from each other.

Gearing   The part of the talent pool review process whereby the manager once removed and direct report managers check and adjust their judgments of the information processing capability of the individuals being assessed.

Human system   A system composed of people and roles.

Immediate manager   The specified manager position for specified direct report positions.

Information processing capability   There are three criteria in matching employees with positions. They are information processing capability, skilled knowledge and application. Information processing capability is the way in which an individual takes information, understands it, reasons with it, and makes plans and decisions. This is a capability that an individual carries, and can be seen when an individual is fully engaged in problem solving. Information processing capability is the maximum level or stratum at which the individual could work at the present time, given the opportunity to do so, having had the opportunity to gain the necessary skilled knowledge, and if that person applied herself fully. Information processing capability matures over time.

Information processing requirement   The requirement of a position for a certain level of information processing. Each stratum is different in the complexity of work. There are two measurements of this complexity. The first is time span, which is a direct measure of the complexity of a position. The second is the information processing that an individual requires to be successful in a position of that complexity. To the extent that there is a mismatch between these two, it is an indication that the position has been poorly designed (e.g., a position with Stratum 2 diagnostic (cumulative) information processing requirement that only has as Stratum 1 time span).

Interim deliverable   An interim deliverable is a deliverable that has a delivery target date that is sooner than the time span of the stratum of the position and that contributes to the achievement of a higher stratum specific deliverable. The characteristic of an interim deliverable is that it is a necessary and measurable component output of a stratum specific deliverable. An interim deliverable is often delegated and may become a stratum specific deliverable of a direct report. However, the manager may choose to directly deliver an interim deliverable. *See also* deliverable

Knowledge   A component of skilled knowledge, this is the knowledge required for success in a position. Knowledge may have indicators such as education, special courses, internal and external qualification, accreditation, and certification.

Leadership   Process of influencing others in a particular direction.

Level of work (LoW)   A characteristic of a position as a result of the complexity of the work in the position as measured by time span and information processing requirement.

Manager   A position in an organization that is accountable for a direct report.

Manager–direct report alignment   The single most important organization design factor driving performance. The alignment can be correct or requisite (manager exactly one stratum above a direct report); compressed (manager and direct report in same stratum); or a gap (manager and direct report more than one stratum apart).

Managerial accountability and authority   Managers have certain accountabilities (e.g., her own personal effectiveness and output) and should have commensurate authorities (e.g., delegating work and assessing performance).

Managerial leadership   Leadership expected from a manager related to accountabilities and authorities. This would include selection, setting context and prescribed limits, providing resources, delegating, development, managing performance, team building, and removal from position.

Manager once removed (MoR)   Manager A is the manager of Manager B. Manager B is the manager of Employee C, and Manager A is the manager once removed of Employee C. *See also* direct reports once removed

Narrow context   The situation when the time span of a position (as established by the manager) is less than the self span of the position (as reported by the incumbent). *See also* broad context; clear context

Optimizing Organization Design   An approach to make an organization design as perfect as possible and reasonable. This approach includes both assessment and implementation, which are based on sound theory, research, and practice.

Organization   A stratified human system.

Organization alignment model   This framework includes the alignment of positions (vertically and functionally), accountabilities and authorities (employee, supervisor, manager, manager once removed and cross functional), people, deliverables, and tasks.

Organization design   The design of an organization including its relationship to its environment and the interrelationships of its parts. We would include the alignment of positions, accountabilities and authorities, people, deliverables, and tasks.

Organization performance   At a macro level, this would be providing better value to stakeholders than alternatives. This would include employee satisfaction, customer satisfaction, and financial performance.

Organization plan   A process and outcome that includes a vision, mission, values, strategic positioning, operational plan, and resource plan.

Organization planning and review   An integrated system that pulls together the often disparate systems of strategic planning, business planning, and performance management. Ensures that individuals at different levels of the organization are producing appropriate deliverables for each stratum level.

People change management   The application of a generally accepted change management methodology, focusing on the people aspect of the change. This may include education and training, and communications.

Personal effectiveness   The effectiveness of an individual direct report in producing outputs.

Position   A role within an organization. It should have a position description with a number of details related to the position.

Prescribed limits   The framework provided by a manager to a direct report that sets limits (i.e., stay within these boundaries). Examples include the following: stay within financial, human resources, and technology budgets; work within the laws of the land; and work within the policies of the organization—there can also be more specific instructions such as, "If you feel you may miss a deadline, I need advance notice."

Proceduralize   This is the process of establishing procedures for doing work. Sometime through this process, work can be automated. However, as well as that, Stratum 1 positions should ideally be proceduralized. Stratum 1 positions will still require judgment, but the judgment and actions can be supported by the understanding and use of procedures.

Process   A series of actions or operations across time and space and carried out in a definite manner leading to a particular goal. A process should have clear providers of input and clear recipients of output. A process should also have an accountable manager and a feedback loop. A process can be thought of as a series of tasks organized horizontally.

Project manager   The position (full time or part time) held accountable by the accountable manager for producing outputs related to a specific problem or situation (the project). Assisting the project manager are one or more project team members (full time or part time). For projects longer than one year, the team members should be direct reports of the project team leader who should be one stratum of capability above the direct reports. Generally in projects of duration of less than one year, neither condition is mandatory. With project teams, it is important to clarify the accountabilities and authorities of the accountable manager, the project manager, the project team members, and the manager(s) of the project team members (when not the project manager).

Recipient   Receiver of requested specified products/services. Has no or only limited choice as to who provides the products/services, as fulfillment is restricted to internal suppliers. Products/services are provided at no direct cost to the receiver (may be funded through a cost-allocation system), and/or are provided on a "user pay" basis for less than full open market value. Not a customer; requires determining the payer to understand the full transaction. Suppliers of products/services, being internal, usually have no or only limited authority to qualify or decline a request from a recipient. This often results in suboptimal utilization of resources through recipients being provided with whatever they want despite the fact they are not paying for it.

Relationship with manager   The most important factor on an employee satisfaction questionnaire. It is strongly related to manager–direct report alignment.

Role   A defined part of a human system that carries a name and related expectations.

Self span   As reported by the incumbent of a position, the deliverable with the longest target completion time that the incumbent believes that his/her manager holds him accountable for. *See* time span

Skilled knowledge   There are three criteria in matching employees with positions. They are information processing capability, skilled knowledge, and application. Skilled knowledge consists of information, facts, procedures, etc., that have been learned, and can be articulated and applied as a capability developed through experience and practice. Three specific components of skilled knowledge are knowledge, technical skills, and social process skills.

Social process skills   A component of skilled knowledge, social process skills are the requirements of effective working relationships, e.g., communication skills, interpersonal skills, managerial leadership skills. The social process skill requirements can be specified at five different levels: intrapersonal, interpersonal, group, intergroup, and organization-wide.

Span of control   Number of direct reports of a manager.

Strategic business unit (SBU)   A relatively separate organization unit within a parent organization with a unique set of characteristics with respect to some combination of products and services; market(s); product and service development; internal factors such as processes, technologies, and specialized skilled knowledge; and alternatives to its products and services (competitors, etc.).

Stratified human system   A human system in which there is a hierarchy of positions and position relationships based upon the differential complexity of the positions.

Stratum   A vertical stratified level in an organization with discrete boundaries. The boundaries define ranges of complexity of work. Each stratum is different in terms of the nature and complexity of work, time span and the required information processing capability to work at that stratum level. Strata can be divided into substrata of low, medium, and high.

Stratum specific deliverable   A stratum specific deliverable is a deliverable that has an appropriate delivery target date that is within the time span range of the stratum of the position. *See also* deliverable

Stress cracks   A term used to define a situation in which the organization is evolving to the next highest stratum. There are two main possible symptoms. The first symptom is compression of management layers as work becomes more complex and additional strata may be required, but the organization has not been properly stratified to the next highest stratum. The second symptom is a gap between management layers as one position moves up to the next highest stratum and the lower position(s) remain in the original stratum.

Subordinate   This is another term for direct report. *See* direct report

System   A set of interrelated parts with a boundary separating it from its environment. Systems have inputs, throughputs, outputs, and feedback. We use this in two ways. First, an organization is a system (human and stratified). Second, we use "system" to describe subparts of organizations (e.g., human resources system, organization planning and review system, etc.).

Talent pool review (TPR)   A process, within a properly stratified organization, of managers ensuring the required capability of employees to meet current and future human resources requirements of the organization. It includes information processing capability, skilled knowledge, and application. The process includes talent pool assessment and analysis, selection, coaching, mentoring, position transfers, and career-development activities.

Task   A task is a particular activity carried out by an individual. A task would generally have input (receiving something), throughput (doing something), and output (delivering something). In defining tasks, it is necessary to decide how micro or macro to be. We generally find that a position would have 10 to 12 tasks on average, with a range of 5 to 20 tasks.

Technical skills   A component of skilled knowledge, technical skills are required for using knowledge. Technical skills consist of information, facts, procedures, etc., that have been learned and can be applied as a capability developed through experience and practice.

Team   There are three main types of teams in an organization. A natural team is a manager and direct reports. A project team is a project manager and project team members. A cross functional team is a team wherein the accountable manager has cross functional accountability and authority with respect to positions that are not direct reports.

Time span   Measure of complexity of work in a position. It is determined by the deliverable within the position that has the longest target completion time. The manager of the position establishes the time span of the position.

Trust   A psychological condition that is important in all relationships and is enhanced by the process of fulfilling commitments.

Vertical alignment   The relationships among positions from a vertical perspective. It includes the optimal number of strata or layers, and the optimal alignment between positions (manager exactly one stratum above direct report in terms of both complexity of work and information processing capability to successfully do work).

Work   Work is the use of discretion and judgment in making decisions and providing deliverables. Work can have varying levels of complexity related to time span and information processing requirement.

REFERENCES

Ambachtsheer, K. P. (1986). *Pension Funds and the Bottom Line: Managing the Corporate Pension Fund as a Financial Business*. Homewood, IL.: Dow Jones-Irwin.

Ambachtsheer, K. P. (2007). *Pension Revolution: A Solution to the Pensions Crisis*. Hoboken, NJ: Wiley.

Ambachtsheer, K., Capelle, R. & Scheibelhut, T. (1998) "Improving Pension Fund Performance." *Financial Analysts Journal* 54(5), 15–20.

Ambachtsheer, K. P., Capelle, R. G. & Lum, H. (2007). "Trustee Competency." *Pensions & Investments* 35(12), 18.

Ambachtsheer, K. P., & Ezra, D. D. (1998). *Pension Fund Excellence: Creating Value for Stockholders*. Hoboken, NJ: Wiley.

Ambachtsheer, K., Capelle, R. & Lum, H. (2008). "The Pension Governance Deficit: Still With Us." *Rotman International Journal of Pension Management* 1.

Ansoff, H. I. (1979). *Strategic Management*. Hoboken, NJ: Wiley.

Ansoff, H. I. & McDonnell, E. J. (1988). *The New Corporate Strategy*. Hoboken, NJ: Wiley.

Bennis, W. G., Benne, K. D. & Chin, R. (1969). *The Planning of Change* (2nd ed.). New York: Holt.

Bennis, W. G., Benne, K. D., Chin, R. & Corey, K. E. (1976). *The Planning of Change* (3rd ed.). New York: Holt, Rinehart and Winston.

Bertalanffy, L. V. (1968). *General System Theory: Foundations, Development, Applications* (Rev. ed.). New York: G. Braziller.

Brock, F. (2003). "Who'll Sit at the Boomers' Desks?" *New York Times*. October 12.

Brooks, E. R. (1998). *Loyal Customers, Enthusiastic Employees and Corporate Performance: Understanding the Linkages*. Ottawa: Conference Board of Canada.

Brown, W. (1971). *Organization*. London: Heinemann.

Brown, W. (1960). *Exploration in Management*. London: Heinemann.

Brown, W. & Jaques, E. (1964). *Product Analysis Pricing: A Method for Setting Policies for the Delegation of Pricing Decisions and the Control of Expense and Profitability*. London: Heinemann.

Brown, W. B. D. & Jaques, E. (1965). *Glacier Project Papers: Some Essays on Organization and Management from the Glacier Project Research*. London: Heinemann.

Buckingham, M. & Coffman, C. (1999). *First, Break All the Rules: What the World's Greatest Managers Do Differently*. New York: Simon & Schuster.

Buzzell, R. D. & Gale, B. T. (1987). *The PIMS Principles: Linking Strategy to Performance*. New York: Free Press; London: Collier Macmillan.

Campbell, D. T., Stanley, J. C. & Gage, N. L. (1969). *Experimental and Quasi-Experimental Designs for Research*. Chicago: Rand McNally.

Capelle, R. G. (1979). *Changing Human Systems*. Toronto: International Human Systems Institute.

Capelle, R. G. (1995). "Optimizing Your Network of Commitments: A Key to Success." *CMA* 69(9), 8.

Capelle, R. G. (2001). "By Design: Insurers of All Sizes Can Benefit from the Simple Principle of Organizing Their Operations According to Employee Skills and Abilities." *Canadian Insurance* 106(5), 41, 43+.

Capelle, R. G. (2007). "The Accountability of the Board of Directors for Organization Design." *Director Magazine* 130(Feb), 6–8.

Capelle Associates (1999). Optimizing Organization Design: Improvements in Manager–Direct Report Alignment, Financial Performance and Employee Satisfaction. Capelle Associates Research Paper #1.

Capelle Associates (2000a). Optimizing Organization Design: Improvements in Organization Design and Employee Satisfaction. Capelle Associates Research Paper #2.

Capelle Associates (2000b). Optimizing Organization Design: Improvements in Manager–Direct Report Alignment, Employee Satisfaction and Customer Satisfaction. Capelle Associates Research Paper #3.

Capelle Associates (2000c). Optimizing Organization Design: Improvements in Manager–Direct Report Alignment and Employee Satisfaction. Capelle Associates Research Paper #4.

Capelle Associates (2000d). Optimizing Organization Design: Improvements in Manager–Direct Report Alignment, Leadership and Direction, and Employee Commitment. Capelle Associates Research Paper #5.

Capelle Associates. (2000e). The Information Processing Capability of an Employee and the Job Grade of a Position: Is There A Relationship? Capelle Associates Research Paper #6.

Capelle Associates. (2000f). Information Processing Capability, Time Span and Job Grade. Capelle Associates Research Paper #7.

Capelle Associates (2003a). Appropriateness of Compensation, Overall Employee Satisfaction, and Employee Satisfaction with Compensation: Review of 20 Organizations. Capelle Associates Research Paper #8.

Capelle Associates (2003b). Organization Design, Manager–Direct Report Alignment and Organization Performance in Canadian Private Sector Companies: Results from Surveys of CEOs and Heads of Human Resources. Capelle Associates Research Paper #9.

Capelle Associates (2004a). Task Alignment: A More Micro Organization Alignment Approach. Capelle Associates Research Paper #10.

Capelle Associates (2004b). Equitable Differential Pay Scale for the Canadian Market. Capelle Associates Research Paper #11.

Capelle Associates (2005a). Relationship between Time Span, Compensation Span and Actual Compensation: Review from 57 Organizations. Capelle Associates Research Paper #12.

Capelle Associates (2005b). Organization Design: From Improvement to Decline. Capelle Associates Research Paper #13.

Capelle Associates (2005c). Manager–Direct Report Alignment is Directly Related to Employee Satisfaction: Review of 30 Organizations. Capelle Associates Research Paper #14.

Capelle Associates (2011). Organization Design, Manager–Direct Alignment and Employee Satisfaction. Capelle Associates Research Paper #15.

Capelle Associates (2012a). Manager–Direct Report Alignment, Delegation and Compensation from Capelle Associates Benchmarking Database. Capelle Associates Research Paper #16.

Capelle Associates (2012b). Capelle Associates Employee Satisfaction Questionnaire. Capelle Associates Research Paper #17.

Capelle Associates (2012c). Relationship among Time Span, Self Span and Compensation Span from Capelle Associates Benchmarking Database. Capelle Associates Research Paper #18.

Capelle Associates (2012d). Relationship among Manager–Direct Report Alignment, Delegation, and Compensation from Capelle Associates Benchmarking Database. Capelle Associates Research Paper #19.

Capelle Associates (2012e). Span of Control and Employee Satisfaction from Capelle Associates Benchmarking Database. Capelle Associates Research Paper #20.

Capelle Associates (2012f). Manager–Direct Report Alignment and Employee Satisfaction for an Analyst Role. Capelle Associates Research Paper #21.

Capelle Associates (2012g). Manager–Direct Report Alignment and Employee Satisfaction in Three Organizations. Capelle Associates Research Paper #22.

Capelle Associates (2012h). Potential Annual Cost Savings from Organization Design Assessments. Capelle Associates Research Paper #23.

Capron, L. (1999). "The Long-Term Performance of Horizontal Acquisitions." *Strategic Management Journal* 20, 987–1018.

Carraher, S. M. & Chait, H. (1999). "Level of Work and Felt Fair Pay: An Examination of Two of Jaques' Constructs of Equitable Payment." *Psychological Reports* 84(2), 654–656.

Carver, J. (1990). *Boards That Make a Difference: A New Design for Leadership in Nonprofit and Public Organizations* (1st ed.). San Francisco: Jossey-Bass.

Charan, R., Drotter, S. J. & Noel, J. L. (2011). *The Leadership Pipeline: How to Build the Leadership Powered Company* (2nd ed.). San Francisco: Jossey-Bass.

Cichocki, P. & Irwin, C. (2011). *Organization Design: A Guide to Building Effective Organizations*. London; Philadelphia: Kogan Page.

Collins, J. C. (2001). *Good to Great: Why Some Companies Make the Leap—and Others Don't* (1st ed.). New York: Harperbusiness.

Conner, D. (1993). *Managing at the Speed of Change: How Resilient Managers Succeed and Prosper Where Others Fail* (1st ed.). New York: Villard.

Cook, T. D. & Campbell, D. T. (1979). *Quasi-Experimentation: Design and Analysis Issues for Field Settings*. Chicago: Rand McNally College.

Covey, S. R. (1991). *Principle-Centered Leadership*. New York: Summit.

Craddock, K. (2009). *Requisite Organization Annotated Bibliography, Fifth Edition*. New York: Columbia University.

Davenport, T. H. (1996). "The Fad That Forgot People." *Fast Company* 1(1), 70–74.

Deming, W. E. (1986). *Out of the Crisis*. Cambridge, MA: Massachusetts Institute of Technology, Center for Advanced Engineering Study.

Dive, B. (2008). *The Accountable Leader: Developing Effective Leadership through Managerial Accountability*. London; Philadelphia: Kogan Page.

Dresner, M. & Xu, K. (1995). "Customer Service, Customer Satisfaction, and Corporate Performance." *Journal of Business Logistics* 16(1), 23–41.

Drucker, P. F. (1974). *Management: Tasks, Responsibilities, Practices* (1st ed.). New York: Harper & Row.

Fairfield, J. (2002). *Levels of Excellence* (1st ed.). Sydney: Random House.

Fairfield, J. (2007). "Profit by Raising a Key Function to the Next Level: Tools to Build a Work Levels Shifting Strategy." In K. Shepard, J. L. Gray, J. G. Hunt & S. McArthur (Eds.), *Organization Design, Levels of Work & Human Capability* (pp. 129–142). Canada: Global Organization Design Society.

Fusaro, R. (2001). "Needed: Experienced Workers." *Harvard Business Review* 79, 20–21.

Galbraith, J. R. (1977). *Organization Design*. Reading, MA.: Addison-Wesley.

Galbraith, J. R. (2000). *Designing the Global Corporation*. San Francisco: Jossey-Bass.

Galbraith, J. R. (2002). *Designing Organizations: An Executive Guide to Strategy, Structure, and Process* (2nd ed.). San Francisco: Jossey-Bass.

Galbraith, J. R. (2005). *Designing the Customer-Centric Organization: a Guide to Strategy, Structure, and Process* (1st ed.). San Francisco: Jossey-Bass.

Galbraith, J. R., Downey, D. & Kates, A. (2002). *Designing Dynamic Organizations: A Hands-on Guide for Leaders at All Levels*. New York: AMACOM.

Gladwell, M. (2008). *Outliers: The Story of Success* (1st ed.). New York: Little, Brown and Co.

Globe and Mail, The (1999). "Management Gaps Can Prove Lethal." *The Globe and Mail*, pp. D.5.

Goold, M. & Campbell, A. (2002). *Designing Effective Organizations: How to Create Structured Networks*. San Francisco; Chichester, UK: Jossey-Bass.

Goold, M., Campbell, A. & Alexander, M. (1994). *Corporate-Level Strategy: Creating Value in the Multibusiness Company.* Hoboken, NJ: Wiley.

Grant, L. (1998). "Happy Workers, High Returns." *Fortune* 137, 81.

Gray, J. L., Hunt, J. G., McArthur, S., Shepard, K. & Global Organization Design Society. (2007). *Organization Design, Levels of Work & Human Capability: Executive Guide.* Toronto: Global Organization Design Society.

Hallowell, R., Schlesinger, L. A. & Zornitsky, J. (1996). "Internal Service Quality, Customer and Job Satisfaction: Linkages and Implications for Management." *Human Resource Planning* 19(2), 20.

Hays, W. L. (1988). *Statistics* (4th ed.). New York: Holt, Rinehart, and Winston.

Heskett, J. L., Jones, T. O., Loveman, G. W., Sasser, W. E. & Schlesinger, L. A. (1994). "Putting the Service Profit Chain to Work." *Harvard Business Review* 72(2), 164–174.

Heskett, J. L., Sasser, W. E. & Wheeler, J. (2008). *The Ownership Quotient: Putting the Service Profit Chain to Work for Unbeatable Competitive Advantage.* Boston: Harvard Business Press.

Heskett, J. L., Sasser, W. E. & Schlesinger, L. A. (1997). *The Service Profit Chain: How Leading Companies Link Profit and Growth to Loyalty, Satisfaction, and Value.* New York: Free Press.

Heskett, J. L., Sasser, W. E. & Schlesinger, L. A. (2003). *The Value Profit Chain: Treat Employees Like Customers and Customers Like Employees.* New York: Free Press.

Hoebeke, L. (1994). *Making Work Systems Better: A Practitioner's Reflections.* Chichester, UK; Hoboken, NJ: Wiley.

Jaques, E. (1952). *The Changing Culture of a Factory.* New York: Dryden.

Jaques, E. (1956). *Measurement of Responsibility a Study of Work, Payment, and Individual Capacity.* Cambridge, MA: Harvard University Press.

Jaques, E. (1961). *Equitable Payment.* Hoboken, NJ: Wiley.

Jaques, E. (1964). *Time-Span Handbook: The Use of Time-Span of Discretion to Measure the Level of Work in Employment Roles and to Arrange an Equitable Payment Structure.* London: Heinemann.

Jaques, E. (1968). *Progression Handbook: How to Use Earnings Progression Data Sheets for Assessing Individual Capacity, for Progression, and for Manpower Planning and Development.* Carbondale, IL: Southern Illinois University Press.

Jaques, E. (1976). *A General Theory of Bureaucracy.* London: Heinemann.

Jaques, E. (1982). *The Form of Time*. New York: Crane, Russak.

Jaques, E. (1982). *Free Enterprise, Fair Employment*. New York: Crane Russak.

Jaques, E. (1990). *Creativity and Work* (9th ed.). Madison, CT: International Universities Press.

Jaques, E. (1996). *Requisite Organization: A Total System for Effective Managerial Organization and Managerial Leadership for the 21st Century* (2nd ed.). Arlington, VA: Cason Hall.

Jaques, E. (2002). *The Life and Behavior of Living Organisms: A General Theory*. Westport, CT: Praeger.

Jaques, E. (2002). *Social Power and the CEO: Leadership and Trust in a Sustainable Free Enterprise System*. Westport, CT: Quorum Books.

Jaques, E. & Brunel Institute of Organization and Social Studies, Health Services Organization Research Unit (1978). *Health Services: Their Nature and Organization, and the Role of Patients, Doctors, Nurses, and the Complementary Professions*. London: Heinemann.

Jaques, E. & Cason, K. (1994). *Human Capability: A Study of Individual Potential and Its Application*. Falls Church, VA: Cason Hall.

Jaques, E. & Clement, S. D. (1991). *Executive Leadership: A Practical Guide to Managing Complexity*. Arlington, VA: Cason Hall.

Jaques, E., Gibson, R. O. & Isaac, D. J. (1978). *Levels of Abstraction in Logic and Human Action: A Theory of Discontinuity in the Structure of Mathematical Logic, Psychological Behaviour, and Social Organization*. London: Heinemann.

Juran, J. M. (1988). *Juran on Planning for Quality*. New York: Free Press; London: Collier Macmillan.

Juran, J. M. (1989). *Juran on Leadership for Quality: An Executive Handbook*. New York: Free Press; London: Collier Macmillan.

Kates, A. & Galbraith, J. R. (2007). *Designing Your Organization: Using the Star Model to Solve 5 Critical Design Challenges* (1st ed.). San Francisco: Jossey-Bass.

Katz, D. & Kahn, R. L. (1966). *The Social Psychology of Organizations*. Hoboken, NJ: Wiley.

Kesler, G. & Kates, A. (2011). *Leading Organization Design: How to Make Organization Design Decisions to Drive the Results You Want* (1st ed.). San Francisco: Jossey-Bass.

Kim, W. C. & Mauborgne, R. E. (2005). *Blue Ocean Strategy: How to Create Uncontested Market Space and Make the Competition Irrelevant*. Boston: Harvard Business School Press.

Kraines, G. (2001). Accountability Leadership: How to Strengthen Productivity through Sound Managerial Leadership. Franklin Lakes, NJ: Career Press.

Kubr, M. (1996). *Management Consulting: A Guide to the Profession* (3rd ed.). Geneva: International Labour Office.

Kuhn, A. (1976). *The Logic of Social Systems: A Unified, Deductive, System-Based Approach to Social Science*. Foreword by Kenneth E. Boulding (1st ed.). San Francisco: Jossey-Bass.

LaMarsh, J. (1995). *Changing the Way We Change: Gaining Control of Major Operational Change*. Reading, MA: Addison-Wesley Pub. Co.

Laurence, C. (1999). "The Long-Term Performance of Horizontal Acquisitions." *Strategic Management Journal* 20(11), 987–987.

Lawrence, P. R. & Lorsch, J. W. (1967). *Organization and Environment; Managing Differentiation and Integration*. Boston: Division of Research, Graduate School of Business Administration, Harvard University.

Lawrence, P. R. & Lorsch, J. W. (1969). *Developing Organizations: Diagnosis and Action*. Reading, MA: Addison-Wesley.

Leeson, N. W. & Whitley, E. (1996). *Rogue Trader* (1st ed.). London: Little, Brown and Company.

Macdonald, I., Burke, C. G. & Stewart, K. (2006). *Systems Leadership: Creating Positive Organisations*. Aldershot, England; Burlington, VT: Gower.

Mahler, W. R. (1975). *Structure, Power, and Results: How to Organize Your Company for Optimum Performance*. Homewood, IL: Dow Jones-Irwin.

Mahler, W. R. & Wrightnour, W. F. (1973). *Executive Continuity: How to Build and Retain an Effective Management Team*. Homewood, IL: Dow Jones-Irwin.

McNaught, T. (2004). "Managing: Most M&As Fail!" *New Zealand Management*, 41–42.

Miller, J. G. (1965a). "Living Systems: Basic Concepts." *Behavioral Science* 10(3), 193–237.

Miller, J. G. (1965b). "Living Systems: Cross-Level Hypotheses." *Behavioral Science* 10(4), 380–411.

Miller, J. G. (1965c). "Living Systems: Structure and Process." *Behavioral Science* 10(4), 337–379.

Miller, J. G. (1971). "Living Systems: The Group." *Behavioral Science* 16(4), 302–398.

Miller, J. G. (1972). "Living Systems: The Organization." *Behavioral Science* 17(1), 1–182.

Miller, J. G. (1975). "Living Systems: The Society." *Behavioral Science* 20(6), 366–535.

Mintzberg, H. (1979). *The Structuring of Organizations: a Synthesis of the Research*. Englewood Cliffs, NJ: Prentice-Hall.

Mintzberg, H. (1994). *The Rise and Fall of Strategic Planning*. New York: Free Press.

Mintzberg, H., Ahlstrand, B. & Lampel, J. (1998). *Strategy Safari: A Guided Tour Through the Wilds of Strategic Management*. New York: Free Press.

Nadler, D., Tushman, M., & Nadler, M. B. (1997). *Competing by Design: The Power of Organizational Architecture*. New York: Oxford University Press.

Pearce, J. A. & Robinson, R. B. (1991). *Strategic Management: Formulation, Implementation, and Control* (4th ed.). Homewood, IL: Irwin.

Peter, L.J. & Hull, R. (1969). *The Peter Principle*. New York: Bantam Books.

Pett, M. A., Lackey, N. R. & Sullivan, J. S. (2003). *Making Sense of Factor Analysis: The Use of Factor Analysis for Instrument Development in Health Care Research*. Thousand Oaks, CA: Sage.

Pitts, G. (2000). "Disciples Preach Organizational Design." *The Globe and Mail*. October 11.

Porter, M. E. (1980). Competitive strategy: techniques for analyzing industries and competitors. New York: Free Press.

Porter, M. E. (1998). *Competitive Advantage: Creating and Sustaining Superior Performance: With a New Introduction* (1st Free Press ed.). New York: Free Press.

Richardson, R. (1971). *Fair Pay and Work: An Empirical Study of Fair Pay Perception and Time Span of Discretion*. London: Heinemann.

Robbins, B. & Davidhizar, R. (2007). "Transformational Leadership in Health Care Today." *The Health Care Manager* 26(3), 234–239.

Rogers, C. R. (1961). *On Becoming a Person: a Therapist's View of Psychotherapy*. Boston: Houghton Mifflin.

Rogers, C. R. (1965). *Client-Centered Therapy: Its Current Practice, Implications, and Theory*. Boston: Houghton Mifflin.

Rowbottom, R. W. & Brunel Institute of Organization and Social Studies, Health Services Organization Research Unit (1973). *Hospital Organization: A Progress Report on the Brunel Health Services Organization Project*. London: Heinemann.

Schein, E. H., Bennis, W. G. and Beckhard, R. (Ed.) (1969–1981). Addison-Wesley Series in Organization Development. Reading, MA: Addison-Wesley.

Senge, P. M. (1990). *The Fifth Discipline: The Art and Practice of the Learning Organization* (1st ed.). New York: Doubleday/Currency.

Shadish, W. R., Cook, T. D. & Campbell, D. T. (2001). *Experimental and Quasi-Experimental Designs for Generalized Causal Inference*. Boston: Houghton Mifflin.

Sharp, I. (2009). *Four Seasons: The Story of a Business Philosophy*. Toronto: Viking Canada.

Simons, R. (2005). *Levers of Organization Design: How Managers Use Accountability Systems for Greater Performance and Commitment*. Boston: Harvard Business School Press.

Ulrich, D., Halbrook, R., Meder, D., Stuchlik, M. & Thorpe, S. (1991). "Employee and Customer Attachment: Synergies for Competitive HR." *Human Resource Planning* 14(2), 89–103.

Worren, N. (2012). *Organisation Design: Redefining Complex Systems*. Essex: Pearson Education.

Weber, G. & Mihalicz, D. (2007). "Redesigning a Global Organization to Deal with Increasing Complexity: The International Federation of Red Cross and Red Crescent Societies" in K. Shepard, J. L. Gray, J. G. Hunt & S. McArthur (Eds.), *Organization Design, Levels of Work & Human Capability* (pp. 211–223). Canada: Global Organization Design Society.

Zar, J. H. (1984). *Biostatistical Analysis* (2nd ed.). Englewood Cliffs, NJ: Prentice-Hall.

ABOUT THE AUTHOR

Ronald G. Capelle has been helping executives for over 35 years to improve organization performance by optimizing organization design. His clients have included virtually all types of organizations in the private, public, and nonprofit sectors. He has supported global clients with operations in North America, South America, Europe, Asia, and Africa. Capelle has a PhD, is a Certified Management Consultant (CMC), a Registered Psychologist (CPsych), a Certified Human Resources Professional (CHRP), and a Certified Organizational Development Consultant.

Capelle Associates Inc. provides organization design consulting services to a wide range of organizations. The firm also does extensive research on organization design, and has shown that better organization design leads to better financial performance, customer satisfaction, and employee engagement.

INDEX